D1497890

CHARLES E. MERRIAM *and the Study of Politics*

(Photo: Moffett Studio, Chicago, Illinois)

CHARLES E. MERRIAM, 1874–1953

CHARLES E. MERRIAM
and the Study of Politics

Barry D. Karl

The University of Chicago Press   Chicago and London

The University of Chicago Press, Chicago 60637
The University of Chicago Press, Ltd., London
© 1974 by The University of Chicago
All rights reserved. Published 1974
Printed in the United States of America
International Standard Book Number: 0-226-42516-9
Library of Congress Catalog Card Number: 74-5731

JA93
M47
K37

Barry D. Karl is professor of history at the University of Chicago. Among his writings are *Executive Reorganization and Reform in the New Deal* and the Foreword to the third edition (1970) of Charles E. Merriam's *New Aspects of Politics*, published by the University of Chicago Press.
[1974]

Arthur Mann
Advisory Editor in American History

To my parents, Anne and Aaron Karl,
for sharing with their children
their love and their respect for one another,
their commitment to the future

Contents

Preface

Charles E. Merriam is generally acknowledged to be the father of the behavioral movement in political science. No one work of his attests to this as effectively as do the generations of students he helped train at the University of Chicago. His own bibliography is extensive; but his reputation as a methodological innovator cannot be made to rest on it very securely, any more than it did during the active phases of his career.[1] Readers searching for clearer evidences of a school of thought developing in the political science of the 1920s and '30s can find what they want in the writings of Harold Gosnell, V. O. Key, Jr., Harold D. Lasswell, Leonard D. White, and Quincy Wright, to name only a few of the figures in the peak generation, as well as in an equally stellar list of students who have managed the profession for the last four decades.

Merriam was an academic entrepreneur whose extraordinary sensitivities to the ideas of his times were combined with a willingness to govern the resources available for the development of those ideas to produce a phenomenon rare even in its day: a genuine school of thought.

Such a statement makes it seem easier to describe than it is, and touches on dilemmas raised by many of the decisions which have gone into the structuring of what I suppose can only loosely be called a biography. An intellectual history based upon the Merriam corpus itself seemed to me to threaten to distort him into a Thorstein Veblen or Frederick Jackson Turner by giving his own sense of political science, as I understood it, a methodological precision he himself never managed to give it. There is, in his Socratic fragments, the material a Plato could shape into the system he himself never actually defined:

and I would not wish even to imply that it could not or should not be done, only that I am no Plato. The entrepreneurial Merriam dominates my account, not because it is the only aspect of his career worth exploring, but because it seemed to me the crucial aspect, perhaps the only one capable of defining his real significance, for his times as well as for ours. For the management of social policy has come to include the methods of funding research and of persuading the political managers of social policy which Merriam, more than any other single figure of his generation, came to master. This was true for the entirety of his career, from his early years as a young faculty member at the University of Chicago, through his political activity in the city reform movements, his national involvement in the Progressive movement, his development of the Social Science Research Council, and his direct involvement in planning the New Deal.

The ideas of his times and the policies they reflected were the ideas of an American academia undergoing a process of modernization and internationalization the agonies of which are still dimly understood, perhaps because close analysis is difficult when the pain is still so intense. The resources for research—university budgets, the funds of philanthropists seeking new methods of organizing their antique sense of charity, and the range of federal, state, and local government looking for advice both useful and politically viable—are the resources Merriam helped reorganize for the entire academic community in the social sciences. The methods he established have remained the essential methods of generating American intellectual life; and it is those methods which I have sought to illustrate by my selection of events in his complex career.

Charles Merriam managed systems of thought and canons of belief in order to increase the size and skills of the community concerned with them, and thereby to insure their continuing utility for a society desperately in need of the good life promised by the Enlightenment, the advent of American democracy, and the riches of technology. His sense of behaviorism was considerably more than a methodological innovation. It was the culmination of an American contribution to the improvement of the human condition throughout the world. If its Americanism did not trouble him as much as it might have, it was certainly in part because of his implicit acceptance of Tocqueville's belief in the unique position of the United States as the inheritor of the democratic crusade.

Preface

Critics of Merriam's impact on political science, the most extensive being Bernard Crick, have caught the problem, I think, in their acceptance of Merriam in the terms his times imposed upon him, although I believe he took himself far less seriously as a social scientist than either his followers or his critics have taken him.[2] The criticisms and the defenses are both justified, in a sense, by the view of political science in particular and social science in general which his efforts as the founder of a school did, in fact, produce. My own view—stated more bluntly here, perhaps, than in my text—is that the continuity between Merriam and his students has been vastly overstated in some very crucial respects. I do not think that Merriam found the triumph of methodology he had helped produce as satisfying as a later generation did. Nor do I believe that the internationalization of social science, which he also helped produce, was without its pains for him. Tang Tsou's very useful and interesting dissertation on Merriam and the Chicago School suggests a kind of recantation on Merriam's part in his later years; but, as I have indicated earlier, arguments of that kind rest on a more systematic view of Merriam as a thinker than I have been able to accept.[3]

The revelation that I am a historian rather than a political scientist should come as no shock by this point. It might explain my conviction that Merriam was an American activist of his generation before he was a political scientist; it was his reason for becoming a political scientist. He saw no conflict between activism and science. Indeed, he saw science as the essential precondition of a useful activism. More important, perhaps, might be my assertion here that he shared the twentieth-century American belief that American nationalism was built firmly and irrevocably on the Constitution of 1787; that the Civil War confirmed that conviction; that American government had already stood the severest tests of modernization and would endure. This antirevolutionary reformism is an ideology shared by reactionaries trying to prevent change, by liberals promoting progress, by radicals calling for major restructuring of social and economic institutions, and by generations of men and women who considered themselves good, practical solvers of problems.

In all of these senses, Merriam's behaviorism was based on the belief that modernization is a fundamentally rational political process prior to and absolutely determining of social and economic change. This political determinism rests, in turn, on the belief that of all forms of political behavior, American political behavior stands the best chance of serving as the model for social change capable of placing all human society on the road to progress. My study of Merriam is, then, an effort to indicate the ideological outlines of the American national creed which supported an intellectual commitment to American society as it was in the first half of the twentieth century. If the events of the past decade make that commitment difficult for a present generation of reformers to understand, then my efforts to explain it may be worthwhile. After all, the problems are still there. The likelihood that they are not going to change may be the best reason for understanding what Merriam and his generation were trying to do.

Acknowledgments

The basic research for this book was done in the papers of Charles E. Merriam, now in the custody of the University of Chicago's Joseph Regenstein Library, but for a crucial period in my custody, first in the library of the Littauer Center, Harvard University, and then the Olin Library at Washington University. Herman Pritchett and Doreen Herlihy were helpful in the initial transfer of the papers, Don K. Price in arranging for their housing at Harvard, and Ralph Morrow for their care at Washington University. Robert Rosenthal and the librarians at the University of Chicago have done a remarkable job of maintaining not only the Merriam papers, but the papers of many of the key faculty figures in the university's history. The papers of the presidents of the university are also part of that collection, and I am grateful to Ben Rothblatt in general and Robert M. Hutchins in particular for permission to use those materials. The Merriam family allowed me to establish my own relationship to their father's career. Robert E. Merriam and his wife, Marguerite, spent many evenings with me at various stages of my developing understanding, answering questions, recalling incidents, and helping me see the perspective only they could have.

The Harold L. Ickes papers in the Library of Congress were opened for research when this book was in page proofs. The extensive correspondence there necessitated the rewriting of several sections in chapters 12 and 14; but the fact that the notes were already numbered and set means that citations could be included only where there were numbers available. This was the case in almost every instance; but readers will still have to be a little patient in fitting the notes to the text.

Acknowledgments

Among the Merriam students and colleagues who submitted to my inexperienced interviewing, I am particularly grateful to Harold Gosnell, Harold D. Lasswell, Albert Lepawsky, Herman Pritchett, Walter Johnson, Bessie Louise Pierce, and especially the late V. O. Key, Jr., and his wife, Luella Gettys Key, and the late John M. Gaus, who lent me very relevant correspondence from his own papers. Both Key and Gaus helped me through some of the early stages of my work with their supportive advice, as well as a kind of humor and forbearance I will always treasure. Key gave me his collection of National Resources Planning Board publications, including some of the working papers for various studies. Eveline Burns, Charles W. Eliot, 2nd, Walter Wanger, and Eleanor Murdock were also helpful in providing recollections of various periods in Merriam's career.

Like all scholars of the period, I am deeply in debt to the remarkable libraries of the National Archives and Records Service and the indefatigable interest of their staffs. The Herbert Hoover Presidential Library at West Branch, Iowa, the Hoover Institute at Palo Alto, California, the Franklin D. Roosevelt Presidential Library at Hyde Park, New York, the Library of Congress Manuscripts Division, and the National Archives all reflect a concept of preservation which makes the study of contemporary history virtually unique. That these institutions reflect the problems of modern history in their organization and incredible variety is a subject of study in itself. Surely not since the days of the pharoahs have past, present, and the dream of an immortal future been jammed together with such effect.

My research has been aided by grants from the American Philosophical Society, the Charles Warren Center at Harvard, Washington University in St. Louis, Brown University, and the University of Chicago. The Warren Center provided not only office space and typing services, both as the project began to take shape and as it reached its conclusion, but that remarkable and essential critical conviviality which younger scholars can offer one another when the circumstances are right; I particularly want to thank William R. Hutchison and Henry D. Shapiro. Like many others, I am grateful for Oscar Handlin's skills in backing his encouragement with generosity and hard reality, and for the very helpful critical support of the editors of *Perspectives in American History*, Bernard Bailyn and Donald Fleming. Stephen R. Graubard of *Daedalus* and Dankmar A. Rustow, who organized a conference on leadership in the fall of 1967, also helped by giving me

Acknowledgments

an opportunity to formulate some of my ideas in a quite different context from that of the biography itself.

Colleagues who have seen sections of the manuscript and commented on it for me have included Rowland Berthoff, A. Hunter Dupree, Neil Harris, Stanley Katz, William G. McLoughlin, Arthur Mann, and George W. Stocking. Professor Mann's careful editorial criticism of the manuscript was particularly important to me, as well as to readers who may appreciate the fact that it is now shorter than it once was. John L. Thomas helped at earlier stages of my work by reading and listening and providing a rich and sustaining friendship.

Graduate assistants at various stages of the work who have been most helpful are Don Klimovich, Marie Schilling, C. H. Sullivan and Marc Hilton. The typing of the final manuscipt was a triumph of cutting and pasting, deciphering of handwriting, and unflagging patience accomplished by Marnie Deering.

I have saved the two most important acknowledgments for last, because I want them to stand alone. I am grateful to Frank Freidel, not only for his thoughtful reading of the manuscript and for his supporting friendship over the years this has taken, but also in recollection of the days early in my career when his encouragement was all I had. There are others in the profession who owe that debt to him and who would want to join me in acknowledging it.

No one knows what's really in this book the way my wife, Alice, knows it; and she will never tell. That gift goes so far beyond acknowledgment it would be pointless to try.

1

Ed Merriam of Iowa

In small towns like Hopkinton, Iowa, the Civil War was kept alive in tales recounted to the young. Battle scenes called to mind by the rhythm of a limp or the pinned fold of an empty sleeve excited young imaginations and reawakened old ones; but there were stories of the daily life of the war years as well to provide a coloring of humor and a richness of community experience. The war experience provided the ever present plank in every campaigner's platform, and gave special meaning to the lists of names in every family Bible, the diaries and letters to be read aloud on winter evenings or by children to one another on rainy days amid storeroom collections of family artifacts.

Big cities also kept the war alive in monuments and parks; but the cities grew in the postwar years, filling with immigrants for whom the war meant little. The obelisks with their engraved names held fewer and fewer memories for the families who picnicked around them or listened to the Fourth of July speeches extolling the virtues of national unity. The war was not forgotten in the cities, but, pressed by the problems of industrial change, it moved into the past. Urban daily life held little room for the war the small towns remembered.

Hopkinton did not change much after the war, which may be why its recollections were so important to it. Its population was not destined to reach a thousand. Located in Delaware County, forty miles southwest of Dubuque, it lay outside the state's major east-west routes. Failing to get the all-important rail connection which many believed would have launched it into the future, it languished, as they might have said. Hopkinton didn't die; it just didn't change.

1

With mingled pricklings of pride and foreboding, the older citizens watched their young move off to the cities or to other more promising communities further west, confident that the training they had given them in their churches and schools would hold firm, and they were right. For a hundred years America would be governed, its history made and interpreted, by men who knew the nineteenth century the way the war generation taught it to them. That education had provided a frame which could contain revision and reform, could even allow a glimpse of revolution; but it was a frame. In its own fashion it gave meaning to the world by excluding disharmonies threatening to a basic national unity.

Charles Edward Merriam, Jr., was born in Hopkinton on 15 November 1874. Ulysses S. Grant was president, a Republican like Lincoln and a war hero, which were important things to remember before you said anything else about him, even after there were a good many other things to say. C. E. Merriam, Sr., had been in the war but had been wounded in his first encounter with the enemy and had waited out his service in Libby prison. He had falsified his age to enlist, quite possibly not out of an excess of unionist enthusiasm but for other urgent reasons. Since his twelfth year his life had been filled with disturbing shifts and adjustments. His father had died of typhus shortly before his birth but his mother had remained in Princeton, Massachusetts, for twelve years before deciding in 1855 to move to Hopkinton. Her eldest sons had settled there several years earlier in a newly formed community of transplanted New Englanders and Scottish Presbyterians. One son had recently been widowed and, left with young children to raise, needed his mother's housekeeping. Both he and his mother remarried within the year, and the following year the mother died. C. E. Merriam was then fifteen. He did not lack shelter, to be sure; but it is likely that even had his brother's new wife been able to give him the patience and support he needed he would still have felt the effects of the displacements of previous years. The outbreak of war offered the opportunity of a kind of revolution, temporary though it may have been, and considerably more brutal than anything he had known. Merriam and his fellow soldiers knew the war as an experience full of privation and disease. Periodic waves of public interest in battle names and the heroics they entailed did not conceal recollections of futility and fear, the unanesthetized pain of an adolescence cut away.[1]

2

The older Merriam brothers eventually established the family as a significant political presence in the state. Speculation in the precariously tandem ventures of railroad and land improvement, carried on in a relatively conservative fashion, served ambitions of solid, Protestant well-being rather than anything even they would have wanted to call wealth. Merriam family members who resettled—in California, for example—kept in touch through correspondence communicating transfers of deeds and repayments of debts-with-interest among news of births, marriages, and deaths, all vital statistics in the measurement of family resources.

As the youngest, separated by some years from his more successfully settled brothers, C. E. Merriam trailed the edge of affluence. His brothers helped him catch up. In 1868 he married the daughter of his brother's business partner. Margaret Campbell Kirkwood was five years his senior, devoutly Presbyterian in keeping with the tenets of her Scottish upbringing, trained to teach school as the outward manifestation of an inward commitment to the righteous governing of the community. She brought to the marriage not only the first really settled home he could identify as his own, but also the sense of culture and education which he himself could no longer hope to attain. The marriage produced three children. John Campbell Merriam was born in 1869 and named for the Scottish uncle with whom his mother had lived while attending school. The second, born five years later, was named for his father, Charles Edward, Jr., and called "Ed" by the family for the rest of his life. When a girl was born in 1876, she was named Susan, after no one in particular. She was the only one, her brothers teased, who had a name of her own.

The children formed a self-supporting, respectful group, aware, as they commented to one another in later life, of the demands placed upon them by their parents. They remembered their mother as a firm, affectionate woman with a sharp and observing wit expressed in the Scottish burr that remained part of her very articulate speech throughout her life. A devout Covenanter, she was committed to an almost punitive keeping of the Sabbath—or so it seemed to her children. And, God's love to the contrary notwithstanding, she had a burning hostility to Catholics. She determined that John's career would be the Presbyterian ministry, even enlisting the aid of the local minister in the evening prayer sessions. On their knees on the kitchen floor they

3

appealed for signs of the call. John's interest in nature developed into a successful career in paleontology and geology; but his speculative later writings describe a hand of God in nature, a hand that bears a resemblance to his mother's vision.

Ed's resistance to her faith was stronger, perhaps, because her religious demands were less upon him than upon John. In his later years he recalled other pressures, particularly those occasioned by her periodic illnesses, and a litany of chronic complaints subsumed under such generic labels as "arthritis." All of the children bore the burdens of managing the household. In addition to normal duties children would in any case have been expected to fulfill, each of the three was trained to prepare and serve family meals. It was a task Ed resented as much in recollection as he did at the time.

Ed lacked John's serious self-sufficiency, the care and precision that ordered the older boy's observations and actions. Ed was his mother's favorite—a fact of life his brother and sister both eventually came to accept—and he was the focus of his father's ambitions. C. E. Merriam wanted a son in politics, not only to take advantage of the family connections, but to fulfill hopes the war and the circumstances of his life had closed off for him. A taciturn man whose relations with others were spare and direct, he watched the development of his younger son's gregarious and articulate personality with satisfaction, if occasional misgiving. A deep involvement in politics had not concealed from him the fact that he was not destined to be a politician. The easy manner and enjoyment of public display of himself so clear in his younger son were not characteristics he had—or wanted, for that matter—although he knew them to be necessary in politics; and he sought to discipline them in his son, at the same time that he nurtured their productive use.

The method of discipline was one his son's students would recognize, although they never knew the source. They all would recall a kind of teasing, wry, some thought biting at times. It made the point without withdrawing respect and support, serving more often to goad than to annoy, although it could do that, too, not without the intended effect. His teasing could show irritation, but with the sting of the nettle rather than the cut of the whip; and it could make shrewd criticism clear without being destructive. It was C. E. Merriam's chief method of managing his growing sons. They knew what he wanted of them, even when they balked at fulfilling his demands. Ed knew, even as a child, what career had been planned for him. Politics would be a center of ambiguous ambition in the life of Ed Merriam, a source of failure and success, and it would sometimes be difficult to tell them apart.

C. E. Merriam, Sr., took part in community politics when politics was inseparable from the other responsible engagements of a man immersed in the daily practical and spiritual life of a small town. Like many of his generation, his commitment to the Republican party had been forged in the heat of the war. The bond created there was as inseparably welded as that between the Democratic party and rebellion. Indeed, his community, like many rapidly developing around it, retained an immunity to political dissidence characteristic of those many regions of the country where one or the other of the parties reigned supreme. Party did not mean the same thing it meant to urban citizens concerned with spoils and national civil service. The war had preserved the union, and the Republican party was the instrument of that preservation. Preservation of the union, like salvation of the soul, was a gift too precious to be compromised by debates over shifting issues.

A silver Republican in the pre-McKinley years, C. E. Merriam bristled with caustic humor at his sons' taunts in 1896 that he had to go down to the train station to wait for the papers so that he would know what he believed. To his son Ed, whose religious questioning of such issues as infant damnation provoked frequent family dispute, the father replied that religious doctrine was like a party platform: you liked some planks, you didn't like others; but a platform was a platform, and you stood on it as a whole.

This sense of political organization influenced the approach of such men ·as the senior C. E. Merriam to the realities of postwar life. Disputes over principle were real enough; but such disputes recalled dangers fresh in the minds of those who had gone through the war. What organization could do, as the experience of Hopkinton so quietly demonstrated, was to assemble a community of the like-minded and tie them to the support of one another. The ties were not always cohesive, clearly held principles, although some of them were. But there were enough of them, even where they were in conflict, to provide everyone with a secure measure of support. There was room for religious difference, although not always enough—Jews, for example, were a much more acceptable group than Catholics—and within boundaries a later generation would find unacceptably narrow, there was room for ethnic and racial difference. Political radicalism was tolerated where it seemed more reasonable to be a Populist than a Democrat.

Chapter One

Political organization in small towns like Hopkinton could be loose and informal, partly because the burdens of community government were borne by a variety of organizations, religious, educational, business, all small enough and all sufficently representative of groups of local citizens to be responsive to community needs. Urban politicians used party organization for purposes the citizens of Hopkinton satisfied in other ways, although ties to state and national party systems made it possible for Hopkinton citizens to identify the problems they read about in their periodicals and to suffer a sense of indignation about them. But political corruption did not damage their sense of the validity of party as an effective means of gaining appropriate political ends.

C. E. Merriam had been prevented by the war from taking full advantage of the education available to him at Hopkinton's Lenox College. The little academy had been built by the community in the first decade of Hopkinton's existence and was run by a local committee in conjunction with the national educational organization of the Presbyterian church. Merriam became a trustee of the school, tending its meager funds as carefully as he tended his own and sending his children there for their first experience with higher education. An elder in the Presbyterian church, he participated in its national policies and politics as well as its local government, serving along with his wife as a delegate to its conclaves, just as he did to gatherings of the state Republican party.

From the vantage point of his general store, he invested as shrewdly as his circumstances allowed in the welfare of the community. He held stock in the local bank, whose policies he influenced and whose advantages were useful to him in the sale and purchase of land. The family's local lumber intersts also were involved in the modest network of financial support he sought to build for himself. In periods of national Republican ascendancy he could be assured the postmastership of Hopkinton, an advantage which served two minor purposes for entrepreneurs like him in towns like Hopkinton. It kept the general store a center of local and national communication and customer traffic, and it kept him on the pipelines to party politics, a service post offices provided all small towns.

Politics was involved with his livelihood in numerous and extended ways, giving at least the illusion of political meaning to debates about currency or tariffs and prices. C. E. Merriam was at the center of an agrarian America that focused its political, religious, and economic forces in small towns where minor entrepreneurs regulated and managed community affairs in accordance with what they conceived to be American democratic values. They sifted those values through a haze of half-articulated metaphors in which biblical morals, political self-sustenance, and the ownership of property became interchangeable. That system of values certified land and the resources of nature as a gift to all men from the hand of God; sanctified an honest business deal shrewdly consummated as an act of political independence; and made political action a holy tribute to the moral cohesion of the community and its common wealth. C. E. Merriam believed in God and accepted the responsibility for managing His gifts intelligently and economically. He trained his children to do the same.

Stiffly astringent photographs of that generation show a side of them their children could recall with envy as the twentieth century rushed on: the thin-lipped certitude in the controlled and ultimately controllable limits of life, the essential justice of death, the alliance of God and country that would carry them and their issue to salvation. In a superficial sense easy to misunderstand—as they and the generations they taught misunderstood it—C. E. Merriam's sons rejected their parents' view of the interrelation of business, religion, and politics. Both John and Ed Merriam contributed to a liberal rebellion which worked to control the excesses of economic privilege, to reshape a rigidly conceived biblical morality, and to sensitize the machinery of politics to changes in public will. At the same time, however, both men shared their father's commitment to capitalism not simply as a historical order of economic life but as a source of social virtue, to American Protestantism not simply as one among many routes to spiritual understanding but as the most potentially liberating route, and to American government as the one closest to the "natural" order of political life toward which all men would ultimately move. In those respects they accepted the fundamental unity of the three as constituting a cohesive structure of values; and they spent their lives modifying that structure with a sensitivity to the changes in cultural development taking place around them. Nonetheless, the basic structure had been learned in Iowa boyhoods and, in at least one important respect, in a brief and abortive search for fortune in California.

In October 1888, C.E. Merriam moved his family westward to Oakland, California, a journey of some four days on the uneven bed of the Union Pacific. In family recollection the reasons for the move had a deceptive clarity. Yet the breaking up of more than twenty years of settled family attachment created deep disturbances, at least for some of the family.

For one thing, the election of 1884 had brought Grover Cleveland and the Democratic party into power. Postmaster Merriam lost his job. There seemed no prospect of regaining it in the upcoming election—a familiar enough error in American political prognostication. While the store was ample enough to sustain the family comfortably, certainly, there was the possibility of greater opportunity elsewhere, and descriptions sent back by the California Merriams of conditions there contributed to the excitement of the move.

Equally important, although in an altogether different realm, were the educational opportunities opened for John by his acceptance at the University of California for advanced study in paleontology and geology. John had just finished the course offered by Lenox. While the resources of the small academy were limited, the fundamentals of training in the natural sciences were not seriously lacking, thanks to the influence of the state university and a legislature which, like many western legislatures, appreciated relationships between scientific study and the utilization of natural resources. Lenox, like many of the private academies in the area, drew heavily on the state university for faculty.[2]

John's teachers had recommended the University of California, then dominated by Joseph Le Conte, one of the students of Louis Agassiz. The state of California had rapidly become the center of geological study in the United States, not only as a result of the influence of men like Le Conte at the university but also as a result of its position in the various geological surveys of the era. Public attention had been attracted to geological research by the lures of gold and silver; but only slightly subtler judgments were required to see the values of other resources—oil, for example.[3]

The final reason for going was the one the children remembered best, although it probably had less to do with the decision than they thought. "The West" connoted a glamour built on an almost total ignorance of variations in climate and geography and on a common belief that westward journeys were good for the health. Mrs. Merriam's rheumatism and arthritis might benefit from the trip, although it seems doubtful that the San Francisco Bay area was singled out as ideal by any doctor she knew.

Together, the three reasons for going, no one of them sufficient in itself, provided a rationale for the move. In the long retrospect—it would be a topic of conversation in family reunions for the rest of their lives—there was a need to understand it. Whatever the move meant for the children, and it meant a great deal, it did not provide the parents with the new and successful opportunities for advancement that they had apparently envisaged. They returned to Hopkinton with their two younger children in little more than two years with a sense of relief that concealed whatever awareness of failure they were willing to admit.

For Ed the move would have been difficult in any case. He was approaching fourteen when they left, sixteen when they returned, and his growing awareness of himself—as evidenced by a fragmentary diary he tried to keep and the school essays he saved—coincided with a period when the family's attention was intensely focused on the launching of his brother John's career and the business failure of his father. In later years when Ed had occasion to refer to the California experience, he made no more than passing mention of either of these family concerns. What he did recall was the loss of his dog, Carlo, a Newfoundland which could not be taken on the trip and which grieved to death, as the story transmitted to them in California had it. Over and over again when he grew older he referred to the incident, even identifying himself as Carlo in the private verses he scribbled for his own satisfaction. Carlo became a private name he used to talk of love and death in his declining years, the "other Charles," for Charles, though his given name, was a name his family never called him.

John's career, like everything about John, had a clarity and direction, even in Hopkinton. While John explored the Iowa landscape, Ed, as he often put it in later descriptions of those early years, "held the bag" for his brother's rock samples, bearing the load in sibling resignation as the price of sufferance. In California such joint expeditions had even greater rewards. Ed's chief contact with scientific analysis came through John's tutelage, and the San Francisco period was by far the most intense and disciplined in this respect. Here were established a vocabulary and point of view important in the careers of both men. The young boy who followed the older brother around the Bay area hills was essentially a passive absorber, but one can see in his later attitudes toward science distinct echoes of beliefs which originated in his brother's teaching. Theories of geological and biological evolution floated about him, their general shape becoming clear from time to time, and the sharpest lines being those which developed from questions of theology.

The religious background of the Merriams, as well as of John's contemporaries in graduate school, gave scientific determinism an engagingly familiar tone. Alongside the bleak prospect threatened by Calvinist doctrines of salvation, the Darwinian belief in the struggle for survival held forth the possibility of a natural world open to rational manipulation. Calvin's God and Darwin's Nature were not irreconcilable, particularly in the peculiar majesty of a region of the country almost biblical in its offering of natural variety and abundance. Whatever the limits of the depths the mind of the adolescent could penetrate in the discussions during the sunny climbs or the cool nights by the campfire, the elements were not altogether unfamiliar. From these discussions came the image of science and the scientist Merriam carried with him throughout his life, the seeds from which grew the model of the productive intellectual community he would spend a lifetime trying to reproduce.

Still other aspects of Ed's observations of his brother John's developing career influenced his own future career. The flourishing California community of natural scientists fed not only on a splendid natural environment but also on a popular enchantment with natural research. John's correspondence reveals his later activities in turning that popularity into research funds for himself and his students, and he was not alone in perfecting the techniques of that transformation. One of the Merriams' companions on local field trips was William Emerson Ritter, an instructor at the university at the time and thirteen years John's senior. Ritter, a zoologist, marine biologist, and oceanographer, later directed the Scripps Institution of Oceanography at La Jolla, founded by his friend E. W. Scripps, who supported Ritter's research projects. The connection between pure scientific research and the industrial utility of the products of scientific research was never far from the minds of both donor and recipient. The relationship was symbiotic, built on a faith in nature and wealth solidly backed by fundamental religious beliefs.

University administrators throughout the early careers of both Merriam brothers continued to view their faculties as teachers, primarily, and the salaries paid them as compensation for that occupation. They did not provide them with funds for research, however much the development of their careers may have depended upon their reputations as research scholars. Men without independent wealth learned to cultivate local resources not only for research materials but

also for funds. Complex alliances among academic institutions, research scientists in those institutions, and industrial entrepreneurs
concerned with systematic development of natural resources changed
the older interests in scientific agriculture and higher education
into a new relationship between state-funded higher education and the
useful resources of the state. What came to be known as the Wisconsin
Idea was already inherent in this approach to the state university as a
research facility for the development of the full potential of the natural
resources of the state. The change in emphasis from agriculture and
engineering to mining and metallurgy, from geology, chemistry,
biology, and paleontology to psychology, sociology, economics, and
political science represented a continuum resulting in significant part
from changing notions of utility and public education. The academic
community's contribution to the Progressive movement was at least two
decades of experience in manipulating the complex of factors relating
pure scientific research to public values and social utility.

Although the metaphors used to describe the resources of the
American West continued to be formed out of the old familiar images
of the pioneer-trapper with his inevitable individualism, the actualities
of those resources and the effort required for their exploitation posed a
set of problems strikingly different from the eastern agrarian past. The
California technologist-scientist was a new kind of colonial on the
American scene, however familiar his cultural evangelicalism may have
been. John Merriam met various family requests that he take a look at
this or that piece of property to see whether it was worth investing in;
but it was the mineral potential he was examining, not the fertility, and
it was a new technology he was using for determining that potential.

The field trips the Merriam brothers took with Ritter and others of
the Berkeley community were part of a by then traditional pattern of
exploration familiar to planners of camping trips. The Le Conte
brothers and others even more specifically entrepreneurs had formalized such programs of exploration for students, colleagues, and
interested local citizens who helped finance the trips. Ideals of camp
life and the reputation of the West for rebuilding body and spirit
combined with concern for scientific knowledge to produce small
summer communities of intellect and conviviality. The environment
became the laboratory. Released from the confinement of museums,
scientists lived outside in the world they sought to understand, measuring the pressures and temperatures of its atmosphere as they breathed

11

it in, growing stronger physically and intellectually, as they saw it, totally absorbing and being absorbed by the new landscape.[4]

For the men who took part in it, the scientific experience contained a mystical experience as well. As the Californian Josiah Royce expressed it in his philosophical writings, it tied discovery to idealism.[5] Joseph Le Conte's later philosophical ramblings, like the much more disciplined writings of John Merriam, have a crudity, philosophically speaking, which conceals too successfully for later generations a deep sense of spiritual and moral meaning in scientific exploration. Charles Merriam's social science, and much of his method in the organization of social research, was derived from exactly the same spiritual sources. For that generation, science was a social experience with nature. The surveys drew friends together from the small academic communities around the nation. Henry Adams and others wrote commentaries on the speculative conversations which enlightened the chill, firelit evening. What most Englishmen of the time went to the Far East to discover, Americans discovered in their own West. Their experience with exotic splendors and fantastic insights into the nature of human behavior and natural environment occurred at home.[6]

The generation which sought to cast the social sciences in the form of the natural sciences was following a tradition born in the moral commitment of the naturalists who were seeking to read the foundations of their own social and historical beliefs in what they so often referred to as "the book of nature." The ultimate compatibility of nature and morality—the frequently unstated assumption of their mutual support—was one of the central beliefs which gave progressivism its thrust.

Charles Edward Merriam, Jr., would ultimately come to be the leader of the movement to transform the socially purposeful study of society into a scientific program of progressive reformation, a reformation built upon the interdependence of social science and natural science. The work of his brother John, not only during the early periods of his education but throughout the careers of both men, served as a model. Charles Merriam's view of science remained very deeply tied to the science he observed in California; and while his sophistication in the methodology and utility of that science deepened as he grew older, he retained an unshakable faith in the moral—and political—principles both men felt were present at the core of scientific understanding where they were convinced nature and society were joined. Neither man regarded a concern for objectivity as precluding a faith in classical American concepts of morality. John would insist throughout his life that an accurate and disciplined understanding of nature proved the existence of God.[7] Charles would find in the "scientific" investigation of human behavior proof of the same fundamental truths of moral purpose.

The California experience had a disrupting number of aspects; and while the close family relationship of the Merriams helped smooth the way for the younger son, it could not do everything, particularly where it was itself the source of demands. Ed's father elected to place him in the University High School, which offered a program, experimental in its day, spurred by the desire of the university faculty to make community education for their children more effective. This was a difficult change for a boy preoccupied with his new environment, but he faced it as well as he could, given the limitations of his preparation. He tried most sports then available in the, to him at least, unique program of organized athletics; and he excelled in track. This helped his self-esteem. He kept records of his physical development— height, chest, biceps—and he read in the university library, whose facilities were one of the most remarkable advantages of the University High School. All in all, he compiled a modest record in Berkeley; but his Hopkinton school experience had been more of a triumph, to say the least.[8]

His brother John's career as a student, sharp and well-defined, with a distinct influence on all aspects of the Merriam family life during those years, produced in Ed a sense of envy, together with a desire to emulate and a habit of critical self-examination, all of which would stay with him in one form or another for the rest of his life. Yet, as he began to see for himself what it was he wished to do, he found the route marked for him, not simply by the name he bore, though that was important, but by periodic urgings, if they could be called that, from the man whose voice never had to say much in the family to be heard.

C. E. Merriam wanted his second son in politics. He probably would have been surprised had he been asked why, for the answer would have seemed obvious. What many of his children's generation looked upon as the road to corruption and mismanagement, C. E. Merriam saw as an opportunity to combine public service and responsible success in proportions a moral man could measure for himself. His generation's heroes were politicians, frequently. Corruption in politics was then an urban phenomenon which small-town westerners like him condemned roundly, but it did not threaten their own interest in political action. The Merriam family, both in California and Iowa, was building a political name for itself. To fail to take advantage of that would be a waste, indeed a sin, he might have said, and his son would know how literally he meant it.

A political career now required a solid training in the law, C. E. Merriam decided, not the apprenticeship his generation had known but a university training. Latin, Greek—all of it—were what a man needed and what he wanted his son to have. A legal training meant something else, too; it meant independence and professional opportunity on its own, a solid haven in case of political defeat. Thus, in his way, the father urged and suggested, guided and cajoled. Ed had no doubt where he was headed. Not that he minded it. Politics fascinated him. Even by the time of the California trip he was interested enough in the battles in the Iowa state legislature to keep up with these local events at long distance; and by the time of his return to Iowa he was already reading the *Congressional Record* with fairly regular interest.

But when the issue was drawn, as it was bound to be, the problem would remain unresolved, or would find its resolution in unexpected ways when the demands of his career pressed resolution upon him. For that career was an uneasy compromise between his brother's science and his father's politics. In a very private sense, troubling to him when critics measured him harshly—even by the standards he himself had helped devise—he faced the failure inherent in an approach to science he knew to be beyond him, and political ambitions he could not fulfill. In his aged reexaminations of his life he tried to rethink the puzzle, but it was too late. The parts of it that belonged in California were lost to him, except for the scattered images he repeated to himself. He kept remembering Carlo. He knew California had cost him more than he wanted to acknowledge, and he never wanted to go back.

Nothing about the California years seemed to mark the family record so significantly as the leaving of it. The story the children told for years after the event seemed to satisfy feelings through repetition only they fully understood—if anyone did. C. E. Merriam had returned to Hopkinton to negotiate the final sale of his property there. He hoped, apparently, that the transaction would provide additional funds for his California business activities. Having ascertained that the sale would probably raise a sufficient amount to justify further gambling, he wired his wife, "If you wish to stay in California, better prepared [*sic*] for business."

What he meant was clear enough to him. Just how much choice he intended to offer his wife is not at all clear, nor is there any indication of her feelings in the matter. The issue was further complicated, as the story goes, by the fact that the telegraph company omitted the "d" from "prepared," so that the message read: "better prepare for business." Her interpretation was clear and unquestioning. Without asking for clarification—or apparently feeling that any was necessary—she wired back, "coming home at once"; and, with Ed and Susan, she did.

All in all, with the exception of John's success in the university, the family had not particularly benefited from the California move. Their living circumstances in Berkeley had been adequate enough—they stayed in the house of a bachelor biology professor who boarded with them—but it was not really home. Mrs. Merriam's chronic ill health showed little improvement in California and may even have been complicated by the homesickness which affected them all.

Most important, perhaps, though least discussed, was the very limited success—it appears indeed to have been failure—of C. E. Merriam's business interests in Berkeley and the Bay area. Whatever help the local cousins may have been able to give him could not really make up for the cultural shock the move involved. Land speculation in California did not follow the leisurely, even gentlemanly, pace to which he had been accustomed in Iowa, although many of the elements were the same: railroads, for example. California urbanization jostled values and eroded confidence. The anger of Henry George against economic inequalities and of Lincoln Steffens against municipal corruption, marked the boundaries of the era of postwar growth in California. Berkeley's development was particularly rapid. Too small to be listed in the census of 1870, classified among places with a population under 4,000 in 1880, its population exceeded 5,000 in 1890 and reached 13,000 in 1900. All of this to younger men might have provided excitement and opportunity, a high gamble and worth it, but to a man of C. E. Merriam's age and experience it was simply a questionable risk.

For the second time in his life he had reached the frontier. The first time, when he had come to Iowa as a child, the frontier had been real. The trip to California came at the peak of a last illusion when the era

15

C. E. Merriam represented had long since made such use as it could of
the limited opportunities open to it on lands increasingly less hospitable
than the familiar countryside of western Massachusetts. His generation,
nurtured on dreams of modest profits from well-tended lands, found the
West puzzling with its new resources, unfamiliar skills, and not easily
attainable riches. The myth of the gold rush, with its sturdy forty-niner
whose pan and axe and mule unlocked treasure from the earth, proved
not much more than an attempt, successful in its day, to bring to life
the Jacksonian legends of the land in a way which seemed appropriate
to the new materials. But it didn't work and it never would. The
individual, alone and ambitious, could sift small successes from the
mountain streams, just as he had scratched them from the reluctant
soil, but they would remain small. John's scientific sophistication, not
his father's simple entrepreneurial energies, was the tool for exploiting
the West; and he stayed. C. E. Merriam came home to Hopkinton
where the small world he could manage with dignity and self-respect
awaited him.

Where young Ed's education was concerned, nothing before so
dramatically clarified his sense of his own ambitions as this move.
Confirmed in a sense of community which involved a commitment to
politics as well as to social service, he would find many of the most
crucial conflicts of his adult life erupting over problems of moving
from one community to another. Aware of the path his father's
political ambitions had established for him, he would have to mark his
own route upon it, in his own way. He would never fully meet his
father's demands, but neither could he deny them. His father's stories
of the war stayed with him like a litany of suffering for the long-range
good. Accepting periodic failure as a subtler achievement of the spirit
than success, he looked to the American community as the source of
compromise and justification. That community had survived the Civil
War and would ultimately make crucial aspects of that experience
seem irrelevant to the long-range nationalism gradually emerging out
of it. The Merriam sons, raised by a generation sick of dissidence,
helped lead that nationalism.

In the later years of his life when Ed Merriam and the other products
of small-town, midwestern America gathered to celebrate the triumphs
of their mode of reform, they would resurrect the stories of the war in
the same twanging accents in which they had first heard them, trying to
communicate to the newer, urban generation they were training some

of the essentials of their own sense of "soul." They were not sure just what it was; but in the warm conviviality of the professional tradition they were creating, it seemed an important thing to do.[9]

2

An Education for Politics

The citizens of Hopkinton used Lenox College to carry out their ambitions for their children, encouraging its administration to keep up with the latest methods of education and the newest innovations in curriculum. They also assumed that the college would vigorously protect their moral and religious traditions, and they enforced that assumption when necessary through their service on the school's governing committees. Academies like Lenox provided the backbone of a system of private secondary education which communities of that era would have considered "public" in every sense of the term long before modernized tax programs, legal reforms, and educational reorganizations formalized the change.

Margaret and C. E. Merriam knew what they wanted for their sons. Lenox made it possible for them to measure their hopes against the best educational standards emerging in the professions and, what is more, for them to feel secure that they themselves would have a voice in any changes. John Merriam did not become a Presbyterian minister and Ed did not become a lawyer-politician. If these facts disappointed the elder Merriams, they knew, nonetheless, that they themselves had played an important part in the professional transformations that did take place. Lenox gave them that assurance.

Lenox Academy became Lenox College in 1884, reflecting the belief held by Hopkinton citizens that education to be worthwhile had to be modern and "college" was the modern term. In 1882 the local board, of which C. E. Merriam was a member, approved a synod decision to appoint a layman to the presidency, J. H. Ritchey, described as "an experienced educator ... well-informed in all the progressive and modern

18

systems of practical and scientific education."[1] "Practical" and "scientific," those were the keys to the future, while the required Bible course and compulsory Sunday church attendance continued to protect the past. The school introduced new courses in commerce, physical education, laboratory science, even Bible criticism. Evolution was subject to serious debate. John Merriam defended the teaching of it, but in language which easily demonstrated to the Presbyterian elders his more fundamental commitment to the community of their beliefs; so they let it pass as a contribution to scientific investigation. But they did debate it; and their sufferance was by no means unanimous.

C. E. Merriam expected Lenox to provide an education which would open opportunities for his children greater than those that had been available to him. What Lenox was prepared to do for his ambitions for his younger son's political career was to pave the way to law school. Like most of the denominational academies-turned-college throughout the state, Lenox considered part of its task the pre-professional training of students who would become degree candidates at the State University at Iowa City. Students could obtain a bachelor's degree from Lenox. The State University offered Lenox graduates a second B.A. in one year if they held the Lenox degree with Greek and Latin, one of several devices whereby the state influenced standards among the varieties of academies. Lenox looked to the State University for guidance as well as faculty, exchanging in an informal system both personnel and ideas.

C. E. Merriam pressed Ed to take the Greek and Latin which would qualify him for admission to State; and he admonished him from time to time—to slight avail—to concentrate more on his studies, as John had done, and to spend less time in such activities as debate, the school newspaper, and the competitive athletic program, the school's first. Ed maintained a B record in a standard classical curriculum which included mathematics, history, rhetoric, and the required Bible course. He relished provocation and conducted a brief and unsuccessful battle against compulsory church attendance. His address at his commencement in 1893 had as its subject, "Have We Freed the Negroes?" and his answer was no. A Fourth of July address the same year blazed with a multi-metaphored nationalist rhetoric calling for enlightened "progress."

Whether or not he could afford it, C. E. Merriam felt that his sons should finance their own educations beyond the Lenox B.A. They agreed, and both took one-year jobs in country schools to save the money to finance the coming year. As it turned out, his one year at Iowa State began and ended Ed's career in law.

What is surprising, perhaps, is the speed with which the decision was made. From the beginning of the year at the State University, with the exception of his studies in jurisprudence, Ed found legal education a distinct disappointment. From a much later vantage point, he would see the problem as the faculty's failure to feed his commitment to ethics and social theory. Certainly the rigors of the case method with its emphasis on the capacity to retain memorized detail left little room for the kind of speculation he preferred; but that problem must be placed in the context of a career which would be spent trying to give scientific reality to social thought by forcing its concentration upon facts. Varieties of case method would remain central to that endeavor, although, characteristically enough, he himself would be much less the practitioner of the method than would the students upon whom he pressed it.

The uncertainty of his commitment to his father's dream also played an important role in his recollections of his law year, as he measured, time and again, the depth of disappointment he aroused and the sense of failure he never lost. It was a disappointment C. E. Merriam did not express directly, although he had made his wishes in the matter clear enough. The touches of irascibility with which he commented upon the academic interests of both of his sons stemmed from his sense of a practical reality of life in which success was marked by money—not greed, he would have argued righteously, but money. "Father," John said to him on the subject, "I hope you understand that my main object in life is not to make money."

"In that case," snapped the father, "you are likely to be an immense success."

Money was not the chief problem, although it provided one way of expressing the fact that Ed was escaping from a small-town entre- preneurial merchandising of life geared to a realism understood by the generation which had suffered the war and its aftermath. He was struggling, too, to escape the pressures placed upon him by the responsibility of fulfilling his father's ambitions for him, not because he failed to share them—he would never escape that, and he would come ultimately to realize it—but because the method pressed upon him rankled somehow, bore in on him in ways which many of the

20

postwar generation found equally disturbing. Of all the professions, the legal could most effectively be made to bear the brunt of the confusions of late nineteenth-century industrial expansion. A system, in the sense of being able to provide a sense of order in an otherwise chaotic struggle to create wealth out of new materials with new methods, it nonetheless encompassed the extremes which enclosed the limits of political debate. The law could be the servant of commerce, a step-by-step pragmatic manipulator of ends determined by political leaders, businessmen, or an aroused, ambitious citizenry; but it could be more than that. Law could also be the embodiment of moral and social order, the established protector and active agent of right against wrong.

What Ed Merriam could easily have seen in the changes taking place in the University of Iowa itself even during his short stay there was that the two functions of law were undergoing a division. It was a division which the requirements of technical specialization were forcing on training in all fields and it would pose important problems well into the next century of American life. Merriam was not the first young American to find in his first year's preparation for the practice of law a disturbing lack of concern for social values, and he would certainly not be the last. Nor was he the first to shift his political ambitions from the practice of law to the investigation of the social sciences. In many of the more sophisticated intellectual circles of his day the view that the profession of politics was built upon a specialized science in which men needed to be trained was taking hold, although the articulation of it—unlike its increasing articulation in the other professions—was severely limited by traditional democratic concepts which made politics the responsibility of all citizens. Woodrow Wilson, Theodore Roosevelt, and Henry Cabot Lodge, to name only the most obvious examples, were already in the process of separating their sense of the politician from their attitude toward the lawyer and looking, in their different ways, for the establishment of a profession that would satisfy their awareness of the new complexities of modern life without conflicting with their commitment to democratic government.[2]

The search moved in the direction of a restructuring of the disciplines through which society could be studied. Changes within the disciplines themselves, related only tangentially to the training of politicians, made the establishment of a relationship among fields like history, political science, and economics central to the reformation of higher

21

education, so that it might then serve the state by training political leaders. In state institutions like Iowa and the much vaunted
Wisconsin the idea of service to the community emphasized even more
the pragmatic requirements of such education. The battle between the
independent development of the disciplines and the utility of education
to the community financing it influenced the growth of the academic
disciplines by forcing them to conform, at least outwardly, to the
demands of their public. At the same time, it educated the public to
require from their academic institutions that they maintain themselves
in accordance with the highest professional standards. The result could
be puzzling. Whether a higher degree in economics, for example, was
preparation for a career in business or a career in the teaching of
economics—or government advising—could be, and would become, a
complex and debatable issue. The same would be true of political
science, whether it was training for law, for public service, or for
scientific research. The disciplines were bound to take their shape from
the successive answers to such questions, and the irresolvability of
many of them would form the basis of continuing professional dispute.

Ed Merriam reached the University of Iowa at an important point in
that institution's approach to the social sciences. While Merriam's
contact with the changing approach was brief, the man who was
bringing it about, Isaac A. Loos, was then one of the faculty luminaries,
an immensely popular teacher who attracted widespread respect among
the student body. Loos held a bachelor of divinity degree from Yale,
where he had been introduced to that most moral of sciences, political
economy, by William Graham Sumner, whose dogmatic manner
alienated the student from the teacher without dimming his interest in
the subject matter. Loos came to Iowa in 1889 from Otterbein College
to take over the teaching of the course in political economy from the
university's former president. He used the course as an entering wedge
in a revolution which was ultimately to create a new and exciting
program in the social sciences.

In eastern schools political economy had come to designate a subject
matter part theoretical and part historical in its survey of economic and
social theory, a descendant of moral philosophy but, probably under
the influence of such books as John Ruskin's *Unto These Last*, rapidly
undergoing a change in focus which would make it the repository of
moderate social and economic reform. Serious conflicts between

British social reform influenced by Ruskin and the German historical methods were beginning to emerge, but in forms still demanding analysis. In the Midwest, at schools like Iowa and Wisconsin, the focus of any subject had to be couched in terms which appealed to school trustees and state legislators concerned with training their sons in the ways of the market and problems of taxation and banking. The result was an at times curious interlarding of conflicts in European social theory with an intense concentration on local problems, political and economic, as models for what analysis there was.

Neither Loos nor Richard Ely of Wisconsin condemned the fact that they were charged with the responsibility of preparing young men for careers in law and commerce: they gloried in it, accepting it as an opportunity to shape the moral ends to which they were also committed. Intellectually, too, the use of local American institutions and practices as the objects of research in social theory was the only "scientific" way, the maintenance of the local "laboratory." Loos's course in political and economic institutions took state and local government as basic material and drew upon current documents from the U.S. Government Printing Office as exercise work. Woodrow Wilson's *The State* served as text for a course in comparative politics, with American state and local government again the basic subject of study. Loos's class in public finance read Charles F. Bastable, and a seminar which he began in 1893 and which drew excited students like Merriam, used James Bryce's *American Commonwealth* as a text for the study of the political and economic history of Iowa. The second half of the seminar was devoted to an examination of monopolies, with special emphasis on railroads and their relation to the state legislature.

Ambitious for his small department, Loos carried on a running battle with the administration for staff. In his efforts to bring the latest point of view to Iowa, he hired Charles Beardsley, a student of the eminent Harvard political economist Frank W. Taussig, and sent one of his staff, Benjamin F. Shambaugh, off to the Wharton School of Finance at the University of Pennsylvania, where the economist Simon Patten and the historian James Harvey Robinson were then teaching, and then to Europe, where he could acquire credentials making him acceptable to an institution with ambition.

Just what influence Ed Merriam got from his experiences with Loos and Beardsley would be difficult to say precisely. Certainly one of

23

Loos's most important contributions to education at Iowa was the establishment of necessary relationships between the abstractions of social and political thought and the realities of current political and economic dispute. Iowa students learned current European principles of socialism, for example, in courses which bore names more acceptable to trustee-conscious administrations than their actual content would have been. State legislators involved in negotiating franchises and rate disputes found their words read by the next crop of young legal talent. Many of the relations between classroom education and current political battles which would make Merriam a leader in his profession over the next half-century were being suggested—cautiously and from the dignity of a professorial podium—in this phase of his education.[3]

Most important, perhaps, was the alternative the experience offered to his previous plan for a career in politics. What his father saw as the right way was no longer the only way. What his much admired brother was doing in university life could be emulated in its way in a newer career. It is significant, perhaps, that the name Ed Merriam gave to his newly discovered pursuit as he looked around for the best way of implementing the exciting new aims was the name Loos used, "political economy."

The selection of a school for Merriam's next academic step posed questions that would play an important role in the way his generation came to view the nature of content and method in the social sciences. As he saw it, the choice came down to Columbia University or Johns Hopkins. In Merriam's view, the Hopkins emphasis upon historical method and comparative institutions was not balanced, as it was at Columbia, by a rigorous program in government administration, by which he meant such subjects as municipal finance and taxation, the programs Loos was seeking to expand at Iowa. Inherent in that comparison, however, was a problem touching, in various forms, every institution where social science was emerging as, on the one hand, a set of scientific disciplines devoted to objective research and analysis and, on the other, a set of community oriented programs seeking to provide newer practical methods for the continuity of rational social reform. The generation of Merriam's teachers, all trained in one way or another in German historical method, were also experienced in the hard facts of American academic life where involvement in community life generally excluded politics as an avocation unfit for those committed to the moral training of the young. In Germany academic reformers lived under sufferance of the government itself, and the close relation between government and the universities established with sharp clarity the lines which could not be crossed and the acts which would lead to expulsion. The American university had no such central ties to government, even the state universities; but there were ties to various communities—religious, local, financial, philanthropic, old and new style reform—which spun out lines like the threads of a web. Whether or not these lines could be crossed, when and by whom, depended upon the individual, the institution, the issue, and the public mood—a seemingly infinite set of variables which bred caution and distance.

The newer generation was growing less cautious. Supported by a waxing reform mood capable of granting enormous respect for their supposed expertise, they made up in boldness what they lacked in skill and moved to develop refinements in reform which separated them sharply from the more conservative frame of their training. One of the consequences of that separation is evident in the reasons Merriam gave for selecting Columbia over Johns Hopkins: the balance between history and administration, as he put it. Although it was not clear at the time—and throughout his career Merriam sought to sidestep the conflict even while he was marshaling forces with which to fight it—the essentially conservative force of historical analysis could blunt an attack mounted by social research committed to examining present evidence in present contexts in order to build immediate solutions.[4]

If one looks at the academic Camelots from which Merriam was making his selection, one can see at least the initial shape of the problem. Johns Hopkins was dominated by Herbert Baxter Adams, whose commitment to *the* historical method was perhaps the strongest of his day. The social sciences at Columbia were dominated by John W. Burgess, head of the School of Political Science, and William A. Dunning, professor of history and political philosophy, each of whom, albeit in quite different fashion, was seeking to find a balance between a science of politics which history would continue to serve and a history which could benefit from the methodological refinements which a rigorous political science could produce. Burgess's political science was essentially the comparative institutionalism which Merriam was trying to balance, while Dunning's moved somewhat closer to the kind of historical sociology which would attract Merriam's interest.

Wisconsin was dominated by Frederick Jackson Turner, a historian, of course, but one whose attention to economic and statistical analysis pushed history out of the orbit of politics into combinations with more recognizably scientific social studies than the institutional abstractions of Burgess or even Adams seemed likely to provide. The Wisconsin position was and would remain more social than political, in many important respects, a complex adaptive response, perhaps, to its relation to its state legislature. Even with the addition of Richard Ely, however, the Wisconsin school did not yet touch what Dean Burgess was building at Columbia. Frederick Giddings taught sociology, E. R. A. Seligman, economics; Richmond Mayo-Smith was working in statistics; and the brilliantly inspirational James Harvey Robinson, recently arrived from the Wharton School, seemed to his spellbound classes to teach everything else.[5]

Merriam arrived in New York City in October 1896. He was twenty-two years old. It is remarkable in retrospect how many of the then seemingly unique aspects of Columbia's history and its relation to the political and intellectual life of the community were to be repeated, in various reshapings, throughout Merriam's career. The president of Columbia, Seth Low, for example, can be considered almost a model of men Merriam would know and respect—and emulate—in his own establishment of an adult identity. It was also an interesting moment for Merriam to be observing Low's career. In 1897 Low left his remarkable presidency of the university to run for mayor of New York, and Merriam moved into the student-supported campaign with enthusiasm.

Low was an intensely political man, actually a prototype of the business reform leader who was to dominate American life until the depression of the 1930s. Heir to one of the classic New York shipping fortunes, Low exemplified a pattern of response to wealth characteristic of many similar New York families, as it was of similarly endowed Bostonians, but in terms of political achievement, often more successful in New York. Over the coming half-century, the Roosevelts, Cuttings, Harrimans, and Rockefellers would actually become politically involved in the reform of the city instead simply of contributing their money to the political activities of others.

By the time he was thirty-five, Low had served two terms as mayor of the city of Brooklyn. At forty he succeeded the aged Frederick Barnard as president of Columbia, his alma mater. His career as mayor of Brooklyn prefigured many of the urban reforms which would not become nationally prominent for another five years, and the range was broad: civil service, city finance, public education, and the appointment of trained administrators.[6]

Two of the problems Low resolved successfully as president of Columbia were problems destined to bedevil a whole generation of university administrators, even contributing to Woodrow Wilson's resignation from Princeton. The first was the relation of graduate education to the liberal arts college. The second, related to the expansion resulting from the various ad hoc solutions to the first, was the physical location of the university.

When Low took over the presidency of Columbia he was faced with what had already become an open, raw dispute. According to critics, graduate and professional study not only threatened to engulf the college but, in an enthusiasm born of envious observation of Johns Hopkins, to abolish it completely. President Barnard had been urged toward such an idea by Dean Burgess. The future location of the university, given the fact that it had outgrown its building at Forty-ninth Street, became an instrument in the battle, with some arguing that the preservation of the college would be assured by removing it from the city entirely into a quiet, suburban environment, and others convinced with equal force that the presence of the school within the city, near hospitals and law offices, was the only means of assuring the success of the new professional modernism.

The arguments could be divided the other way, with advocates of the new professionalism urging removal from the city where there were expanses of cheaper land available for laboratories, libraries, and classrooms, old college sympathizers pleading to protect the tradition of identification of the school with the heart of New York. The problem had become invasive. No discussion, from curriculum on down, escaped it. It touched heart issues like fund-raising; but it was a problem that attracted an important number of similarly beset college administrators such as William Rainey Harper of the new University of Chicago. Indeed, young professionals being trained at Columbia during Merriam's generation would find the continuing debate affecting most of their own careers.

The knot could well have attracted a Gordian solution: and Low had both the power and the authority to use the direct slice. That he chose not to, electing instead to untie it strand by strand, was the mark of his rather remarkable sense of administration. With a respect for professorial dignity and sensitivity reflecting his own awareness of his academic limits, with the devotion of an alumnus dedicated to keeping the city spirit of his college alive, and with the sure entrepreneurial sense of the measure and management of his own wealth and the wealth of his friends, he moved step by step, reorganizing the schools which clustered about the college, selecting the location on the high tableland on the northern edge of the city with its stunning view of the Hudson, and tapping the resources of friends and associates for new endowment for expansion.

In 1896 when Merriam arrived there, Columbia College formally became Columbia University. The School of Arts retained the old name, Columbia College, and the complex of schools shared the new. Low had given sizable sums from his personal fortune to the university—a million dollars for land, another million for the library building in memory of his father, and the initial endowment of the university press. Despite misgivings among faculty and friends of the university, all of whom had their various reasons for criticizing some of his decisions, supporting others, he had put the university's vast and ambitious expansion program on a financial footing which rested on the continuing involvement of the New York economic and philanthropic community in the future of the university. It was an astonishing tour de force involving skills which approached the highest and most precarious order of speculative gambling—a charge political critics were willing enough to make when the time came. Seth Low was then forty-seven years of age.

Students such as Merriam were attracted to the mayoralty campaign of 1897 not only by their interest in politics or even by their admiration for Low but by the multiple uniquenesses of the campaign itself. For one thing, it was the first mayoralty campaign since the formation of Greater New York as a political unit. It therefore represented numerous complexities for party organization, all of which were compounded not only by Low's acceptance of the nomination by the Citizens Union as a reform candidate but by Henry George's place at the head of the Jeffersonian Democracy ticket. Although both the regular parties fielded candidates and ultimately carried the day, for many of the students the race was between George and Low, between idealistic radicalism and sane, practical intelligence. For others the issue was the breaking of partisan party hold on the city government, and either George or Low would have served their purposes. In a rare and oddly inclusive moment in urban politics of the day practical partisanship and ideological conflict were both present. Merriam rode the tailgate of a horse-drawn wagon over cobblestone streets to campaign for Low; and with George to draw the votes from the Tammany group, Low's success appeared to be a real possibility.

Henry George died toward the end of the campaign and Low's chances died with him as Democrats moved back to familiar leadership. Had the Republicans been willing to throw more support to Low, he could possibly have won easily. Running second to the regular Democrat, Robert A. Van Wyck, Low polled more than 50,000 votes more than the Republican candidate, General Benjamin F. Tracy, who, together with Low, ran some 20,000 votes ahead of Van Wyck. Low had come to politics a Republican; but the James G. Blaine nomination in 1884 had offended him as it had Theodore Roosevelt—only Low had bolted. Mugwumpery was a crime that didn't pay, although Low may have consoled himself with the recollection that Roosevelt's loyalty in '84 hadn't helped him in his mayoralty bid in '86.

Low was a hero. American students who read James Bryce, as most of them did, knew of Bryce's admiration for Low. As early as 1888 in his chapter for Bryce's *American Commonwealth,* Low had set forth arguments that would become central to movements for the reorganization of urban management over the next twenty years.[7] Chief among them was the assertion that the city was a corporation and therefore *not* an integral part of the state. It was a device which would appeal to those who, like Low, wished to emphasize the need for business leadership and management, as well as for reformers less committed to the business community who nonetheless wished to underscore the need to separate city government from partisan politics. However much appeal such arguments may have had for Merriam at the time, when he came to examine his own reform experiences, the business analogy with its denial of the utility of political power proved to be a dangerous one to use carelessly. It is clear that his view of the function of the university in relation to the community and the political responsibilities of the academic shared much more with Low than with the other university administrators with whom he was to deal in later years. Principled commitments to staying aloof from "dirty" politics, undoubtedly aided by an awareness of the political opinions of trustees and alumni, served to keep the social service role of the academic pretty well confined to standard philanthropic occupations. While not himself an academic,

29

Low apparently felt free to move from the university to politics and back again with the kind of impunity which Merriam, though never a university president, would come to feel in similar situations. Certainly as a model of the intellectual, enlightened businessman, the energetic young man of wealth and community stature, Low could have sat for the portrait the Progressive generation would impress upon American politics for more than half a century, until even the once cudgeled name of Rockefeller could join names like Roosevelt in the pursuit of respected political power.

For Ed Merriam the Low campaign was considerably more than an initiation into the particular complexities of urban politics where party commitment meant something different from what it had meant in Iowa. Low served well as the epitome of the belief in involved responsibility shared by many, though by no means all, of the Faculty of Political Science, that to teach politics and to act politically were not conflicting aims, that their conjunction might indeed be a new, modern necessity. He reflected a familiar sense of the political responsibility of the citizen whose material resources were a part of the community he was committed to protecting, to serve simultaneously his own interest and the interests of all. As Ed Merriam knew, communities like Hopkinton depended upon leadership for such government as they had or needed, and C. E. Merriam had been a leader all of his life. On any economic scale, Seth Low and C. E. Merriam were so far apart that comparisons were pointless; but where certain values were concerned, their positions were identical. thrift and responsible management, muscular Christian charity, a view of politics as a viable and necessary instrument in the functioning of democratic life were some of them. Ed Merriam would find traces of the same essential elements in all the philanthropists he sought to provide him with the base of his own career.

Over and above politics itself, there were opportunities for students to engage themselves in the life of the city of New York, opportunities which touched crucial issues of social organization: slums, factories, the city's penal, medical, and charitable institutions. These opportunities were facilitated by an eagerness on the part of many in the university to make such relationships part of formal training. Richmond Mayo-Smith, one of several Burgess students elevated to the rapidly growing Faculty of Political Science, had devised plans for extending work in social science beyond historical and theoretical instruction. President Low had submitted them to the trustees in 1894 with his recommendation for approval. In addition to the development of a statistical laboratory for the accumulation and analysis of data concerning social conditions in the city, "field work" was also introduced in cooperation with philanthropic groups in the city. "The city," Mayo-Smith had argued, "is the natural laboratory of social science, just as the hospitals are of medical science."[8]   Such groups as the Charity Organization Society, the Brooklyn Bureau of Charities, the State Charities Aid Association, the University Settlement Society, and the East Side House opened their offices to interested students and instructors.

Merriam tramped up and down stairs in tenement sweatshops, attended labor union meetings, and taught a course in economics in the John Elliott settlement house. His neighbor for a time was Adna F. Weber, whose study of cities and their growth was one of the pioneering documents to come out of the period.[9]   Equally important, he met members of the growing group of service professionals, men and women who were not the new academic reformers or the older volunteer officials but the paid staffs of charity and social welfare agencies. As unsympathetic to intellectual abstraction based on little or no hard experience as they were to ignorant if well-meaning do-goodism, they exacted respect of their standards from the eager young academics, just as they competed with them for control of the policies they were called upon to execute.

For the rest of his life Merriam credited William A. Dunning with the major influence on his career, and in a very personal sense that was true. But the obviousness of it tends to obscure elements important to an understanding of the community which had been created in the Faculty of Political Science during those years; and the creator of that community was not Dunning but John W. Burgess. Where students of Merriam's generation were concerned, the influence of Burgess was difficult to acknowledge, though no one at the time would have dared to deny it. Burgess was a presence, like an Old Testament deity, calm and forbidding, whose dogmatisms one endured. The emotional base of his intense, articulate nationalism had been shaped in the Civil War; but the intellectual base had been formed in Germany. He was committed to a collection of beliefs fairly typical of that training: a Kantian set of pure categories according to which history and politics were to be understood; a Hegelian sense of the unfolding process of life

31

toward the ideal Teutonic civilization; a conviction that geographical location combined with race to create cultural development—the latitudes were what mattered, not the longitudes; and, as the capstone of his philosophy, an assurance that "sovereignty," by which he meant "the original underived power to command and to enforce commands by punishment" was the ultimate and distinguishing characteristic of the state.[10]

Burgess guided students, Merriam among them, through the constitutions of the states, impressing upon them his devotion to the idea that it was not "states rights" but "state rights" which mattered, the ultimate generalization of legal authority which made the nation whole, despite the differences among the various constitutional units which comprised it. In order to understand the development of the American states one had to understand not only their historical origins but their different geographies and natural economies, their ethnic groupings, their traditional methods of governing. But the purpose of such understanding was to comprehend the ultimate generalizations which blended all American states into one national state. The investigation and classification of differences was the method by which difference could be transcended and the ultimate unity achieved. But there were other fixed elements which were evoking less and less agreement. In his opinion the enfranchisement of the Negro had been an error for which the nation would long pay. His nationalism was built upon concepts of race and culture shared by many of his students, but only up to a point and with an increasing flexibility which, by the outbreak of World War I Burgess would have to repudiate.

By the time Merriam's generation arrived at Columbia Burgess's commitments to his times could no longer be viewed with sympathy or understanding. The Civil War was a legend for them, a living and still smoldering memory for him. Most of the historical experiences which colored the concerns Burgess felt were well beyond their attention. The readmission of the Confederate states to the union had raised arguments in constitutional theory and practice in which students were no longer interested. Reform methods had been embodied in debates over amendments to the federal constitution as well as the reorganized state constitutions. Those were not the abstract issues they seemed to Merriam's generation, but hard political realities of another time. Between 1876 and 1912 eleven new states would be added to the union, organizing the remaining mass of western land under new constitutions with new local governments and in an environment of national reform which emphasized methods and procedures, charters, and the like.

In its way, Burgess's influence was as great as Dunning's, but the way was largely a negative one. If there were few Burgess students, there were many anti-Burgess students in a quiet and subtle fashion. They shaped their beliefs in a crucible of rigid formalism whose fires Burgess himself tended precisely and energetically. Disagreeing with Burgess was a training more rigorous than agreement with others tended to be. The intellectual rebellion against Burgess, if it can be called that, was perhaps one of the strongest forces the Columbia environment produced.

Dunning was some thirteen years younger than Burgess and succeeded him in the Lieber chair when Burgess's tasks were confined more and more to administration. While both men spent a large part of their time working in the same period of American history—what would today be called "recent history" was to them the era of reconstruction—their personal contacts with the period and their attitudes toward it, despite very real similarities in fundamental position, were necessarily different. The differences were largely a result of the difference in age. While obviously not what would be called a generation, it was enough to have made Burgess a participant in the war, Dunning a child with the sort of recollection that Woodrow Wilson had of it. Dunning's nationalist commitments, therefore, were much more flexible, in a sense, than Burgess's. He had an openness in point of view which made his personal approach to his teaching and writing less specific and dogmatic, more amenable to what he seemed to sense as basic disciplinary changes going on in his students' work. His interests seemed to them catholic and inclusive. He encouraged and supported much with which some felt he might well have disagreed. In the context of Columbia education he provided a perfect foil to Burgess's effect and became, in a very important sense, an intermediary between the generations. He was seventeen years older than Merriam.

Dunning shared Burgess's concern with the development of political science and its relation to history, but with a much more active sensitivity to the development of the other social sciences. The priority of political science and the elaboration of a methodology governing it were central to Burgess's position but not to Dunning's. Although it would not be obvious in their day, this difference constituted a problem which would grow increasingly sharp as the separate disciplines developed and sought to establish necessary working relationships with one another. The diligence with which Merriam worked out a course to avoid the problem is perhaps one of the most significant aspects of the relation between his career and the elements which produced it.

Although Dunning accepted a Hegelian process in the development of political thought and historical experience, he discarded the concept of an ideal purpose or end to the process, thereby allowing himself a critical distance from his material. The Teutonic elements recede to the background, as does the conviction that civilizations are ordered in any fixed form. The two collections of essays published by Dunning's students in his honor indicate not only the scope of his interests but their rigorous separation. The first, published in 1914, is devoted to articles on southern history and politics. Walter L. Fleming and Ulrich B. Phillips are there, as are Charles Merriam and James W. Garner. The second volume of papers reflects the other aspect of Dunning's teaching: the interest in social science theory. Edited by Merriam and Harry Elmer Barnes, the essays include papers on theory and international law by E. M. Borchard, socialist economics by Paul Douglas, social psychology, anthropology, and racial theory by other students whose associations with special disciplines had long separated them from the more traditional approaches of Dunning.[11]

Dunning's wit and warm intelligence attracted students and kept his relationships with them alive. His criticisms were sharp and incisive, but helpful always, and delivered with a light humor to assuage the pain of the barb without dulling the point. Students stood in awe of his reception of their work long after they had left the tutelage of his classroom and long after their own reputations had been established. And they were more often than not surprised by the way in which his mind would open to welcome the companionship of their most revolutionary doctrines. A fearful Charles Beard sent him his *Economic Interpretation of the Constitution* and received in a few days the following acknowledgment: "This is the true milk of the word, but it will cause the heathen to rage."[12]

Burgess and Dunning, at the peak of their relationship in the '90s and until 1910, formed what could be called the new poles of an approach to social science, about the axis of which moved the remarkable world containing Frank Goodnow in administrative law, Munro Smith in jurisprudence, Mayo-Smith in statistics, Seligman in public finance and economic history, Frederick Giddings in sociology, John Bates

Clark in economics, and James Harvey Robinson, Herbert L. Osgood, and William M. Sloane in history.

Burgess's differences with colleagues and students, built as they were upon the firm foundation of rigorous principle which was his political science, were never less than serious. He was probably deeply involved in Goodnow's leaving Columbia—at least students like Merriam were well aware of Burgess's running feud with Goodnow. But the most serious—and in many ways most profoundly telling—dispute occurred over growing anti-German attitudes in the academic community after the outbreak of the European war in 1914. Burgess and Dunning split irrevocably, but in a fashion as characteristic of fundamental differences between them as it was of the specific event itself. Burgess's defense of the German-American alliance was based upon an analysis of the objective relation of the aims and national circumstances of the two nations—a similarity that Progressives like Herbert Croly had once pointed to with assurance. It was, in a sense, a "natural" alliance with nations having very similar interests at similar points in their national and international lives. Dunning's defense of an Anglo-American alliance rested upon a detailed analysis of the traditional relationship between America and England, the historical and emotional interdependence of the two nations.[13]

The differences between the two points of view were in effect the differences between two minds in search of two concepts of reality, the one built upon the observation of factors which technically should have constituted the reality upon which rational men would act, the other constituting an observation of behavior as part of a social pattern in which historical and psychological ties would ultimately overshadow all other considerations. It was a difference epitomizing the social science debate with which Merriam's generation would cope. It summed up essential incompatibilities in the meaning of social science and its relation to social change.

Merriam's first year at Columbia was spent in seminars with Dunning and Robinson, and in Burgess's lecture course on constitutional theory. Burgess, whose course was small, would enter the room and signal immediately to a student who would close the window so that the quiet voice could be heard above the traffic noises outside. The lectures, the same year after year, were meticulously shaped, wide ranging and erudite, and available to students in copy machine reproduction. The moments for which one waited were the recitation breaks.

Students would be called to the front of the room to expound details of constitutional cases and to respond to the questions Burgess posed. Merriam and his classmate Harlan Fiske Stone competed for honors.

The visit of James Bryce to Columbia that year was one of the most stirring events Merriam could recall, second only perhaps to the Seth Low political campaign. Bryce's writings were of course familiar from Merriam's earlier Iowa training; but the impact of the man's advice to younger generations, delivered with an avuncular assurance, had perhaps even greater effect. The best way to learn politics, he argued, was in political life itself, and a practical commitment to political action was the only way of assuring a continuing level of intellectual force in American politics. Bryce's call to action had a ring which sounded appropriate to American students like Merriam, caught midway between a Jacksonian faith in participatory democracy and the newer elitist professionalism. German science to the contrary notwithstanding, British utilitarianism—the acceptance of controlled participation in political life as the necessary training for political responsibility—rested its faith in democracy on the educational values of political experience, not on a mystical attraction to natural democracy.

The influence of that point of view in the education of Merriam's generation was as important as the influence of German laboratory method, in some respects more so. Modern forms of representative government—the short ballot, proportional representation, the responsible cabinet system—were products of contact with exponents of British government, not with German universities. The popular influence of German scholarship on American government was to raise the call for greater efficiency. The popular effect of such a man as Bryce was to argue for more effective democracy. Bryce was to the young intellectuals of the twentieth century what Tocqueville was to those of the nineteenth: a warm friend to American democratic government, given to criticism, but an affectionate criticism that called for the fulfilling of American ideals.

Dunning's tutelage of Merriam was careful and sustained. Two years formed a teacher-student friendship which lasted for twenty years, until Dunning's death in 1922. Bryce died the same year, and Merriam wrote appreciative professional obituaries for both.[14] In Merriam's second year at Columbia, Dunning gave a seminar on American political theory with Merriam the only student. Dunning treated the course as a tutorial, requiring weekly papers which were discussed and dissected. At the end of that year when Dunning announced that he was leaving for a year's sabbatical, he had already arranged for Merriam to teach his lecture course on political theory, as well as a seminar in American political theory, requiring that his protégé write out his lectures in full.

That second year was an exciting one for Merriam. His new position enabled him to sit in on the faculty discussion seminars where many of the central disputes were aired. Here he was treated with a paternalistic affection that enabled him to overcome the nervousness he felt in the presence of so distinguished a group. The seminar in American political theory produced a set of notes later to become the basis of several books he wrote on the subject.

In the fall of 1899 Merriam sailed for Germany to study with the giants whose work had formed the center of the education he had been receiving. It was a brief sojourn, one year spent paying homage to his teachers' teachers, but an experience which seemed to him outdated, even at that time. The great Otto Gierke of Berlin intoned magisterial phrases already familiar from Columbia and indeed from Iowa. It was difficult to evaluate the relationship between the echo and the source, a relationship rapidly becoming irrelevant. As he later learned, Heidelberg would probably have been the better choice, given his interests. In economics and psychology it was the center of the newer ideas. Even in jurisprudence it seemed to him more advanced than the formalistic state constitutionalism he was exposed to in Berlin. But the city itself offered other possibilities for intellectual excitement. Merriam organized a discussion group in German municipal government, a topic interesting both to American and German students; and he joined his class in a foot-stomping tribute to Hugo Preuss, a professor and member of the Berlin city council who had been rebuked by the empress for his use of scriptural quotations in council sessions. Interestingly enough, the event would recur, in a way, in Merriam's own experience in the Chicago City Council, where scriptural quotation was more familiar though, in context, more out of place; and there seems no doubt that his young idealization of Professor Preuss played an important role in his relation to his own students as professor-politician. After the war, however, Merriam tended more to deny the relationship than to affirm it, though his vacillation on the subject of his German intellectual forebears was characteristic of the problems his generation faced.

Merriam's doctoral thesis was begun before he left Columbia and finished by the time of his return. Under Dunning's direction and with considerable advice from Gierke, he wrote *History of the Theory of Sovereignty since Rousseau* which won him a place for that year in the Columbia University series called Studies in History, Economics, and Public Law.[15] In an interesting way, the subject was Burgess, the method Dunning. By the end of Merriam's career the term "sovereignty" had an antique sound, and he used the title of his dissertation as a seeming joke to dangle before students who considered his contribution to political science of an altogether different order of analysis. They laughed at the term, too, without realizing the close relation which the concept bore to "political power" in Merriam's later writing. Nor was he inclined to confess that he had written the article on the subject for the 1904 edition of the *New International Encyclopedia*, then defunct. Burgess's definition, "the original underived power to command and to enforce commands by punishment," was to undergo much refinement in Merriam's later treatments of it; and the behavioral context gave it the appearance of an altogether different shape. But the debt was strong, even in the rebellion against it that Merriam found himself leading.

By 1900, then, Merriam's student years in the classroom were over. The celebrated turning of the century cast its light in both directions. The adjective "new" adhered to all things as an appreciation of the necessity of change—of "progress" as they all would have agreed. Merriam turned twenty-six in November of that year, all of his energy thrust toward the new century. Dunning at forty-three stood astride two eras, uncomfortable at times but wryly amused at his presence in both. Burgess had led his own revolution and it was done. Although he did not know it, his generation had fifteen years to go. World War I ended it; but he defended it until his death in 1931.

Dunning sought to place Merriam at Dartmouth, his own alma mater. There seems no doubt that he saw Merriam as his heir and pressed for every vestige of continuity. But Merriam found his own job—and with Dunning's enthusiastic recommendation—by going to Chicago himself to apply to Harry Pratt Judson, chairman of the Department of Political Science at William Rainey Harper's rapidly growing new univer-

sity. It was, by Columbia standards, a conservative department, more
Burgess than Dunning and more Dunning than Goodnow, in short,
much less concerned with the political activism which Merriam was
coming to see at the base of a science of politics. Harper's raids on
eastern schools had assembled a stellar group, but unlike Loos at Iowa
or Burgess at Columbia, he had been more concerned with the individual intensities of the stars than with their relation to one another.
Harper, too, did not share all of Low's sense of the political relation of
the university to the community; and quite possibly his reasons were
valid. Low was independently very wealthy; Harper was not. Low was a
New Yorker by birth and tradition; and while Chicago had a social
openness which eastern cities did not—it was experienced at absorbing
new entrepreneurs into its upper social orders—there were limits which
a university president seeking to ingratiate himself with local sources of
wealth could not transgress. On a more philosophical level, Harper was
an educator by training and profession; Low was not. Harper viewed
his relation to the local community as that of an expert, a specialist in
education willing to put that service at the disposal of the community if
it requested it. His interest did not encompass Low's more general
concept of the citizen-politician. Merriam was soon to find that efforts
on his part to model his position at Chicago along lines similar to many
in his Columbia experience would be met by a coolness, even an
opposition, from an administration less sympathetic to the new sense of
politics.

That Merriam had committed himself to a new sense of politics is,
however, clear. In a deeply personal way he had resolved through his
education, at least for a time, the dilemma of his own career and its
relation to politics. There were various factors involved, and their
conflicting relation to one another raises many puzzles. The establishment of a firmer, more coherent set of relationships among these
factors was to occupy the next twenty years of his life.

First of all, Merriam considered himself a student of political theory.
Insofar as that designation involved a relation of theory to political
science, he had yet to resolve the conflict between the views of Burgess
and Dunning: Burgess's concept of political science as the construction
of a theoretical framework of the ideal state, buttressed by moral
imperatives to be taught to a leadership who could guide civilization to
the realization of that ideal, and Dunning's descriptive science of

39

politics involving collection and classifying information to provide the trusted processes of history with analyzed and organized evidence and so to keep the process intact and in motion. Dunning's political theory—as reviewers of his later books often pointed out—was always in danger of desiccation, of a pleasant if somewhat mordant separation from the realities and necessities of the human life so uniquely characterized by politics. Burgess, on the other hand, suggested theory as an activating force in political life, a process of speculation which could, in its enunciation of ideals and its articulation of moral purpose, give energy to the intellectual process itself. A science of politics shaped by Dunning shaped nothing but itself, in the sense of leaving to the forces of politics the uses to which its independent analysis might be put. The forces of Burgess's science ultimately pressed everything before it, restructuring the world as it structured itself, reshaping itself as it analyzed the world. Dunning's use of science was democratic; Burgess's was not. Dunning's commitment to democracy was not scientific; Burgess's view of the state limited the uses to which any specific form of government could be put—including democracy.[16]

Second, although an important drive behind his sense of it would have put it first, Merriam believed that participation in politics was the only base for an experimental approach to the study of politics. Bryce had said it; but C. E. Merriam had made it an integral part of his son's view of himself many years earlier. Loos had used Bryce to teach it; but he had used himself and his own view of the political life of the community in which he taught to make the same point. Being a politician was a unique kind of learning about politics—not only unique but essential to the fact of learning itself. A career in politics and a science of politics were thereby irrevocably intertwined. One could not have one without the other. It was a concept of political science which came to Americans from Bentham, was enriched by Jackson, and reached modernity with Bryce. Even so, it contained its contradictions for Merriam's generation. Was the commitment to political action best served directly in politics, by running for office, or by writing for the critical media and so bringing understanding of politics to a broader public? This question separated the American academic from the British journalist in a very important sense. The familiarly tight relation existing in England among the institutions—universities, government, and the intellectual news and opinion media—created individuals who moved freely among all three and could transfer their involvement equally freely when they visited the United States. One need only look at the American acknowledgments in Bryce's prefaces to see how easily he found his American social and intellectual position. But various factors, chief among them the number and geographical diversity of the institutions involved, made such professional mobility difficult in the United States. Like the young Henry Adams in the previous generation, however, Merriam was determined to bring intellectual life and political life together into a working relation.

Finally, Merriam's upbringing had given him a Tocquevillian faith which his more cosmopolitan education had served to reinforce. He believed in American democracy as an emergent form of "natural" government, in that the direction in which it was moving was destined to bring it as close to a government appropriate to the nature of man as civilization had yet produced. The function of politics in that emergent development was twofold: to come to understand scientifically the political mechanisms necessary to the furthering of that development, and to thwart and destroy, again through scientific analysis of them, the mechanisms which inhibited that development. The test was always the same: is it more rather than less democratic? This was not necessarily a blind faith in democracy, nor was it a naive view that democratic judgment, instance by instance, was always correct. It was a conviction that the continuous development of more democratic processes of government was the only way of testing the validity of hypotheses which could be framed about social and political life, and the only way, ultimately, of assuring their effect. Error would be revealed only in the test of belief, not in the struggle over its dogmatic assertion, and democracy was the only way of insuring that revelation.

The move to Chicago for the academic year 1900–1901 began Merriam's professional career.[17] Although he would continue to look upon Dunning as his mentor and career adviser and to eastern academia as the focus of his ambitions for a good many years to come, Chicago was to be his home for the rest of his career. He returned east the following summer to marry Elizabeth Hilda Doyle, of Constableville, New York, the sister of a Columbia classmate. He was a grown man, a docent at the lowest rung of Chicago's academic scale. It was a place to begin.

3

Harper's University

The University of Chicago was built with the energies of William Rainey Harper, the money of John D. Rockefeller, and the affections of a local midwestern community of affluent middle-class Americans concerned with the education of their young. A national university at the outset—Harper, many faculty luminaries, and, indeed, the principal benefactor were outlanders—the school was nonetheless profoundly in and, as its title says, "of Chicago." It shared significantly in the renaissance embodied in the Exposition of 1893 and the boosterism which swept the city into the twentieth century.

Located on the stretch of land which had formed the Midway of the Columbian celebration, the university stood at a safe suburban distance from the successive waves of disruption and reform that mark the city's transition into the 1900s. Turn-of-the-century urban universities, far more than other American cultural institutions, sought to establish a compromise between an elitist role in the training of leaders and a traditional democratic commitment to all who could meet their standards. The University of Chicago's suburban setting helped it meet that compromise. It was to be a half-century or more before the life of the city seriously threatened the institutional foundations of the university, although the pressures were there from the beginning.

Two often conflicting ideals governed the university's reform role. One emphasized the necessary protection of the educational environment of the young from the forces of change and the disruptions of day-to-day community involvement. Only through such protection, it was felt, could a long-range goal to preserve the values of the community and its leadership be reached. The other ideal conceived of

42

the city as a source of excitement, its torments and turmoils an incitement to reform. According to this point of view, the university was uniquely qualified to provide experts to study the city, to test the generalizations to be drawn from the direct experience, and to change the particulars open to change. Academic investigators invaded settlement houses, hospitals, prisons, and schools seeking to develop expertise to be used as the central bargaining point in their reform campaigns: the fact that they had learned more than mere do-gooders could learn and were therefore more qualified to organize change.

Where the two ideals met in institutions of general public welfare— bureaus of research, schools of philanthropy and social work—they could generate a sense of cooperation built on a mutual respect for professional training and its social and economic utility. Within the university, however, the relationship between commitment to the moral and intellectual development of the young in their formative years and commitment to the training of technical specialists was not so easily compromised. The complex of issues raised thereby called for special skills in administrators, who needed, on the one hand, to convince prospective donors and alumni that life at the college would develop their children along traditional lines of social growth, and, on the other, to create a modern university to train professionals in law, medicine, business, and education. John D. Rockefeller, like so many of the entrepreneurs who financed the development of the modern American university, had had no such education himself. Whatever recollections of academy training any of them may have had did little to acquaint them with the concepts they were being asked to support. Their reform impulses and their industrial experience may have led them to support more complex intellectual ventures than they had any hope of understanding; but their moral commitments and their concern for the nurture of the young set limits and restrictions no intellectual rhetoric could obscure.

For the first quarter of a century of its existence, Harper's university spent as much of its energies on the collegiate training of the young as it did on the rare research of the first stellar group Harper had so brilliantly assembled. For the first six years undergraduate enrollment constituted approximately one-half the total enrollment. While the addition of professional schools in law, education, and medicine changed the proportion after 1900, it is worth noting that until 1923 the undergraduate enrollment was greater than that in the graduate divisions, and that from the 1920s through World War II, the proportion of undergraduate, graduate, and professional enrollments was approximately equal. The figures fluctuate with the general state of the economy; but one point seems clear. The need for tuition-paying students and the relatively more economical methods of undergraduate instruction always stood at the edge of every generation's vision of the great university.

Harper's vision was just that: a vision. Periodic backsliders, their faith in his promises threatened by deficiencies necessarily produced by the task of creating a university from scratch, were treated to Harper's rhetoric in the confines of his office where he could display to them the drawings of the buildings sure to come. Some, like Robert Herrick, found the dream uninhabitable and turned angrily against the effort and its rhetoric. Others, like Thorstein Veblen and to some extent John Dewey, recognized the paradoxes involved in Harper's search for a bridge between the business leaders who supported his dreams and the academics who were to realize it.[1]

C. E. Merriam, Jr.—he began his career with his father's name—was attracted to Chicago by what Harper was doing there; but he was not one of the stars for whom Harper had searched in the academic firmaments of his day. Merriam was thus to inhabit Harper's reality, not his dream, and the difference was significant. Younger staff members bore the heaviest burdens of the undergraduate teaching load and came to look upon their graduate teaching as their only opportunity for research in their fields of study. Harper controlled academic policy through a baronage of "head professors," departmental chairmen who held their offices secure until retirement.

Political science was the smallest of the social science departments; it was dwarfed by Political Economy, headed by J. Lawrence Laughlin, and History, headed by J. Franklin Jameson. Albion Small's Sociology dominated in spirit, regardless of the numbers involved, for it was not only the world's first academic department to bear that title, it was also the symbol for reform-minded intellectuals of the major shifts taking place in the relation between the university and the practices of modern social reform.

The Department of Political Science was headed by Harry Pratt Judson, professor of comparative constitutional law and diplomacy, and included Edmund J. James, professor of public administration, and Ernst Freund, associate professor of jurisprudence and public law.

Merriam's was the only appointment designated as "political science"; and the difference in title was, in its way, an accurate reflection of his relative isolation in what by then he considered an old-fashioned, constitutional-legal environment. Only James interested himself in the problems Merriam had grown accustomed to considering at Columbia, and he left in 1902 to become president of Northwestern University and then the University of Illinois. Judson did not replace him but gave Merriam his courses in municipal politics and government to teach.

Merriam taught the introductory course, "Civil Government in the United States," as well as courses in political theory. During his first five years, from 1900 to 1905, students could also have taken John Dewey's "History of Political Ethics," Albion Small's "Sociological Concepts" and "Philosophy of the State and of Government," or Thorstein Veblen's "History of Political Economy" or his "Scope and Methods of Political Economy." Wesley C. Mitchell, a young associate in the Department of Political Economy, and a man who would be associated with Merriam in numerous projects throughout their careers, taught "Economic and Social History."

In those first five years Merriam added courses in American political parties, state administration, and comparative state governments. Advanced courses in political theory were always added at the cost of an increased workload, and, as was the case where his research was concerned, the university expected him to bear his own burdens. Harper's interest in faculty research extended to the provision of a well-funded university press; but it often both started and ended there. The better-known members of the faculty were free to find their own patrons.

Merriam's problem in the search for patronage resulted, in part, from the nature of the new field, political science. Sociology could be viewed as a modernization of the reform sciences. Connections with the settlement house tradition, the charity and philanthropy groups in the city—Graham Taylor was one of the leading figures—and the rapidly developing field of social work kept sociology in an acceptable direction. Economics, too, had a respectability—Veblen to the contrary notwithstanding—which held it within the bounds of patronage. Political science posed problems, particularly if the field were to move from its constitutional and historical concern with legal frameworks like charters and constitutional revision to participation in the political process itself. Urban patrons were partisans in the privacy of their own political opinions. Social and economic issues could become partisan issues; but it was possible to pretend that they were not. The separation between politics and partisanship was harder to achieve, even as a pretense. Faculty members who interested themselves in a scientific approach to poverty could attract a wide range of nonpartisan support from some very partisan patrons. The same was not true of politics.

Merriam wrote Harper in December 1904 asking to discuss with him the possibility of Merriam's entering the forthcoming aldermanic primary. Harper did not reply. He was extremely ill at that point, which may explain his silence; but his successor, Harry Pratt Judson, did not look very approvingly on Merriam's political ambitions. Merriam's views of the future of political science were already tightly tied to participatory politics. Judson's quite clearly were not. Judson retained his own chairmanship of the Department of Political Science when he succeeded Harper in the presidency of the university in 1907, running the department by curt messages to the staff issued from the president's office on presidential stationery.

Merriam poured his discontent with his academic situation into letters to Dunning, who replied with avuncular advice laced with sarcasm. "Your acquisition of the great academic truth that a 'call' is the open sesame to promotion is a cause for congratulation," he wrote in 1902. "But don't fancy for a moment that the truth is limited to the latitude of Chicago. It is as widespread as the instinct of 'business' which is the foundation of our national greatness." On a more sober note, Dunning went on to assure Merriam that his "old instructors" were aware of his difficulties and would help him along whenever the opportunity appeared. He also made it clear that "thoughtful revision" of the manuscript which Merriam had been sending him chapter by chapter would spur that opportunity considerably.[2]

A History of American Political Theories appeared the following spring but was not greeted with the acclaim Dunning quite honestly thought it deserved. Both Dunning and Otto Gierke, Merriam's mentors, had reason to laud a piece of work so eagerly cast in their molds. Merriam forwarded an enthusiastic note he received from Gierke to Dunning who already had in hand a review written by Andrew C. McLaughlin for the *Political Science Quarterly*, edited by Dunning. Dunning warned Merriam, as jovially as he could, that Gierke's praise would probably be "sufficiently counteracted by a review in the Political Science Quarterly... which may, however, give you a little temporary discomposure, and cause a little searching of heart. This also, however, will be good for you!"[3]

McLaughlin thought that Merriam had paid too little attention to political actions, too much to obvious theoretic materials. W. W. Willoughby, reviewing the book for the *American Historical Review,* came to exactly the opposite conclusion.[4] Both men found the book too brief, but concluded that the author had promise. "Don't worry about the reviews," Dunning reassured Merriam. "If you get six notices that manifest enough intelligence in the writers to enter a high school, you will be lucky. *Crede experto.*"

The book won Merriam a promotion from docent to instructor, but a minimal salary increase, he complained to Dunning, who was beginning to be annoyed. "Why do you repine and groan at the rate of speed?" Dunning asked. "I served Columbia for three years ... at the magnificent salary of $500 per annum, and taught history under the cover of a tutorial fellowship in physics. . . . It seems to me that you are prospering fairly; and you are not grey-haired yet."[5]

Merriam's disappointment with the critical reception of *A History of American Political Theories* is understandable in the light of its subsequent usefulness in the field. Not many of Merriam's generation in 1903 shared the essential insight he was trying to voice, although it would rapidly become the rallying ideal of the emerging Progressive movement. But the Dunning-like historical catalog of successive periods of political thought did rather obscure the book's best insights.[6]

In brief, Merriam sees the Civil War as a moment of central ideological change in the history of American thought, from the dominance of a "revolutionary" ideology based upon natural rights and a contract theory of government to a "nationalist" ideology which had thus far failed to achieve a similar base in theory capable of being considered part of a "systematic politics."[7] The "revolutionary" ideology begins with Locke and Paine, achieving success as systematic theory but utter failure as history with Calhoun. The Civil War thus represented the triumph of Daniel Webster's nationalism without a Webster to give it a voice consistent with the tradition of American democratic theory. Merriam argued not that there had been no attempts to voice such an ideology in the post–Civil War years but that those attempts had been if not antidemocratic, certainly pessimistic in their view of the future of democracy. Here Merriam avoided broadening his attack, largely, one might presume, because Burgess would have been the most obvious object of attack. He cites Burgess—as well as Lester Ward, E. A. Ross, and E. L. Godkin—as a man who considers democracy severely limited by the demands of scientific development, industrial progress, and the drive for a stable world social order, with nationalism a step along the way of historical progress. Not only did Merriam disagree, but he asserted—as he would continue to assert for the rest of his life—"that the charge that democracy is on the decline in the United States is not proven. There are certain tendencies, which, if taken alone, might seem to point in such a direction; but when we consider as a whole the numerous tendencies of which democracy is made up, it is found that there are other and counterbalancing influences, equally important and significant."[8]

Thus, almost a decade ahead of the celebrations of change called for by Herbert Croly in *The Promise of American Life* and Walter Lippmann in *Drift and Mastery* Merriam was laying out the historical canon of Progressivism's support of a traditional American politics as the base of reform, not of revolution, and a new scientific order of thought consistent with democracy. A Republican populism which could easily reject Bryan is joined with social science to produce—what? It would take the rest of Merriam's life to figure it out. His belief in the future of democratic government, American style, rested on an essential optimism. The appearance of inconsistency in such a point of view was evidence of scientific error or ignorance, and that required research, not revolution. The Civil War had been the necessary revolution and the last one. What was needed now was an orderly organization of the changes that revolution had represented.

Having dedicated his first book to Dunning, as his mentor, Merriam invited Dunning's guidance in choosing his next project. Merriam wanted to do further studies in political theory, to become, as he had implied, the first American Tocqueville or Bryce; but Dunning urged him away from that youthful ambition, suggesting instead that too little attention had been paid to the "comparative constitutional law of the states of our Union, or as Prof. Burgess would write them, 'States.' " He directed Merriam back to the first volume of the *Political Science Quarterly*, to Burgess's article on the subject. That the volume also contained Woodrow Wilson's "The Study of Administration" was not mentioned by Dunning, although it was in the direction of Wilson's injunctions that Merriam later decided to move, not in the direction indicated by Burgess.[9]

Indeed, Merriam had already paid as much filial respect as he could to Burgess and Dunning's preoccupation with the states, a logical concern for their generation but too distant from the problems of Merriam's. The concept of sovereignty which Merriam had dutifully searched out in his dissertation and in his *History* was a German vessel borrowed to hold the outpourings of the earlier generation's need to understand the upheaval of the war, its violation of the voluntary cooperation of rational men which was the American meaning of self-government as these men had been taught it and as they would continue to teach it. By focusing their sense of wrong on the supposedly outmoded demand for sovereignty by the states and then demolishing the intellectual bases of that demand, they solved their problems for a time, but not those of their successors. In his analysis of Burgess's position, Merriam suggested that "attention is called to the diminishing importance of the 'states' in our political system, in contrast with the rapidly increasing power and influence of the modern city, and serious doubt is raised as to the ability of the 'state' to hold its place as a unit of government in our political system, if the influences operating during the last half century continue uninterrupted."[10] And in his own efforts to continue an interest in state government as the base of a representative, local government, Merriam tried to face the consequences of that decline. Urbanization would ultimately overshadow the preoccupation with states, a process now beginning.

For an urban reformer in 1900 the alternatives seemed clear enough, though the effort to make them useful alternatives produced numerous ambiguities. With state legislatures acting as roadblocks to reform, one could either attack them and work at reorganizing them, or try to separate cities from them and appeal for such federal involvement as was available in the years before World War I. The whole period was filled with confusing efforts in both directions and conflicting interpretations of their success or failure. The New York State Library, for example, served as a model for the development of a state agency oriented toward reform through the collection of useful legislative data and its referral not only to the New York Legislature but to the rapidly growing group of state reference libraries carrying on the same kind of work for other legislatures. Writing a general survey of the field of state government for the *New York State Library Bulletin, Review of Legislation* in 1902, Merriam commented that state governments were much slower in developing needed reforms in civil service and in administrative organization than were either municipal governments or the federal government.[11] For many critics the villain was political parties, and the two reforms Merriam noted in city and federal government had specific virtues with respect to that problem. Civil service curbed the misuses generated by "spoils," and administrative centralization encouraged party responsibility.

For academics interested in reform, legislative reference libraries and their various developing counterparts in cities—bureaus of municipal research, the periodic surveys, and the charity and social work associations—served as communications systems through which they could learn of new governmental methods and their effects. As informal committees of correspondence they documented the local Progressive programs and maintained a continuing national community of interested participants. The system was essential to academics financing their own research because it provided them not only intellectual contact with others interested in similar problems but data for their own research projects. Funding of such projects might come from state legislatures or from local groups of interested citizens and business leaders.

Merriam's reputation began to develop among that small band which, in 1903, gathered to form the American Political Science Association as an offshoot of the American Historical Association. Significantly, Merriam led an elite within that group which did not have to identify itself as former historians and whose concerns had always rested exclusively on investigations of the methods of government. When the University of Illinois made Merriam an offer in 1904 Merriam reported it to Dunning, who advised that the offer might best be used to force a promotion to professorial rank at Chicago. But if the promotion was not forthcoming, Illinois, in Dunning's opinion, was as good a place as Chicago to await a call to one of "our big eastern institutions during the next five or ten years."[12] He was voicing a common academic parochialism Merriam shared. The Chicago promotion was promised, in spite of Judson's coolness, and in 1905 Merriam became assistant professor of political science at a salary of $2,000.

Chicago's chief links to national research and reform were the Commercial Club and the City Club of Chicago. The Commercial Club announced in 1905 the promotion of a program of city planning prepared by Daniel Burnham and financed by the club. At the same time, the City Club was given money by a private donor, Miss Helen

Culver, to aid "in the investigation and improvement of municipal conditions in the City of Chicago." The following year Merriam was appointed by the governor to the Chicago charter convention as a member of the steering committee and chairman of the committee on revenue and taxation. The combination of involvements drew him into the city, and for the first time gave his research interests funding independent of the university. Whatever the university administrators chose to think now of Merriam's role in the university, he was in the process of making himself visible to—and indispensable to—the same wealthy leadership to which the university looked for its sustenance.

For Miss Culver and other like-minded philanthropists the university was one of several city institutions capable of satisfying an interest in reform and cultural development; and if such donors had a tendency to look upon the staffs of the institutions as a part of their own philanthropic entourage, no university administrator dared block access. Miss Culver expected results. A hospital matron for the Sanitary Commission during the Civil War, she had settled in Chicago as a real estate entrepreneur after the war, traveling to Atlanta briefly to set up a night school for Negroes to teach them the rudiments of property ownership which she believed to be the route to social responsibility and political success. Her business partner was Charles Hull, Jane Addams was her friend, and the founding of Hull House was influenced by her persuasions. Race and immigration were her lifelong interests—one of her last benefactions was the financing of the first major study of American immigration, the five-volume *Polish Peasant in Europe and America* (1918–20) by W. I. Thomas and Florian Znaniecki. She believed in giving to relatively small, precisely focused activities rather than large, continuing projects, and the gift to the City Club was a typical example.[13]

On Merriam's advice and under his direction, the committee selected the municipal revenue system as its topic. The choice is a tribute to Merriam's entrepreneurial skills as both academic and politician. As Merriam knew, municipal revenues were of much interest in the reform-research movement with which he had been working. While there were undoubtedly other topics more specifically concerned with Chicago—the Commercial Club with its Burnham plan was one—Merriam seized the opportunity to link Chicago with a national problem capable of national generalization rather than to emphasize

51

issues unique to Chicago. Such a project might thereby engender a wide spread interest not only in Chicago as an American city but in Merriam as an effective investigator.

The form Merriam chose was one which had long been familiar both to eastern reform elites who traveled to European cities to compare public gardens, hospitals, or school systems in preparation for local projects and to academics interested in comparative method. With his graduate student Frederick D. Bramhall as assistant, Merriam gathered evidence on revenue machinery and revenues from the cities of New York, Philadelphia, St. Louis, Boston, and Toronto. Materials on London, Paris, Berlin, Vienna, and Glasgow were contributed by John A. Fairlie of the University of Michigan and compared with corresponding facts about American cities in sets of parallel tables and commentaries.

His professional relationships in various parts of the country enabled Merriam to produce in short order and with modest funds a report of impressive proportions and scope. The conclusions were not startlingly new: American cities had insufficient revenues for their operation and growth; unity and responsibility in the local revenue system required greater consolidation; publicity was necessary for public support and criticism—all points surely familiar enough. But the collection in one volume of over one hundred and fifty pages of diverse material, the application of so broad a research frame to a single major city, and the use by urban reformers of such a professional array of evidence and personnel to document an old-fashioned reform interest gave the report a remarkable currency. It was published in January of 1906 and reprinted, revised, the following month.[14] The second edition carried a brief preface by Merriam announcing that investigations spurred by the report were underway in the county and the city and were uncovering instances of corruption which would undoubtedly lead to reform. Merriam's sense of political drama was never less than acute. Among those concerned with establishing new lines of control and new methods of research in philanthropy, academic research, and government, the report was enthusiastically received. It did much to establish Merriam's name in a very influential national group of urban reformers.

Relationships established at the City Club of Chicago were to form some of the central influences in Merriam's career. The club met weekly, and beginning in 1907 it published transcripts of those

neetings. Discussions varied. Leading political figures from other cities
s well as from foreign countries were invited, and symposia on local and
ational political programs and campaigns were arranged. Harold L.
ckes, a young lawyer with an interest in public utilities and traction
ontrol, chaired discussions of those issues. Jane Addams and George
Ierbert Mead discussed welfare and public education. Mrs. Ella Flagg
'oung debated issues of public and parochial education with Catholic
ducators in the city. Socialists appeared with business leaders, ward
osses with good-government enthusiasts.

The City Club had begun as an exclusive association of the wealthy in
earch of a society in "the west" but by 1907 included professionals of
nodest means as well as members of ethnic groups once restricted from
uch fellowship. The common interest was the city. Merriam lunched
vith Charles R. Crane, Lessing Rosenthal, and Julius Rosenwald, as
vell as with fellow members of the University of Chicago faculty, and
vith political leaders and members of important local law firms.

The common language of the City Club was business. The inherent
norality of that language rested on concepts of responsibility and
philanthropic duty with which Merriam had been familiar all his life.
Great differences in the distribution of wealth were clearly acceptable;
but the underlying community of understanding brought the teachings
of Merriam's family and the social motives of John D. Rockefeller into
a cooperation which was at the heart of their definition of progress.
Dunning had spoken of "the instinct of 'business' as the foundation of
our national greatness" and he meant something very significant by that.
The acceptance of business leadership in the half-century before the
1930s was based on an adulation of strength, a vital force which was, in
its emergence as myth, the transformation of the rugged frontiersman
into the financier. That it could be an untutored strength magnificent
in its power but dangerous in its effects had become an American
mythology.

Even by 1909 Merriam's views were not so sanguine. He liked to see
university faculty involved in research which could be useful to the
business community as well as the political community, and he thought
the relationship would become a necessary one for businessmen, even
though they might take to it reluctantly. "The modern university has
something which the community, including the business world, ought
to know about and make use of. The businessman's idea of a university
is likely to be about as far behind the times as a stagecoach is behind

53

the Pennsylvania Limited."[15] Still, Veblen was almost alone in his assertion of the dangers inherent in that relationship.

What Merriam and other academics shared with their industrial benefactors and what the generation of Harper and Low had sought to embed in the structure of the university was the responsibility for guiding that power in socially responsible directions. For most of them the endeavor did not imply a denigration of that power, let alone the necessity of destroying it. It was deemed by many a distinctive—perhaps *the* distinctive—American contribution to the world's store of natural energy, the extraordinary physical dynamo of American power in the world. The motive was in part Androclean: removing the splinter from the paw of the lion would not only save Androcles but transform the lion. The regulation of business power through education could lead to a restatement in modern industrial and scientific terms of one of the few ancient adages Americans could claim: that good business and good works were mutually beneficial.

A charter convention authorized by the Illinois state legislature, under the charter amendment adopted in 1904, met in Chicago through much of 1906 and 1907. Merriam served as a member of its committee on taxation and revenues and played a significant role in the complex lobbying which went on. The convention brought together representatives of the various interested groups: businessmen, churchmen administrators of charitable welfare organizations, the Chicago Federation of Teachers, and associations of immigrants, among others. The idea of home rule—the basic aim of Progressives and the nightmare of politicians eager to retain control of the patronage resources of the city—was inundated in the sea of proposals which had to be agreed upon by the many interests represented in the convention. The proposals then had to be pressed through the state legislature itself, and changed in accordance with demands put forward there. The resulting document, finally, had to be presented to the voters at a referendum.

The compromises insured disaster as group after group withdrew in the face of changes sure to sacrifice the interests of constituents. The Federation of Teachers withdrew its support when legislators inserted provisions nullifying, in effect, its fight against patronage in the distribution of teaching positions. The legislature had also denied the teachers the authority to change textbooks oftener than every four

years, an economy measure which the teachers considered an infringement on their control of curriculum.

The United Societies of Chicago, an association of some 490
immigrant societies said to control, or, as its leaders put it, to
"represent" some 90,000 voters, attacked provisions requiring enforcement of laws closing saloons on Sundays. That issue became a central
one for Merriam's career in Chicago politics, unifying in a solid wall of
opposition middle-class families who considered their Sunday beer
garden excursions a significant social ritual and lower-class workers for
whom Sunday was no special occasion for abstaining from a daily need.
The convention's reasons for running in the face of that opposition
were clear enough. The flouting of existing legislation, as Chicago
saloon keepers were accustomed to dealing with the problem, led to
police corruption and made saloons the clearing houses of vice and all
the political chicanery associated with payoffs. At the same time, a
state legislature dominated by rural politicians could not fail to support
its religious enthusiasms and urban-ethnic prejudices. Chicago police
could not enforce such a law and Chicago politicians could not press
them to. The convention's solution was to provide recourse through the
courts for the enforcement of state statutes, a compromise destined to
be no more effective than the problem warranted, but effective enough to
solidify the opposition. As the representative of the United Societies
put it to the City Club, "This charter would enforce puritanical ideas
upon men who have acquired for generations certain ideas and customs
that are dearer to them then the power of the council to sell more
bonds, and the power to build a political machine in this city."[16]

In the September referendum fewer than 180,000 of the more than
360,000 registered voters turned out, and the charter was defeated by
more than two to one. In a letter to Dunning, Merriam attributed the
loss to an alliance between the Democratic party which had opposed
the charter all along, and the United Societies. The alliance would have
continuing effect on his career in Chicago politics.[17]

As secretary to the Chicago Harbor Commission, Merriam worked
with Charles Wacker and Frederic A. Delano in a program for the
development of the Chicago harbor area which would satisfy local
business and shipping interests, on the one hand, and the promoters of
the plans for the beautiful city on the lakefront, on the other. The
complex of conflicts and pressures, the local business interests, the

railroads, the port city political patronage, the army engineers in the War Department, and the Treasury and Interior professionals who had long dreamed of a North American seaway through the Great Lakes to the Atlantic, provided a rich if at times frustrating experience in the problems of urban planning. Merriam saw to it that experts were appointed to the commission: J. Paul Goode, professor of economic geography at the University of Chicago, and George C. Sikes, a leading Chicago journalist, who did comparative studies of the principal ports of Europe, as well as of Boston, New York, and Philadelphia as a base for the projection of the Chicago plan.[18]

Merriam's writing during this period remains bound to his immediate political involvements, usually as generalized abstractions of his own experiences. To watch him moving away from the concept of sovereignty to what would become a concern with behavior, one can compare his article for the *New International Encyclopedia* of 1904 on "Sovereignty," written in terms removed by scarcely a step from his Burgess notes, with an article written the same year for the *Political Science Quarterly*, "State Central Committees," in which he wrote, "The possession of the central committee is, if not conclusive, at least presumptive evidence of party authority and control—one of the external marks of sovereignty." The interest in party and an effort to understand its role as the base of political control was obviously part of his involvement with Chicago politics; but he had just read M. Ostrogorski's two-volume study, *Democracy and the Organization of Political Parties*, and was eager to work out some approach of his own to the problem. By 1907 when Ostrogorski visited the United States and accepted an invitation to speak at the University of Chicago, Merriam was at work on his study of primary elections; the two had long discussions about the subject, and the following year Ostrogorski wrote Merriam from Paris reminding him of his promise to send a copy of the finished work.[19]

Primary Elections appeared in 1908, the year the city of Chicago in citywide elections, adopted primary elections as the method for choosing political candidates. Merriam spent about a year surveying the attitudes of political scientists around the country, as well as selected members of his acquaintance in city and state governments who were interested in primaries. His questionnaire consisted of nine points, such as "Does the direct primary bring out a larger vote than the convention system?" and "Is the class of nominees any higher under the direct

rimary system than under the convention plan?" The questions were,
ll in all, a transparent acknowledgment of the reform motives of the
nquiry and the inquirer. Merriam sent out probably more than sixty
uch questionnaires and did not make very systematic use of the
eplies, most of which followed, in general, the line which Merriam
iimself took in the book: that where the voting population is literate
nd intelligent and the community small, direct primaries work. Other-
vise, their utility is questionable.

In its revision with Louise Overacker in 1928, the book takes a quite
lifferent form, having been expanded from a high-level reform pam-
ohlet of the Progressive era into a political science analysis of the 1920s.
Merriam contributed a more comprehensive analysis and more mate-
ial to the revision, and Luella Gettys provided a fully researched
ummary of primary laws and bibliography. Although material from
he first edition appears in the second, the difference between the two is
nteresting as an example of the change between the Progressive Meriam of 1908 and the political science Merriam of 1928. Nonetheless,
he level and quality of the first effort are extremely important. Meriam's search for scientific objectivity consistent with his progressive
political method and his informed analytical skepticism of reform
deals move his 1908 work well beyond the general reform tract of the
period. Indeed, the 1928 book is far more insistent on pressing the
theme of progressive optimism than the 1908 work. In 1908, on the
threshold of the movement whose momentum would carry through the
next thirty years, Merriam tended to be suspicious of the growing
emphasis upon institutional reforms, although not perhaps as sharply
acid as Henry Jones Ford, whose reply to the questionnaire summed up
the new reaction. "My opinion," Ford wrote, "is that what are termed
the newer institutional forms of democracy are simply the latest fash-
ions in political nostrums, addressed to symptoms rather than to the
malady itself; which is the lack of responsible government due to defects
in the organization of public authority. I think that after the patient
has been well dosed with these nostrums he will be worse off than
before.[20]

While Ford's terms are different from those which Merriam tended
to use, "the organization of public authority" did indeed point to the
same center of weakness that attracted Merriam's attention. What was
different, perhaps, was Merriam's continuing insistence that "institutional forms of democracy" would provide the only real route to re-

57

form. The question was finding the right forms, not seeking alternatives to democratic forms. Given the mood of social and political
thought in Europe during Merriam's lifetime—the increasingly visible
background against which the intellectual problems of his lifetime were
to be projected—the persistence is significant. Ford's doubts implied a
radicalism which Merriam saw no reason to accept.

The year 1907 had brought several interesting job offers which
Merriam discussed with his brother John and, of course, with Dunning
President David Starr Jordan of Stanford offered him an assistant
professorship at $3,000 and Merriam was inclined to bargain, although
John, being at the University of California and therefore more familiar
with the neighboring institution and its difficulties, warned him against
it. Western Reserve in Ohio had raised $100,000 to endow a chair in
political science, and the opportunity there of a separate department—
which Stanford did not then have—appealed to Merriam. The role of
research in both institutions worried him. The question of whether or
not Stanford really intended to become a "university," by which he
meant to "abandon or at least lay less emphasis upon their collegiate
work, and devote themselves primarily to research," was the one to
which he directed himself. John had already been engaged in a running
battle with Jordan on precisely the same subject and had written to one
inquirer that same year that "Stanford as a University looks rather
large to people, but from what I learn it is the hardest place in the
world to obtain money for research at present, and has the further
disadvantage that no one is allowed to solicit or receive outside funds
for assistance." The last point was crucial. John solicited money from
wealthy San Franciscans for his work. His brother was already doing
the same thing at Chicago. Jordan was obviously trying to plug leaks
which diverted funds from the university's coffers, and the new breed
of academic entrepreneurs was not inclined to accept that interference.[21]

Not that Merriam's situation at Chicago seemed very much better to
him. His dissatisfactions were the product of ambitions which Judson
as an adminstrator was willing to try to cope with, but not in ways
which Merriam could completely understand. However much Judson
valued Merriam as a member of the university community, he mis-
trusted his ambitions although he had somewhat grudgingly come to
accept Merriam's increasing involvement in politics. He made Merriam
associate professor but refused him backing for research and rebuffed

his early efforts to develop a school of government or politics in the university. Merriam was trying to see beyond the idea of a Bureau of Research to something else; but he wasn't sure what it was. Neither was Judson. He offered to make Merriam dean of the College of Commerce and Administration—the closest he could get to what he thought Merriam wanted; and Merriam accepted. But he held the post only through 1909, after which his involvement in other matters apparently made the position less attractive to him. While the disagreements between Judson and Merriam were rarely crucial, they do indicate fundamental differences which neither could resolve. For example, Judson consulted Merriam on the subject of a school to train foreign service officers, to be founded by the federal government. His advice had been asked and he turned to Merriam for what he apparently thought would be support, but Merriam strongly opposed such an idea. The universities, he felt, were in a position to do such training more comprehensively and much less expensively. Judson could not agree.[22]

Increasingly, the city became the focus of Merriam's interests, his research, and his ambitions. Judson inherited Harper's university but not his entrepreneurial skills. He also inherited Harper's problems, chief among them the question of how far the university's backers were really willing to be pressed. Merriam quite logically turned to the city, free enough to build there on his own. With his acute sense of presence before any audience, he was much in demand as a speaker before the many groups whose interests he shared. He could be professorial enough to satisfy businessmen and university alumni who preferred that manner in his approach. Yet he retained a midwestern easiness which could slide into good honest farm talk with an Iowa twang and a wry humor. He spoke in German at beer festivals, and he lectured to the members of the Chicago Institute of Social Science, as it was called, which stated as its purpose the training of "men and women for positions in settlements, charitable societies and institutions, juvenile court and truant work, and other social sciences."[23] He met Edith Abbott, who headed what was then the Chicago School of Civics and Philanthropy. Both organizations, with their leaders would eventually become the university's School of Social Service Administration.

By 1909 as his first decade in Chicago was closing, Merriam had assumed full status as a citizen in his adopted community. His position in the university and in his profession was secure. Temptations to leave would come again; but there would not be the depth of dissatisfaction which had marked this first stage of his career. At the edge of his university career stood a career in politics, not simply in the study of it but in profession of it. In 1909 a vacancy appeared on the City Council's seventh ward representation—the "silk-stocking" ward in which Merriam lived—he was a logical candidate. He was popular in the university and well known among the local groups concerned with Chicago politics. Despite objections from the Republican organization which considered itself in control of its politics, Merriam's community was ready to assert its identity. So was Merriam.

4

The Scholar in Politics

Merriam entered the Chicago aldermanic primary in 1909 as "C. Edward Merriam," but his party manager rebelled. "It's bad enough to have a university professor on the ticket," the older veteran complained, "without having his name parted in the middle."[1] He became "Charles E. Merriam." His father had not lived to see his son in politics, and so the old issue of the name resolved itself.

Although the Republican organization had opposed his candidacy, the strength of reform in the ward was too great, as Merriam's unexpectedly strong showing in the primary proved. It was tantamount, of course, to election. His opponent in the primary had charged him with seeking to turn the ward over to John D. Rockefeller, an accusation with which Merriam was to become very familiar. Republican Mayor Fred A. Busse had called him a socialist from the University of Chicago. After the primary, however, the regular organization perked up. Governor Charles S. Deneen wrote to congratulate him,[2] and the reform group with which Merriam was associated throughout the country gave his candidacy considerably more attention than aldermanic races were usually likely to get. Advisers of Charles Evans Hughes were using Merriam's book on primaries and his reputation as an active participant in politics was becoming well established.[3]

Dunning wrote warm and enthusiastic congratulations, although not without his customary *caveat*. He saluted his student as "that wholly admirable phenomenon, the scholar in politics." But unwilling to leave it at that, he added, "remember Henry Cabot Lodge."[4] If Merriam considered that a warning, the success of Woodrow Wilson in New Jersey the following year must certainly have weakened its effect.

The Chicago City Council in 1909 consisted of seventy members, two from each of thirty-five wards. Half the total, one per ward, came up for reelection every two years. Primary elections required by the new law were added to the aldermanic elections, producing a continuous stream of discussion about the city, its council, and the affairs with which it dealt. In 1909 the chief issues involved transportation disputes produced, in part, by the electric revolution, the use of transportation tunnels under the city for telephone and electric lines, and the location and distribution of gas lines. River and harbor innovations affected all the other issues. Franchises to be authorized by the council and interfered with by the state affected property values and the inevitable land speculation. The railroads which entered the city and the banking relationship with those railroads attached the Chicago and New York financial community to the political affairs of the city. "Aldermanic courtesy," a device much lamented by reform groups, allowed each alderman to influence the franchise votes of other aldermen through the threat of a veto. This miniature federalism produced a lively political situation difficult for voters to understand or influence.[5]

Merriam's first term in the council was exciting and intellectually invigorating. The council's extraordinary control over Chicago affairs, coupled with the relatively successful effects of a decade of reform on the council's personnel, made it an effective forum for a young man seeking influence and authority. The council controlled a budget of close to fifty million dollars and conducted its business largely through some twenty-four committees. Party control of committee assignments and chairmanships had been broken ten years earlier, and while posts were subject to negotiation, a young man who entertained reform ambitions was assured of as immediate an involvement as he wanted to have.

Merriam pressed first for appointment by the mayor of a commission to investigate the city's finances, a request which Merriam's recent prominence in the City Club's report and his work on the charter commission made eminently reasonable. As chairman of this commission he bore in on building frauds, irregularities in the handling of bids, and the more flagrant misuses of patronage. Under pressure from Merriam, the council also created a "bureau of efficiency," which centered its interests on standards of civil service. Merriam's most important work was on the committee on gas, oil, and electric lights, which included the telephone system, and which brought him into conflict with the city's major suppliers of business services, the leading figure among whom was Samuel Insull.⁶

Unlike many of his contemporaries in urban reform whose training followed nonpolitical routes, Merriam's education in urban planning was from within politics itself, as a politician using the processes of city politics to gain political ends. What he was discovering was that planning took place whether planners controlled it or not. Samuel Insull planned; traction companies planned, and their planning shaped the city to meet their needs. The reformers did not use the concept of "public interest" to destroy these private interests or to substitute for them. The idea was simpler than that: to give the public a voice to balance its needs against those of private interests, a modest enough aim. The people's representatives like Merriam conceived themselves as serving this aim. The image of the watchdog fitted the role these politicians set for themselves, just as it characterized the methods they tended to select. The bark was often considered a political tool just as effective as a bite, at times even more so.

That many reform-minded politicians were professional academics followed a pattern made nationally familiar by Seth Low and even Woodrow Wilson. Merriam found his own meager economic resources as a political figure limiting and frustrating; but he found he could depend on donors who, not eager themselves for even short-term political careers, respected the academics as men more like themselves intellectually than the professional politicians whose careers the less reform-minded business leaders chose to finance. The "donors" distinguished themselves from the "graftors" in that they considered their motives in financing political careers a demonstration of community interest rather than crass self-interest. In later years students of the period would have difficulty seeing a difference between the two as sharp as it seemed in its day.

The life of an alderman brought Merriam close to his constituents in the university community. He must also have felt some sense of the citizen-leadership his father had enjoyed in his Hopkinton general store. Merriam served as intermediary between the citizen who felt himself dealt with unjustly or ineffectively by some city department, an "ombudsman" whose services were constantly in demand. Although the Municipal Voters' League saw the necessity of such demands as a persistent sign of "inefficient and slovenly administration" on the part of the departments the alderman had to nudge to action, the service was part of daily life in a city rapidly growing too large to provide both needed services and the small-town illusion of freedom from government. In this situation the ambiguities inherent in the relation between bureaucracy and democracy were not easily resolved.

Merriam enjoyed tending his ward. He could be called upon to defend a city employee under fire, a schoolteacher, for example, whose parents resided in Merriam's ward but whose job was controlled by another alderman, who had needed to consider that job as his responsibility. Trades of influence could be arranged between the two aldermen. The alderman served, too, as fund raiser for individual charities, the beneficiaries of which were citizens come unexpectedly on hard times. While the alderman prodded existing city services into more efficient operation, he also provided services himself which the city had not yet discovered the need of offering. As long as the manipulation of influence and power benefited citizens of the community as a whole rather than the personal fortunes of the manipulator, it was considered public service not corruption; but the difference was not always so clear to business interests who considered the success of their ventures a public service in a way too.[7]

As head of the council's finance commission, Merriam was in a position to attract city-wide attention. Equally important, and perhaps more so to a public in danger of overexposure to cries of corruption, Merriam's personality and his skill in projecting it, his humor and his awareness of the utility of the press assured reporters seeking to brighten an otherwise dull story from City Hall of a bright anecdote and a sharp quotation. Also, Merriam used his experience in city government to create a constituency in his profession. Notes concerning the changes in Chicago city government appeared over his name in social science journals throughout the period. Indeed, there is little indication during his term that he had an interest in being anything other than alderman-professor, like Professor Hugo Preuss of Berlin, perhaps, or following Bryce's injunction to learn the science of politics from experience in politics rather than from theorizing about politics. At times Merriam called upon Plato's myth of the cave to justify his life to students who were open in their admiration of the man whose classrooms they filled during the day and whose battles with the "gray wolves" of the council they flocked to see in the evening meetings of that august body.

The approaching mayoralty campaign of 1911 was important to Merriam for one reason only: as a Republican loyal to the party he was committed to reform and as head of a commission which found much to criticize in Republican Mayor Busse's conduct of his office, Merriam held a highly sensitive place in the public's view of the party and the party's battles with itself. While Merriam played his part in such a way as to avoid direct embarrassment to the mayor, concentrating criticism on functionaries within the administration, by the end of his two-year term he was an obvious alternative to the mayor and ultimately a focus for public gossip.

While President Taft's leadership had aroused dissatisfaction among many reform Republicans in the nation, the situation in Illinois Republican politics was exacerbated by the emergence of the Lorimer scandal in 1910. William Lorimer, a state party boss of immense power, was accused of having bought his seat in the United States Senate. A lively newspaper campaign kept the issue going for long enough to pressure the Senate into taking action, the outcome of which was a vote to refuse Lorimer his seat. Unlike the scandals of the Grant and Harding administrations—and much more like the present-day Watergate—the Lorimer scandal forced a reexamination not simply of the transgression but of the very acceptance of the practices being transgressed. The selection of United States senators by their state legislatures had always raised questions of patronage and the misuse of financial power, so much so that the vote against Lorimer could scarcely avoid raising a sense of embarrassment—if not outright hypocrisy—among many of the legislators who joined in it. Taft's avoidance of a stand on the issue, appropriate to the separation of powers though it may have been, did not satisfy reformers who wanted only to separate the sheep from the goats. The presidential ambitions of Senator Robert La Follette were given a forward thrust.

The Lorimer scandal in Illinois was not only a public scandal, but a professional scandal as well, calling attention to the necessity for the review of practices as only the professional politicians understood them. It enabled reform Republicans to identify the entire regular party organization in the state as "the Lorimer faction" and to make all political leaders associated with it the objects of reform. The label gave increasing impetus to concern over the possibility of Taft's reelection and, more importantly perhaps, to the question of its appropriateness.

Many Illinois Republicans, particularly in the small towns, still liked to consider themselves descendants of a Lincolnian liberalism. On the national scene Theodore Roosevelt represented it; Taft most certainly did not. The addition of the Lorimer scandal to Taft's growing difficulties threatened to have the effect of associating the president not only with national big business but with the shoddiest local corruption.[8]

Merriam's candidacy in the mayoralty campaign of 1911 began simply as an attempt on the part of more extreme reform groups within the Republican party to take control of the party by forcing Mayor Busse to withdraw. Support from within the party's core of regulars came from those who felt that the mayor's association with the Lorimer forces might lose him the election in any case, particularly after the announcement by Carter Harrison, Jr., in January 1911 that he would enter the Democratic primary. The son of one of the city's most important nineteenth-century mayors, and a former mayor himself, Harrison's popularity—or the popularity of his name—plus the national and local pressures on the Republicans, gave some impetus to the possibility of a Republican reform candidate who might help recoup the party's reputation, even if he lost. From the organization's point of view, it might even be better if he lost.[9]

Merriam's candidacy was given further aid by a group of city contractors who were faced with increasing public criticism brought on by revelations of the Merriam commission and who, having failed to pressure the council sufficiently to stop the investigations, sought and were granted a temporary injunction cutting off the commission's funds as an unwarranted expenditure of public tax money. While their case would probably have been lost, the time and expense involved would also have done serious damage to the commission's work. The action angered Julius Rosenwald, who had hitherto confined his philanthropy to nonpolitical causes, and he agreed to underwrite the commission's expenses, announcing himself thereby as an active backer of Alderman Merriam.

Merriam's initial intention, then, was to force Busse out of the primaries, possibly to open the way to a more acceptable candidate, not necessarily himself. He selected as his manager Harold Le Clair Ickes, a young lawyer and Republican reformer who shared Merriam's interests in city government. His partnership in the firm of Richberg, Richberg, and Ickes had thrown Ickes into many of the same public utilities battles that Alderman Merriam had been fighting.

Both Ickes and Merriam looked upon their membership in the Illinois Republican party as a responsibility requiring their active participation. They had both been delegates to the state Republican convention at Springfield in 1910, a convention that had made clear the depth and disruption of the struggle for power within the party. It was on the train home from Springfield that Merriam and Ickes had first discussed the possibility of Merriam's mayoralty candidacy.

Merriam's decision was made by November of that year and his campaign for the February party primary launched by December, a month or so ahead of Carter Harrison's announcement of his decision. Busse withdrew reluctantly, certain that the combination of Merriam's already well-publicized criticisms and recent discussions of his personal life would bring about his defeat.

Merriam and his reform followers saw the primary as a reaction against the operating machinery of the Republican party regulars. The fact that they saw it that way is an important element in explaining their ultimate defeat. Indeed, much of the subsequent history of the reform movement—the peak of progressivism—continues to be distorted by their vision of themselves as the true reformers, their opponents as the corrupt enemy. The leaders of the Illinois Republican party were not willing to take the position which Boss Jim Smith of the New Jersey Democratic party had taken with respect to Woodrow Wilson: back a reformer or face defeat. Nor were the conditions similar enough to make such a position possible. But in their fashion, they tried. All candidates in the primary could claim connections with reform. All could be criticized for their relationships with one or another of the wealthy interests of the city. Reform interests of the period were never quite what the defending and attacking rhetoric so clearly sought to imply.

Governor Deneen of Illinois had had the backing of the reform forces of 1904. He now supported the former city treasurer John F. Smulski, Chicago's best-known Polish-American politician. Busse and some of the so-called Lorimer faction backed John R. Thompson, wealthy restaurateur who had little experience in politics but a desire for office. Merriam had the backing of a wealthy group, and many of his supporters were experienced political reformers. In addition to Julius Rosenwald, the only avowed political innocent, Merriam received support from Charles R. Crane, the plumbing heir whose secretary and assistant, Walter S. Rogers, kept close tabs on politics, and Cyrus H.

McCormick, Harold F. McCormick, Mrs. Emmons McCormick Blaine, and Miss Helen Culver, among others. It was solid backing; and it financed a very active and expensive campaign.

Merriam won the primary with a 54,000 vote majority. Thompson received 26,000 and Smulski 24,000. Although the total vote in the Democratic primary was 40,000 more than the total in the Republican primary, Harrison's narrow victory over his nearest opponent indicated the possibility of serious division among the Democrats, plus the possibility of a certain dimming of the traditional Harrison luster. Whether the Republicans would be able to exploit the unexpected popularity of their reformer depended upon changes in strategy and a drawing together of factions which would have to be accomplished in the weeks separating the February primary from the April election.

The battle between the two candidates rested on the issues of experience and reputation, puritan reform and personal freedom—the saloon debate with all its crucial ethnic overtones. Harrison could draw a sure and derisive laugh from many audiences by referring to "the Professor," a term which to many still indicated the orchestra conductor in a vaudeville show, to others the epitome of impracticality and radicalism. Religion—both Merriam and Harrison were Protestants who had married Catholics—became an element in the fight. Pamphlets were distributed suggesting that Mrs. Merriam attended a Baptist church and had refused to baptize her children in the Catholic church. Counter charges implied that Mrs. Harrison no longer practiced her faith. Since neither marriage could be said to have the sanction of the church, the issue of practice was the more embarrassing. Mrs. Harrison was a Catholic communicant who was raising her children in the faith. Her husband was not a religious man, as he frequently put it, although, as he was also quick to add, he had attended a Catholic school and did not feel uncomfortable at the Catholic services. Mrs. Merriam, on the other hand, had not continued the practice of her Catholicism after her marriage, and while she did have her children baptized by the church, she did not give them a Catholic education. Nor had she joined another church.

Both Harrison and Merriam appealed to ethnic groups, particularly the Irish and the Germans. Both could speak German sufficiently to do a reasonable job of campaigning in the language, although in the German districts the reform label—and its unavoidably prohibitionist implications—stuck firmly to Merriam. Years later Merriam would insist to students that Harrison had envied his German; but the fact that Harrison had spent three years of his adolescence in schools in Germany while Merriam had one postgraduate year there makes the story somewhat unlikely.

The fact remains that, on balance and as all of the foregoing detail indicates, Merriam and Harrison were probably more alike in what they really represented than they were unlike. Mayor Busse and Lorimerism were the only real villains; and they were out of the way. Both Merriam and Harrison could identify themselves as reformers. True, Merriam was "a professor" but one with two years in the City Council behind him and with a sense of the politics of Chicago based on active engagement in the city and the party over the previous five years. Harrison, as a former mayor, was a professional; but his father's years as mayor and his own career were both part of a tradition associated with the good government interests of the city. Each within his party opposed an existing machine. Where they differed sharply was in their control of the potential coalitions within their respective parties. Coalitions were possible, not only within the party but between factions of the two parties with interests in common, and the management of these coalitions required a skill at which Harrison was experienced and Merriam not. Even so, indications are that Merriam would have been pleased to gain the experience, the short time allotted him to do so notwithstanding.

That Merriam's political inclinations were opposed by Harold Ickes may have been more responsible for the closeness of the mayoral race than any of the factors one can elicit from a study of the campaign itself. Ickes's nonpartisanship was more intense than partisanship. Although he continued to identify himself as a Republican, when the Republicans nominated Taft, Ickes cast his vote for Bryan. He voted against every Republican candidate for president from 1920 through 1944; but he opposed Truman's candidacy in 1948 with the same vehemence with which he had opposed Hoover's in 1928. Yet he considered himself a committed progressive Republican, devoted to an ideal of party which was profoundly partisan. Even if no such party ever came to be, he could not be faulted for having failed to try to produce it.

Ickes felt that Merriam had won his primary battle without the aid of the party factions of the Illinois Republicans, indeed in spite of them; and he saw no reason to consort with men who had given no support in the part and who could not, he felt, be trusted to cooperate now. Merriam thought otherwise and sought through negotiation with the regular leadership to establish relationships with ward and precinct groups—some less savory than others. Ickes gave in, but grudgingly and with a distaste he did nothing to conceal. He resented what he considered the patronizing manner of Roy O. West, one of the necessary architects of any party compromise and a figure deeply involved both socially and financially with the city's business leadership, but a man also known as a close associate of Governor Deneen.

Among the paradoxes of Ickes's chronic mistrust was his willingness to deal with Democratic leaders who resented Harrison's takeover of the party and claimed at least to be willing to aid in his defeat. Ickes believed from them what he could not believe in his own party: that there was a confusing disagreement among party regulars—the professionals—on the question of just how to deal with reformers in the party. True, the whole question of reform was tangled in rhetoric which often misstated the realities of politics. The definition of graft and the precise pinpointing of what one meant by corruption had to be balanced against the necessity of financing political campaigns—reformer and regular alike. Ickes, even given the angularities of his personality, illustrates beautifully the dilemmas of reform. Willing enough to engage in the grating irregularities of ward politics at its very worst—and as knowledgeable as any man about the ways to do it—he nonetheless abhorred the manipulative methods he had managed to learn, with the result that he hobbled his victories with a belief in the necessity of reforming the methods by which he had achieved them. Julius Rosenwald, beginning to be interested in his new venture in backing a political candidate, suggested that Ickes pay his precinct workers a modest fee for their services; Rosenwald would provide the funds. It seemed to him a sensible way of compensating them for their efforts, and it would scarcely be enough to be considered dishonest. Other faction leaders in local politics had obviously thought similar things useful and had not hesitated to employ them. Ickes objected, not because he thought it dishonest, but because he thought it would not do any good.

The two men, candidate Merriam and his manager Ickes, were a marvelously contrasting pair whose very relationship spelled defeat. Even so, the issue between them and its consequences can be seen as more than a local matter. The Republican party as a majority party throughout the nation was having difficulty using its reformers. Reform in the Democratic party, identified for almost two decades with Bryan and his supposed agrarian radicalism, was in a position to be more inventive and more compromising. Republicans were caught between the necessity of holding onto past gains to sustain effective organization and the necessity of accommodating themselves to the growing reform mood. Even Roosevelt found it necessary to refuse to speak on Merriam's behalf during a Chicago visit while the primary campaign was in process, at the same time that he refused to appear at a Republican banquet if Lorimer were also to be present. The balance between supporting reform and supporting a going and clearly effective political organization was a difficult one to strike. The rhetoric of reform was the necessary base of any political campaign; but believing it could be suicidal.

Election day, 4 April 1911, finally came, and the vote was close: 177,977 for Harrison, 160,627 for Merriam, and 24,825 for the Socialist candidate. Merriam was convinced that he had been the victim of fraudulent voting and vote counting, and he was probably right. Close votes in Chicago elections were then, as now, subject to such charges by either side. Taking a very local view, Merriam analyzed the Socialist vote as the result of Democratic regulars who could not accept Harrison and would not vote Republican, although the national increase in Socialist voting over the period makes that argument somewhat suspect. Merriam also charged Republican regulars with foot dragging, and both he and the regulars defended themselves by post-election analyses of wards and precincts which could have been expected to demonstrate their positions.

Ickes's law partner Donald Richberg wrote Merriam an impassioned and supportive defense: "It was painfully clear in the early returns last evening that your defeat was to be laid to your supposed political allies and not to your supposed opponents." And in an interestingly revealing forecast of the dilemma which was to produce the party split, he continued:

> You may remember that at the start of the primary campaign I refused to become a member of a republican organization (just as I have refused to become a member of any democratic organization), although I worked consistently and avowedly for you from the day you entered the race. I do not care to dub myself a republican as long as the leaders of the republican party are men of the Busse, Lorimer, Thompson, Deneen, Pease type

of unprincipled political traders and tricksters. Nor do I care to dub myself a democrat under the leadership of Harrison, Sullivan, Kenna, Coughlin, Burke and other buyers and sellers of public rights, privileges and principles and licenses for crime.... [A] decent man who wished to be elected to a place where he may give good government in exchange for votes has nothing in common with those who only exchange votes for personal profit.[10]

Merriam blamed part of his loss on Ickes's intransigence with respect to the party regulars, particularly the aldermen who controlled wards most open to attack by reformers and who simply wanted assurances—so it was argued—that a reform administration would not deal too harshly with their livelihoods. Certainly more could have been done to appease such interests than Ickes was willing to do or than Merriam had had time to do. The kind of hard realism with which Harrison juggled his alliances was at least a tacit recognition of the inherent weakness of the whole campaign: the genuine similarities of the two candidates as potential progressives. The election had to rest on a careful organization of forces. Harrison could do that; Merriam could not. Harrison's analysis of his own campaign is as close to the truth as anyone needs to get. "Beyond a shadow of a doubt I owed my victory to the loyalty of the foreign nationalities backed by the flophouse ballots of the first and eighteenth wards," he wrote later, adding philosophically, "In politics you must take them as they come."[11]

Merriam's race put him in an unusually strong position as a Republican leader in the state. Frederick A. Cleveland, chairman of President Taft's Commission on Economy and Efficiency, wrote that "few in this part of the country thought you would get as large a vote as you did, considering the alignment of forces there, and the very marked democratic swing in politics." He invited Merriam to "assume responsibility for the political science end" of the commission's work, offering him appointment to the proposed five-man commission at a salary of $6,000. "While we were not in the attitude of hoping that you would be defeated, we watched the returns of the morning with added interest, for the reason that in case you were defeated we hoped that you might be available," Cleveland added.[12] Merriam refused the offer.

On the thirtieth of the month Merriam was in Washington as part of the three-man Progressive Republican contingent from Illinois, which included Senator W. Clyde Jones and Walter S. Rogers, representing his employer, Charles R. Crane. They met with the congressional group which had gathered to back the candidacy of Robert M. La Follette as leader of the party's progressives. By early June, Senator Jones wrote Merriam in detail about his current conversations with La Follette and the latter's decision to "tear the hide off" the president in his reciprocity speech.[13] La Follette also confided to Jones that he intended to show Taft's unavailability for the nomination. La Follette commented on a campaign fund of $60,000 plus the promise of an additional $25,000 from Crane, whose only condition was that he be allowed to name the campaign manager.[14]

Rumor was beginning to circulate that Merriam intended to support Taft, and despite Merriam's ultimate commitment to the Progressive movement—once Roosevelt's direct involvement in it was clear—the suggestion in the summer of 1911 had more than just a breath of truth. Merriam had met Taft during the campaign of 1908 when the Chicago Association of Commerce, in an absurd burst of bipartisanship that did not reflect the traditional views of its members, invited both Taft and Bryan to be present at a dinner. The invitations were issued in such a way as to make refusal by either one difficult. Bryan seemed to enjoy the evening; Taft very obviously did not. But Taft managed to charm Merriam; and, while Merriam came to question his capacities as politician and party leader, he respected Taft's administrative intelligence and his grasp of national problems. When Merriam entered the Chicago mayoralty race he had Taft's support. Taft, who had just appointed Chicago conservationist Walter L. Fisher as Richard A. Ballinger's replacement in the Department of the Interior, sent Fisher to speak for Merriam in Chicago, hoping to extend one reach further the peace bridge to the progressives which Fisher's appointment had been intended to be in the first place. In fact, Taft was apparently willing to consider backing Merriam either for the Illinois governorship or a Senate seat as part of a new liberal program intended to counter progressive criticism of his administration.

Taft's move came too late; but it created serious confusion for Merriam. La Follette had sought Merriam's support—his magazine referred to Merriam as "the Woodrow Wilson of the West"—and Merriam, while not enthusiastic, seems to have found La Follette a reasonably attractive leader. Senator Jones sought assurances from Merriam that he would support La Follette and that he would reject compromise with Deneen, quoting La Follette's opinion that Deneen was a man without courage, a "trimmer," the term soon to be applied to anyone who sought compromise with the party regulars. So committed was La Follette to independence from the regulars that as early as 1911 he encouraged progressives in Illinois to boycott the state party convention, to meet on their own instead, and to provide a slate of their own candidates. He planned to work out a program whereby public interest would be sustained throughout the coming summer through speaking engagements on the Chautauqua circuits.

Although both Merriam and Jones felt that La Follette underestimated the problems faced by Illinois Republicans, they were willing to agree with his view of Illinois as the chief battleground of the Progressive insurgency. The Lorimer fight was attracting national attention. The Chicago *Tribune,* in La Follette's opinion, owed him a debt for his pursuit of the Lorimer hearings which they would have to repay. The formation of the Progressive Republican League of Illinois, which had as its purpose the naming of a slate of candidates in the face of the opposition of the Deneen faction, was the beginning of a debacle which, to observers even as relatively unseasoned as Merriam, was clear from the outset. Funds for the league's support were not forthcoming in anywhere near the necessary amounts. The regular Chautauqua programs had been booked since April and space was available only where unexpected cancellations occurred. Downstate Republicans—with headquarters at Morris, Illinois—may have had more reform enthusiasm than their urban counterparts, but they didn't have the money. The chief question seems to have been the general reluctance of local parties to commit themselves to a break with the national party and its incumbent president a full year before the national convention. "Patronage, patronage, patronage," an American Bryce might have chanted, and he would have been painfully close to the facts.[15]

Merriam had avoided Roosevelt overtures on at least two occasions during the winter of 1911 and spring of 1912, one at a dinner in Chicago at which a petition was circulated and the other when intermediaries of "the Colonel," sought his support. Merriam continued to speak for La Follette throughout the state and followed up requests from Walter L. Houser, La Follette's campaign manager, concerning engagements in nearby states. But by January 1912 the issue of La Follette's health was weighing heavily with even the most enthusiastic supporters. His physical "collapse," as the newspapers were reporting it, threatened to bring the Illinois progressives down with him, even though they had a majority in the state Republican committee. Increasingly nervous about their own position in the state, they accepted Roosevelt's official announcement of his candidacy on 23 February with a sudden relief that allowed no time for consultation among them. Senators Jones and George Magill had come out for Roosevelt without speaking about the matter with either Merriam or Walter Rogers. As a result, Merriam's supporters requested of Houser that Merriam be "released" by La Follette lest he be put in a "position where to keep his word means to sacrifice his position as leader in Illinois government."[16] The issue was Merriam's continuing leadership in Illinois and a political future which seemed at the moment very promising. The mayoralty defeat had turned out to be a victory.

When Merriam switched to Roosevelt is unclear. He continued to speak for La Follette through the early spring; but he supported TR at the Republican convention in June. Early in July Merriam joined a delegation of visitors to Oyster Bay, there to ascertain for himself whether Roosevelt was really willing to lead a losing cause or whether he planned some form of compromise. Here, in what was perhaps one of the momentous decisions of his political career—as well as of his intellectual life—Merriam entered the American dream world of third party politics, committing himself to a realignment of American political parties on ideological lines, a position he would in effect repudiate in his subsequent writing. He admired Roosevelt as a politician, a party leader, a charismatic colossus embodying everything the concept of leadership would mean to Merriam for the rest of his life. Later, when Merriam was with TR during the assassination attempt in Milwaukee, the colonel's melodramatic bravery illustrated this concept with a sharpness Merriam would never forget.

As a member of the resolutions committee of the national Progressive party, Merriam watched the threatened dissolution of coalitions of reform groups averted by compromises made possible only by the personality of the man they had, in many instances reluctantly, chosen to lead them. In later years Merriam frequently recounted to students tales of the meetings that went on until three in the morning, with William Allen White stretched out on a sofa, periodically lifting his pudgy hand to register his vote. Merriam watched the traffic moving back and forth between the rooms of the resolutions committee and Roosevelt's rooms. Irritated progressives, threatened with the loss of some one or the other of their pet reforms, greeted the colonel angrily, and left his presence in smiles. When Merriam asked him what it was he had done to effect such transformations, he replied, "I held their hot little hands. I crossed a 't' and dotted an 'i' and they went away happy."

Merriam addressed the state convention of the Progressive party as temporary chairman when it met on 3 August. He outlined a fairly straightforward Progressive program, but began significantly with initiative, referendum, recall, and direct election of senators, the "changes in political machinery" which would "place the Government in the hands of our people." The importance of free choice had become the red flag of the Progressive movement. Waved with skill by those who had been through months of victorious primary campaigning and felt the more deeply the "theft" of the Republican nomination by the Taft forces, the flag aroused a particularly vehement rage among those who found its populism the threat against which they had long been fighting in their battles with Bryan and the radical westerners. Taft, who had expressed his absolute hostility to Roosevelt's espousal of judicial recall and who would in later years, seek to make the Supreme Court a bulwark against such excesses of democracy, had spoken out as well against initiative and referendum. "Mr. Taft says: 'Referendums do not pay rent or furnish homes. Recalls do not furnish clothing: Initiatives do not supply employment,'" Merriam quoted in his address;[17] and the reminder was sufficient to provoke the desired identification of Taft with the anti-democrats of the party.

Much of the address had to be a justification for the founding of a new party. Roosevelt and the Progressives had sustained much criticism, not only from those who felt that the desertion of the two-party tradition was a shameful, spiteful, and even ungentlemanly act, but from those who, in the interests of practical politics, viewed the timing as poor. Party primaries had already been held; and those who had voted in them had bound themselves to support the party candidates. To launch a new ticket at so late a date was an invitation to confusion.

Merriam sought to counter both these arguments, calling for a genuine realignment of parties, Republican progressives with Democratic progressives, insisting that such a genuine realignment transcended prior commitments. The moral justification rested ultimately on identifying the regular machinery of both parties with corruption.

For Merriam, Roosevelt's chief function in the 1912 campaign was not to win but to lose in such a way as to insure continuity of his cause. In mid-November when Merriam wrote to the colonel to congratulate him on his "splendid fight" and to comment on the 35,000 majority which the city of Chicago had given him, he reminded him of the visit to Oyster Bay the previous July and of his conviction then that Roosevelt's willingness to make the fight was not "in the hope of winning the election of 1912, but of establishing permanently a Liberal Party."[18]

The colonel's reply, still heated by hostility to the Republican regulars, was in complete support of Merriam's view. "[W]hen the bosses not merely cheated us at Chicago and stole the nomination," he steamed, "but perfected their organization so as to render it certain that they could cheat us just as readily four years hence, it became in my judgment our clear duty to start a permanent progressive party, a liberal party, a radical party—and therefore in the long run the only true conservative party." But he disagreed strongly, albeit patiently, with Merriam's contention that George W. Perkins's continued involvement in the party was damaging to its future. "We are far stronger in men who can portray our principles," he told Merriam as he told the numerous others who had written the same complaint, "than we are in men who can organize victory."

Perkins had been the organizer and the financial architect of Roosevelt's campaign. He was indispensable to the practical existence of the party, a J. P. Morgan partner, to be sure, but that testified to only one of his skills. As TR put it, "Perkins is almost alone among the leading men of the party in being able and anxious to do the organizing work which is vitally necessary if we are to keep the party up during the years when there is no presidential campaign to inflame our people to enthusiasm."[19]

The hardcore reformers at flood tide—and for once Merriam and Ickes thought as one—were offended by Perkins's management of the party. For whereas the Merriam of 1907 and the Merriam of 1920 both had respect for men with money who wanted to commit themselves to political reform, the Merriam of the 1912 Progressive campaign and its aftermath was a far more radical figure. Political alignment with Perkins was plainly distasteful.

By April 1913 the early outlines of the Wilson program were beginning to appear to Merriam to be proof of the inevitable victory of reform, regardless of party. The Illinois Republicans were clearly out for Merriam's blood. They opposed his campaign for reelection as alderman and managed to gerrymander the most important part of his constituency out of his ward. Merriam nonetheless won reelection to the council as an Independent. Roosevelt was elated. "I regard your victory as of the highest importance to the Progressive Party," he wrote, underlining the ideal Merriam was trying to construct for himself with the statement that "it is much more than a local triumph." Interestingly enough, Merriam's opponent was a Progressive who wrote his complaints to Roosevelt. "Then let me explain something which will probably amuse you," Roosevelt chortled. "I did not even know that Hess was running against you!"[20]

Governor Deneen had lost the governorship in 1912 and loved the Progressives no more than they loved him; but he had been looked upon as a reformer in the days when a man had to stand in less of a glare to accept the title, and he could find his way there again. A more obvious candidate for party peacemaker was Frank O. Lowden, whose health had conveniently prevented him from showing his colors in 1912 but who was willing enough to take more public stands now that the heat was off.

William Jennings Bryan, as part of the political service he would perform so ably for Wilson, visited Illinois just before the inauguration in 1913 to see if some use might be made of the fact that both Senate seats would be up for filling, a short term and a long term. The hope was to give Wilson both Progressive and Democratic senators from Illinois. A member of the state legislature had already written to Roosevelt asking his views of such a proposition and indicating that state patronage would go to the Progressives if they could agree to some such arrangement. Roosevelt referred the matter to Merriam, among others, for an opinion. "Sooner than do anything that was in the least way tainted with Lorimerism, or with anything else that was improper, I would prefer to see the Democrats and the Republicans forced into a deal," he wrote, seeming to wash his hands of the issue.[21]

As the 1915 Chicago mayoralty election approached, Merriam's work on the crime commission succeeded in keeping his name before the public. Former Governor Deneen had moved back to Chicago to rebuild the party organization, and while the source of Deneen's troubles in 1912 had probably been Ickes rather than Merriam, Merriam bore the public banner, and that was enough for Deneen. The Lorimer organization was also being reconstructed in a fashion which included Frank O. Lowden as a very respectable ally. Its mayoral candidate was the then very attractive William Hale (later "Big Bill") Thompson, a man whose charm and energy were sufficient to obscure some rather questionable earlier years in the City Council. Still, there seemed no doubt that anyone the Deneen faction could agree upon would defeat handily anyone bearing the Lorimer seal. The Democrats were certain to renominate Harrison, despite the inroads made upon his reputation by the continuing investigations by Merriam and his Commission on City Expenditures. If Merriam could get Deneen's approval, defeat Lorimer's Thompson in the primary, and move on to a replay of the Harrison battle, the 1915 mayoralty election would be his.

Deneen would have none of it. That Ickes once again had to serve as Merriam's intermediary did not help matters; but the resurgence of regular control of the Republican party after 1914 kept the Illinois Progressive party in existence as an extremist reform group, and Ickes was its leader. Despite Merriam's personal eagerness to talk "fusion," as it was called by those still insistent upon maintaining Progressive identity, Ickes was his spokesman, and Ickes believed in the Progressive party. Merriam and Ickes, in compromises which found Deneen's favored candidate and Merriam's candidacy blocking each other, agreed on a third candidate, Municipal Judge Harry Olson, who seemed assured of the Republican nomination if Deneen approved. One of the few things that 1912 seemed to prove to those who had gone through it was that a split Republican party did nothing but elect Democrats.

That both regulars and Progressives were overstating the virtues of fusion—or underestimating the skills of William Hale Thompson—did not occur to any of them. Both primaries were political upsets. Harrison lost the Democratic primary, thus weakening the opposition the Republicans were to have; and Thompson won the Republican primary, beginning a new era in Chicago politics as Progressive reformers and the respectable party professionals found themselves cut out. Power fell to a man who was capable of using techniques perfected by both, but for ends both would have abhorred. Under the direction of his lieutenant Fred Lundin, whose acute analyses of local interests in the city's wards and precincts led him to plan Thompson's speeches with brilliant effect, zeroing in with ruthless precision on ethnic prejudices and hostilities, Thompson sought to appeal and he did. His was a triumph of publicity, emphasizing warmth and appeal over program and deliberately cultivating women, newly enfranchised by the state. It ended the tradition of city reform politics which had brought Chicago through the difficult first years of industrialization and urbanization at the close of the previous century. Harrison had never been Merriam's enemy, and both of them may have realized this in the years following the election of 1915. They represented different wings of Chicago's Brahmin elite, whereas Thompson was part of a new order of urban politics, building on an older ethnic approach to politics with a shrewd brutality the older alliances would never have condoned.

William Hale Thompson was as much a product of the techniques of Progressive reform as Woodrow Wilson. He may indeed have been the logical outcome of an era which saw inherent democratic virtue in scientific techniques, a successful apprentice to a singularly sincere bunch of sorcerers. Merriam came to hate him with an at times unreasoning venom. Thompson's bossism was a post-progressive phenomenon which Merriam did not see as continuous with the old concepts of corruption. "Bill the Builder," as he came to be known, used the new technology of modern urban growth and the new social dilemmas of urban life for corrupt purposes mind-boggling to the old Progressive mentality. The post-Progressive city included administrative agencies in fields like health, education, public utilities, and transportation, the triumphs of Progressive reform, all now to be subjected to the new political control manipulated by Thompson. Merriam's Progressive utopianism had to be transformed.

The election of Thompson also ended the political career of Charles Merriam, although like many Progressives he had to wait until 1920 to feel the shock of that fact. The effect on his intellectual life was profound. His progressivism had followed a pattern one could trace through the Progressive movement itself, from a realistic concern with practical politics in the era of the McKinley and Roosevelt presidencies through the fighting idealism of 1912 to the disillusionment of 1920. The cycle suited his personality. He felt the peaks and troughs with an intensity requiring an active engagement as total as the intellectual withdrawal and reexamination in the period which followed. The Progressive period influenced his political thought the way all his experiences influenced him. It gave him a reality to intellectualize, to reorganize, and to mythologize.

Merriam had joined in the dream of a genuinely new party reorganization at the peak period of 1912; but he dropped that dream much more quickly than did many of his contemporaries. Unlike his friend Harold Ickes he did not continue to lament the failure of the dream and to search for its causes. Quite possibly he saw that the continuing defection of prominent Progressives back to the regular party would give the regulars the balance of power they needed in order to retain control over the "loaves and fishes," the patronage which had so often offended the Progressives. Once in control of the party in the states, the regulars could manipulate election machinery, not by the old-fashioned methods alone, now, but by turning to the methods the Progressives had fought to create: the systems of primary election and registration. Running for his Senate seat in 1916, Hiram Johnson of California was forced to make his way through a Republican primary, even though he knew that at least 300,000 of his most faithful constituents were Independents and would not be able to vote in the primary. "[A]ll the old machine crowd have but one thought—the punishment of Progressives," he wrote to John Callan O'Laughlin. "They'd rather defeat us than elect Hughes."[22]

Intraparty enmity was not alone in influencing the changes taking place. Merriam had begun to find himself drawn to President Wilson, who was making efforts to attract academics. In 1917 Merriam was offered a place on the president's Tariff Commission, not because he knew anything about tariffs, he was told, but because the president wanted people like him closer at hand. Merriam turned it down but he was interested. He even attempted on one occasion to convince Roosevelt that Wilson was doing a fair job of pressing forward with progressive programs, but the angry Roosevelt would have none of it. Merriam could not understand him.

Merriam's agreement to back Judge Olson, the fusion candidate in 1915, plus the publicity attendant upon his own campaign, brought him renomination in the primaries for his seat in City Council, this time, significantly, on the Republican ticket. He was reelected easily; but his battle with Thompson was beginning. So were the personal attacks which would be painful for him and for his family as he struggled with the costs of prominence as a party reformer.

Merriam had never before used his investigative powers in the council to attack a Republican mayor directly; now he did. Thompson was engaged in a rollback of civil service and efficiency reforms that was producing patronage powers Chicago mayors hadn't had since the days before the first Carter Harrison. Thompson accepted the challenge of Merriam's opposition head on. Even reform-oriented regulars like Lowden, who became governor in 1916, could do little but compromise with Thompson. All the divisive energies were spent. The party would have to accommodate itself to men like Thompson. As Roosevelt wrote

Lowden in his congratulatory letter, "What I most desire is that you shall help bring the Republicans far enough forward to enable us to hold the progressives far enough back to keep a substantial alignment."[23] Merriam would have to find his compromise or go under.

Merriam was counted out in the aldermanic primary of 1917 by five votes, a decision reached by a municipal judge and hence, under the law, unappealable. Although an independent petition was circulated and three thousand signatures obtained, this, too, was thrown out through a series of maneuvers masterminded by the Thompson forces. In the campaign Merriam received over ten thousand write-in votes, falling short of victory by fifteen hundred votes. The Thompson opposition had held; Merriam had gone under.

Students who knew Merriam later in his career were convinced that his failure to become mayor of Chicago was the source of a deep tragedy in his life. In a sense, perhaps, they were right. He was clearly on the verge of a career in politics, perhaps a major one, and the fulfilling of his father's ambitions. Yet it is not clear that he wanted such a career, that he saw in himself enough of the qualities of leadership he thought necessary for attaining his deepest ambitions for himself. In the privacy of the verses he composed, he referred to himself as lazy and indecisive. In effect he acknowledged publicly his lack of physical stamina by his periodic ailments, most of them imaginary, a characteristic which by his own definition would disqualify him for leadership. A career in politics would pose problems for him.

At the time of his defeat Merriam's progressivism underwent a wrenching change tied irrevocably to his abortive political career as well as to the subsequent career of Big Bill Thompson. Although teacher and students alike would tend to see in Thompson the classical corrupt boss whom reformers had been describing for years, there was a difference. Progressive reform rested on small-town moral values which could not easily be pressed on urban life. Thompson's audience and the source of his power were the urban public itself, a hard reality for traditional reformers to absorb. Big Bill was a nightmare for them because the city he appealed to was closer to reality than the city they were trying to build. They called him a demagogue, and rightly; but the term had a common root with the democracy they were fighting to preserve.

In 1915 Thompson resembled a prehistoric monster unexpectedly awakened in a dark valley. He had lumbered into one of the most promising of America's modern cities and was bent upon its destruction, as Merriam saw it. Over the next decade Merriam was going to have to cope with that reality and everything it represented. His view of politics and of science would seem in his later years to bear little relation to progressivism. Changes of that order are painful. Whether or not they are tragic is another matter.

5

The Shock of War

World War I brought an organization to Amercian life more total in its effect than any event since the Civil War. The war struck like a tornado, sudden and oddly unexpected, even to those who watched the signals of its coming. Americans went into the war from diverse backgrounds and experienced a disruptive change which marked them all in different ways but at the same time. For Merriam, who spent his war service in Italy, the war touched everything and changed everything it touched. The relation of the changes to one another was never clear to him, but the cause very definitely was.

Where the Merriams' marriage was concerned, the wartime separation provided the occasion for a disruption inherent in the relationship from the beginning. The Merriams were not well suited to each other, although there was a strong sense of family which provided ties of loyalty and affection considerably sturdier than was apparent to the friends and students in whom they confided. Merriam was a warm, sociable man who enjoyed flirtation. The fact that women whose intelligence he admired found him attractive flattered and fed a need his wife had obviously met at the beginning of their courtship when she, the sister of a Columbia classmate of Merriam's, was attending Hunter College. She gave up her educational career, whatever that might have been, when she married him; and he did not encourage her periodic attempts to resume it. Although Merriam strongly supported academic careers for women, even in fields like political science, he seems to have assumed that marriage brought a proper end to such ambitions.

Unable or unwilling to provide her husband with the adulation and support he seemed to crave, Mrs. Merriam responded with an increasngly intense jealousy and suspicion to any attention he paid to other women. She channeled her affection and support to their children, the only really shared interest of their life together, and contented herself with what she fancied to be the vigorous protection of her home.

Some of the differences were clear at the beginning. Elizabeth Hilda Doyle was a Catholic and a Democrat. Her father became postmaster in Constableville, New York, in the same national victory which lost the Hopkinton office for C. E. Merriam. Ed Merriam might have known that his father would forgive Hilda her politics sooner than his mother would forgive her her religion. C. E. Merriam's Presbyterianism had been filtered through the same two and a half centuries of New England Congregationalism that characterized his politics. His wife's view of Catholicism was still governed by that Scottish sense of the meaning of "toleration," which wasted no time with niceties and recognized the devil for what he was. She could not acknowledge her son's marriage in a Catholic ceremony, and she never welcomed the new Mrs. Merriam into the family. Only during the last years of her life did she speak to her daughter-in-law, and then only to establish communication with her grandchildren.

The Merriams were married in the Doyle family home in Constableville, New York, in August 1901. Their honeymoon was the train ride to Chicago. Hilda Merriam's life was shaped by her husband's career, and while she toyed with compromising that convention toward a career of her own, her efforts never extended beyond soliciting the advice of career women on the faculty. Late in her life she wrote a history of the New York region in which she had grown up, arranging secretly for its publication in maneuvers her husband found more embarrassing than he had reason to. The act was characteristic on both sides of the frustrations neither of them could resolve.

There were two widely separated sets of children: Charles James, born in 1903, and John Francis, born in 1904; their daughter Elizabeth was born in 1912 and Robert Edward in 1918. A sense of family held them all together. The tie was more than the present-day view of the responsibility of parents toward their childeren. Family—the parents' siblings and the children of their marriages—provided an extended community to celebrate and enjoy on summer visits and in the correspondence which all of them maintained. Summers not spent in Europe were spent in the Doyle family house at Constableville. There was family security in touching the symbols of the past.

Chapter Five

The house at 6041 University Avenue in Chicago was Mrs. Merriam's to manage, and she did it with an authority derived from the standards of the worlds from which both of them had come. Students who visited Merriam there would find the sophisticated and convivial man of the twentieth century surrounded by the massive mission oak and mahogany furniture, heavy drapery, and darkly framed monochromes of the nineteenth century. Merriam's study, unlike his cluttered university office, contained neatly arranged furniture covered with flowered chintz. Not only did Mrs. Merriam not wish liquor kept in the house, but she gradually limited and then entirely abolished evening meals at home. For this she gave a variety of reasons, all having to do in one way or another with the problem of managing a household with children so widely separated in age and with social arrangements of their own. Merriam took it as a criticism of his self-indulgence, complained to friends about the chronic emptiness of the cupboards, and dutifully led the family procession to the university's Quadrangle Club for evening meals. The public legend of the unhappy marriage grew.[1]

Given their backgrounds and the contrasting professional, urban environment in which they lived, the difficulties of their marriage were as much a part of the great American transition into the twentieth century as were the marriage's basic satisfactions. The responsibilities his mother's religion and his father's politics thrust upon Merriam could not be mitigated by his successes in the world. His wife kept the old standards before him in her own fashion, to punish him when that seemed necessary, but also to give him the special comfort of returning to his supportive past. He could lapse into the surefire method his generation was the last to use with total impunity: hypochondria. Both he and his older brother, John, used periodic lapses in health as convenient releases of tension, allowing them acceptable episodes of escape and rarely inhibiting their work but straining family life when periods of morbid concern would reflect and underscore confusions of decision. Victorian women had the various and innumerable mysteries of their physiology to depend upon, with childbirth, of course, the center of responsible suffering. Victorian men had to be more inventive. Merriam's father died of stomach cancer in his fifty-eighth year, and his son struggled with the recurring fantasy that he would die of the same disease at the same age.

Hilda Merriam shared more with her Presbyterian mother-in-law than either could probably have admitted, not only in the fundamental

86

quality of their moral conviction and its timelessness in a rapidly changing world, but in the function they served for Charles Merriam. Their home was the base from which Merriam moved into his professional world. His wife kept their home, their family, and the circle of friends she was willing to share with her husband as a sanctuary devoted to the preservation of those things worth valuing. Her husband could join her there when he wished to and when he needed to. They bore one another as burdens with a necessary and vital sense of sufferance.

The time Merriam spent in Italy during World War I was relatively brief, like the American involvement itself, but it was the longest stretch of time the Merriams had been separated. An encounter with a young Italian noblewoman gave Merriam the occasion for a romantic adventure. It was not to be the last such occasion in his life, although each would provide him with the self-romanticization he needed. His wife always "discovered" and punished; his students always seemed to know and in any case to gossip.

Merriam's awareness of the effect any kind of scandal might have had on his career at the university was reinforced, certainly, by the university's dismissal in 1918 of W. I. Thomas, the distinguished sociologist, following charges that Thomas had violated the Mann Act. Although the charges were later thrown out of court, the newspaper publicity was sufficient to provoke the president and the board of trustees to actions considerably more hysterical—and less humane—than those Harper had taken against Veblen. The university press was ordered to cease publication and distribution of his books. Remaining copies, as well as the plates, were turned over to the author. The faculty looked on in tragic resignation, accepting a decision which was inevitable by their standards, even if it was not just. Merriam tried to help the man who was, perhaps of all the Chicago sociologists, the most influential on his own thought, but the best he could do, at least at first, was to continue to provide his personal friendship. Merriam went to Thomas's home, where he had closed himself away, accepting the disgrace he had brought upon himself, and, taking him by the arm, led him to the faculty club for lunch, where he could be greeted by his friends. Merriam understood, and he never forgot.[2]

The war years were hard years for the university. No one avoided being caught up in a sense of nationalism, logical enough in the light of the Progressive mood, but unreal with respect to the evolution of an

American internationalism which seemed, by turns, the glorious future and the impending cataclysm. American involvement in the war was long enough to have significant repercussions in the organization of American life, yet brief enough to be seriously misunderstood. The rationalization for American involvement changed so rapidly that disputes about it among intellectuals tended to be transformed before they were resolved. The result was that the experience could be understood only later, in recollection, the actual event having been too muddled by speed and enthusiasm.

Like many of his contemporaries, Merriam had not been inclined at first to take the outbreak of European war as a serious problem for Americans, interpreting it instead in rather straightforward Progressive terms. An industrially based military aristocracy in the process of decay had come to control the will of people who had few effective methods of opposing such control. The key terms were "will of the people" and "methods" of expressing opposition. The solution would have to come in the development of new methods after the overthrow of the oppressing aristocracies. Neither the British nor the Continental monarchies came off blameless in newspaper accounts of the period from 1910 to 1914 covering not only their disagreements with one another but, perhaps even more importantly, the Irish conflicts, debates over the role of the House of Lords, and woman suffrage. American neutrality was a useful concept. It underlay a good bit of Progressive analysis of the situation and it satisfied those who had studied in Germany or who, as politicians, had German or Irish constituents. It was a view not far from various arguments proposed by American Socialists, and it attracted Bryanite midwesterners and conservative business leaders alike. That America would involve itself in a war to defend any of the monarchies governing Europe seemed unthinkable.

If Merriam was at all typical of men in his position, what is remarkable is their lack of attention to foreign affairs in the period between 1910 and 1917, particularly during the first Wilson administration. The engagement of American troops in Mexico plays absolutely no part in Merriam's political discussions. That event was romanticized rather than analyzed, even by journalists such as John Reed. Popular accounts tend to see the Victorian monarchy as moving in the direction of greater democracy, the empire of William II in the opposite direction. Louis Brownlow, then traveling for the Frederick J

Haskin news service, provided such views for American readers,[3] which were supported, too, by the widespread circulation of materials like Friedrich von Bernhardi's *Germany and the Next War* (1914) and Owen Wister's *The Pentecost of Calamity* (1915). While later critics of American intervention emphasized the effects of European propaganda on American attitudes, the propaganda at home, resulting from the emergence during the period of the American foreign correspondent, may have had as much, if not more, influence. Newspapermen's influence on policy making and their role in developing alternatives to information disseminated by the State Department were formalized in the Committee on Public Information, the Creel Committee of World War I.

With the American entry into the war, Merriam accepted a commission as captain in the Signal Corps and was assigned as an examiner to an aviation board in Chicago. Glamorous enough as an idea, it had little practical consequence except for the contacts it gave Merriam with the slowly developing intelligence services of wartime America. Although the war would revolutionize this approach, aircraft were first looked upon more as effective sources of surveillance and information than as offensive or defensive weapons, and their function in the Signal Corps reflected that early view.

Merriam had the influence, largely through Walter Rogers, to move into what turned out to be higher level intelligence work once the Committee on Public Information expanded its function beyond a role as a public news source. Established initially as a device for managing domestic information, the committee undertook the operation of offices in thirty-two foreign countries before the war ended. While its defenders and supporters described it as America's answer to enemy propaganda and as a means of keeping America's war aims clear both at home and abroad, its function was in fact somewhat more complex than that. Its wartime activities came to serve as a kind of bypass of the State Department through which journalist-advisers and others considered "specialist" in some loose sense of the term could have their attitudes channeled directly to the White House. The State Department had been placed on the patronage block in 1913 as was the custom in major party change, and under the direction of Secretary Bryan and with the approval of Wilson's virtually total focus on domestic concerns and Democratic party buildup, the lower echelons of staff both at home and abroad had gone to "deserving Democrats." While this had

89

not been equally true of the always troublesome ambassadorial posts—on balance Wilson had done about as well as any president of his day—the embassy staffs were obviously not drawn from the experienced Republican—and often Progressive Republican—groups whose long experience had given them at least the rudiments of knowledge and skill. The Creel Committee became their center of involvement in the war.[4]

The Russian revolution triggered more extensive operation of the committee in the building of an American war policy as the fear of an erosion of the Allied cause through antiwar revolutions in Europe combined with the conviction that American embassies were not sufficiently in touch with antigovernment sentiment in their various countries to produce real concern on the part of the administration. The possibility that Italy might follow the course already taken by Russia led, in March 1918, to the establishment of an office of the Committee on Public Information in Rome with Charles E. Merriam as its head. Its announced function was to spread knowledge of America's war aims in Italy and to encourage the belief that America's involvement in the war meant new hope for the cause of democracy in Europe. Its function beyond that was to keep channels of useful intelligence open directly to the White House along a route which moved through the committee's New York office and to Colonel House, and then, it was hoped, to the president.[5]

Traveling journalists who reported both to House and to Wilson, as well as to Creel, that Italian socialist and labor leaders distrusted American purposes almost as much as they did those of the French and British, not to mention the Germans, did not agree with reports coming from the embassy in Rome where Ambassador Thomas Nelson Page presided. Page, distantly related to Walter Hines Page, American ambassador in London, was the Hanover County, Virginia, novelist. Although his letters to Colonel House indicate that he was not at all the ineffective fool that his critics in Merriam's circle pictured him, his habit of serving Smithfield ham and spoon bread at embassy dinners as his means of introducing America to Roman society endeared him neither to Italians nor to Americans. Too, his approach to his official responsibilities did not give him the mobility to look beyond information being fed to him through diplomatic channels.[6]

Merriam was charged with rebuilding the American image in Italy by appealing to middle-class and working-class Italians on behalf of their expatriate countrymen in America. He was to combat the combination of enemy and antiwar Italian propaganda which pictured the United States as both unprepared and unwilling to support the war. Ironically enough, as it turned out, the leading anti-American claim was that the United States would lend money for the war but would demand repayment with interest. The committee sought to counter this with projections of a view of Americans as generous and compassionate people, a view underscored by the presence of the American Red Cross in Rome.

The methods employed were very similar to those the committee was using at home: a speaker's bureau run by American professors of Italian, newspaper articles fed out of Walter Rogers's office in New York detailing American preparations, movies and movie stars, picture postcards of little Italys in America, and pictures of President Wilson, whose fourteen points were becoming the rallying ground for political and social idealists on the Continent. The committee's buildup of Wilson was a massive public relations campaign the success of which could be measured by the crowds who cheered him when he arrived on his well-prepared postwar triumphal tour.

Merriam's office finally succeeded in persuading the American military forces to land one ambulance unit at Genoa—where it was scarcely of much use—so that Italians could get their first glimpse of American uniforms en masse; and on 24 May 1918, while the American committee staged sympathy-for-Italy celebrations in New York, the Italian committee produced a near-riot public celebration of the third anniversary of the Italian entry into the war. Under committee direction, Italians celebrated the Fourth of July with fireworks and festivities. An elaborate campaign initiated by the writer Will Irwin and realized finally through visits by Merriam persuaded Gabriele D'Annunzio to provide a sixty-stanza poem in commemoration of American-Italian friendship and American independence.[7]

American violinist Albert Spaulding played for Italian audiences, and Fiorello La Guardia, who had served with the United States air service until 1917, traveled the countryside in his airplane, speaking to peasant groups and struggling—under persistent advice from Merriam —to keep his antigovernment, antiaristocratic sentiments in check, despite the obvious eagerness with which his audiences received them.

Although the offices of the committee in Italy were at 2 via S. Susanna, the lobby and bar of the Grand Hotel, open then only to a very exclusive society, served as a meeting place for Merriam and his chief assistants, an Irish-American journalist named John Hearley and the young movie enthusiast Walter Wanger.[8] Much attracted to Merriam, and he to her, an Italian noblewoman, Contessina Loschi put her social and political skills to work for Merriam's committee. Her loyalty and shrewd advice did a great deal to help Merriam move quickly into friendly relations with members of the Italian coalition cabinet. V. E. Orlando, head of the cabinet, had been a professor of political science at the University of Naples. Francesco Saverio Nitti who was in charge of the treasury and the man with whom Merriam established the closest relationship, was a former professor of political economy at the University of Naples. By September Merriam's dispatches were going directly to Creel and from him to Colonel House. "Captain Merriam," Creel wrote House, "our representative in Rome is in very close touch with the Italian leaders by reasons of his work and has come to enjoy their confidence in a very large degree." Merriam had come to be a source of some confusion to the Italians as well: this professor who was only a captain but bore the title "High Commissioner" and seemed indeed to outrank the ambassador and who seemed to have some connection with the important Colonel House—American government was indeed a puzzle.

House saw the mission clearly enough: to stop the spread of bolshevism. Merriam and Ray Stannard Baker saw it somewhat differently. Baker's travels for his journalistic projects were also supplying information which confirmed what House was learning from Merriam. House commented in his diary early in November, after a conversation with Baker, "I wish him to keep in touch with the liberal movements there so as to keep us informed"; and when Baker and Ambassador Page returned briefly in December for consultations, it was clear that their views of the Italian situation were in serious conflict. "Ambassador Thomas Nelson Page has arrived from Rome," House wrote. "He gave us a full account of conditions in Italy as he saw them. Ray Stannard Baker returned with him. He sees things from another angle and I get an entirely [different] viewpoint." House preferred to accept Page's position in spite of Baker's persistent attacks on Page in his letters to House. Baker tried to make it clear that Page's unreliability, as Baker saw it, stemmed from his lack of association with men whom Baker considered the real forces. He urged House to bring Wilson into touch with the labor leaders of Italy who were in fact he proof of the Creel committee's success: they believed Wilson a great liberal leader and were willing to follow him to the conference table.[10]

Merriam had been working toward that end, pressing for some rapprochement between American and Italian liberals. He invited the American Socialist commission—which A. M. Simmons chaired and which included John Spargo, president of the American Social Democratic Federation, and John Howitt, president of the Kansas Miners Union—to meet with Italian socialists and labor leaders. The Creel Committee sent Samuel Gompers to talk with Italian labor leaders, but while Gompers did his best to give the rousing speeches he thought required of him, he was more interested in touring Italy, taking particular care to sample its nightlife. As Baker wrote to House, "he never touched the labor group at all," and that was putting it politely.[11]

In addition to Gompers, other American junketeers not eager to return to the farm used the staff of the committee as tour guides. Congressional groups checking on the American role in the war effort expected to examine unrelated sights as well. Assistant Secretary of the Navy Franklin D. Roosevelt was introduced to Italian officialdom and the public by Merriam, who guided his visit personally. One group, which Wanger was directed to take to Venice, was headed by a southern senator whose familiarity with the landscape was summed up by his horrified response to the Venetian canals. "Do you mean to tell me," he gasped, "those dirty Huns flooded this beautiful city?"[12]

Such visits added to the "information" being fed back to Washington. At the same time, the maneuvering which all the traveling about entailed could scarcely have been more damaging to embassy efforts to maintain some semblance of orderly control. As would be the case all over Europe in the months preceding the peace conference, Americans were suddenly and chaotically ubiquitous, all claiming to represent some source of power in the mysterious American government, or some committee, commission, or association whose relation to the government was obscure. Even the presence of the American Red Cross was a not inconsequential addition to the utter confusion that dominated the scene in Rome and other centers of Europe.

The confusion reached the very top in the personal animosity afflicting relationships between George Creel and Robert Lansing; the latter, according to Colonel House, threatened an open collision. House pleaded with Wilson to pay more attention to keeping Lansing informed so as not to disrupt the network of communications which the

State Department had evolved even if—as they were all only too willing to agree—it was not entirely satisfactory.[13]

The immediate impass in the Italian office of the committee arose from the fact that all messages to the United States had to be coded and sent from the embassy where the military attaché, a man spoken of as a young protégé of Mrs. Wilson, held and operated the official codes. It was in the power of the ambassador to stop the sending of messages from the committee any time he was willing to risk an open break. Creel was impressed with Merriam's work. Over two million postcards were distributed to American servicemen of Italian extraction, to be used to send words of encouragement to relations in Italy. Merriam called for photographs of President Wilson, George and Martha Washington, and Abraham Lincoln for distribution to Italian audiences. He had fifty thousand flags displayed.[14] But he was also using embassy personnel to code and send messages directly to House; and when the embassy staff rebelled, he used his influence with Nitti to get access to Italian telegraph services. Page and his staff seethed. Page wrote Creel accusing Merriam of using his office for a political campaign in Chicago; but Page was already suffering under what seemed to him intense competition from other sources, particularly the Red Cross. Merriam became known as the "black Pope" to Page's staff; and Merriam's staff began receiving notes of warning from the embassy staff.[15]

Page was ready to press the issue with Creel; and Creel knew that he would ultimately have to give in to his demands, once it was clear that Merriam and Page were not going to compromise.[16] While Merriam, Hearley, and Baker were certainly to the left of House in what they considered their responsibilities in Italy, they shared a view that a radical revolution along lines they would have considered Bolshevik was not the answer. The problem with the embassy was not that it differed from House or Merriam in the fundamental aims it sought to further but that it was so out of touch with any reasonable alternatives.

The break between Merriam and Page did not become official only because of events in Chicago. By September Merriam had already decided that he wanted to return home for a conference, but he had been refused permission to do so on the grounds that his work in Italy was too important. With the 1919 mayoralty campaign approaching, Merriam's friends began to press for his return to lead them; and that seemed to provide a more effective reason as far as the committee was concerned. He departed in October 1918, after scarcely seven months of service abroad, and with the apparent intention of returning. Hearley was made acting commissioner, and the war with the embassy continued. By that time Creel knew who was going to win, and when Page began his crack-down on Hearley's efforts to continue the committee's independent activities, Creel did nothing to prevent it. By November, of course, the war was over; and by January the Committee on Public Information was preparing for its own demise. "George Creel was an afternoon caller," House wrote. "He is disgruntled with the President and pretty much everyone else. He says he will resign tomorrow."[17]

The war had been an unanticipated accident, perhaps, as had America's crusading entry into it; and now it would end as it had begun, in a collection of angry disaffections. Winning the war had provided a needed unity; but it was really the only unity. The cries of victory would be for the public and they could wave the flags and wipe away the tears. From the disgruntled heap of those who knew exactly what they wanted—or had at least decided that they knew as the crusade progressed—came the muffled sounds of pain and disappointment. It would be a relief to forget the war, or better still, to remember it in a way which justified the sacrifices at the same time that it made their repetition impossible. A war to end war could do that, too.

Most of Merriam's generation recalled the war without the ambivalence which had marked their first reaction to it. When revisionist interpretations in the 1920s and '30s tried to help them recall it, they resented the effort. Nothing by then could be allowed to damage a general historical recollection of the Great War as an event dominated by the figure of Wilson, the giant of international peacemaking brought to ruin by a narrow-minded and confused senatorial clique characterized, at one extreme, by Henry Cabot Lodge in the role of the villain and, at the other, by Warren G. Harding in the role of the fool. Such an interpretation made it possible to look upon the decade that followed as an aberration, a needless and costly pause in the inevitable onrush of progressivism.

Such a view vastly oversimplified the experience of the war, just as it vastly overstated the successes of progressivism. In what may be one of modern American history's most significant acts of intellectual self-delusion, the failures of 1912 and 1920 were looked upon as triumphs of educational experience, as though learning-by-failing had been what

John Dewey had been writing about all the time. Indeed, what the process-oriented pragmatism of that generation would share with the behavioral orientation of the generation which followed was a capacity to confuse the meaning of results in the search for ends and the analysis of their achievement. The success or failure of any activity came to be measured too easily by the depth of the psychological experience the activity was supposed to create rather than the objective result of the activity itself.

Merriam and Walter Lippmann both wrote about the war as, in some ways, a useful experience. They differed on just what lessons were taught but justified the methods by which they had learned and the war itself as their teacher. Harry Elmer Barnes, and eventually Charles Beard, came to take a decidedly different view of the experience. World War II later reaffirmed a division in American social thought which may have had its first modern statement in World War I. The lessons involved, with the disputes they generated, were more far reaching than the issue of American internationalism, since they rested on progressive views of the presidency, on legislative policy making, and on the function of American social and economic thought as a body of doctrine for world reform.

For Merriam the effect of the war hit with shocking force the triumphal return to Chicago politics he had anticipated making as Captain Merriam. He had every reason to believe that he would be successful. Chicago had had its share—and a good bit more—of the patriotic fervor which had marked the furious nationalism marketed by the Committee on Public Information. The anti-German outrages perpetrated in the city had formed a background against which the outspoken antiwar stand of the mayor, Big Bill Thompson, seemed an utterly suicidal act of public conscience from a most unlikely source. Thompson's initial antiwar stand could be explained easily as a politician's confusion over the relevance of the German vote. Others did the same. The motive may indeed have accounted for Merriam's initial reluctance to take a position on the European war.

By 1917 and American entry, however, Thompson seemed to be not only sticking to his guns but turning them on himself. He became a militant pacifist. But he finally agreed to march in a preparedness parade and rescinded his initial order refusing to permit the selling of war bonds in City Hall. He endured the criticism of an angry public and of equally angry members of his own Republican party, not to mention public condemnation by Theodore Roosevelt. His audacity reached its peak and earned what many considered its appropriate reward in 1918 when he campaigned loudly and angrily for the Republican senatorial nomination, attacking not only Wilson's war policy but the war itself. As a kind of urban neopopulist, he saw the war as a conspiracy of business and banking to involve the country in European affairs; and he proclaimed his allegiance to "America first." What was good enough for George Washington, he shouted to angry and hostile crowds, was good enough for Big Bill Thompson. He lost the campaign; but he retained the platform intact. When the war enthusiasm crashed with the suddenness of a tidal wave receding, the only political edifice which could still be seen standing on the mid-American landscape was the wartime platform of William Hale Thompson. Midwestern progressives of both parties would find it a firm base for another twenty years.[18]

That it did not look that way in 1919 as the mayoralty race approached was so obvious to everyone as to require no comment beyond the sound of potential candidates rushing to benefit from Thompson's certain defeat. Deneen once again refused to accept Merriam as candidate and put forth Judge Olson. But this time, unwilling to accept a compromise and convinced that the uniform was one additional weight in the balance, the militant reformers—Ickes, Jane Addams, and Donald Richberg—persuaded Merriam to run in the primary. As evidence of their increased shrewdness, they hired a recently discarded Thompson lieutenant, James Pugh, as a guide through the intricacies of the Thompson organization.

The campaign was a brutal display of tactics for which Merriam and the progressives were totally unprepared. When they hired a theater for a rally, Thompson supporters filled the seats and boo'd and heckled Merriam into a shouting, white-knuckled rage. Following the war's passion for patriotism, both sides used "Americanism" as an issue. Convinced that Wilson represented the new wave in American internationalism, Merriam confidently attacked Thompson's antiwar, anti-British approach, while Olson concentrated his thrust on city policies and the corruption of the Thompson regime. Even torn in two, the Progressive banner seemed sure to triumph; but when the votes were in —proper counting or no—the evidence showed a miscalculation almost beyond belief. Between them Merriam and Olson had not beaten Big Bill. His majority over Olson was 40,000. Merriam trailed sadly behind. Thompson once again faced a weak Democratic opponent in April and won.

The voters liked Thompson. His wartime daring was unique to him and it paid off. Lundin, still his adviser and his manager, had calculated well the mood of the voting population of Chicago, giving backing once again to Thompson's intuitions. He reflected something—a new mood? If so, it ran so counter to everything Merriam had wanted to assume was true and everything urban progressivism had stood for that its meaning could tear the definitions of progressive politics to shreds. More than a year before the election of 1920 and with the treaty decisions liquidating the war still a subject of public debate, the reaction to the war could be heard, but not by Merriam and the reformers, still caught up in their decade of triumph. What the coming decade would mean to them would involve a massive reshaping of their whole conception of reform, including a rejection of the term itself. What would come out of it would have to be the sense, at least, of a redefinition of politics if their commitment to democracy were to survive. Whatever they thought of William Hale Thompson and Warren Gamaliel Harding, the public thought enough of them and their kind to see in them a leadership worth following, a conception of self, of success worth emulating.

Merriam had returned from the war with a sense of renewed urgency and concern for the future that contrasted starkly with the political mood expressed in the postwar elections. He had tried to indicate that urgency in his 1919 campaign. "The morning of victory which we now enjoy. . . is a dangerous period, because America faces a great period of readjustment and reorganization and reconstruction," he told his audiences. "And that period will tax the energies, the character, the ability, the resources, the equilibrium of our country as the shock of war perhaps has never taxed it."[19] Yet the "shock of war" had already taken its toll.

The young academics rethinking their wartime service, the older Progressives rethinking their reform politics, the young lawyers and ambitious industrial managers rethinking their first real experience with a national industrial system, all faced that shock. The Progressive view of public opinion and its infinite capacity for enlightenment had to be reexamined. Walter Lippmann's *Public Opinion* in 1922 began the process in a subtle questioning of assumptions established by Bryce and the core of the Progressive's education. Bryce had reinforced an American tendency to accept the interest theory of Madison's *Federalist No. 10*, the view that interest was essentially rational, subject to irrationality only in conflict with other interests. The wartime experience with propaganda had been an at times harrowing experience with public irrationality, nationally and internationally. It had to be understood; but when Merriam sought the encouragement of the University of Chicago Press for a book on his wartime experiences with propaganda, he was told that there would be no audience for it. He had to be content to wait.[20]

A note in the Preface to *The American Party System* indicates at least one of the directions in which by 1922 he had determined to move. "The objective, the detailed study of political behavior will unquestionably enlarge our knowledge of the system of social and political control under which we now operate," he wrote, adding in a tone which did nothing to conceal his frustration, "but such inquiries will call for funds and personnel not now available to me." He had not been very clear about the purpose, but those who might have read those words a decade later could easily have seen that the method was obvious to him.[21]

The shock of war had been brief, but it was profound. The things it touched—his marriage, his career, his intellectual commitments—were all subject to change and all in the process of changing. The war quickened change, fusing with its own peculiar intensity processes of life that might better have been left apart. He was not alone in his frustrations, although at times it felt that way. In the aftermath of the war a periodic sense of the loneliness of the experience touched a whole generation.

6

The Aftermath

The last year of Woodrow Wilson's second term in the White House began in 1920. It was a year of disheartening silences and distressing sounds to citizens concerned with the functioning of government. It would get worse in the decade ahead, although that scarcely seemed possible as one watched the political parties stumbling like wounded animals toward summer conventions and fall elections.

Merriam was forty-four, turning forty-five. As an experienced Progressive he listened to talk about "Reds" and observed the real fear of radicalism with the unavoidable realization that a reform politics of the future would have to be separated, cautiously and carefully, from the events of the past. Progressives and regulars alike had their own definitions of "normalcy" when time and the processes of politics brought that term into being. Although by 1932 Harding, Coolidge, and Hoover could be lumped together like partners in a permanently defunct corporation, in 1920 the intellectual base of "normalcy" was much stronger, the idea of appropriate withdrawal from previous concepts of reform much more acceptable. In March of that year Wesley C. Mitchell announced the opening of the New School for Social Research. He called for a new kind of man for the years ahead, a man of "facts" rather than "hunches," was the way he put it. "The man of hunches may combine native shrewdness with wide experience, but he is an erratic performer. Sometimes he scores uncanny successes and sometimes he makes bad blunders. The man of facts is less brilliant but more consistent." The aims of the new movement, he concluded, were "to supplant guesswork, however brilliant, by genuine knowledge, however laborious."[1] Therein lay an intellectual "normalcy" which

100

The Aftermath

rejected at least some of the excesses of progressivism. The rejection was as significant as the mood of the Republican presidents.

Like many Progressives in the 1920s, Merriam puzzled over the problem of leadership with less assurance then Mitchell, and with a more obvious sense of loss. Indeed, the struggle to define leadership had split Progressives from populists, just as it would the social science movement of the two decades to come, far more profoundly than such working friendships as that between Mitchell and Merriam indicated. Merriam published *American Political Ideas* in 1920 and in his conclusion to what was essentially a summary of the political debates of the Progressive era he pointed to the attacks by students of politics on the dogmas of "separation of powers." "Of the three powers of government, the executive was the greatest gainer in public esteem, in practical and effective organization and in political theory. Executive leadership emerged as a definite feature and was supported by a strong body of sentiment and theory. When Woodrow Wilson said that he intended to assume the initiative in the government of New Jersey, if elected governor of the State, and that if that was unconstitutional, he intended to be an unconstitutional governor, he stated the whole situation in a nutshell."[2] Yet in more youthful arguments, Wilson had worked the other side of that street, and the issue of American democracy as a battle between the executive and the legislature, each struggling for a modernization that claimed efficiency as its benchmark, was only entering a new phase.

Nor was there complete agreement, to say the least, among the group which even Merriam, by that time, would have called "the old Progressives." The theme was the same: Progressivism was not dead, but it lacked the leadership necessary to organize and focus the continuing progressive interest in many communities throughout the country. Merriam and William Allen White agreed; Herbert Croly did not. In answer to Merriam's criticism of an article Croly published in 1921 lamenting the death of Progressivism, Croly admitted that he did perhaps underestimate "the raw material," as Merriam had put it, of progressive opinion in the United States. But he was still willing to defend his basic position. "In the first place," he argued, "the middle-class resident of the small towns, who formed the bulk of Roosevelt's support in 1912, is probably more reactionary now than he was then."[3] The reasons for the reaction Croly thought clear enough: a fear of labor, of social unrest, of the new sense of class in the debates over concerns he would once have labeled "reform." Croly saw no chance of unity on a common platform. Even California's Hiram Johnson, whose following Croly had called "local"—Merriam completely disagreed—could not manage to create a sense of national direction out of his popularity.

By 1923 both Merriam and White were completely disillusioned with Johnson. His anti-internationalism offended them both. "He has been a disappointment to me since he bit Wilson and went mad," White wrote, and the study of Wilson that White was preparing indicated he knew the taste well enough. "He has compromised domestic economic issues and questions for not very important international issues and questions. Too bad." And when Merriam read White's *Cycles of Cathay* three years later, he sent a letter of praise which touched once again on their common concern. "I wonder where our next leaders are coming from, for I have not in my time passed through such a barren period. Possibly Al Smith may be our next one, although I suppose to you bone-dry Kansans that would be anathema." White was quick to agree; but his concern about Smith was Smith's religion, not his position on prohibition. He felt that Smith could be the leader they were looking for "if his political friends had sense enough to put him in the United States Senate for ten or a dozen years so that he could become national." But even that prospect did not move him out of the despondency which had trapped them all. "I think we are in a time of reaction and might as well admit it. Reaction makes no leaders. It is only where great causes arise that great leaders come, it seems to me."[4]

The sense of helplessness, like the later labels characterizing the twenties as a trough of progressive lassitude and frustration, obscure the degree to which progressive intellectuals shared essential commitments of the period. By the mid-1930s many attitudes intellectually acceptable in the 1920s—isolationism was one of the key ones, of course—represented ignorant reaction. Equally important, while thoughtful men took positions against the Red Scare of the twenties, they committed themselves to strong anticommunist, antisocialist political views as the intellectual foundation of the Americanism they were trying to support. To define an American national identity distinct from other national identities took on an urgency in the aftermath of the war that bore distinct and embarrassing relation to the prewar progressive concept of nationalism.

In respects which they could not have anticipated and with which they did not tend to associate themselves, postwar Progressives shared nationalist commitments with the architects of the popular anti-European mood. They could even be accused of providing, by whatever inadvertence, a sound intellectual foundation for some of the very extremism they deplored. Their wartime energy expended on the work of the Committee on Public Information was an obvious example; but their struggle to bring the European training of their social science into the scale of reform in the 1920s and '30s touched many of the same issues. Education and the creation of a responsible Americanism built on national rather than local identification required the construction of a national ideology strong enough by itself to be free of the threat of surrender to an always dangerous Europe but enough like older national ideologies to be competitive in the postwar world. The answer was to make capitalism socially responsible without changing the structure of American government—and, perhaps more important, without seeming to threaten the necessary historical base which post-Civil War nationalism had given that government.

Merriam's *American Political Ideas: Studies in the Development of American Political Thought, 1865-1917* is a survey of progressivism, but underneath its copybook summaries and blandly enumerative accounts of the changes in American government since the Civil War runs a theme which had not been a serious concern in Merriam's earlier writing: criticism of socialism as an effective alternative for American government coupled with the more familiar criticism of industrial capitalism as "free enterprise." Unlike Charles Beard or Walter Lippmann. Merriam had never found socialism attractive in the period when many Progressives were seriously considering it; but with the exception of a graduate school essay on the subject—which did not win a prize in the Columbia competition for which it was written—he had not made the criticism of socialism the center of any of his approaches to American government. The war changed that.

Merriam's argument consists, briefly, of the following points. He sees the post-Civil War constitutional doctrine applying the concepts of individual freedom to the new industrial corporation as an error. Individual freedom in its preindustrial form, he argues, was a freedom of political action from coercion by the state—not a freedom of economic action from regulation. The American industrial revolution, then, was turned into a political revolution by the courts. They gave modern industry political power unsanctioned by public will, making industry, in effect, a political power outside democratic political control. This is a familiar enough argument in the Progressive debate, and the term Merriam uses to describe it, "Invisible Government," is taken directly from Theodore Roosevelt. The function of reform is to make that government "visible" by bringing it under public regulation.

The fact that it is regulation rather than control marks the difference between progressive reform and socialism. While it is true that under progressive reform some corporate activities might best be operated directly by the state, such activities would generally fall into a relatively narrow category which could be designated "public service" as distinct from industrial production. The latter could remain private but regulated. The debate over the range of public service and its distinction from private enterprise split Progressives of the twenties, many of whom looked to younger leaders such as Herbert Hoover for a rationalization of its meaning and application, but the defense of whatever free enterprise remained would be the same: that government ownership of all production would erase the necessary democratic distinction between politics and economics, replacing one form of coercion with another. The crucial factor seemed to be the insistence on the priority of politics as the crucially "free" factor determining democratic behavior. Politics, the conscious process of selection among alternative leaders and policies, is the ultimate and sole preservation of democratic government.

This "politicism" in Merriam's approach is the key to such system as he managed to devise. To be an antirevolutionary force, it needed a base in the American historical tradition. *American Political Ideas* provides that. The primacy of politics becomes the American preindustrial insight which industrialism has neither need nor right to change. In America, industrialization did not call for revolutionary change and the courts were wrong to make it happen. Progressivism thus becomes a counter-revolutionary force against a usurpation of political power by nongovernmental groups hidden from public control.

This view of industrialization recognizes its economic significance historically but denies a necessary corresponding political significance—but only in America, where, presumably, the political insight happened to take practical effect before industrialization, not after it, as it did, again presumably, in Europe. Therefore, whatever sense socialism may make in the European historical setting is not transferable to America.. Denuded of political significance in the "true" traditions of American government, industrialism can be brought into the framework of American governmental processes by a manipulation of those processes in order to "modernize" them. All that socialism would do in America would be to impose a nonhistorical and coercive solution on a much purer form of indigenous social democracy evolved out of the history of American politics. Getting Americans to vote, educating them as citizens, and defining the nature and training of the men who would lead them were all issues which grew out of the effort to redefine reform in postwar America. The elements of a new concept of reform were being collected, but for the moment only in the familiar vessels of the Progressive era.

Merriam had been active in the American Political Science Association since its founding; but the leadership of the association still rested with a generation whose primary professional concern had been the separation of political science from history. In December 1920 the association held its sixteenth annual meeting in Washington, D. C., once again as a joint meeting with the American Historical Association. Although the two professional groups had separated formally sixteen years earlier, and although the alliance had long since ceased to serve the interests of the younger generation now coming to leadership in the profession, the number of departments still designated as both history and political science gave a practical convenience to their continued association. Two of the papers indicated the nature of the shift in focus which was taking place. Harry Elmer Barnes discussed "Some Contributions of Sociology to Modern Political Theory," celebrating the occasion as an infusing of a new interdisciplinary interest for both sociology and political science. Charles E. Merriam delivered a paper entitled "A Survey of the Present State of the Study of Politics." When it was published in the association's journal the following year, it appeared without the "survey" as "The Present State of the Study of Politics,"[5] a change of some importance. Merriam had apparently planned something in the nature of a summary of his book, which had just come out—and to some extent that is what he did—but the textbook detachment is gone, replaced by a tone the profession was going to hear more and more over the coming years. It is a tone combining exhortation and prophecy, protection of the past and a call for a new future. Merriam's politics was shifting from the public polling places into the profession.

"The original plan of this paper included a general survey and critique of the leading tendencies in the study of politics during the last thirty or forty years. . . . It would have been an interesting and perhaps a useful task." And so his text proceeds in a chain of conditional verbs: "It would have been useful possibly. . . It might have been possible to discuss. . . It would perhaps have been useful to offer a critique. . ."[6]

Its style is a skillful variation of the politician's tearing up of his prepared text, a dramatic search for a new departure in a carefully planned direction. Its substance was to have an impact on political science not unlike Turner's announcement almost thirty years earlier of the meaning of the closed frontier, and its concepts of change were those already being discussed by John Dewey and firmly part of the older tradition of pragmatic thought.

Merriam called for a new approach to research in political science, for new, modern methods in the collection and utilization of information from public and private sources, and for the involvement in political science of methods and materials from the other social sciences. Barnes had opened his discussion with a frank statement of his awareness of this significance of the occasion. "The fact that a sociologist had been requested to appear upon the program of the American Political Science Association is in itself far more significant than any remarks which may be made upon the subject of the relation of sociology to political theory."[7]

Merriam's pleas for revision in the study of politics involved at least four elements familiar from the progressive tradition but reshaped now in the light of that experience. First, the call for more improved methodological equipment for the collection and analysis of political material was an old reform demand most recently met in such institutions as legislative reference libraries in the states and bureaus of governmental research in the cities. But Merriam added another concern, suggesting that even where such institutions do exist, the possibility of their domination by political reform interests distorts the information, making it less reliable for objective analysis. Inherent in this is the rejection by the new academics of the status of reformer, one of the significant elements of the new progressive mode. Accomplished politely enough for the most part, it was nonetheless one of the major sources of friction in the various associations which brought old-line reformers into communication with new-line academics.

Second, Merriam suggested that what he called "political prudence"—the experience of men actively engaged in politics—needed to be utilized more effectively as a source of knowledge about politics. Such experience "constitutes a body of knowledge which, though not demonstrably and technically exact, is nevertheless a precious asset of the race."[8] To be sure, Merriam placed a high value on his own political experience and made the fullest possible use of it anecdotally in his teaching and in his persuasive professional exhortations. But there is more to it. One of the strongest progressive-reform tenets to survive into the twenties intact was the hostility to politics as a profession—the regulars are viewed as the enemy and the system they manipulated as the basic machinery of evil. While Merriam did not outline a realpolitik in the sense in which the generation he taught would try to spell it out, he did insistently argue for a respect for nonscientific, professional political experience as a kind of knowledge different from and equal to scientific knowledge. Merriam's growing interest in analytical biography of political leaders was one direction in which this concern was to move.

Third, he requested "broader use of the instruments of social observation in statistics, and of the analytical technique and results of psychology,"[9] as well as more involvement with those sciences concerned with man and his relation to his environment. Interestingly enough, the restructuring of this set of issues in the 1920s in the fields of economics, geography, sociology, and the statistical approach to political research was what Merriam's name would most often be associated with by those who knew him through the "Chicago School"; but it is the area in which his individual contribution both as writer and as teacher was always the weakest. It seems not accidental that the point is the third on his list rather than the first.

Finally, he asks for "more adequate organization of our technical research, and its coordination with other and closely allied fields of inquiry."[10] And he concludes his article with a definition of science that indicates an approach rather different from the classical academic position of his predecessors. "Science is a great cooperative enterprise in which many intelligences must labor together. There must always be wide scope for the spontaneous and unregimented activity of the individual, but the success of the expedition is conditioned upon some general plan of organization. Least of all can there be anarchy in social science, or chaos in the theory of political order."[11] Merriam was proposing a concept of community in social research that would render obsolete the traditional picture of the university as a collection of isolated monuments to contemplation whose treasured protection from the world was exceeded only by their preservation from one another. Like Mitchell's distinction between the man of facts and the man of hunches, Merriam's view of research would provide little comfort for those still seeking to support the romantic concept of genius as a unique social event nurtured by privacy and marked by the eccentric individualism of a Veblen.

The two aspects of Merriam's approach to political science to be found in this paper of 1920 and to become the hallmarks of the new career which he was in the process of forming for himself were these: First, he emphasized the multiplicity of methods which could be appropriate to the study of politics. What he called his "pluralism" gave him an interest in the testing of method and a rejection of a fixed commitment to any one of them. Second, he believed in social research as the product of a loosely but purposefully organized community to which each made his contribution and from which all benefited. Yet his efforts to reconcile a number of different methods in a free community of research with his "general plan of organization" which would abolish "anarchy in social science" later subjected him to criticism from those who found such a definition of science a contradiction of the term and his manipulation of that contradiction an exercise in a new kind of politics.

Although Merriam was credited with the founding of a new school of political science, he did not do it by specifying a distinctly new method of research or even by clearly articulating an old one. If he can be said in any sense to have restructured political science itself, it seems more likely that the method was far more political than it was scientific. Yet his eagerness to utilize other social sciences in the development of a new concept of politics looked very much to the exactness of those disciplines as the basis of their use in the study of politics.

Methodologically speaking, he left political science sufficiently neutral—his critics might have said "vague" or "impressionistic"—to enable it to absorb methods from the other social sciences without being dominated by them. Thus, the study of politics could use the methods and revelations of economics and statistics without accepting a mathematical sense of the determination of political events, the insights of Freud without being bound by a Freudian framework of social development, and so on, adopting techniques which tended to become deterministic in their own disciplines but adapting them to what he considered the free choices of politics.

This methodological eclecticism directed by a classically rationalist definition of politics gave Merriam a capacity to relate himself and his sense of organization to other disciplines without either identifying with them or arousing from their adherents an inhibiting concern over competition in the development of their mutual interests. This methodological eclecticism involved no sacrifice, in his terms, of the subject matter of politics and the principles guiding political behavior; and his writings, therefore, were generally directed toward such concerns rather than method.

It is important here to compare Merriam's interests at this stage of his career with those of his fellow luminary, Wesley Clair Mitchell, who was moving in directions similar enough to enable the two men to be mutually supportive but different enough to mark essential oppositions which were ultimately to separate them. Both had begun their professional careers at the University of Chicago and both had come under the influence there of John Dewey and Thorstein Veblen. By the time Merriam came within the reach of Dewey and Veblen he had already worked with Burgess and Dunning. But the Chicago experience had been more seminal for Mitchell, who began his intellectual career there. Mitchell left Chicago in 1903 to teach at the University of California; and from there he moved eventually to New York, to Columbia and the New School for Social Research. In an important sense, the two men's careers, like their points of view, criss-crossed each other, one beginning where the other ended. Their most productive period of contact was from 1923 until 1936, when Mitchell left the New Deal at the end of Roosevelt's first term. It was a working relationship rather than a friendship; both men were capable of profound friendship, but not with each other.[12]

Mitchell and Merriam were among the group of American scholars who returned from the war in varying states of confusion and concern, their optimism tempered—not to say dampened—by the war experience. Mitchell had headed the price section of the War Industries Board and had, just three days after the Armistice was signed and in the face of a massive and irrational mood of demobilization, brazened through a request that he be allowed to increase his staff so that the information gained about price movements could be retained and made available to economists and businessmen. The resulting fifty-seven bulletins—*History of Prices during the War*—was one of the most comprehensive efforts to preserve useful collections of domestic data from the war experience.

Mitchell was among the many called to government service who found that government habitually acted on abysmally inadequate information. The war dramatized the problem at the same time that it gave interested enthusiasts money and opportunity to do something about it. It also dramatized the unwillingness of Congress or the public to continue to support such efforts on anything other than a wartime basis; in the concluding days of the immediate liquidation of the war effort agencies seemed almost literally to vanish from sight. Men who had seen the experience from that standpoint were not inclined to trust the scientific objectivity of a government operating under the pressures of politics.[13]

Mitchell's commitment to a genuinely scientific examination of society had come not only from his own research interests but also from his profound, critical affection for Veblen, Mitchell had helped nourish and tend the erratic career of the strange and stubborn man who had taught him so much. "What drew me to him was his artistic side," Mitchell wrote in 1928. "There was a man who could really play with ideas!...But if anything were needed to convince me that the standard procedure of orthodox economics could meet no scientific tests, it was that Veblen got nothing more certain by his dazzling performances with another set of premises. Compared with other economists at Chicago, he was a giant. His working conceptions of human nature might be a vast improvement; he might have uncanny insights; but he could do no more than make certain conclusions plausible—like the rest. How important were the factors he dealt with and the factors he scamped was never established."[14]

Mitchell might have come to feel similarly critical of Merriam in the later years of their relationship. For reasons Mitchell could have ascribed to the quirks of a different personality, Merriam remained committed to hunches and insights.

Both men viewed themselves as students of behavior; but the primary difference between them was not only the disciplines themselves but a difference in the histories of the disciplines over the previous two decades. Mitchell was fond of quoting Alfred Marshall's statement of 1907 to the effect that the work of qualitative analysis was done and would have to give way now to the "higher and more difficult task" of quantitative analysis—once the statistical evidence had been assembled. Like Merriam, however, Mitchell did not see qualitative and quantitative methods as mutually exclusive, or as old-fashioned and inaccurate methods to be replaced by new "scientific" methods.

"I shall say little of qualitative analysis," Mitchell told the American Economic Association in his presidential address of 1924, "beyond making the obvious remark that it cannot be dispensed with, if for no other reason, because quantitative work itself involves distinctions of kind, and distinctions of kind start with distinctions of quality." Mitchell disputed Joseph Schumpeter's prediction that American economists were about to undergo a serious division over quantification, arguing that good statisticians saw as many reasons to issue warnings about the misuses of numbers as Schumpeter purveyed to readers of his qualitative analyses. Economics, in Mitchell's somewhat optimistic terms, had already undergone its era of acrimonious methodological debate. It had moved from a state of concern over the "verification" of hypotheses to one of the "testing" of hypotheses; and the change, he felt, heralded an era of cooperation which would prove far more fruitful than an era of debate.[15]

From the standpoint of such reasoning, political science was at least twenty years behind economics. Even so, there were important differences in the disciplines which might indicate that the problem was more than a matter of timing. The breakdown in America of the field known as political economy had had more immediately beneficial effects on the study of economics than on the study of politics. While this reorganization seems to have been consistent with Mitchell's aims, it had side effects which worried him. The old political economy courses had actually served to educate young businessmen-to-be for their roles in the national community. The new economics was tending away from that function, either because of the change in the discipline or because of the emergence of the business school curriculum with its own tailored courses of economics. It was difficult to tell which was cause and which effect; but Mitchell deplored the effects of the separation, finding the lack of communication between the two groups of economists a contradiction of what seemed to him the basic view of economics as a study of behavior.[16]

A similar separation of functions was beginning to affect political science. The science of government could be made attractive to business leaders if it were clear that it was government—not politics—which was being made scientific. Throughout the twenties the funding of new institutes for the study of government indicated that the reform-minded benefactors of the Progressive era were capable of rethinking their commitments. The little empire being constructed by Robert S.

111

Brookings in Washington, D. C., was only one example. To be sure, the orientation toward economics was strong; but the acknowledgment that new legislation had to be the means of bringing about economic change helped expand the boundaries of systematic research acceptable to philanthropists ordinarily cautious about contacts with politics. By the end of the twenties the economist was on the way to becoming a professional whose expertise could compete openly with that of the businessman or banker he had once sought to advise. Could political science professionalize in that direction? Political science was in the process of changing; but the change was not going to be the same, however much it paralleled the changes in economics. Envious glances and ambitious methodological designs to the contrary notwithstanding, American political scientists would have difficulty assuming expert status in a society historically attached to beliefs about the relationship between democracy and individual political judgment.

The legal and constitutional orientation of the older schools of politics—in combination with the newer emphasis upon the study of administration—made political science useful as a field for training those interested in careers in law or business, as well as politics and public service. Many men in the profession, even those as research-minded in their point of view as A. B. Hall and even at institutions as committed to the new scientific politics as the University of Iowa, continued to argue that the teaching of political science at the undergraduate level was the teaching of citizenship, not the teaching of scientific descriptions of the operation of government or generalized principles about the functions of government, as Merriam's view of the science seemed to suggest.

In the aftermath of World War I the use of political science in the teaching of citizenship took on an importance influenced not only by the patriotic confusions of the war and the continuing concern with Americanizing immigrants but also by the increasingly revolutionary atmosphere of Europe. The new Soviet Union dramatized the role of government in the training of the young to support the aims of that government. Then, the revolutions in Italy and Germany brought an emphasis upon youth training, and the distinction between citizenship and indoctrination became blurred. Citizenship was to political science what the education of responsible businessmen was to the economists of a scant generation earlier. Both interests were gradually shoved to the periphery of their respective disciplines as the pursuit of scientific method became the dominant concern. Mitchell and Merriam, still concerned with the utility of social science, could only lament the barriers which disciplinary specialization placed in the way of communication between social scientists and the public. In their views, such interaction was not only socially useful but the fundamental source of their kind of knowledge; the essential experience of social science was, for them, not an abstract manipulation of theory but the observation in the theater of public behavior of the results of a tested hypothesis. They devoted their careers to the carving of new routes of communication as old ones closed. As essential as the pursuit of science was to the increased utilization of social knowledge by mankind, if the increase took place at the expense of public understanding of and respect for social knowledge, it could scarcely avoid defeating its own purposes. The relation between social knowledge and democracy required communication of that knowledge at a level capable of generating public support if democracy were to continue to work. Their fundamental belief that it could and would continue to work was the sustaining spark which kept them moving.

The important difference between Mitchell and Merriam, and the one which would do most to cast their careers and their influence in different directions, rested on the relation of their respective disciplines to the other social sciences. Despite their recognition of the importance of interdisciplinary relationships, Mitchell's basic commitment was to economics as one among the several social sciences, an equal among equals in the search for knowledge. Research for him was fundamentally research in the materials of economics. His sympathies with other disciplines were the sympathies of a reformer and dedicated humanist; but he carefully qualified his relation to them, avoiding any pretense of competence beyond the range of the only area of involvement which he was willing to call his "work." This humility did not stand in the way of his influence on his generation; indeed, it enhanced it. One need only check the leaders since Mitchell in the establishment of the relationship between professional economists and the federal government to see the depth of this influence. Nonetheless, he did not seek Merriam's range. He deepened economics; Merriam broadened political science.[17]

Merriam's concern with the interrelation and interdependence of the social sciences was far more comprehensive than Mitchell's, but it was purchased at the expense of a concern with a definition of political science which called for a rigor Merriam himself seemed almost deliberately to eschew. While Merriam's students of the 1920s tended each to adopt one of the methods with which Merriam toyed—psychoanalysis, quantification, comparative behavior, and the like—and to become, like Mitchell, specialists in the evolution of a method, Merriam continued to move about from one method to another. In many respects, Merriam was the last of a generation of generalists. He might have taken the old title "sociologist" had it still been the designation appropriate to the generation of Sumner and Ward rather than to one specialization among a growing number.

Whether Merriam was a political scientist or even a social scientist in the sense in which many of his students were seeking to use the terms was a subject of subtle debate in his own time. It is important to note that, while he exhorted others to ever more scientific endeavor, he consistently avoided the use of the term "science" in the titles of his works, preferring to speak of "politics" in which "study" and "research" are to be done. His concern was for the "state of politics" or "new aspects of politics" rather than for a science of politics as such. A strong group within the profession—important among them, one of his earliest students, Arnold Bennett Hall, and Robert Treat Crane of the University of Michigan—accepted Merriam's leadership but debated, at times vociferously, the limitations he seemed to them to place upon the development of what they considered scientific techniques.

In a review of Lippmann's *The Phantom Public* Hall stated the case in what were perhaps its gentler terms:

> Most writing that appears under the name of political theory might better be called political literature. Certainly it is not theory in any scientific sense, for a true political theory is a generalization that accurately explains the facts of political behavior. Unfortunately, most so-called political theory consists either in retroactive rationalization in defense of official actions, or political dogmas, or pure speculation for the joy of the game, or propaganda in behalf of specific proposals. It seems to derive its influence from the lure of the literary form in which it is expressed, from the splendid emotional ideals in which it is conceived, from the occasional flashes of intimate insight into human nature it evidences, or from the intriguing ingenuity displayed in its formulation.[18]

The same accusations could well have been made against Merriam.

At its extreme the scientific school could be identified by its belief that in political science impressionistic statements were the result of

114

scientific ignorance or a failure of research and would ultimately be replaced by accurate data and generalizations drawn from such data. Merriam insisted that he believed in a similar future, but he kept adding warnings, pleading for a kind of patience with the past which modified the threat of revolution, scientific or otherwise. Patient for the time with the necessity of accepting other approaches, the true scientists looked forward to the gradual decline of the "literary" in political science itself; and so Merriam seemed to believe, too, until he began talking about "prudence" and citing the evidences of his own political experience.

While Merriam still identified himself with political theory, he also drew fire from critics as diverse as William Yandell Elliott and Charles A. Beard, both of whom, in rather different fashion to be sure, were unwilling to relinquish a conviction that political theory required more of a commitment to traditional system than Merriam thought it necessary to observe. In *American Political Ideas* he had specifically sought to transfer the label of theory to such statements as court decisions, party programs, and the reports of committees or groups investigating particular problems. Beard continued to insist that Merriam managed to find political theory in an unusually broad range of social and political utterances. And Elliott, in 1925, reviewing Merriam and Barnes, *A History of Political Theories: Recent Times*, expressed a well-considered puzzlement at the authors' selection of a title. "To this reviewer," he wrote, "it seems that political theory, although it cannot slight the problem of the methodology of research, is chiefly concerned with a political evaluation of the descriptive material that is properly the concern of the other social sciences, and of the administrative and structural fields of political science. In this respect many of the essays . . . may seem to the student of theory incompletely assimilated to the field of politics." In the same review, however, Elliott acknowledged Merriam as the man "who has become the dean of American theorists."[19]

Elliott's bestowal of title might have raised one eyebrow on most of the leading political scientists of Merriam's generation—but only one eyebrow, and that was significant. By the time Elliott made the remark in 1925 there was no doubt of Merriam's importance in the field, but the nature of that importance was considerably more complicated to define than the phrase "dean of American theorists" could be taken to imply. Even those who might have thought the phrase misdirected would nonetheless have conceded Merriam the stature such a phrase carries with it.

The public sounds of dissatisfaction with Merriam's leadership were generally muted, however critical commentators may have felt about him privately. Harold J. Laski disliked Merriam's work. He took the occasion of the reprinting of Merriam's *American Political Ideas* in 1925, over two decades after its initial appearance, for a polite critique of Merriam's emphasis upon political rather than economic theory, but he acknowledged Merriam's importance. Privately, Laski was considerably less guarded. He told Oliver Wendell Holmes that he thought the book "a dull flat book which catalogues names without I think showing any real ability in their measurement." And when *New Aspects of Politics* appeared the same year, Laski refused Herbert Croly's invitation to review it on the ground that one public attack was sufficient. Croly's invitation to review may also be another indication of the rapidly crumbling line of the old Progressives.[20]

Had Merriam chosen to follow Mitchell's course, developing political science primarily through his own researches, the effect would have been altogether different from what it was, and, in many respects, much easier to define. One would cite a succession of significant monographs and trace their origins in the work of his teachers and the effects in the work of his students. Merriam, however, was a crucial figure because of his implicit recognition of the distinction between political science as a discipline and political science as a profession. For he saw in the profession the means whereby the discipline would be sustained, enriched, and perpetuated, and he recognized that in the context of a society so intellectually and geographically disparate as the America of his day, the task of creating a national profession might be different from the task of developing the discipline itself. Merriam could quiet whatever qualms he might have had from time to time about the quality of his own work by insisting that the priority of politics in human behavior gave political science a uniquely entrepreneurial role to play in the organization of social sciences. If that were the case, then political science *was* the organizational theory of social science in some ideal sense.

The focus of his career, then, from 1925 on, was on the organization of the social sciences. While the degree to which his writings establish the intellectual base for that organization is open to debate, the fact that he established the economic organization is beyond question. In an era when the old philanthropic sources of social research were ques-

ioning the validity of their previous endeavors, when the disciplines
hemselves were reviewing the depth and limits of their own intellectual
esources, when the return to "normalcy" attracted a far wider variety
f Americans seeking the good life than commentary on the decade
sually suggests, Merriam committed himself to the broadening of the
ocial sciences and to the reexamination of an inherently American
iew of social theory which that entailed.

7

An Organization for Social Research

Merriam's leadership in the profession was built on his skill in the manipulation of the three factors needed for the management of a national system of social research: exhortation, organization, and money. The hortatory phase of his work can be seen most clearly in the essays in *New Aspects of Politics*, which appeared in 1925, the year of his presidency of the American Political Science Association. The organizational phase of his work can be documented in the formation of the Social Science Research Council in 1923 and the building of the political science faculty at the University of Chicago. The financial aspect of his method can be shown by outlining his relationship with philanthropic organizations in the twenties: the Rockefeller Foundation, the Spelman Fund, the Public Administration Clearing House, and his friendships with Beardsley Ruml and Louis Brownlow.

New Aspects of Politics is in part distillation and in part restatement of various pronouncements Merriam made to the profession, beginning at the December meeting of the American Political Science Association in 1921. In support of a resolution passed by the executive council calling for the appointment of a committee on political research, Merriam emphasized the concept of cooperative enterprise. In a fashion typical of his loose and rather jovial approach, he suggested recent and unspecified discoveries of Aristotle's use of "scores of men who scoured all of the countries of the world for political information to be placed at his disposal." The parable gave him a characteristic gambit: that what was new was really very old and very respectable. "In view of the fact that Aristotle was the teacher of . . . Alexander the Great," he continued in what would also be a familiar line, "it is conceivable that he may have had a sufficient influence with his powerful pupil to bring this about." And he added wryly, "In this respect none of us is as well off as was Aristotle."[1]

William A. Dunning became president of the association in 1922, and in accordance with the council's mandate, appointed a committee with Merriam as chairman. In addition to Merriam, the committee included Robert T. Crane of the University of Michigan, John A. Fairlie of the University of Illinois, and Clyde L. King of the University of Pennsylvania. In its first report, the committee surveyed existing research agencies and methods. The surveys were divided into studies of recent advances in political methods, the work of government research bodies, legislative and municipal reference agencies, research and equipment in universities and colleges, and research carried on by social and industrial agencies bordering on the field of government. The sections on research methods and on research in the universities were written by Merriam. In his analysis of recent methods, he outlined a history of political thought over the previous century, concluding that there were four periods through which the study of political processes had moved: the use of the a priori and deductive method down to 1850; the historical and comparative method, 1850 to 1900; the tendency toward observation, survey, measurement, 1900 to the present; and the beginnings of the psychological treatment of politics.

The placing of psychology last on the list and its implied relation to observation, survey, and measurement are an important indication of the position Merriam had begun to take. What he meant by psychology is unclear, although it seems to combine laboratory and Freudian psychology with a more classic attitude toward "human nature." Graham Wallas is credited by Merriam with a seminal role in the development of modern political psychology, although his work is described as being "brilliant, stimulating, and suggestive, rather than systematic." Walter Lippmann is cited repeatedly as the student of Wallas most likely to advance and systematize the work of his teacher.[2]

Robert Crane's section on the bureau method of political research is, characteristically, critical, even though he recognized the independent bureau's contribution to the recent history of such research. The bureau's dependence on the production of results, its emphasis upon economy and efficiency, and its need to produce propaganda in both the furtherance and the justification of its work weaken, in Crane's opinion, the "scientific" nature of its work by making it more "applied" than "pure." Crane recommends closer cooperation between bureaus and universities, particularly in view of the fact that the former have sources of funds for research which are sorely lacking in the latter, while the latter have the independence of mind which is presumably more "scientific." As he would continue to do, Crane voiced in sharpest terms the basic criticism of the method Merriam was developing in his efforts to reconcile the positions Crane was trying to keep separate. In his argument about the bureaus, Crane saw, without at first realizing it, the potentially destructive effects of the very relation between pure and applied research that many in Merriam's generation were convinced needed to be created. At almost this very moment Herbert Hoover and other public leaders were seeking support for research in the natural sciences by arguing the necessary relation between pure and applied science as a general good to be achieved, not an interference to be feared. And despite his own argument Crane recognized the unavoidable consequences of that interdependence.

The legislative research libraries in the states were surveyed by John Fairlie with results similar to those reached by Crane. Fairlie found that the legislative libraries suffered more from lack of adequate financing than did the municipal research bureaus. The reluctance of states to invest sufficiently in the libraries and the increasing lack of interest in state reform among municipal reform philanthropic groups (Fairlie does not mention the latter point) had combined to weaken a movement which went back to the 1890s but which, by the 1920s, had gone the way of all state reform movements in giving way to the growing emphasis upon urban reform. Indeed, one of the most important political phenomena of the 1920s is the progressive weakening—in every sense of the term—of the state governments.

Merriam was sharply critical of the state of research in the universities. Classwork and administrative duties made time available for research "wholly inadequate." Most institutions failed to provide stenographic or clerical aid, research assistants, or allowances for field work and provided only inadequate research and publication funds. "It may therefore be concluded," he stated flatly, "that the time available for political research and the equipment for intensive inquiries is deplorably inadequate in view of the needs of scientific inquiry."[3]

Merriam's work as chairman of the Committee on Political Research involved him in competition with other efforts in the field to undertake similarly critical and constructive assessments of the state of scientific research in politics. The disputes were deeper and the stakes higher than the relatively bland intellectual exchanges reported by the journals indicated. The funds were limited by many factors, including a reluctance on the part of philanthropists to engage in any matter as subject to criticism as politics—scientific or no. The intellectual differences were also far more extreme than is revealed by the rational tone of the debate.

A. B. Hall and R. T. Crane organized a National Conference on the Science of Politics, the first meeting of which was held in early September 1923 in Madison, Wisconsin. Merriam chaired the group that discussed the relation between psychology and politics. It is clear from the reports of the three successive years of the conference that the majority represented, or came to represent, a position in political science considerably more specialized and separatist than Merriam's. Crane, who became Merriam's critic, though their differences did not surface publicly, saw the necessity of separating pure from applied science; his views formed the center of an opposition which threatened the most fundamental of Merriam's motives by removing the science of politics from direct involvement with political life. While the conference ultimately blended its work and its personnel with the larger social research group which Merriam sought to form, and Crane became a leading figure in the group, the relationship was a significantly uneasy one.

In effect the dispute boiled down to Merriam's commitment to some form of publicly available generalization as the ultimate end of social science research, but actively designed for that purpose, not, as critics of Crane's view of pure science might have put it, as an accidental by-product which the public could understand in whatever way it needed to or wanted to, like the principles of physics or biology. This meant the maintenance of a common language of discourse in the midst of increasing specialization and all the difficulties attendant upon such a combination: specialized and particularized terminology, refined methods of statistical calculation open only to the trained, the necessity for specialist training at ever more advanced levels. Merriam accepted the technical paraphernalia of specialization, but his support of democracy as a scientific process of government and his view of the introduction of science as a nonrevolutionary extension of a democratic tradition rested on the maintenance of a continuous balance between the development of new scientific techniques, on the one hand, and the development somehow of more rapid advances in public education, on the other.

While it would be all too easy to see Merriam and Crane as the opposing extremes in the profession—and many of their contemporaries undoubtedly did—Merriam's role was much more significantly an effort to mediate between Crane and the intellectual proponents of the "bureau method" represented among academics by Charles Beard but in a more public sense by the professional practitioners of the new kind of governmental reform. These new reformers were the public educators, administrators, social workers, and a whole new group of public service technicians. Crane's political science looked to them like a withdrawal from the reality they wished to serve. Their political science looked to Crane like a thin veiling of the old amateur reform business leadership. Both sides were right; but the victory of either one in the profession would have meant the expulsion of the other. Crane correctly saw that his opponents had access to more money than he did, but he seemed to underestimate the reason for that, if he understood it at all. Merriam had spent the bulk of his career convincing men with money that the work of the university was a good investment in reform, and he knew that pure research was acceptable to such men only as a by-product of a promise to improve the human condition.

A case in point is Merriam's response to the Scopes trial. His brother John wrote him condemning Bryan for the damage to science and the scientific community which Bryan's espousal of the battle against the teaching of evolution was doing. Merriam did not agree. He supported Bryan's contention that public education was a responsibility of the people speaking through their legislatures, not through the courts. "The voters undoubtedly have a clear right to determine what doctrine shall be taught in the public schools," he wrote, "and the courts neither can nor will stop them." His solution to the problem was again consistent with his view of the relation between science and democracy. "What is really needed is not a judicial decision, but popular education on the fundamental principles involved, and if this is not effectively done, the consequence may be very disastrous for perhaps a generation or at any rate a number of years. In the long run, to be sure, the intelligent point of view will prevail, but in the meantime much popular damage may be done both intellectually and politically." He went on to suggest that a movement be formed for the repeal of the anti-evolution laws, and that such a movement might be headed by Charles Evans Hughes or Elihu Root or Secretary Hoover. "Unless a highly organized and highly intelligent move is made, Mr. Bryan is likely to sweep the board, for he has now found an issue which involves no special economic considerations and where his well-known eloquence and piety give him enormous strength."[4]

This was a response typical of Merriam's point of view, replete with the circles of involvement which seemed to him the key to the political process in American society: the use of recognized social-political leaders to respond to an alliance of intellectuals and the public they had educated to press for legislative action for reform. It illustrated a method based on his belief in the marshaling of communities in conflict to pursue common ends.

The construction of mechanisms to facilitate continuity was central to the maintenance of those ends; but this required compromises that bordered on violation of the meaning of rationality in science. Merriam as leader set himself up as an opponent of both anarchy and autocracy. In *New Aspects of Politics* he wrote:

> And if there were a benevolent despot of science, he would compel the union of all the scientific agencies centering around the welfare of the race. Geneticist and environmentalist, psychologist, anthropologist, biologist, social scientist would all be brought together to consider the fundamental social problems in which they are all concerned and which cannot be effectively solved without their joint consideration and action.

But he stepped back from that solution: "Fortunately there is no such despot, and we live in a world of freedom, but the necessity of co-operation remains the same."[5]

Cooperation was the key. Others in other fields were talking about "voluntarism." Some were remembering the war years as the great example of national fervor brought to the service of the state. It was possible now to minimize the recollection of the legal and administrative coercions—not to mention the social·and intellectual ones—which had put the teeth in that cooperation.

The organization and development of the Social Science Research Council became the best example of Merriam's concept of cooperation. While he is often considered its founder, this label misstates or at least misdirects the attention which needs to be given his involvement in the beginnings of that organization. The organization of such a group was in fact the product of a community facing postwar stringencies in the financing of their research. The growth of international scholarly cooperation in a variety of fields, coeval with the development of the League of Nations, had led to the founding of the American Council of

Learned Societies devoted to Humanistic Studies in the United States as a super-academic association. A parallel movement in the natural sciences had led to a reorganization of the National Research Council, initially a wartime agency funded by the armed services and the Council of National Defense. The distinction between "humanistic studies" and "natural sciences" placed political science, economics, and sociology, as well as history, among the humanistic studies.

The wartime phase of academic international cooperation declined rapidly. The federal government was certainly not willing to sustain such a movement—even· assuming that American academics would have wanted it—and the period immediately following the war was, for the relatively new foundations, a period of rethinking of purpose and direction accompanied by extensive reorganization. The search for more effective means of financing research led academics to organize their joint programs for better presentation of their interests. It also led philanthropists to seek through such organizations a more efficient use of their gifts. The effect, by comparison with the prewar years of academic development and philanthropic support, was to weaken the older system of individual support of specific scholars and their projects—and certainly of specific institutions and their administrations—in favor of a growing view of philanthropy as an organized, professional system of national research and reform. The supra-academic associations could now begin to attract funds of their own.

For many, and particularly during the early postwar years, the formation of yet another organization in addition to the ACLS and the NRC seemed excessive competition for the resources available. Although it was not stated as such, part of the problem hinged on the difference between the concepts of "learned society" and "research council." The efforts of the social scientists to find a mid-position between the humanists and the natural scientists produced internal strains in the academic community which reflected the disagreements Merriam had sought to compromise. Political scientists like Crane felt far more comfortable in the discussions of the NRC, with its new divisions of psychology and anthropology, and in state and federal research relationships, than they did in the ACLS, where Egyptology and the study of English literature were equally "learned"—and equally competitive for research funds—as political science.

Yet one fact remained: philanthropic interest in research had an unmistakably utilitarian base. Funding for the sciences—social or natural

—like funding for the arts, was dependent upon a proof of utility, however small the group for which it might be useful. Crane's concerns about the purity of research and the dangers of an interfering interest in efficiency or reform became a frank invitation to bankruptcy. In that sense, Egyptologists looking for backers for the investigation of a pyramid, like opera impresarios looking for funding for a new production of *Aida*, stood a better chance of getting money than a researcher insisting upon the purity of his research aims.

Nonetheless, there were many in the various social science fields who were skeptical of Merriam's arguments for the general intellectual utility of a new association. Henry R. Seager, for example, recognized the various practical advantages which such an organization would have but wondered "whether any of the associations are far enough along in their respective fields to provide fruitful joint discussion." The American Economic Association, he felt, had done very little as an association of economists to develop and promote research. It seemed highly conceivable to him that economists would be better off pursuing their separate interests.[6] Wesley Mitchell remained torn between research in his own field and his interest in interdisciplinary research. As his organization and funding of the National Bureau of Economic Research in New York amply demonstrated, economists had already found it possible to feather a highly inhabitable nest for themselves.

Doubts among the historians, particularly those who had recently been engaged in the organization of the ACLS, had strongly economic overtones. The proliferation of academic agencies could only bring more competition. Skepticism among historians concerning the validity of "social science" was balanced by experience with philanthropists who considered the editing of rare literary and historical texts single ventures which could be tidily liquidated on publication. The scientific reorganization of human society, however, was a continuing problem in need of continuing support.

Merriam managed to get agreement for a meeting in Chicago in February 1923 to discuss the organization of a research group in the social sciences. A good deal of political effort had gone into getting the various academic meetings during the 1922 Christmas week to recommend the establishment of such a council, or at least to indicate a willingness to discuss the problem, although there were notable dissents. The historians and the economists both disapproved. The historians found it inconvenient to send a representative even as

125

observer—another meeting to be paid for out of one's personal funds seemed too much—and the economists sent a man specifically restricted to "confer" on the subject.

In March the council of the American Economic Association finally agreed to authorize Wesley Mitchell to write Merriam of the association's cautious willingness to join a Social Research Council, as it was still being called. "You will note that the resolution is in the form drafted by Professor Crane and forwarded by you," he remarked; "but that the Council dropped this clause in the preamble, 'and for the advancement of other common interests.' This emendation was deemed wise because we have in the American Economic Association a considerable sprinkling of strict constructionists who live in constant fear of entangling alliances."[7]

The historians, and particularly the American Historical Association's president, Charles Homer Haskins of Harvard, had not been sympathetic to the development of a separate social research group. Their reasons were complex enough as far as their intellectual base was concerned. They felt a definite commitment both to what Haskins called the "literary and archaeological studies" and to the social sciences. They were also willing to see a social science group given special status within the ACLS. The financial reasons were less complex, to say the least. "Have you any means in sight for the council of the four subjects which you propose, or do you expect that to be financed by the constituent societies," he asked, adding dryly, "The Historical Association would find it difficult to help finance any new undertakings."

When the cards were down, however, Haskins was willing to engage in a little realistic negotiation. "I ask these financial questions because a good deal depends on them," he went on in the avuncular tone of the older professional. "If there is sufficient money available for the continuation of the work of the Council of Learned Societies, and adequate money available for a research organization of the social sciences, the practical reasons must be given due weight."[8]

His hand called—and his bluff along with it—Merriam had no reply. There was then no money available outside the associations themselves, and Haskins suspected as much. "Cooperation" would work only if Merriam had a purse to contribute. If he did—Haskins was willing to leave that possibility open—then the historians might want to rethink the problem. Haskins was as aware of the game as Merriam, and considerably more experienced.

The next president of the association, Edward P. Cheyney of the University of Pennsylvania, was far more interested in the idea but apparently less aware of the base which Haskins's opposition had reflected. In March 1923, the month after the failure of the historians to attend the Chicago meeting, Cheyney wrote Merriam an apparently unsolicited and very enthusiastic letter supporting the idea of a new association. He recognized the pledge of the historians to the ACLS but added, "Personally I am not altogether convinced of the wisdom of this arrangement."[9]

Merriam jumped quickly to respond to the first sign of encouragement he had received from the historians. Unlike Crane and several others among the social science group, he did not see any utility inherent in a boycott by the historians but continued to hope for and to work for their involvement. The historians had formed the first of the modern professional academic associations and as such represented the academic establishment against which Merriam and his colleagues were allied. Yet the historians, a generation earlier, had sought similar professional identity in their separation from the American Social Science Association and had struggled with many of the questions of the reform role of the intellectual which were now driving the social scientists away from the ACLS. That many of the historians considered that association the successful climax of their professional dreams did little either to illuminate or "correct," as they might have seen it, the ambitions of a younger group setting its sights on goals the older group could only vaguely remember sighting—and rejecting—many years earlier.

Cheyney innocently suggested to Merriam that Haskins and J. Franklin Jameson of the Carnegie Institution would be the historians' representatives at the very next meeting of the social research group; and Merriam quickly forwarded an invitation to them. Haskins's reply left no doubt that Cheyney had overreached his position as president of the association by a good bit, and that both Merriam and Cheyney had underestimated the degree of Haskins's opposition. "Our general position remains as before," he wrote from a firm grounding in the first person plural, "namely, that the American Historical Association is friendly to cooperation for research in the social sciences, but it does not see the necessity of forming a new organization for that purpose."[10]

In an effort to acknowledge a factor which played no small role in Merriam's concern, though he did not acknowledge it often, Haskins suggested that more representation from the "Middle West" in the councils of eastern academia might be a good idea. Merriam would have been a logical choice for the next opening, and the concentration of establishment power in the east had long been a problem which the associations had tried to contain by various attempts at regionalization and the scheduling of meetings in midwestern urban centers. These efforts were no longer enough.

Following what was apparently an agreed upon strategy among the historians, Jameson also declined the invitation. He, too, feared the economic consequences of a separation and the competition it would be bound to entail. Jameson hoped that decisions could be held in abeyance until the December meetings when he wanted to try to convince Merriam that the work of the Social Research Council could be done perfectly well within the ACLS, although he admitted that "body had at present little means of action."[11] Neither, at that point, did Merriam, so he avoided discussion of the issue. The competition for resources, can easily obscure the parallel competition among ideas. Central as the economic threads are to the dispute, they are by no means more crucial than the sharper differences over the meaning and function of social science research. This aspect of the argument is clear in the role played by the report of the Committee on Research and its opposition from other quarters of the social research community. William H. Allen was by then one of the old-line public service professionals who had devoted his career to participation in the reform process as a trained expert, and a practicing social worker, not to the privacy of the academy. Writing from the Institute for Public Service, he indignantly attacked Crane's "libelous" comments about the role of bureaus. He accused Merriam of having "put the soft pedal upon one of the most important aspects of political research, namely, putting the research virus into the lay mind." Crane's use of "scientific" had a dangerously "private" meaning, he felt. "I think it is a pity, too, that on that same page, he implies that there is some superiority in investigations 'for the furtherance of science' that does not inhere in investigations for the promotion of good government," he raged, in a tone which he himself later characterized—in a guarded apology to Crane—as "Irish hyperbole."[12]

Crane was not beyond returning any blast, particularly one against a position so central to his whole definition of science. Whether he liked it or not, Allen had interpreted him correctly and their differences were far more irreconcilable than the necessity of continued involvement in the same community could allow them to admit. Gingerly lifting Allen's "virus" metaphor as though intent upon avoiding infection himself, he admitted that "the 'inoculation' of 'the lay mind' 'with the research virus' may be desirable, as you say, but the phrases seem to me ambiguous. If you mean getting officials and public to appreciate the value of research in government, everyone must agree. If you mean, as I gather, turning the lay mind into channels of research on its own account, I cannot agree with you. Research is a highly specialized task of which the lay mind is incapable," he announced with an Olympian dispatch which sought to obliterate with one swift bolt the entrenched Jacksonianism which had supported the utility of social research.

Crane went on to insist upon a sharp difference between investigations for the furtherance of a science and investigations for the promotion of good government. He claimed "no shadow of implication in my paragraph that experiments lucifera are superior to experiments fructifera," only that they were distinctly different from each other.

> As far as I can see, research presents two entirely separable processes. The work of the academic chemist . . . is work that would never be performed in the scientific laboratories of a manufacturing industry. . . . [T]he purposes of the two are unlike . . . [and] the pursuit of distinct purposes quickly produces unlike attitudes of mind. . . . [Y]ou want everyone, even the individual citizen, to play both of these roles . . . while I maintain that the roles of the academic scientist and of the practical scientist, in politics as in all else, are distinct; that neither can properly perform the task of the others; that their work is mutually complementary.[13]

Clarity like Crane's sharpened issues but did little to further the compromises required. That there was a relation between pure and applied—even Crane had to withdraw into a mutual complementariness which was scarcely consistent with his best arguments—was an article of faith that had to be observed. Merriam believed in it deeply, and so, in his way, did Crane; and so, in their way, did the philanthropists who could be convinced that social research was a good investment.

Individual institutions and individual professors were no longer as attractive to those controlling the funds for research as they had been in the recent past. Individuals would therefore have to form an association to meet this trend head on, or they would not benefit at all.

129

The temporary Social Research Council had no money. Its support in the academic profession came from the younger ranks, the men no older than fifty, while its opposition was the established group which had built organizations like the American Historical Association and the American Economic Association and could consider the ACLS the acme of their own endeavors, the more than adequate link not only to the sources of funds but to the future. The group that Merriam was trying to lead saw otherwise, but with no clear vision of their objective.

Merriam's brother John had just moved to Washington, D. C., to become president of the National Research Council. When Miss Mary Van Kleeck of the Russell Sage Foundation had written to the NRC on matters concerning the Foundation's support of the NRC's forthcoming study of the scientific aspects of human migration, John Merriam suggested that she get in touch with his brother's new social research group to ask if they would help with the study. The Russell Sage Foundation had contributed $10,000 to the project and, for the year 1922–23, the Laura Spelman Rockefeller Memorial gave $60,000. The Committee on Human Migration voted to seek relationships with workers in the development of a "correlation computing mechanism" for dealing with new statistical data. For these purposes, the committee formed a connection with the National Bureau of Economic Research and the new social research group, an indication of both a broadening and a deepening of ambition and scope. The migration study was, at least in its conception, an unusual effort at international academic cooperation financed with American funds.[14]

Then, in February of 1924, the American Sociological Society proposed a survey of the sources and distribution of international news, a project which touched many fields other than sociology, particularly given the anti-internationalist policies adopted by many American newspapers. The Social Research Council used this proposal as the basis for its first request for funds. Merriam led the negotiations but found himself suddenly facing a difficulty which was to serve rather sharply to educate him on the subject of dealing with the new competing foundations. When the philanthropist E. A. Filene learned that appeal was also being made to the Rockefellers, he withdrew the tentative support he had offered. Cooperation had its limitations and confusions.[15]

Not until May 1924, a year after the organization of the council, did it begin to acquire independent funds. First, $18,000 as assistance for its role in the study of migration and the mechanization of industry. Another grant of $2,500 supported committee and conference work for the proposed international news study. And, finally, the grantors, the Laura Spelman Rockefeller Memorial, agreed to provide for the first time for meetings of the council and travel expenses for members. This recognized the existence of the council itself as an acceptable object of support, not just its research projects. Independent funds to administer the council required its incorporation in December 1924. The Social Science Research Council thus became a legal entity.

The financing of social research during this period was a more complex matter than the financing of research in the natural sciences. From research in medicine to industrial chemistry and its offshoots, a general public consensus agreed that scientific discovery was a good thing—almost mystically so. Social science, particularly in the ideologically charged postwar years, could not generate the same optimism. Crane and others had pointed to the fact that local bureaus had adequate financing from reform-minded philanthropists; and Robert S. Brookings was one of those attempting to implement that concept on a national scale. But Congress had on previous occasions demonstrated a reluctance to accept philanthropic services, indeed had expressed a hostility as though faced with a threat to national liberty at the idea, but presidents from Theodore Roosevelt on had quietly accepted support from philanthropists for the study of specific governmental problems.

At the level of local politics, philanthropists were accustomed to the criticism of politicians who scarcely stood to benefit from the results of "scientific research," if that's what it was to be called. For the modestly knowledgeable politician the veil of scientific research scantily concealed a familiar reform shape; and his defense was an attack upon the revealed reformer as a man with evil motives bent upon the harassment of liberty.

At the same time, the association of social science with European ideology, or the possibility of arguing the inevitability of such an association, put reforming philanthropists in the paradoxical position of being open to the accusation of supporting various social control ideologies—socialism, communism, and, by the 1920s, fascism. The financing of medical research was therefore a comfortable withdrawal from attack without withdrawing from reform.

As Merriam knew, the reluctance of philanthropists to become

131

involved in politics—even "scientific" politics—was a continuous threat to the financing of research. Whether consciously or not, he devoted much of his intellectual energy in the twenties to convincing philanthropists that it was possible to finance political reform without being politically involved. This sleight-of-hand feat often depended on a distinction between politics and administration that could sound more naive than anyone with Merriam's experience could possibly have been. During the whole Progressive movement, however, the idea of "public administration" often operated as the intellectually acceptable surrogate for what "politics" had once been before the "machines" took it over.

In some ways the aspect of Merriam's career in the 1920s which gave it the most distinction was his ability to sell the concept of political research to philanthropists suspicious of politics and experienced enough to know why. In some respects, Crane and his antipolitical, pure-research-oriented colleagues should have been better at it than Merriam; but that was where the dilemma lay. Philanthropists were motivated toward reform; pure research rejected reform as detrimental to research. Whatever the antipolitical bias of philanthropic reformers, their commitment to bringing about change could not be translated effectively into pure research. Nor could it be translated into politics. But Merriam could ease the dilemma, by his commitment, his personality, and his skillful rhetoric.

All of this activity required direct contact between Merriam and philanthropists, and on the national scene, not just the Chicago-based group with which he had long been familiar. Beardsley Ruml, a twenty-seven-year-old graduate of the University of Chicago who had put his interest in the new field of psychological testing to the service of the wartime government as co-director of the Division of Trade Tests, was the vehicle. Ruml's spectacular career started with a proper conspiracy between Abraham Flexner and President James Angell of Yale to persuade the ambitious young man to turn aside more lucrative business employment for a career in philanthropy, even though, as Angell wrote him, the salaries would be low. Raymond Fosdick of the Rockefeller Foundation had asked Flexner to recommend a bright young man to help manage the new programs under the foundation's General Education Fund. Flexner and Angell agreed on Ruml as their choice; and, as Angell wrote Ruml, the reasons for taking the job were clear: "You will have all sorts of chances to give and make good."[16] Ruml took the job.

Ruml's acceptance of the post was to have extraordinary significance for Merriam's interest in the financing of research. Rockefeller had not sustained his personal interest in the University of Chicago, although branches of the Foundation continued to support specific ventures, particularly in medical research. Too, though relations with the Rockefeller Foundation were by tradition the province of the president of the University of Chicago, not its faculty, Merriam, with his practical experience with philanthropy, was now in a position to deal with them.[17]

Merriam knew two important facts: Ruml was a loyal alumnus who had admired Merriam, and Rockefeller took part in the financing of political reform movements in New York through his backing of the New York Bureau of Municipal Research. That organization, following reform trends with which Merriam was also familiar, had recently been reorganized, establishing as an offshoot the Institute of Public Administration.

In a letter to Fosdick in April 1922 Merriam had offered advice to the foundation, using a recent publication of the institute, A. E. Buck's study of budget making, as his stalking horse. The book, he thought, was an example of precisely the sort of work which limited both the authenticity and the utility of social research. To continue the study of laws and mechanistic regulation was, Merriam wrote, "wooden" and "not scientific from the technical point of view." Pressing his counter approach, he called for more attention to the examination of the practical makeup of various budget systems through the use of fieldwork investigations. That would be treating the problem of budgeting "scientifically" by seeing its relation to the attitudes of a given community.[18]

The criticism of Buck illustrates as well as anything can, perhaps, both the distinction which Merriam saw between his "psychological" view of politics and the views of the public administration group with which he was, in effect, competing. The construction of generalizations in the form of laws or principles of budget making and the construction of models in the form of systems or charters, although acceptable as at least part of the meaning of science for many in the field, seems to have had serious limitations from Merriam's point of view. He emphasized particular methods of research and committed himself to the treatment of the community as a special and individual case, the analysis of which would depend upon a particular case history and a "popular psychology" of its own. The failure of the school administrative reform which Buck and the institute represented was the level of generalization at which they worked. For Merriam as for many of the men and women he trained, the mechanisms of politics had to be examined and observed in operation, which meant within the reality of an actual political situation. That was the science of politics. Its appeal to the reshaping of reform and reformers was clear.

Merriam's friendship with "B" Ruml was lifelong, convivial, and useful for both men. They enjoyed each other's company. While Merriam's appeal to younger colleagues would always be strong, he maintained a distance with most of them which he did not with Ruml. He enjoyed Ruml's calculated lack of caution, the enthusiasm and rambunctious inventiveness which had a strong sense of economic practicality underneath. Ruml wielded the power of Rockefeller money with a flair which might have been frightening to the conservative philanthropists had it not been accompanied by a skillful adherence to the rhetoric of sound business principles. Like Merriam, although on an often more dramatic scale, he projected a sense of practical invention, safe and jolly revolution. Beginning in 1925 he became the initial and sustaining source of the reality behind Merriam's organizational theories in social science.

The first step was the Social Science Research Council's decision—backed by Ruml and Rockefeller—to hold a general conference at Hanover, New Hampshire. Meeting in the Dartmouth College Alpha Delta Phi fraternity house, they began what was to be a most important series of yearly meetings on the development of American social science. In fact the incorporation of the SSRC and the reorganization of the Laura Spelman Rockefeller Memorial, once the vehicle of Mrs. Rockefeller's charities and now of the research interests of Ruml and Merriam, coincided. The capital of the memorial was increased to $80,000,000. The memorial's backing of the conference was thus the beginning of a new network of philanthropy and social research, with Merriam at its head.

Styled originally as a conference of psychologists, the meetings brought together the luminaries of three generations: James R. Angell of Yale, Frederick J. E. Woodbridge, the "Dean" of Columbia, and the leading social scientists of the current generation—not only Merriam and Wesley Mitchell, but Howard W. Odum of North Carolina, Guy Stanton Ford of Minnesota, and numerous others—and the younger group of Chicago graduate students as well as students and young faculty from other institutions. Ruml in his welcome to the group set a new note for the meetings and their purpose.

"The conference has been organized not so much for the purpose of securing an interchange of ideas as for the purpose of creating a vision from which new ideas may emerge." It was a point of view which, by the next year, had drawn to the New Hampshire hills an even wider range of social scientists who had come to present their programs to the council, to the representatives of the donor foundations, as well as to one another. James T. Shotwell joined the meetings in 1926, along with a sprinkling of foreign scholars, Harvard's Dean Roscoe Pound, and Felix Frankfurter, whose midnight fireside recapitulation of the Sacco and Vanzetti case as it then stood both informed and crystallized whatever opinion still needed either; and discussions were interspersed with golf, hillside walks, food, drink, and convivial conversation. A highly modernized version of the western camp meetings which had educated and entertained America's scientists half a generation earlier, as well as the church conclaves which had held western Protestantism in its various organized molds, the Hanover meetings marked a new phase in the distribution of resources for research in the sciences of society.[19]

The business, as Ruml had suggested, was not just the interchange of ideas but their reformation as well as their creation. But the real difference between these conferences and the conferences on various social science research interests with which all of them were familiar was the opportunity afforded by the central purpose of the gathering: to give the SSRC and its financial backers the means of deciding on the distribution of research funds for the coming year. Through the council members, made up of two from each of the academic associations, social scientists were to decide the course of research, acting upon proposals not passively as if they were finished programs but after hearing debate and reshaping by members of the disciplines concerned.

The presence of representatives from the various foundations, Carnegie, Rockefeller, and Russell Sage, among others, also hinted at broader support beyond the decisions of the council. Any accounting of the resources which went into the social sciences and allied studies during the twenties and thirties must include not only the distribution of funds through the council but its channeling into numerous other centers and agencies concerned with social research. Representatives of research bureaus in state and municipal government, as well as in federal departments, came to observe. It was an extraordinary assemblage year after year, as the ample transcripts testify. It was testimony, too, to the concept of the self-judging, self-generating community which Merriam sought and which he intended the council to reflect.

Over the first decade of its existence, the council was to find its search for funds increasingly rewarded. Grants to the council in 1926 amounted to $226,000. In 1927 it received its first lump sum extended over a period of years: $1,958,000. At the end of the decade—by 30 June 1933—the council had granted well over $4,000,000 for research in social science and had broadened its sources of funds considerably. It acknowledged support from the Carnegie Corporation, the Carnegie Foundation for the Advancement of Teaching, the Commonwealth Fund, the Maurice and Laura Falk Foundation, the General Education Board of the Rockefeller Foundation, the Laura Spelman Rockefeller Memorial, the Rockefeller Foundation, the Rosenwald Fund, the late Julius Rosenwald, the Rosenwald Family Association, and the Russell Sage Foundation. More important even than the sum total for the ten-year period is the amount of increase per year in the second five years and the fact that contributions would continue throughout the depression years.[20]

Nor should the figures be allowed to mislead anyone seeking to calculate the virtually incalculable sums going into various forms of social research during the period independently of the SSRC but directly related to the efforts of its managers. As the letter files of those involved in the SSRC during the period indicate, social scientists and their research programs were persistently interlocked with local and regional philanthropic research projects of various kinds. The personnel involved was often duplicated, and the sources of funding were the same. Universities, too, were responding to the demand by increasing the size and number of social science departments. Money channeled into the building of new buildings for social research with "equipped laboratories," as William F. Ogburn called the new University of Chicago social science building, does not show up in grants to associations or councils, although the Chicago building was built by Rockefeller money provided to Merriam by Ruml. Eventually Ruml would move to the University of Chicago as dean of the Division of the Social Sciences, Merriam would take over the Spelman Fund, as the memorial was later renamed, Ruml later would move to New York as

an executive in the R. H. Macy Company and act as adviser to the
federal government through the National Resources Planning Board,
of which Merriam was a member. The network which tied universities,
the government, the social sciences, philanthropy, and American
business together to implement their various programs of social reform
remained intact. Merriam's leadership in his profession rested on his
continuing relationship to the group and on his ability to manipulate it
to achieve his aims.

Merriam's presidential address to the American Political Science
Association at its meeting in 1925 noted the celebration of the
organization's twenty-first birthday, its coming of age. His theme, with
the title "Progress in Political Research," marked the sixth consecutive
year of his leadership, summing up his views, once again, of their
professional responsibilities. His mood was expansive, his approach to
politics touched by the kind of experience which made him, before the
assembled professionals, a figure of complexity and interests who could
exhort them to science and research at the same time that he could
warn them not to take themselves too seriously, citing his "fellow-
townsman, Mr. Dooley" as "one of the greatest teachers in politics in
his time, although he was never awarded a doctor's degree." In the
midst of a search for more refined data and greater methodological
precision, Merriam could still call upon his fellows to remember that
"whatever it may become in print, in real life politics is vivid in tone
and color. Its flavor is in no sense mild and bland, but meaty, savory,
salty.... But politics itself is full of life and action, of dramatic
situations and interesting moments."[21]

Merriam commented wryly on the tendency among his social science
colleagues to use the phrase "Well, of course, that is purely political" to
express "the absolute absence of science in any subject." And he went
on to say,

We are even solemnly warned that politics is disappearing. I have read
with great interest the comments of those who seem to believe that we are
about to pass into a world from which the wicked spirit of politics has
been exorcised, into a depoliticized, denatured state—no, not state but
status—in which nonpolitical rule has taken the place of the outlawed
scape-goat once called politics. It is easy to understand what these writers
feel and sometimes even what they mean, but I am unable to share their
convictions, and it is difficult to escape the conclusion that they are

deceiving themselves with euphonious verbalisms. Whether the ruling authority is called economic, or social, or political, or by some other name hereafter to be determined, a set of relations similar to those of politics seems to be inevitable.[22]

If the utility of politics as a continuing force in human behavior separated Merriam from one central strand of the Progressive tradition, his faith in the necessary public responsibilities of social science would remain as the sign of the deeper, unbreakable bond. Social theory, whatever its claim to purity and abstraction, could not assert its claim to science until it returned for testing to the empirical ground from which it had sprung. The ultimate return to experience was thus not only the beginning point of all research; it was as well the end point of all social practice, the necessary enriching of the empirical ground out of which new research would come. That this cyclical process was voluntary, at the same time that it produced the clarity and certitude of science, was what necessitated the dependence upon the kind of social politics which Merriam summed up in the term *prudence.*

In his address, he pointed toward the possibility of a new era with new reconciliations of limitations. "Some day we may take another angle of approach than the formal...and begin to look at political behavior as one of the essential objects of inquiry."[23] He called for a new integration of the social sciences, and of the social sciences and research in the natural sciences. "But this is fundamental—that politics and social science see face to face; that social science and natural science come together in a common effort and unite their forces in the greatest task that humanity has yet faced—the intelligent understanding and control of human behavior."[24] And in a peroration which stirred his listeners and which had become the mark of what Merriam signified to those touched by his aims and his eloquence, he called for:

> A freer spirit, a forward outlook, an emancipation from clinging categories not outgrown, a greater creativeness in technique, a quicker fertility of investigation, a more intimate touch with life, a balanced judgment, a more intense attack upon our problems, closer relations with other social sciences and with natural science—with these we may go on the reconstruction of the "purely political" into a more intelligent influence on the progress of the race toward conscious control over its own evolution.[25]

Those who listened to that address in December 1925 all knew that for a year now, since the incorporation of the Social Science Research Council the previous December, he had had the means to attempt, at least, the realization of his ambitions.

8

The University and the Chicago School

Merriam's efforts at the building of a national program for social research had to rest ultimately on what he himself was able to do as scholar, as teacher, and as influence upon the policy makers of the University of Chicago. On that last point in particular, any survey he might have done of his first twenty years at the university would have given him precious little hope. Harry Pratt Judson still did not like Merriam's political science. His refusal to give Merriam the chairmanship of the department—indeed, his refusal to give it to anyone through the entire fifteen years of his presidency of the university—was the tacit acknowledgment of his opinion. Merriam's research was funded in large part through his political activities, given the fact that virtually all of his publication during those years was the product of his work in Chicago politics. The two books on political theory are the obvious exceptions; but they were not reflections of anything he would then have wanted to call "research."

Offers continued to come in. President David P. Barrows of the University of California offered him $6,000 in 1921; but Merriam thought the $1,000 increase over his Chicago salary insufficient to justify the move. His feelings about California undoubtedly had something to do with his decision; but he enjoyed toying with the idea.[1] Twenty years of such active attachment to the city had had its effect. Merriam's influence in both city and state politics was still an important investment that anyone with Merriam's interest could not discard easily, or expect to duplicate elsewhere.

When William A. Dunning died in 1922, Merriam was assumed throughout the profession to be his successor as Columbia's Lieber

140

Professor. Nicholas Murray Butler, president of Columbia, wrote Merriam in December offering him the Lieber Professorship of History and Political Science at an annual salary of $7,500. The position itself should have been the ultimate temptation. In a letter to his brother John, Merriam expressed doubts whether "after 23 years of intimate connection with this community, I might not regret severing my relationship with Chicago. I do not have any desire for public office," he added, "but of course I am in an unusual position of influence and power in the community, in no wise dependent upon office holding."[2] His musings to John include nothing about the university or his feelings toward Judson. Judson's retirement was imminent and his successor, Ernest D. Burton, already chosen, so there was at least some possibility of change.

Merriam wrote a delaying letter to Butler, claiming to be busy with other things. The American Political Science Association meetings at Chicago that year were to be the platform for the report of the committee on political research, and Merriam was working to finish the final manuscript. While he felt that he would eventually make his career in New York, at Columbia, and as Dunning's successor, or at least he thought that he did, he was waiting for some sense of a "right time" and this seemed not to be it—or perhaps not, he was not sure. In any case he planned a trip to New York for January.

His journey was spurred by a shocking piece of news. Burton had made such promises to Merriam as his suspended position as president-designate allowed him to make, including the chairmanship of the department, so that Merriam might carry the knowledge with him on his trip. But when Burton confided his decision to Judson, he discovered that Judson, without consulting anyone, had already offered the chairmanship to Barrows of California, a final act as president with which he hoped to confirm, once and for all, his opinion of Merriam. Merriam left for New York knowing this and with his own decision all but made.

Burton began a barrage of telegrams to Merriam in New York. Judson had assured Burton that Barrows was practically certain to decline the invitation; indeed Judson's offer had been little more than a friendly tribute to Barrows, however insulting it may have been intended to be to Merriam. Burton announced to Merriam that he, too, was on his way to New York and was willing to accede to virtually any demands Merriam made. The university was in difficulty, threatened

141

on a number of fronts with loss of key faculty, and Merriam's resignation would likely trigger others.

Merriam returned to Chicago, his decision still unmade. He found awaiting him a letter from Butler, no mean recruiter himself, announcing the intention of the trustees to raise the salary of the Lieber Professorship from $7,500 to $10,000. As Butler probably knew, Burton was blocked. University of Chicago statutes limited professors to salaries of $8,000. Burton, still traveling in the east, felt convinced that, given enough time and the security of his position, he could meet any demand Merriam might make. The question was whether Merriam would give him the time. Burton pleaded with Merriam at least not to accept the offer without answering the telegram and giving him the opportunity of still another reply.[3]

Merriam accepted Burton's terms on the condition that the latitude given him as chairman be considerably wider than anything then in practice in the university. He wanted freedom from the kind of cautious skepticism that had been the mark of Judson's tenure. When he became chairman in 1923, Merriam did receive the power to use his position in the university as an independent base for his own local and national interests in social research. Although Burton was not asked to guarantee him funds, he could agree not to stand in the way of Merriam's own search for support for the building and equipping of a major center for social research. At that point Burton was not really gambling anything on Merriam's dreams; and he had already hedged his position somewhat by making all departmental chairmanships renewable yearly.

Indeed, the events of the next decade in Merriam's career were to cast some question on the logic of his decision. It turned out well enough, but his trust in administration promises gained him less than the continual fight for freedom had already gained him. In two years Burton was dead, and his successor, Max Mason, held the post for scarcely four years. And his successor, Robert M. Hutchins, had interests in the educational function of the university which could at times run counter to Merriam's.

Merriam explained his decision to Butler by pointing to the embarrassment his resignation at that moment would cause the university, and to the probable election in the forthcoming mayoralty race of Alderman William E. Dever, a candidate whom Merriam described as "leaning heavily on me for advice." Regardless of personalities, sense of duty to the university, or, quite obviously, the money involved, the overriding issue seems to have been the promise of leadership in the Chicago department. Yet this was the attraction on which Merriam had the least objective reason to depend. In every professional sense one can project, a move to Columbia should have been the next step. Many years later, after Merriam's death, Lindsay Rogers commented on the significance he felt the refusal to move had for Merriam's role in American political science—of which Rogers was wryly critical—specifically in the disjoining from Columbia of a school of thought which had in fact originated there. Rogers felt, too, that the Columbia move would have brought Merriam's work a discipline it lacked, although that is hard to see.[4]

Basically Merriam probably made the correct decision. Chicago had become a whole community to him. The house on University Avenue, about which he enjoyed complaining a certain amount, the political failure with its minor sense of tragedy to be played upon in convivial moments of recollection, all combined with the new promise of power to sustain something which both preceded and transcended his professionalism. Professional mobility was new still to his generation and he looked upon the ease with which younger men like Ruml and near-contemporaries like Louis Brownlow shifted from place to place with a certain amount of awe. Despite the nationalism of his intellectual persuasion, his personal point of view was established in a sense of home modeled on a small-town community like the one in which he had been raised. Not naive by any means in his sense of the elements of that community which were transferable to a metropolitan environment, he was nonetheless dependent upon the idea as a lens through which he saw the world. Chicago and the neighborhood communities which surrounded the university gave a realistic support to that idea which could not be duplicated in any American city even approximating the size and power of Chicago.

Indeed, the Chicago academics in all the social sciences received extraordinary support for the small-community orientation of their social theories from the fact that the urban context in which they worked had the capacity to provide them not only with impressive examples of the evils they were seeking to reform but also with impressive examples of successful attempts at reform. The reforms may, in the long run, have been less impressive—or at least less persistent in their effects—than the evils; but they shared a quality of idealism more

143

characteristic of the middle American town of the early twentieth century than of the older cities of the east coast. Eastern academics like Mitchell and Lindsay Rogers could see New York as a field of opportunity from which they could select what they wanted for their own intellectual purposes, not necessarily as a community to be invaded by their power. Merriam had the drive for power which Chicago could encourage, not always by inviting him, but by not excluding him either, and by giving him a place to sit among the local elites who managed to retain a significant control of the affairs of the city, even during periods of political failure.

Merriam's Chicago politics had always been underwritten by his kind of research. The Chicago school of sociology had already developed the habit of using the city as its laboratory, and long before the date usually assigned to it as its beginning, 1920. The vice studies undertaken by Chicago sociologists during Merriam's aldermanic years had become famous both in the professions which admired their method and in the public press which enjoyed details lurid enough to be banned from the mails. Merriam had taken part in such projects and had encouraged their proliferation; but he envied the fact that other departments of the university got the credit, while political science struggled along with new appointments only to cover undergraduate instruction. In the year 1920-21 the roster still listed Judson, Ernst Freund, and Merriam as its only senior faculty. Frederick Bramhall and the newly appointed Leonard D. White carried undergraduate instruction. The sole departmental fellow for that year was Harold F. Gosnell.

Burton offered Merriam the opportunity to take the lead in changing what even he must have seen as the anomalous position of political science among the Chicago departments of social science. Chicago sociology had started with Albion Small as Harper's luminary, and it had evolved into a school responsible for the training of the leadership in the new profession. That was where Merriam wanted to begin.

His first three appointments were Quincy Wright and Rodney L. Mott from the University of Minnesota and Jerome G. Kerwin from Dartmouth College. The Wright appointment was intended to open up the field of international law and diplomacy, while the Mott and Kerwin appointments, initially to expand undergraduate education, freed Leonard White to begin graduate teaching in public administration. Appointments thereafter tended to come from two sources: the public service officers Merriam was seeking to bring to Chicago to

establish centers there for their various associations (Clarence Ridley of
the International City Managers' Association and Fred Telford of the
Bureau of Public Personnel Administration were two such appointments) and the leading figures from the graduate student body who, as
they received their degrees from the university, were appointed to
teaching positions. Harold D. Lasswell, Harold F. Gosnell, Frederick
Schuman, and Carroll D. Wooddy were the most prominent among the
first group; yet they subjected Merriam to the most serious criticism
from successive university administrators, who, throughout the peak
years of Merriam's chairmanship, tended to see such appointments as
examples of the kind of inbreeding they considered debilitating, particularly for an institution so committed to looking outside itself for its
great figures.

Merriam's view of the communal nature of social research invited
criticism, yet it was the hallmark of his method of academic administration. It was the *department* which engaged in research, and the
projects announced to the profession at various times were referred to
as departmental enterprises. Junior members were not distinguished
from senior members in such announcements, and joint citations were
the custom. The Chicago department was conceived of by Merriam as a
community of researchers. If the ideas tended to be ideas Merriam had
long been indicating were worth investigation, and if the investigators
were former students whose initial interest had been stimulated by
Merriam, and if their research and, indeed, their careers at that stage
were being supported by funds Merriam had solicited from boards
whose judgments he influenced, he saw nothing to justify criticism.

For the next twenty years, the figure of Merriam was, in a way, a
symbol of familial continuity in the university community and in
the extended community of political science researchers which ultimately spread out from it. He knew his students and their families,
collecting personal details like tidbits of small-town gossip to be passed
around to create for each personality a friendly legend. His Jewish
students knew how much he enjoyed anecdotes about their homelife
and customs. Doctrinal differences among midwestern Protestant
sects provided material for banter among students who could still share
his recollection of disputes no longer relevant to their concerns. His
correspondence chronicles marriages, births, and deaths much as his
parents' correspondence did. Merriam's community did not survive
him; but then neither did the communal sense which had produced it in

the first place. The national research system Merriam was working to build had as its inevitable outcome the erosion of many of the local values which had stimulated Merriam to develop it. Merriam made his department an exciting place to be, partly by generating a sense of camaraderie in a common crusade, partly by making certain that the resources for maintaining the crusade were always there. Since many of those resources were from the same coffers which funded the other social sciences, and indeed the university itself, the level of competition could become intense. Political science was a new field among some very established fields; but Merriam's reputation as a local leader put him in a group which transcended discipline among a generation of academic administrators and foundation managers still capable of thinking of social science as a single moral pursuit, however much they may have acknowledged the necessity of scientific research. Merriam's linkage of the generation he taught and the generation responsible for funding that teaching was again the crucial element.[5] To some of those involved in the peak years, from 1923 to 1943, the ending seemed difficult to explain, yet the conditions for a kind of failure were always there.

Harold Lasswell's career at Chicago is a case in point. Few men of the period more effectively exemplified the triumphs of the Chicago school of political science. Bright and articulate, master of the most romantic of the period's new social sciences, Freudian psychology, and capable of generating enthusiasm among his students, Lasswell often seemed to represent to Merriam the kind of youthful intellectual attainment men in the later phases of their careers can see—and envy—in the generations which will succeed them. Lasswell spent part of the period between 1922 and 1926, when he was working on his doctorate and assisting in the department, traveling in Europe, studying and paying homage, on Merriam's behalf, to some of the older masters who were still alive. His letters to Merriam are a witty chronicle of intellectual life in Europe during the early twenties. Merriam absorbed and incorporated the experience, and admired it.[6] Merriam's pre-1920s Europe had included Ludwig Gomplowicz, Gustav Ratzenhofer, Emile Durkheim, and Georg Simmel; but Sigmund Freud, Vilfredo Pareto, and Robert Michels stood at the outer edges of the experience, when they were there at all.

Merriam found the idea of psychoanalysis attractive; but he was past the point of pursuing the matter any further. He saw a Freudian interpretation of political behavior as part of an older tradition of interpretation he traced from Ratzenhofer's *Wesen und Zweck der Politik* (1893) to Albion Small's *General Sociology* (1905) and thence to Arthur F. Bentley's *The Process of Government* (1908), citing Bentley, as he was wont to do, as "a pupil of Small." Merriam recalled an interesting Small quotation from Ratzenhofer, "The science of politics, however, is primarily a psychopathology of human beings, and with reference to such a science the truth is always rather of a depressing than an exhilarating nature."[7] Lasswell was engaged in pressing the issue of psychology and politics considerably farther than Merriam did, and with results Merriam might have found it difficult to accept; but that was not the issue of Lasswell's career at Chicago. The university administration was inclined to view Lasswell as an extension of Merriam—which in every crucial respect he was not—and ultimately to refuse to give him the status in the university his work deserved.

The same was partly true of Harold F. Gosnell, whom many Chicago graduates considered one of the great influences on their years there. His application of statistical analysis to political behavior pioneered in the joining of the survey methods worked out by the Chicago sociologists and the political science Merriam was seeking to create; but even his impressive bibliography did not protect him from the criticism that he was another of Merriam's *epigone*. For Merriam the building of a distinctive school of political science did tend to work from within the research community he had created. He thus had to withstand criticism from administrators who looked for judgments from other departments of political science at other universities, or from other departments within the university's Division of Social Sciences. A community of research did not mean a community of agreement on what research was to be done and who was to do it.

Between 1892 and 1920 the university awarded thirteen doctorates in political science. Between 1920 and 1940 it awarded eighty such degrees. By bringing Louis Brownlow to Chicago in 1931 and helping to create for him the Public Administration Clearing House, Merriam enriched not only the programs of the department but the range of staff to teach, to involve itself in the research projects, and to increase national attention on Chicago as the place where the practice of politics and the theory of politics were being brought together in their most exciting form. It was the place for the young professionals to be, to learn, and to launch productive careers. However one analyzes the differences of opinion or interprets the years after Merriam's career came to its close, for the years of his management of a Chicago school of political science, there was such an entity in the profession. Its results are far clearer in its definable impact on the discipline than any analysis of philosophical plan or methodological system can justify or explain.

Non-Voting: Causes and Methods of Control, written with H. F. Gosnell and published in 1924, provides a remarkable demonstration of Merriam's vision of a Chicago school of political science in operation. It was in fact the public debut of what came to be known as the Chicago School. The motivation for the study, at least on Merriam's part, was a classic Progressive concern. Despite the increase in voting population brought about by the woman suffrage amendment, elections in the years immediately after 1920 showed a drop in voting participation which seemed to threaten the whole American tradition of democratic reform. To find out why, Merriam and Gosnell, utilizing a large research staff of students, undergraduate as well as graduate, studied the Chicago mayoralty campaign of 1923. The first major study in political science to use both random sampling and the statistics of attributes, the book combines new methodology and familiar concern in a fashion which startled and delighted the profession. As the introduction acknowledges, the chapters discussing method were largely by Merriam, the remaining chapters—the bulk of the book—by Gosnell, although the "cooperative" nature of the enterprise was what they both chose to emphasize. In *Non-Voting* the community of research was the center of attention.

The focus on cooperation had been carefully publicized for over a year through the planting in several social science journals of notes describing a large-scale research project being undertaken by the University of Chicago department. "Progress reports" appeared in follow-up issues, and so by the time the book appeared its audience had been primed to accept not only the innovations in the book itself but the innovative process by which it had been produced. It was a technique Merriam knew well, an effective means of attracting support from donors with money to give, from legislatures with appropriations to approve, and now from a national academic community whose support might be less direct, in its way, but just as crucial in the system Merriam was trying to build.[8]

The tone of *Non-Voting* is strikingly reminiscent of the studies undertaken during Merriam's years in the city council. Merriam and Gosnell give color to their statistical materials by adding quotations from interviewees which provide the numerical evidences of "Disgust with Politics" and "General Indifference and Inertia" with a more familiar kind of evidence. It is a most skillful "bridge" book, moving from one generation of thinking to the next with an impressively deft touch.

Non-Voting also illustrates the sort of relationship that Merriam had during the period to the work of some of his best students. He generalized method effectively, and smoothed the way of novelty by making sure that abstractions always rested on the richest of available examples. One of the impressive features of the book—again a characteristic of Merriam's work—is the fact that its innovations in technique do not separate the untrained reader from his material but rather draw him into it from a different perspective. This refusal to use new methodology itself as the base of an intellectual revolution and to depend, instead, on relating familiar to unfamiliar concepts and conclusions is a sign in the profession which seemed frequently to mark the products of the school most closely associated with Merriam and his work. One finds him playing a similar role in the work of many of the books produced during the period, either as co-author or as the writer of forewords and certainly as critic and financier of research. Merriam's forte was cooperation; and he softened the more radical qualities of innovation by his very presence in the process.

In retrospect many of his more innovative students recalled their ideas as their own, not his, or as having been swayed by others than Merriam; but that, too, was characteristic. Although he would perhaps not have appreciated the metaphor, Merriam's mind seemed to work like one of the mirror reflectors which decorated the ceilings of dance halls of the period, where, from the center of the room, beams of light from many sources would be caught on the fragmented surface of the turning ball and flashed around the room, marking everything and everyone momentarily with a particular touch of color. Part of the effectiveness of the ball of mirrors stemmed from its lack of color of its own, that it did not seek to transform what fell upon it as much as it did to disseminate it as quickly and as broadly as possible. It transmitted and it did not compete.[9]

Merriam had not originated the call for cooperation among the social sciences at the University of Chicago and he acknowledged that.

He and many others in the 1920s remembered Albion Small's efforts to persuade the social scientists to listen more to one another. By 1923, several years after Small's initial discussions, a group had come into being under the title "Local Community Research Committee" with members of the Department of Sociology, Merriam, and others among the social sciences concerned with using the city as a research laboratory as its original core. Merriam was instrumental in obtaining support from the Laura Spelman Rockefeller Memorial by 1924, and the committee's work grew at a pace which, by 1929, had expanded its interests and its publications well beyond the city of Chicago. *Non-Voting* was one of the first of its major projects. *Chicago: An Experiment in Social Science Research*, edited by T. V. Smith and Leonard D. White, appeared in 1929 as a demonstration of the committee's success in producing cooperative work and as an indication of the future programs of Chicago's social scientists. The list of publications and unpublished dissertations in its appendix reveals the extent of the survey work undertaken by the committee.

The new methodologies and the new scientific aims transformed the approaches Merriam had been familiar with long before the new era. The Union League Club, the Commonwealth Club, and the Regional Planning Association contributed familiar support to the new ventures. Merriam's interest in what he was beginning to call "metropolitan regionalism" suggests new directions in urban planning. It was in connection with this interest that he stepped up his efforts to bring organization headquarters for planners and local government officials to Chicago. Since it could be shown that the Chicago region was in the process of developing at a rate approximately three times that of New York, Chicago seemed a much more obvious point for centralizing research in this subject. He argued that planning should be "American" and "futurist" rather than dominated by European traditionalism or the complex political concerns of Washington, D. C., where most groups tended to establish themselves. And, finally, he wanted urban research to be "functional" rather than "informational," able to take account of interests as well as ideas, capable of cooperating with the practical forces which would in any case shape the region.

In an argument which reflects his critique of the Buck book and the approach of the Institute of Public Administration in New York, he contended that true planning resulted from the establishment of a relationship between a "scientific" conception of a given area and the practical needs and interests of the public most immediately concerned. In an important sense, Merriam was continually acknowledging somewhat indirectly a debt to the same sources of thought which had motivated Frederick Jackson Turner in his studies of the frontier, that is, the important localisms on which any American nationalism would have to be based, no matter how complex their relation to one another. Turner had sent Merriam a copy of "Sections and Nations" in 1922; and in his reply, Merriam referred Turner to his discussion in the *American Party System*, trying to reconcile Turner's concept and his own. "There are of course regions within regions and classes within regions which may affect the intensity of the regional attitude or the vigor of its actions," he wrote Turner. "You are of course entirely familiar with these developments and illustrate them in your lectures." But then he sought to press the argument one step further. "Even in city politics there is distinct evidence of sectionalism or localism going down to the roots of representative government. Often the sentiment is much more pronounced or at any rate more effective politically than any other single sentiment."[10]

Ultimately, Merriam sought to base planning on a commitment to scientific study of regions and locales, drawing generalizations not as principles of planning for all regions but as methods of analyzing all regions for purposes of discovering the particular approach to planning appropriate to each. Only on such a building, study by study, could a generalized sense of "causes and methods of control," as the subtitle of *Non-Voting* had it, be achieved. This concept would be most severely tested in the context of the nationalism of the New Deal, but in the 1920s it touched the sympathies and the intellectual concerns of sociologists like Howard W. Odum and neo-agrarian regionalists like the twelve authors of *I'll Take My Stand*.[11]

The development of Merriam's extra-university affluence in the 1920s had a dramatic effect upon the social sciences at the University of Chicago, and the Local Community Research Committee in particular. By the end of June 1926, the LCRC had a budget of almost $132,500, but an analysis of the sources of those funds indicates the span of support Merriam sought to sustain locally as well as nationally. The Rockefellers through the Spelman Fund gave $50,000. The Rockefeller Foundation gave an additional $25,000, but as a "matching" sum in response to Merriam's local fund-raising efforts and those of the groups supporting individual research projects. The Wieboldt Foundation contributed the small sum of $50, and the Commonwealth Club gave $11,000.[12] Merriam's influence among the city's wealthy had not changed; but his methods of using their resources had expanded well beyond his approaches of twenty years earlier.

The money provided research and travel funds, as well as fellowship funds for student assistants. Merriam's interest in political leadership produced at least a half-dozen studies by graduate students assisted by grants from the Local Community Research Committee. In his introduction to Claudius O. Johnson's *Carter Henry Harrison I* Merriam cites Gosnell's excellent study of Boss Platt as a pioneering work in the field and indicates several similar projects under way, among them Leonard White's work on the city manager movement, another LCRC project.[13] By 1928 the committee consisted of Ellsworth Faris from sociology, L. C. Marshall from economics, M. W. Jernegan from history, J. H. Tufts from philosophy, Merriam, and Leonard White, who was secretary and, in effect, general manager. The idea was to draw in the reigning lights in all fields of social science research.

Even with the many evidences of the committee's success, however, by 1929 it had begun to run into problems that were to mark the recurrent weaknesses of the kind of cooperation Merriam continued to try to establish. In a confidential memo to Merriam, White complained that the committee lacked initiative, cohesion, and planning capacity. Citing the test of true research organization as the "capacity to develop systematic, well-rounded and significant programs," White suggested paring down the committee to three from the social science faculty alone and broadening representation from the professional schools of law and medicine.[14] He did not need to complain specifically about philosophy and history, but the implication was there. Still, there was a generalization inherent in what he said that went beyond the personalities involved. The tendency of a committee of widely dispersed interests to become either a passive board of review or a tense anarchy of competing pressure groups could be moderated only by some sustained sense of direction. Yet a sense of direction, specified in a program of research, would have to be able to elude coercion, for the very nature of the intellectual community—even if one confined one's view to the social sciences—required agreement on goals and a voluntary commitment to them. One could successfully coerce inferiors; one had to persuade equals.

The problems were real enough. The increasing availability of funds for study and research had unleashed a difficult debate about management. The ACLS, for example, as a new organization, preferred initially to follow the traditional method of using funds to reward proven research scholars and to encourage further production from them. It was generally acknowledged that donors of funds wanted to see results and that risks had to be limited by that need. Yet, in a social science convinced of the necessity of innovation, a dependence upon the young and untried was crucial. As Merriam had pointed out in his presidential address to the American Political Science Association in 1925, a new generation of students would have to "take over an unfinished work," and he acknowledged that "[f]undamental readjustment is the problem of another and younger generation." Of that generation he concluded, "We rely confidently on their insight, technique, judgment, and vision to effect the more perfect development of a science on which we labored long but left so much to do."[15] As the work of Gosnell and Lasswell would demonstrate, the Chicago School's effectiveness and efficiency in selecting promising young men more than made up for the risks involved, and Merriam's reputation flourished accordingly.

Concerned over the very real possibility of a rapid proliferation of unrelated projects, members of the SSRC created the Committee on Problems and Policy with the responsibility of overseeing programs as well as encouraging new work and guiding younger research energies into them. The Hanover meetings were intended to serve not simply a watchdog function in the screening of applicants for funds but, more importantly, as a continuing opportunity for open discussion and debate with the selected committee and among the entire research community.

Also, as a counterbalance to the potential autocracy inherent in project research, the SSRC established the Committee on Research Fellowships under the direction of Wesley Mitchell. Its purpose was quite explicitly the development of research workers rather than research projects, and its focus was announced at the beginning as being on "candidates in the late 20s or early 30s," the "newly-fledged doctor" who, as Mitchell's description acknowledged, was overworked and ill used by the academic system. The program was planned to avoid overlapping with the projects of the Committee on Problems and Policy.[16]

Merriam's effort to create in the university a research community parallel to that which the SSRC was building threatened the autonomy of the university as a liberal arts institution in a society rapidly becoming professional. The pressures, on the one hand, to formulate fixed programs of research which would use powerful outside resources to dominate the local academic community and, on the other, to leave initiative entirely in the hands of individuals interested primarily in their own formulations of problems created the sensitive and shifting political ground on which Merriam sought to build his empire. In the vast uncertainty of choices available to the disciplinary approaches, just at the threshold of discovery, Merriam considered the domination by any one point of view or even by a group of points of view as great a danger to inquiry as a passive acceptance of the chaos of alternatives passing in review before boards and committees lacking appropriate criteria for selection. The first would destroy the meaning of initiative. The second would render absurd the notion of rational and informed choice.

The Rockefeller financing of the Social Science Research Building at the university provided a dramatic setting for Merriam's enterprise. Symbolic of his approach was the compromise in a debate over the very construction of the building itself. While Merriam took a relatively loose and jovial view of the actual construction, William F. Ogburn reveled in floor plans and designs. He corresponded at length with social scientists around the country, determined to arrive at the ideal conditions for statistical laboratories and their equipment, as well as other factors related to the size and location of lecture and seminar rooms.[17] Furthermore, the building was to be festooned with decorative comments on its function in the form of stone carvings, rosters of names, and mottos. As chairman of the Committee on Symbolism, Ogburn conducted surveys of lists of names to be memorialized in the stone, objects to be carved on the cornices, and a phrase to be engraved on the central outside bay above the street. The objects were relatively easy: Ogburn selected an adding machine, the sign of the Greek psephos, the sphere enclosed in a cube, and representations of a graph. Members of the departments responded with lists of names for the cornices and a sprinkling of relevant quotations for the bay, the most popular of the latter being Aristotle's *Anthropos Zoon Politikon.* Only Edward Sapir refused to supply either motto or list and objected roundly to the whole idea. He opposed lettering in architectural design, arguing that he looked upon lettering "with its nonarchitectural meanings, as an intrusion, not as an inspiration." As for a list of names, he felt that "opinions differ widely and the verdict of 25 or 50 years from now is likely to be very different indeed from present day opinion. I think we should adopt a much more modest point of view in the social science and not stress the idea of the great man at all."[18] As far as Ogburn was concerned, Sapir stood alone.

Ogburn's favorite phrase from the beginning had been a quotation from Lord Kelvin much too long for the space available, to say the least, although Ogburn spent page after page of graph paper trying to block it out. "When you can measure what you are speaking about and express it in numbers, you know something about it; but when you cannot measure it, when you cannot express it in numbers your knowledge is of a meagre and unsatisfactory kind." The terse convenience of Aristotle, even in translation, threatened to win out—and would undoubtedly have been the "popular" choice, but Ogburn finally managed to carve the cumbrous Kelvin into shape. "When you cannot measure...," it finally read, "your knowledge is...meagre...and... unsatisfactory...."[19] An imaginative stonemason marked the lacunae with roses.

Merriam returned from an extended summer trip to find the commandment engraved, the stones in place. Standing there alone as the sole statement of the building's function, it sent him into a rage. He considered having it removed. Kelvin's "law" clearly would have had a place in whatever decalogue Merriam might have constructed, but not at the top. Measurement, for Merriam, was only one of the essentials of scientific knowledge. It shared with intuition, observation, and experience a place none of them held alone and all of them competed to maintain. Kelvin's words, therefore, hammered into the building, never ceased to offend Merriam's eye, for they threatened to deny everything the building symbolized for him. If there was only one kind of truth in social science, then everything he was trying to do was false. Merriam and Ogburn were to spend most of both of their careers in a reasonably genial debate, never friends and always in more fundamental disagreement than it would ever seem desirable to admit.

The formal dedication of the building was held in mid-December 1929. It brought a national and international galaxy of social scientists to Chicago. The two-day program consisted of formal addresses by Wesley Mitchell, Franz Boas, E. B. Wilson, and other Americans, as well as the Europeans Albrecht Mendelssohn Bartholdy, professor of comparative jurisprudence at Hamburg, Sir William Beveridge, director of the London School of Economics, and Celestin Bougle, professor of social philosophy at the Sorbonne. It was a carefully planned "grand occasion," and Merriam's delivery of the "Word in Conclusion" was the acknowledgment of his role in the Chicago School. The building had become an active symbol of the life of social science at Chicago. From it, over the next two decades, would emerge the leaders in their respective fields.[20]

The dedication took place at the conclusion of a crisis in the life of the university. The brief presidency of Ernest Burton had been followed by the equally brief and more troubled administration of Max Mason. The trouble centered on an issue which had split American university faculties and administrations ever since the major modernizations of the late nineteenth century had grafted graduate education onto the various denominational structures for collegiate training of the young. By 1920 the new academics were themselves a remarkably schizoid group whose professional training had come under the by then secure guidance of the new system but whose collegiate experience had for the most part been under the old. Merriam and many of his older colleagues had not been trained at Chicago, as had increasing numbers of the younger faculty, but had come up through the small-college system of the late nineteenth century.

The resulting conflicts in image of the ideal university were exacerbated at Chicago by its tradition of ambitious self-adulation. Like the city's indefatigable boosters, the university's faculty, administration, and trustees tended to translate the city's motto, "I will," into the command, "you must," as they pressed for progress in the good years of the century and dignified survival in the bad years. During the leaner years, undergraduate education with its steady assurances of tuition and conservative community support provided a more secure base for development than the ideals of graduate education, although the fact that the university had come into being on the strength of the latter revolution created a problem. There was always a limit to how far back one could go in the one area and how far forward one could go in the other. Nor was the dispute simply between an administration looking toward community and trustees, on the one hand, and a faculty looking toward the expansion of its professional aims on the other. The split moved like a jagged edge through all the groups involved, and the politics it generated could be found in every camp.

When Mason's unexpected resignation was announced in the Sunday papers of 6 May 1928, the news spread immediately to the various participants in the most recent disputes over university reorganization. Whatever relief any of the groups felt turned rapidly into indignation with the discovery that the resignation had been in the hands of the board of trustees since the previous January. The trustees had withheld announcement in order not to interfere with a movement to reorganize undergraduate programs favored by several powerful trustees and supported within the faculty and administration—although not by Merriam's group. Seemingly innocuous enough, the reorganization would have established a direction for the university quite different from that represented by so obvious and recent a monument as the Social Sciences Building.[21] To the extent that Merriam's plans rested on a firm base of support in his own university, the change in presidency, particularly given the debates of the previous year, constituted real jeopardy.

The next day, Monday the seventh, Mason went before the University Senate, a body made up of senior faculty from all of the departments, to discuss a plan presented by C. S. Boucher, a junior member of the History Department and an administrator in the undergraduate college. The restructuring would have separated the four-year B. A. program into two parts: a two-year junior college under its own administration and committed to curriculum reform, and a two-year senior program which would remain under the direction of the departments. The faculty appeared in greater numbers than usual, but Mason cut off discussion and quickly brought the meeting to a close. The next day at a meeting called by Vice-President Frederic C. Woodward an indirect apology was issued, and the topic of faculty representation on the committee was finally chosen from the list of ten names voted by the reorganization plan, thus tying the two issues together. A five-man committee was finally chosen from the list of ten names voted by the Senate. William E. Dodd was made chairman of the group, which included Merriam, Henry Gale, Gordon Laing, and Vice-President Woodward. The selection was considered a "victory" for the faculty group opposing the reorganization plan, since Woodward, the trustees' leading candidate for the presidency, was the only member of the pro-college faculty.[22]

Although the issue was to be debated in terms of curriculum, undergraduate teaching, and the like, there were added dimensions which, to someone with Merriam's aims, posed a serious threat to everything he was trying to do. Julius Rosenwald, one of Merriam's constant benefac-

157

tors, had offered the university $2 million to build a dormitory system across the Midway. This generosity would not.have been objectionable in itself had it not contained the provision that the university match the gift with an additional $3 million, thereby earmarking a sizable amount from scarce university resources for a program its critics could see only as dormitory expansion.

Within the administration and faculty, however, there developed support for a program that would make a dormitory complex considerably more than just housing for undergraduates. What this intended, apparently, was a parallel to the developing Harvard house system. Angry Chicago faculty referred to the "Harkness" invasion of the university. Merriam and Dodd, who had both been actively engaged in the building of important departments in the university, took the plan as an attack upon their aims. In some senses it was, although that misstates the complex of interests involved in the post-World War I concern with liberal arts education, professional training, and the "generalization" of education for the young. What had already become a movement for "general education" was in part a response to the very educational nationalism Merriam and others were seeking in public education, although they were not inclined to see it that way.

As Merriam told Dodd, "we are in a Hell of a fix; it we seek to do our duty, we shall have to fight the Board of Trustees and perhaps be beaten and then have our departments suffer under the new regime." Others were less cautious than Merriam and saw the problem as posing less of an impasse, though more of an opportunity for dramatics. Laing wanted to fight the scheme and force the appointment of Ray Lyman Wilbur of Stanford, although how he thought he could accomplish that was unclear, even to him, and highly naive. Gale argued that the four of them (Woodward, of course, favored the proposal) should resign if the plan were forced through. As Dodd saw it, the basic issue was whether Chicago would become a graduate research institution like Johns Hopkins or, as he put it, with "athletics, frats and the like," like Princeton or Yale. That the same issue was splitting many of the very schools they mentioned, or that it even went back as far as Woodrow Wilson's fight with Princeton, seems not to have occurred to them in their remarkably myopic institutionalism.[23]

At a faculty meeting on 15 May the administration offered a compromise on the college plan, primarily to lessen the faculty opposition to a Woodward presidency. But by then it was clear the faculty strength in the committee would prolong the search, and that the only hope the trustees could hold would rest on the possible fruits of exhaustion and delay. The committee began compiling lists and bringing in candidates for interview.

The interview sessions that followed were not calculated to arouse faculty support. One of the trustees asked candidate Chase, president of the University of North Carolina, "how do you get rid of professors who make fool speeches?" To which Chase replied, "we do not get rid of them." The trustee was probably not surprised at the answer, although he continued to mumble his annoyance at "radical faculty members who talk of 'free love' and the like." And Chase's candidacy came to an end. The luncheon for Beardsley Ruml impressed all the faculty present, although to be sure by that time most of them were accustomed to being impressed with Ruml. But the trustees thought he was too young and too fat to be considered a candidate.[24]

It was clear to the faculty as the June convocation approached that the waiting game being played by the pro-Woodward trustees was having the desired effect. At the June meeting, faced with summer adjournment, the faculty committee resolved to declare itself firmly in opposition to Woodward and elected Merriam as its spokesman to the trustees. Taking advantage of the planned absence of Woodward from the joint faculty-trustees meeting, Merriam stated his case, although lamely, much to the surprise of Dodd, who expected and desired a stronger statement. The fact of the matter was that Merriam would have been willing to accept Woodward as president and did not wish to do anything to alienate him in the event that that came about. He was much more strongly opposed to Laing, whose candidacy he thought more threatening on personal grounds, apparently, even though all the other faculty members disagreed with him.

At a July meeting composed mostly of trustees, the names of Dwight Morrow and Owen D. Young were raised and, while trustee Harold Swift was absent from the room, his name was suggested, which Dodd took to be a revelation of the true purpose of the delay: if not Woodward then Swift. He wrote Merriam accordingly and received in reply Merriam's opinion that "we are in urgent need of someone who can qualify now or a little later as an outstanding leader in the field of education and research. . . . I have the highest regard for Mr. Swift, and a personal attachment to him, dating from the time he was one of my students," but he did not think him an appropriate figure for the

159

job. "I do not see how the University can hold its own with the fierce competition of the rising and powerful state universities unless we once more be pioneers and path breakers as we were in the days of Harper."[25]

By the end of July, Dodd was beside himself, convinced that Swift would have his way. The new president would be Woodward and, Dodd wrote Merriam, "that means that the larger, if not all the gifts of the next few years will be devoted to that new 'Harkness' across the midway." Dodd had reasons to predict serious difficulties for his department under the new regime. "Only last time I saw Woodward," he wrote, "he said 'if you must have [Ferdinand] Schevill, you will have to find the money.' " For Dodd that was the issue. He was a competent fund raiser, as Woodward well knew, although his own most immediate benefactor had refused to contribute money to the university despite his willingness to fund Dodd directly and indefinitely. Privately Dodd began negotiations for an appointment elsewhere. Carl Becker was willing to get him a generous invitation to Cornell, and Daniel Roper would use his considerable influence at Johns Hopkins.[26]

Merriam's approach is interesting and typical. Although he did not say so, he took a much harder view of the political situation. "Regardless of who is elected President," he wrote Dodd, "I am strongly inclined to think that the position of the social sciences will be more favorable—pleasanter than heretofore." After all, Woodward was willing to let Dodd "find the money" himself, and that, from Merriam's point of view, was half the battle. But Dodd was off to Europe for a two-quarter leave. He hedged his position with Swift by threatening to resign if the committee acted in his absence. The stalemate had produced a polite exhaustion which made delay possible—aided no doubt by Woodward's willingness to continue to bear the administrative burdens of the university.[27]

The name of Robert Maynard Hutchins had not appeared on any of the elaborate lists of candidates. As the young dean of the Yale Law School he had attended a meeting of lawyers held in Chicago in December 1927, and some of the members of the committee met him then. Although he was a man of impressive and imposing appearance, witty and capable of projecting a sense of a sharp and efficient intellect, he seemed to many too young, although there were those ready to remind exponents of such criticism that William Rainey Harper had also been "too young." Even so, the name was only discussed and never entered on the lists. On 11 March 1929 the committe voted on three names: Ernest Martin Hopkins of Dartmouth, E. E. Day of the Rockefeller Foundation, and H. G. Moulton of the Brookings Institution. Merriam opposed Hopkins, the favorite in the last vote, not out of personal or intellectual objection but out of a political conviction— quite the correct one —that Hopkins would refuse, and that his refusal would be part of a design to throw the decision back to the trustees. Actually, Merriam still had no objection to Woodward as president but he did object to the continued waste of his time in meetings. Others agreed. Sentiment in the faculty began to move to Woodward. George Herbert Mead, a strong figure in the Philosophy Department and a proponent of the undergraduate reorganization, had been lobbying extensively for Woodward, and William F. Ogburn had come out for Woodward. Only Dodd seemed to stand in adamant opposition and that could not last for long.[28]

On 19 March, Edwin R. Embree, president of the Julius Rosenwald Fund, wrote a letter to Swift, a copy of which he sent to Dodd with a covering note. "You were good enough to ask me to send from time to time the names of candidates that occurred to me for the presidency of the University of Chicago," he wrote. "I now have one. It is Robert Maynard Hutchins." He recognized all of the pitfalls inherent in the choice of so young a man, and a man already marked by a reputation for some unconventionality. "A conventional leader may continue the University as a respectable institution," he countered. "A brilliant choice may enable the University to return to its earlier role of a real leader in American education." And to Dodd he added, "the amusing thing is that if anything happened to Angell, I think Yale would elect him its president immediately, but the conservative East is much more courageous in such matters than the supposedly radical or progressive Middle West!"[29]

Committee meetings picked up. In many ways, Hutchins with Rosenwald's Embree behind him seemed a compromise even more miraculous than Dodd could have dreamed possible. He was thrilled. The offer was made on 16 April at noon. It was accepted, and Dodd assumed the pose of victor.

As the events of the next two decades were to demonstrate, the issues in conflict were not ones that an appointment, however brilliant, could solve, for they went to the roots of the revolution in twentieth-century higher education, which was by no means at an end. The trustees who managed the funds found the gradual absorption of the college by the graduate schools a threat not only to the traditions they wanted to remember and preserve but also to their authority over the future direction of the school as it met what they considered to be the responsibilities of the new society.

In addition, the sustaining of a certain economic class of undergraduate meant a predictable flow of tuition receipts and loyal alumni gifts, not so much dependence upon the less predictable flow of philanthropic gifts directed to problem-solving projects of researchers. To expand the enrollment of the undergraduate college beyond 2,000—as the new program hinted but did not clearly state—would require expansion of faculty. Dodd did not say that the sort of faculty hired for such a purpose might be different from the kind he and Merriam were interested in hiring. But he did point to the fact that the trustees had recently cut salaries of younger instructors to $2,000 from the previous year's $2,200 and $2,400. The trustees had countered criticism with a move to raise tuition; but Dodd and others objected. To raise tuition, Dodd contended, would lower the caliber of the student body, turning Chicago into a "Harvard," a name synonymous with a high level of faculty but a low level of undergraduates, the wealthy, "gentleman C" students.[30]

In a way, Merriam and Dodd were caught in the conjunction of two major revolutions taking place in American higher education; and so was Hutchins. One, the professionalization of graduate training and research, had moved far enough outside specific educational institutions to place itself on a national base—but only partly. Still dependent upon the individual universities in which they continued to place their professional roots, system-builders like Merriam threatened to exhaust the resources of the ground on which they stood, overpowering and throwing off balance the myriad interests that were also part of an institution's central function. True, they could raise the name of the university to national eminence, but at what cost, with what changes in the role of the university? At the same time, universities were rethinking their own roles in the years after World War I, and that was the second revolution. Though part of the same professional development, the university could conceive of its role as a counterbalance to the very professionalism to which it was contributing, by, on the one hand, eschewing the image of playground for a select local group of wealthy sons and daughters and, on the other hand, seeking a pattern for the "general" education of a national elite. The transition from local to national in undergraduate education came on the heels of a similar movement in graduate education, and caught up with it and collided with it in the competition for the resources available for the two revolutions. Not that those resources were as scarce as they seemed to the competitors; they had grown remarkably in the years under discussion. But so had the ambitions and the needs of the competitors.

The University of Chicago, like other important universities in the country, was reevaluating its function with an insensitivity to the general nature of the problem. In May 1929 the *Chicago Tribune* carried an article by Westbrook Pegler reporting that President Lowell of Harvard favored only one football game a year—the Yale game. Pegler discoursed at length on the anti-athletic trend on American campuses—and Hutchins, who would become something of a legend for abolishing football at Chicago, had not yet become its president. Nor would Pegler necessarily have known or been interested in knowing that Lowell was pushing a plan for a house system at Harvard over a negative vote from his faculty, or that he was to set up a fellowship program at Harvard with the express purpose of short-circuiting the professional interest in a Ph.D. But then, it is unlikely that many of the Chicago faculty knew about the parallels either. The localism of American university life successfully obscured the national process under way, at the same time that it served to intensify the fights on individual campuses.

In April 1929 Vice-President Woodward aroused the wrath of his faculty with a letter to the alumni in which he sought to scotch rumors that the university intended to abolish undergraduate education or set its entrance requirements so high as to discourage the traditional elements of college life—by which he meant football, fraternities, and the happy days they all thought they remembered sufficiently well to continue their liberal contributions to the university. The rift was deep, and pressure from alumni did not help solve the problems of trustees, who sought reasonable and responsible solutions from what everything they had been taught led them to believe was a community of the nation's most rational minds.

The appointment of Robert Maynard Hutchins put in a very difficult job an extraordinarily talented but very inexperienced young man. It was an environment still seething with the discontent of some of the losers who felt that Woodward was still the right man and who assumed from the satisfied smiles of those who presumed themselves the winners that the young canary was obviously trained to sing their song: no college revolution. But Swift still led the trustees. Woodward was still vice-president. Mead still had no intention of giving up his fight, even to the extent of circulating a letter critical of the president-designate and his wife, purportedly written to Mrs. Mead by Mrs. Angell, the wife of Yale's president. The new president of the University of Chicago, apparently unaware that the warm glow around him was not entirely fueled by welcome, poured his sometimes volatile wit on it. The year-old embers were quickly brought to blaze.

Hutchins pressed the college plan on the faculty Senate in December 1930, and in a manner too clearly recalling the Mason episode. Underneath the manner, however, was a shrewd compromise which could have succeeded in canceling out the opposition. Hutchins had separated the educational aspects of the plan from the building program, thus buying his support from the faculty at the expense, apparently, of Rosenwald's millions, or at least so the proponents of the combined program saw it. The discontent still rankling among the Woodward supporters led those who felt themselves the architects of Mason's downfall to consider the possibility of forcing Hutchins to resign, a movement which would have gained little ground but for a tactical error on Hutchins's part that galvanized faculty concern.

Hutchins had been seeking to add departmental faculty, over departmental vote if necessary. The term "unwelcome recruits" was being delicately applied by faculty members to such figures as Mortimer Adler, whom the Philosophy Department had rejected. James H. Tufts, who had been chairman of that department for twenty-five years, retired in what was virtually a resignation; and, about the same time, George Herbert Mead, a supporter of Woodward, went to Columbia. Hutchins could and did back down from the specific issue by finding a place for Adler in the Law School, but he could not escape the principle of departmental autonomy in appointments. The issue could have been used by the trustees and Woodward to force his resignation and pave the way for the whole "Harkness" building program.

While Merriam and Hutchins were never to see eye to eye on the question of appointments—and over the years it was to become the chief issue that divided them—the separation of the college plan from the building program, the appointment of Beardsley Ruml, a supporter of the plan, as dean of the Social Sciences, and the autonomy of the social sciences under Hutchins's administrative plans, all then seemed more important. Merriam had also found Tufts a dissident member of the Local Community Research Committee and considered Mead old-fashioned. The issue, then, could be viewed not as Hutchins against the faculty but as Hutchins and the faculty against the trustee-bound administrative staff he had inherited, and for the moment it worked.

On 7 March 1931, the Saturday before the scheduled Monday "showdown" meeting of the faculty Senate, Hutchins lunched with Merriam, Dodd, Ruml, and a few other selected supporters on the faculty to ask their advice. They advised a speech detailing the unreasonableness of the faculty attacks on Hutchins and their true basis in the plans of the trustees. Hutchins listened, undoubtedly aware that such a course of opposition was well enough for them to advise but a difficult course for him to take.

Merriam and Dodd spent the weekend rounding up votes; and when the meeting opened on Monday afternoon, the first action was the introduction of a motion of confidence which, in the absence of an opportunity to call for an investigation, passed unanimously. Apparently well aware that his Saturday luncheon circle had spread the "facts" with sufficient breadth, Hutchins followed with a speech the brevity of which shocked both sides. He made no defense of himself, launched no attack upon trustees or faculty opposition, but simply announced that he had been advised to review recent administrative difficulties in the university, that he was willing to do so if a majority of the Senate wished it, and that they should now proceed to decide for themselves if they wished him to do so.[31]

It was a stunning performance. He was asking them to call for an investigation, not maneuvering to avoid their demand. When the motion of investigation was made, Merriam introduced a motion to postpone action until October. The motion to postpone carried 64 to 47. For the years to come Merriam retained his role as a manipulator of the balance of power among that portion of the faculty which could be brought to the support of the president against the trustees. While he maintained a strong dislike for many of Hutchins's appointments to the faculty and administration of the university, his attitude toward Hutchins himself was that of one political power toward another with whom compromise was always possible because victory could only be Pyrrhic.

The University of Chicago had to be Merriam's base; and there could be no stepping back from that. He had built power there for himself in the community as well as in the university, and as he grew older he could manipulate that power with an economy of motion satisfying to his sense of his own energies. In the last decade of his career he would have enjoyed an offer from Harvard or Yale, but he probably would not have accepted it. His identity as founder of the Chicago School included everything the term implied, the university and the city. By January 1931, as the nation struggled against the slow and seemingly inevitable slide toward further depression, Merriam published a preface to the second edition of his *New Aspects of Politics*. The five years since its first publication he saw as years of advance, years of success in the achievements of social science. He surveyed what were in effect the triumphs of his own career, the founding of the Social Science Research Council, the increased activity of the American Political Science Association. He pointed to a critic of his view of communal research, Harold Laski, "who protests against co-operative research and against the realistic forms of investigation, sometimes characterized as 'field work,' at least to the extent that they interfere with the 'lonely thinker' and with appropriate diet of principles." And he noted the objection of Charles A. Beard, that scientific research endangered the humanistic aspects of social research. But Merriam pushed both of them aside. Social research was pressing the world in new directions and the world was following.[32]

In the ensuing battles, as in those which had led to Hutchins's appointment in the first place, Merriam's role was governed by the dilemma he had chosen in his decision to stay with the university. Both Judson and Burton had struggled with the problem of fitting Harper's ideals to the realities they inherited; and the relation between graduate and undergraduate training, the German model of the university and the British model of the college, became only one way of expressing the issues involved. General education versus professional specialization was another version of the battle. Hutchins added a touch of his own, a gentlemanly Veblenism which attacked the university's image of its own greatness by calling attention to the faculty's supposed failure to meet its own standards, but doing so in a fashion that left it increasingly clear that it was the standards themselves which were at fault. Late in Hutchins's career as chancellor of the university, when he informed the faculty and trustees at their annual dinner that the university had the responsibility of producing a national "revolution" in values, he provoked a faculty split as profound as anything he had produced in the previous fifteen years. Embellishing his attack with his customary humor, he called for the abolition of faculty rank, for the turning over to the university of all income received by faculty for outside professional work, and for the establishment of a salary scale that gave higher salaries to younger faculty raising families and lower salaries to senior faculty chairing departments. Nor did he stop there. These innovations were to be coupled with curriculum reforms designed to release higher education from the grip of professionalism and its control of training and evaluation. Hutchins had titled one of his first major commentaries on American university life *The Higher Learning in America*. That was in 1934. Ten years later in his address to the faculty and trustees he was fulfilling whatever promise to Veblen the title was intended to imply; and if the cackle of Veblen's ghost could be heard around the dining room of Chicago's swank South Shore Country Club, it was surely accompanied by the raging shade of William Rainey Harper.[33]

Merriam and Hutchins enjoyed one another when their joint endeavors brought them together; and Hutchins tended to allow Merriam the same leeway in the raising of funds for social research that Merriam had had in his promise from Burton. They differed seriously on the meaning of research in social science and, consequently, on the judgments to be made about permanent university faculty to do research and to teach the future researchers. Not that Merriam ever committed himself deeply to social research as an abstract science divorced from public policy, and hence as a pursuit to be preserved in the university along with Sanskrit and epigraphy; but Merriam supported and, indeed, had sought to generate a professionalism in social research that had to conflict, in the long run, with Hutchins's view of the university.

Dodd's triumph in the selection of Hutchins changed the shape of the presumed catastrophe he and Merriam had been working to avoid; but it did not avoid it entirely. Other members of the faculty looking toward a Harper revival in the young president were also disappointed. The hope that a relationship with the Rockefellers might also be revived did not work out, although it looked promising enough at the beginning. John D. Rockefeller, Jr., extended his own firm welcome to the new president by offering him a "summer place" at his Maine estate for whatever rental the Hutchinses had been accustomed to pay for summer lodgings. They were young, of course, and what they had been paying was a nominal rental on a family place; but that was enough for Mr. Rockefeller. He provided them with a house fully furnished with linen, silver, china, and art. At another time, again early in their relationship, Hutchins made a trip to New York to speak to Mr. Rockefeller's men's Bible class, a successful performance for which Mr. Rockefeller paid expenses for both Hutchinses, brushing aside Hutchins's insistence that he pay at least his wife's way himself.[34]

Merriam's generation of entrepreneurs paid homage to Mr. Rockefeller, but they spent their time working to manipulate the ideas of the new officials of the foundations who were taking over the management of philanthropy. At the same time, Merriam was not inclined to view Hutchins's interests as necessarily competitive, or as the total threat others began to see them as being. Compromises could be made as long as the issues did not become too strident. The focus on educational issues—the college and its identity—could even be useful, as he saw it, but only up to a point.

9

Civic Education

Concern with the troubled relation between ideology and public education was not new to American educators in the 1920s, most of whom could remember an earlier instance of the old controversy between science and religion. The eruption of that issue in the Scopes trial shocked few of them, no matter how much it may have worried them. And everyone could recall World War I, when German language teaching in the schools was attacked and when the government urged the schools to inculcate an intense and fervent Americanism. At the end of the war the Red Scare touched public education as vigilante Americanist groups in local communities examined textbooks to assure proper indoctrination.

Professional educators and other intellectuals were no less concerned, although they often disagreed with the methods of the vigilantes. Progressive education earlier had emphasized the totality of the educational experience and had drawn materials relating to public affairs into the classroom. The creation of citizens, once the preserve of those concerned only with immigrants, became a subject significant for the training of all Americans. The transfer to the schools of educational responsibilities once left to family and church in small communities now both broadened and complicated the meaning of civic education.

Such concerns, logical enough in the process of urbanization and nationalization of American society, were given a more troubled context by the international temper of the times. In the increasingly critical aftermath of World War I Americans became conscious of the influence of propaganda in international affairs, although they saw sharp differences between the patriotism Americans had the right to demand of one another and the nationalism which had infected prewar Germany. As the years passed they would see the same distinction between the demands for good citizenship training in American schools and the reports about education of the young in Lenin's Russia, Mussolini's Italy, and Hitler's Germany.

Merriam's concern with education in the 1920s moved in two directions, one of which had for a long time been part of his urban experience and academic interest, the other of which can be more tightly tied to the new aspects of the era. Education, on the one hand, was the most traditional of local-nationalist issues, and Merriam spent a large part of the period fighting the patronage attacks on the school board by Mayor Thompson and serving on the American Historical Association's committee to study the teaching of the social sciences in the schools. On the other hand, education was one of the keys to nationalism and internationalism. The responsibility of the citizen to his community was the democratic center of an American upbringing, and its translation to world responsibility the most logical of progressions. Educating Americans to vote and to the acceptance of world responsibility was part of the same battle.

The basic issue—the use of public education to generate national loyalty and responsibility—was an old concept in European history, but one which Americans had turned to their own peculiar uses. The tradition of local control of public education had seriously hobbled the development of a national educational system; and the recent progressive insistence that the schools be kept out of partisan politics had raised the threat of indoctrination in curious forms. Big Bill Thompson had succeeded in turning Merriam's efforts to preserve the Chicago schools from spoils patronage into an issue of elitist indoctrination, with Merriam's "ideas" the threat, while Americanist groups like the DAR and the American Legion were seeking to control the national image being taught in the schools. In a sense, then, Merriam and his community of new social scientists were to find themselves in an odd agreement with the very fundamentalist Americanist groups whose points of view they so often deplored. They agreed on the necessity of using the schools to train loyal citizens. They disagreed on the meaning of loyalty.

Merriam's position on the issue is perhaps one of the most important examples of his capacity for original insight in the often eclectic processes of his management of his academic empire. Studies in the Making of Citizens (SMC), the series of monographs on civic education which he conceived during the period and which was concluded by his own comparative study of the subject, did not survive very successfully as one of his more influential productions, although recent revivals of it in some circles indicate an interesting resurgence of awareness of some of the subtler aspects of his insight.

With all the interest American writers have shown toward the use of the schools as institutions for socializing or even Americanizing the child, the idea that public education should "indoctrinate" children has tended to be repugnant as an abstraction. The schools are supposed to teach American children how their government works; but the schools are not supposed to teach children to "love" their government —to respect it, to participate in it, even to reform it, but not to "love" it—for the concept of blind devotion to the state is built upon irrationalities unacceptable in principle to Americans, however necessary they may in fact be to order and continuity. As a result, the tradition of civics education since the 1920s has been away from the emotional contexts of loyalty so obvious to Americans of Merriam's generation—Bible reading, flag ceremonies, and pledges of allegiance —and toward behavioral understanding of the processes of government and their consequences, an approach one would be more inclined to associate with Merriam's general attitude toward politics.

The purpose of the monograph series on civic education was to examine the bases of the methods used by various societies to indoctrinate children with a love of the state, and more than any other project of Merriam's career, it suggests the consciousness of the nonrational or irrational components of political behavior which Merriam's optimistic rationalism ordinarily tends to blur. While his emphasis upon the necessary nonrational core of loyalty puts him unfashionably close to both the superpatriots of his day in America and the social theorists of European politics who in the 1920s were questioning the utility of rationalism as a framework for democracy, his demand for rational investigation of the process as a necessary condition for escaping it is consistent with his general point of view toward an American uniqueness capable of serving as a model for the rest of the world.

First of all, the collection of studies was to be genuinely international, to include nonwestern as well as western societies. This aspect of the plan was to test the principle that all human culture, regardless of historic context, had to produce civic education in order to survive. Second, the studies were to be conducted by researchers who were not members of the societies they were examining. Neither aim—most particularly the latter—was actually realized to any extent; but Merriam's consciousness of them indicates both his ambitions for proving the universality of the kind of social science he was promoting and his belief in the objective neutrality which that universality was presumed to reflect. Within both one can catch important hints of the basic humanism which sought the breakdown of national and racial barriers, a rejection, once again, of Burgess. Human behavior was not to be historically or culturally contained by national ideology, geography, or race, precisely because it was human and prior, therefore, to all factors in the developing patterns of society. Like many in his generation, Merriam apparently tended to conceive of his Americanism as a neutral factor and the values of his own upbringing as a clear window on the world, any distortions removable by scientific understanding, when necessary, and by education.

John M. Gaus agreed to do the study of Great Britain; Samuel N. Harper undertook that of the Soviet Union; Oscar Jaszi, the Austro-Hungarian empire; Paul Kosak, Germany; Carleton J. H. Hayes, France; Elizabeth Weber, the Duk-Duks of Melanesia; and Robert C. Brooks, Switzerland. Merriam asked Carl Brinkmann of Heidelberg to do the United States, and Robert Michels the study of Italy. Merriam was to contribute the systematic overview of the project, and the Laura Spelman Rockefeller Memorial agreed to a financing which was generous enough to include not only the expensive international research involved, but payment to the authors for manuscripts as well as subsidies for the costs of publication.

Few of Merriam's efforts during these years are more revealing of the limitations on the conditions for fulfilling his dream of the university of cooperative research in the social sciences, although he seems not to have interpreted it that way. While it is true that his critical opinion and his sense of the design he wished the research to follow carried weight with American colleagues like Gaus who shared his ideals even when he did not share his judgments, the international plan was a fiasco which produced virtually nothing for public use.

Brinkmann's manuscript was, in Merriam's terms, an utter disaster. Although the selection of Brinkmann was singularly appropriate—his

Geschichte der Vereinigten Staaten von Amerika had appeared in 1924 and a Yale lecture, published in 1927,[1] had as its subject theories of citizenship and government—he produced a collection of highly inaccurate reflections (Merriam called them "opinions"), written in a crude and inept style. Actually, the manuscript offers an interesting set of insights into the European view of American society in the 1920s and could have served to suggest the distance yet to be covered before any such dream of intellectual cooperation would even approach realization, but not to Merriam. He wrote Brinkmann that the manuscript did not do justice to his "scientific reputation for grundlich work," which Brinkmann took as a gratuitous insult. There was not even a basis for revision. The American scene was eventually represented by Bessie L. Pierce's *Civic Attitudes in American Textbooks*, but as a member of the Chicago community working at the edges of the Chicago School, she could not reflect the international implications Merriam's plan had originally envisaged.[2]

The Michels volume on Italy provided the most interesting battle. Brinkmann was receiving a certain amount of American academic lionizing for his interest in American history and was a kind of latter-day Von Holst, though with considerably less analytic talent. Michels, a major European theorist, was another matter. Attracting him to his series was quite a coup for Merriam—at first. Michels's study of political parties had been widely read by American academics, particularly in the post-World War I era when his criticisms of progressive democracy were accepted on firmer intellectual grounds. Such criticism had been in any case a significant undercurrent in the Progressive movement itself. Political parties were suspect as part of the democratic method by many Progressives, although whether in the institutional form in which European critics like Ostrogorski and Michels saw them or for their extralegal, extraconstitutional status as Americans were inclined to see them is a moot point. One-party government had its attractions for Americans looking at the early twenties in Italy or the Soviet Union, and Americans toyed with such ideas—usually without quite seeing the connection—when they talked about nonpartisan elections in local government and the virtues of city management, but not when they discussed the federal government. It is difficult to tell just what Merriam thought he would get when he invited Michels to do the book; but it is certain he did not get what he wanted.

From the beginning of their correspondence in 1926 Merriam had in mind a study which would eventually focus on Italian fascism; but he failed, apparently, to make this clear to Michels. The initial letter outlining the project was clear enough to Americans who read it, though it is possible to see how Michels may have misunderstood it. Merriam asked for a study which would be analytical and dynamic, as he put it, rather than historical and descriptive. He wanted to emphasize the "making" of citizens. He wanted Michels to analyze the processes by which historical traditions were used by educators and made a part of education. He did add one point to the Michels letter which he did not include in the others. "To what extent and in what fashion," he asked, "do they seek to build up civic interest in one nation by preaching doctrines of hate or indifference or misrepresentation of other nations?"

All of Merriam's assumptions about Michels's attitude are a great deal clearer than his understanding of his own values; but then Michels either did not see that, or did not wish to, given the opportunity to appear in the distinguished American series. In addition, Merriam knew that Michels, then at Basel, was eager for an appointment at an Italian university, and that his sympathies for the Fascist movement in Italy were strong. Merriam himself was interested enough in Michels's work not only to invite him to join the series but to issue an invitation to him to teach a course on political parties and recent political and social theory at Chicago during the summer session of 1927—an invitation which Michels accepted. Merriam apparently took Michels's interest in fascism as an example of a kind of political opportunism which he was willing to accept, not as a genuine commitment.[3]

Merriam had visited with Michels the previous summer and knew that long before his move from Switzerland to Italy Michels had given his services to various Italian universities. "I find that he really is giving half-time to the University of Turin," Merriam wrote Gaus. "He is also a member of the new faculty of political science recently organized in Rome. I am inclined to think he may be something of a Fascist; but perhaps he may be able to understand all the better the peculiar methods employed in the development of his system." He may also not have thought those methods so peculiar, but that was not the point.

After a July visit with Michels in that same summer, Merriam wrote that "in his early days he was a friend of Sorel and in his later years he swung around toward Fascism . . . [and] he seems to feel himself to be an Italian rather than a German or Swiss." He was also beginning to sign his letters "Roberto Michels" rather than "Robert."[4]

When the manuscript arrived in Chicago Merriam was shocked to find the subject of fascism completely ignored. Hoping to jog him to revision, Merriam wrote that Harper's study of Russia "has developed many interesting phases of instruction designed to produce good communists. I am wondering whether the Fascists in Italy are developing similar types of instruction for the education of good Fascisti." If Michels knew, he was not eager to say; but he promised, finally, to add a preface and "some pages on Fascism" when he got to Chicago the coming summer. Merriam and others continued to believe that Michels was unwilling to put anything down on paper which might throw him into a critical position with Italian ideologues. What is surprising is that they continued to think that he could or would say such things if he only wanted to.[5]

Actually, Michels, like Brinkmann, apparently, did not understand how American scholars could take such a project as Merriam's series so seriously. Michels thought it overly ambitious, possibly even ill conceived, and certainly something a European scholar would have labored on for years, even a lifetime, not something which, as the Americans thought, could be done in the space of a few small books. He did not tell Merriam his doubts, but his derision both to and about a younger colleague, Paul Kosak, was close to brutal. Michels wrote Merriam that he thought Kosak, who visited him early in 1927, "rather young and feeble for so tremendous a task as the volume on Germany."[6] To Merriam Kosak related his conversation with Michels jibe for jibe.

"I am sorry to say that I got very little out of Professor Michels," Kosak reported. "He considered my outline (as well as Professor Harper's) as hopeless 'American' which would take years of study to complete. He considers it useless at all to work out all large parts of my outline. He thinks I ought to write out the history of the ideas of German nationalism. He himself is not going to treat the modern period very much. He told me he will not touch on Fascism, schools, bureaucracy, sports, organizations and other 'secondary' matter."[7] From Merriam's point of view it is hard to see what there was left, but Merriam still hoped the summer would bring some kind of compromise. He assigned Harold Lasswell the task of working with Michels on a revision.

Merriam was not unaware of some of the bases of his disagreement with Michels. In the 1920s Merriam, like many of his generation, found much to be interested in in European theories of social control, although his public rhetoric of the period does not indicate the extent of that interest. "As you know," he wrote to Kosak, "I myself am primarily concerned with the problem of civic training as a control problem in a given situation."[8] As society becomes more directive in its self-evaluation, he felt, conscious devices for control become more important. The study of Italy, which had finally become in Merriam's open statements about it a study of fascism, was so obviously a central focus of such control devices that to have ignored fascism would be to make the study irrelevant.

Michels, on the other hand, was no better at stating his own position clearly. His agreement to do the book in the first place did not jibe with his carping about the scope of the project. He did feel that materials and methods for dealing with the questions which Merriam wanted posed had not yet been developed and were unlikely to be in the course of so brief a study. Merriam agreed; but his whole view of the nature of research was built on a sense of urgency which no European could easily understand. The alliance between research and reform which Merriam took for granted was not alien to European social theorists obviously, but it was built upon a long tradition of mediation by class bureaucracy, and a far more sophisticated history of the role of academia in public affairs than Americans could usually understand. Equally important, perhaps, although it can be overstated easily, Michels's concept of scholarship was deeply dependent upon precisely the kind of "historical and descriptive" approach which Merriam's initial charge had specifically ruled out. Michels apparently did not understand American social science well enough to realize just how serious a threat a commitment to a historical approach had become, and Merriam was too deeply inured to the danger to realize the wall it created between American and European concepts of social thought.

By November 1927, after what was apparently a thoroughly unpleasant summer for everyone, Merriam was looking around for someone else to do the study of Italy. "He wrote an admirable essay on the history of Italian patriotism," Merriam wrote Robert C. Brooks in asking for his advice, "but he seemed a little shy about describing the system now operating." That was surely an understatement, but it indicates a conviction that Merriam was not going to reveal to Michels for some time yet to come. Michels wrote Merriam complaining about Merriam's failure to reply to the postcard he wrote him before leaving America and asking for a copy of the Lasswell revisions of his Italian study. Merriam stalled as Michels's temper mounted.[9]

176

The correspondence dragged on in increasing annoyance. Finally in February 1929 Merriam wrote, blaming the delay in publication—he had still not rejected the manuscript although he was in fact negotiating with someone else—on the difficulty of finding a publisher for the series. The University of Chicago Press had long since agreed to publication—no difficult decision in view of the fact that the costs were to be liberally subscribed by the Laura Spelman Rockefeller Memorial. He did spell out in the bluntest and most precise terms just what revisions he wanted. He asked for reduction in size, agreeing to publish it as a study of Italian patriotism and stating that he had "found it necessary to have a further study made of the technique of civic training under the Fascist system."[10]

Michels's reply to Merriam was filled with underlinings which threatened to demolish the paper. Angry not only at the judgment but at the "year and a half of *tenacious* and, let me say, *strange silence*," he accepted the proposal to have the manuscript shortened but said also that he would seek to have it published under other auspices. Merriam sent Michels full payment and informed him that this gave the University of Chicago full ownership of rights in the manuscript. The manuscript never appeared in the series. Two years later Michels asked for a copy of his book and was informed that it had not yet been published. Merriam said he still hoped to bring the volume out, but suggested that the depression might make that rather difficult. Michels tried to force the issue, claiming a legal and moral obligation, but to no avail.[11]

Merriam had persuaded Herbert W. Schneider and Shepard B. Clough to do the study of fascism. "I should suggest that you make your own study entirely independent of [Michels's]," Merriam wrote Clough, "as he has become an Italian citizen and has accepted a position in a fascist university, a situation which undoubtedly makes it difficult for him to express his judgment as freely as otherwise." Brooks had informed Merriam that Michels wrote to say he had accepted "an honorable call to the University of Perugia" in March 1928.[12]

Merriam continued to feel that Michels's "free judgment" would somehow be different from the one he would express in print—if he were to express it—and that intellectuals who approved of, not to say praised, fascism were manipulating a lie which they would privately have been willing to admit. One can see in Merriam's behavior toward Michels, the very honest invitation in 1926 and the eventual rejection in 1931, a pattern of the American intellectual response to fascism in Italy as well as even more basic differences in point of view between Europeans and Americans on the nature of social science.

Prior to the rise of Hitler, and to a lesser but still significant degree thereafter, the Italian experience had drawn considerable attention in the United States. Italian social scientists published articles in American scholarly journals pointing out the structure in politics which underlay the revolution for which Mussolini was the shrewd and dramatic leader—a position held in great part by Michels. William Yandell Elliott, taking account of such arguments, referred to Mussolini as the "prophet of the pragmatic era in politics," using a term which, in its American context, had significant meaning. Acknowledging the interest and its base in postwar thought, Elliott pointed out in a 1926 issue of *The Political Science Quarterly* that "the public press, not only of this country but of England and of continental Europe as well, is full of current prophecies that the age of democratic liberalism is dead and done for. It is a phenomenon of curious portent, following as it does upon the heels of the late crusade to 'make the world safe for democracy.' " And in a statement which drew uncomfortable lines of relationship between some aspects of the social science which Merriam represented and the Italian fascism which Merriam opposed, Elliott pointed out that "the pragmatic desire for progress that is impatient with representative government in any form, that demands facts, not theories, and action, not programs, is quite as lopsided a view of politics as its intellectualistic antithesis." [13]

While Merriam emphatically denied any impatience with representative government, the essential pragmatism of his approach, the search for a scientific commitment to the reality of facts, required an acceptance of representative democracy which could also allow for "social control" but "in a given situation," as he puts it. One of the inevitable effects of the influence of science upon society would be an ever narrowing scope for the area in which the processes of democratic choice would be relevant, perhaps, but that the area would never disappear, would never even become so small as to lose its significance, was a primary article of faith which separated Merriam from the "pragmatic revolt," though by what his critics saw as a remarkably thin line.

The arguments of the twenties and thirties, in the social sciences as well as in more public debates, sought the drawing of sharp distinctions between American democracy and Italian fascism, particularly after the rise of Hitler in Germany. Important as those distinctions are—or seemed to be to those who made them—it is equally important to draw the possible lines of similarity. In the years before Hitler, social planning in Russia and in Italy provided useful background to debates over the alternatives for social planning in America. The idea of comparative studies of "civic training" was an important device for evaluating the relevant and irrelevant experiences of other countries in their search for the pragmatic base of a modern nationalist identity.

Merriam's inherent rationalism kept him from adopting a mystical base for his concern with leadership, but the concern itself is clear. Although the absence of a Weberian influence on American thought throughout the twenties kept Weber's definition of charisma from surfacing, much of the Progressive tradition with which Merriam was identified had centered its attention on the search for leaders. One of Merriam's best books of the period, a series of lectures entitled *Four American Party Leaders* (1926), opened with the statement, "Leadership is one of the basic factors in the organization of life, and its implications are everywhere of profound significance. Wherever we look, whether among plants, animals or humans, we find dominant centers emerging and the relations of dominance and subordination developing." The purpose of his analyses of Theodore Roosevelt, Abraham Lincoln, Woodrow Wilson, and William Jennings Bryan was to suggest the patterns of study which might make it possible "that studies of the qualities of political leadership be energetically and intelligently prosecuted." And he concludes, "We cannot hope to maufacture at will our Lincolns, Roosevelts, Wilsons and Bryans, but we may reasonably look forward to a more intelligent view of the whole problem of leadership, to more intelligent training of potential leaders, and to progressively intelligent popular discrimination in the selection and rejection of the personnel of leadership, and in the circumscription of its metes and bounds."[14]

As with so many of his concerns, he directed graduate students and willing colleagues toward the investigations he marked out. Harold Gosnell's study of Boss Platt and Claudius O. Johnson's book on the first Carter Harrison were the most significant examples, probably, of a group which included dissertations on William Jennings Bryan and a plan for one on Jane Addams.[15] He toyed with ideas of interviewing current and surviving political leaders with the same end in view. But, in contrast to his friend William Allen White, there was no mystical historicism in his plan; indeed, the ideas of scientific investigation and analysis implicitly denied such a sense of historical causation, let alone mystique.

The selection and training of leaders was the other side of the coin of citizenship, and those, like Merriam, interested in both facets were within the lines of argument being explored by Weber and Michels; but the conclusions reached by each side produced lines of difference too serious, seemingly, even to be discussed. Michels's objections to Merriam's approach were obviously an extreme among responses possible from Europeans faced with Merriam's drive to confront whatever obstacle stood in the way of uniting American and European traditions of social and political thought—under American leadership, to be sure—although the difference was only a matter of degree. John Gaus's study of Great Britain may have been the most successful volume of the series in fulfilling Merriam's program. No less a figure than Graham Wallas praised it highly, but he was not without serious concern for its American "style."[16] As the response to the European volumes suggests, the insistent "presentness" of American social sciences was as disturbing to the European tradition of historical analysis as it was to those in America who were trying to sustain older historical methods. Michels was voicing, albeit more derisively than others did, a view of American scholarship not unlike Merriam's response to Brinkmann—that it was overambitious and superficial, and that it lacked a genuine historical perspective.

Europeans reading John Dewey, for example, could see relationships between the pragmatic drive for reconstruction in social and philosophic thought and the antidemocratic developments in European thinking—a point which Elliott's use of the term "pragmatic" seemed so clearly to imply. But faced with the question of whether their own society was moving away from liberalism—to, to what? to something different—Americans drew back in alarm. Americans seemed capable of attacking the very roots of their own liberal tradition at the same time that they asserted liberalism to be their fundamental cause. They viewed their own history as unique, and good, and then proceeded to deny the relevance of historical experience as the basis of social and political reformation. Americans were quick enough to see the weaknesses in efforts of the Italians to revive Rome, or of the Germans, certainly, to rebuild Valhalla, but they talked about the "rugged individualism" of the "frontier" and glorified its heroes as mythical types as though they had found some special answer to an altogether different set of problems.

American intellectuals who accepted industrial technology as a non-revolutionary force and capitalism as an economic system capable of transforming itself to meet the demands of industrialism had less to say to Europeans facing the issues of social change in the years after World War I than either Merriam or Michels could have believed. That so deep a rift in intellectual communication could exist—and the evidences that it did in fact exist—did not prevent them from trying. That was as true for Americans seeking to use American social science to answer Europe's social problems as it was for Europeans striving for American approval of their new ideologies. The debate over Italian fascism was presented to Americans by Michels and Luigi Villari, who sought to emphasize its new utility, and by Luigi Sturzo and Giuseppe Prezzòlini, who presented more critical approaches. Both sides were given platforms in eminent academic publications: Michels in the *American Political Science Review*, Villari by the Institute of Politics organized by H. A. Garfield, president of Williams College.[17]

William Yandell Elliott used his publication of *The Pragmatic Revolt in Politics* in 1928 not only to provide further analysis of the depth of attack on liberal, constitutional democracy in Western society but also to suggest that Americans had made significant contributions to the intellectual base of that movement through the writings of William James and John Dewey. Critics wondered, some of them angrily, at so blatant an attack upon Pragmatism, indeed, upon the scientific behavioralism Americans were working to build into a new concept of reform. Harold Lasswell wrote that "the process of extending pragmatism has succeeded in distending it," but he was one of the few who faced the issue even that directly.[18]

It was an issue much easier to avoid in 1928 than it was by 1933 when Mussolini and Franklin Roosevelt could appraise one another cautiously and not altogether critically as long as the problem of ideology did not have to be raised.[19] Pragmatism had that kind of convenience, whether it was the philosophic rejection of abstract principles as controls of behavior or the more or less random selection of handy solutions to social and economic problems.

For Merriam and the social researchers he led, the period from 1928 to 1933 constituted an era of acute crisis; and until the appearance on the scene of Franklin Roosevelt—and as dramatic president, not as somewhat ambiguous candidate for the presidency—the question of ideology was considerably more open than it was after Roosevelt's first term in office. That openness did not mean that European ideology in any of its forms would be more useful to American reformers than it had ever been; but the 1920s had been a period of interest at many levels in the possibility of using America's new position in the world as a means of aiding world social problems and stabilizing American economic problems at the same time. Merriam's philanthropists were willing enough, some of them, to subscribe to peace movements in the earlier phase of their international interest; but by the 1920s they were concerned with practical, long-range aims to benefit American agriculture and to find markets for American industrial products. That American industrial skills would be useful for the development of new industrial societies and the modernization of older ones was part of the belief held by E. A. Filene and other social Taylorites of the twenties who supported Herbert Hoover in his belief that good business was good philanthropy, and vice versa.

Throughout 1926 Merriam and Ruml discussed what was in effect to be a joint Merriam-Rockefeller invasion of Europe. Putting it in that form overstates the case, of course, but only relatively. Ruml had become the financial entrepreneur behind Merriam's intellectual politics. The problem was simply one of finding the appropriate method of organization for Merriam's new international activities.

By the end of 1926 they had it. Merriam agreed to open what was to be an office of the Rockefeller Foundation in Paris, returning to Chicago for the autumn quarter of each year but spending the remaining time abroad. His salary was to be $16,000 per year, plus whatever assistance was necessary at the University of Chicago for the continuation of his research interests there. The first of January 1928 was set as the official beginning of his appointment, although he would spend the intervening summer in Europe beginning the organization.

Actually there was a firmer basis for such an organization than simply the institutionalization of Merriam, although Ruml continued to see it that way. Various agencies of the Rockefeller philanthropic interests had been engaged in international activities at least since the war. Research projects like the migration study, for example, had numerous connections with foreign groups. The social interests of the many international health and welfare organizations associated with the League of Nations brought them into contact with American philanthropic efforts. The NRC, the ACLS, and now the SSRC were all in periodic touch with international associations of scholars, and the move to internationalize many of the American public service associations—Civil Service and the City Managers groups among them—sparked a connecting interest in the foundations which had supplied many of them with support in their earlier reform years and could be counted upon for continuing project support.

An office in Paris which could serve as an international meeting place—a clearinghouse—for social scientists seemed a useful idea. American social scientists were coming to the belief that they were developing programs which European colleagues needed, whether they knew it or not. Merriam, too, wanted to see more "modern" social science taught abroad; and in the furtherance of that aim the Laura Spelman Rockefeller Memorial gave £30,000 to Cambridge University for the founding of a chair in political science. Merriam's ambitions for the civic education studies, conceived at about the same time, added impetus to his own interest in an international platform, and the summers in Europe during the period were financed in part with Rockefeller money.[20]

Yet Merriam kept the plan a secret from everyone but his brother John. He may have discussed it with top university officials, but this is unclear. He mentioned it to no one in his family in Chicago. He allowed Ruml to keep pressing plans through 1927 while he himself struggled with what would become an increasingly complicated year for him emotionally. His home life was beset by problems of late middle age in a marriage sufficiently full of conflict in any case but marked now by his conviction as he approached the age at which his father had died that he would die, too, and of the same disease, cancer of the stomach. The university's medical specialists had diagnosed his condition as ulcers and had given him a diet and pressed upon him restrictions which he found morbidly satisfying, at least temporarily.

The romance of a return to Europe interested him, but perhaps not, it was hard to tell. The Contessina Loschi had made a trip to the United States—Mrs. Merriam thought for the purpose of trying to reawaken whatever had happened between them during the war, but that seems not to have been anything more than a peripheral concern. This was the Roaring Twenties, and academic life at the University of Chicago had its share of the sound, as the anonymously authored novel *Grey Towers* published in 1923 gives moderately lurid testimony. It was no longer Veblen's day, but it was still dangerously close to W. I. Thomas's.

The struggle with Michels in the summer of 1927 may have provided a trigger to a chain of reactions all of which must have hung on the possibility once again of dissociating himself from Chicago, the university, and the protective environment of his family. Although the plan was surely the most efficient and effective compromise which could have been found for him—Ruml had that kind of genius without a doubt—Merriam was in the hospital by October, healing another ulcer.

In November he wrote a formal letter of resignation to the Rockefeller Foundation, agreeing as he had promised Ruml he would, to serve as a summer adviser. He followed the letter with a personal note to Ruml. "This has been a bad year for me, in more ways than one," he wrote. "I cannot tell you how greatly I appreciate your many courtesies during my long prospective and ephemeral actual membership on the staff. Nor can I say how much you have helped me in the most trying period of my intellectual life—my belated reorientation after the shipwreck of the war." Merriam typed the letter himself on the machine he kept in his office. He made a carbon of it. It was an important moment in his life and he wanted to remember it. [21]

He never mentioned the plan again, not even in his late years when, in the throes of attempting to write his autobiography, he kept repeating the story of the boyhood California trip, the grieving pet, and the return home. He also, perhaps, was looking at a frontier which was no longer really open to him, and the recognition of that was too much to take. He stepped back from the threatening barrier and for a moment felt a sense of relief he had not known in some time.

Whatever the shipwreck of the war, the political career and the struggle to make the academic profession the successful surrogate of that lost endeavor, he was at least partly correct in identifying his own reorientation, its success, and his debt to Ruml in achieving it. Within the course of the next year, the whole system of social research in which Merriam was involved would begin to push toward an important kind of fulfillment, a reestablishment of contact with a progressive optimism which even the coming years of depression could not shake.

The continuing experiment with internationalism would never quite fulfill the optimistic forecast, but Merriam and other social scientists of his generation continued to try. True, the course of the developing relation between ideology and politics in Europe subjected the beliefs of interested Americans to one blow after another in Italy, Germany, Spain, and the Soviet Union, with the emergence in France of Leon

Blum a sole glimmering of light in the lowering shadows which began in Ethiopia and ended in the Nazi-Soviet pact. Still, the almost total unacceptability of socialism on grounds which rested more often on a practical view of American public opinion than on a fundamental ideological clarity led American intellectuals nearer than they could afford to get to tacit even if totally unintentional support of the belief that responsible national planning for social welfare was un-American. Socialism was all right for Europeans because their historically benighted traditions prevented them from doing any better. Some would even be willing to justify fascism on similar grounds. Merriam's dispute with Michels reveals a condescension and mistrust on both sides. Merriam suppressed the American publication of a book with which he disagreed—hardly a completely responsible academic act.[22] Michels committed himself to a project for which he had no respect for reasons which suited his own ambitions. They were using each other and both lost.

"Shipwreck of the war" was a good phrase, better perhaps than Merriam could know. No one could avoid the fight; no one could win; no one could stop wanting to win. Insulated by traditions which seemed, to those optimistically inclined, unreal, they sought communication which could lead to reform—but of whom and by whom and with what utopian end in view? It was an old dilemma. Americans who could not see it in their own heterogeneous accumulation of states and races and interest groups were not to be expected to see it when they sailed abroad. That the most devastating shipwrecks, when they came, would be on their own shores on the return voyage was perhaps as characteristic as it was, sadly, unavoidable.

10

Social Studies and Public Education

In 1926, following discussions held during the Christmas meetings of 1925, the American Historical Association appointed a group to examine the teaching of the social studies in American schools. Designated initially as the Committee on the Social Studies, the group ultimately accommodated itself to its expanding membership by renaming itself the Commission on the Social Studies, the series title given to the sixteen monographs which finally appeared.

While the historians had been appointing committees and issuing reports on education ever since the founding of their organization, the new commission signified a departure from the tradition. Its appointment had been initiated by a movement in the Institute for Educational Research of Teachers College of Columbia University and by the National Council for Social Studies. As the use of the term "social studies" indicates, the commission was intended to represent a broader range of interests than the historians had previously admitted, as well as an acknowledgment of the expansion of the educational profession itself.

Certainly as far back as 1899, the historians were reporting that "the most essential result of secondary education is acquaintance with political and social environment, some appreciation of the nature of the state and society, and some sense of the *duties and responsibilities* of citizenship,"[1] but it was "the study of past times and conditions" that they emphasized—an important difference. As the commission's chairman, medievalist A. C. Krey of the University of Minnesota, pointed out with statistical reports on the expansion of urban public education since the 1899 study, the new group faced problems quite different from those envisaged by previous committees. He could hardly have been more prophetic.

Merriam's membership on the commission brought into focus several concerns which contrast sharply with the issues raised by the civic education series. If civic education necessarily involved the training of the young, to what degree could social science serve as the vehicle for such training? Changing the name from social science to social studies resolved nothing and may indeed have concealed serious differences. Second, if one agreed that the teaching of the social studies—assuming one agreed on a definition of them—was an acceptable method of civic education, then where did one go for the civic principles being inculcated? To the communities which controlled education in the schools? To the social sciences themselves? To some particular ideological commitment about the nature of society and the relation of the social studies to that nature?

Merriam found himself embroiled in a dispute over ideology once again, but this time it was a somewhat shadowy left-wing ideology he was debating, not the sharper right-wing issue of fascism. The dispute was complicated further by the fact that the leading "radical"—and one must use the term with considerably more leeway even than it normally requires—was Charles A. Beard. There, too, the issue of ideology refused to surface in any definitive form, given the fact that Beard's position on the commission was represented less by the two studies he did for the commission than by his support of the commission's director of research, George S. Counts.

Beard and Merriam would have had reason to dispute each other even had the question of ideology never entered the picture. Beard rather enjoyed reviewing Merriam's books, particularly the ones on political theory. Basically, he thought Merriam overemphasized politics at the expense of economics, which was, of course, a logical basis for intellectual conflict between the two.[2] The trouble was, neither man was so committed to a clear, deterministic position that contemporary observers could understand why, whenever occasions arose, they took such delight in sniping at each other. By the 1930s when Beard's positions vis-à-vis the New Deal and American foreign policy gave the anti-Beardians in the Merriam camp sufficient ammunition, as they saw it, for discrediting him, the opposition was clearer; but it had been there all along. Part of it was personal. Merriam envied the greater public acclaim Beard's writings achieved for him. Beard had sufficient occasion to feel that Merriam's management of funds for research was designed to exclude him and everything he felt he represented. More important, perhaps, the two men reflected the decisions about the relation between the academic community and the tradition of intellectual social reform which all participants in the process of American social reform would have to make in the years after 1920. Merriam had chosen an academic approach to social science, a definition of the nature of research, and a commitment to the professionalization of academic social reform—a term his decision would have forbade him to use—that Beard could scarcely have helped finding threatening.

Beard was his generation's Veblen, in many significant respects, a self-appointed pariah who walked the fences with which the academic community separated itself from the world like a small boy determined not to fall off lest he lose his spectacular vantage point and the demonstration of skill it so obviously signified. His resignation from Columbia during World War I had represented in part at least his hostility to the control of the university by its wealthy trustees. But his withdrawal had been voluntary, unlike Veblen's, and Beard did maintain important contacts with academia and its new professions. He played the role of conscience to the academic professions, accepting their honors—the presidencies of both the American Historical Association and the American Political Science Association—but, like a genial Jeremiah, repaying the gifts with a recital of sins.

Merriam tried to involve Beard in various projects but rarely received more than a quick, vaguely disgruntled rejection. Beard's suggestions to Merriam of personnel for research projects were likely to be met with the reply that so and so was really a journalist, or, worse still, a reformer. The two men were inclined to take occasions for compromise as opportunities for new confrontation, and the Commission on the Social Studies was, in its way, a well-designed platform for both men.

In addition to Krey, the commission included, initially, William E. Lingelbach, John S. Bassett, Guy Stanton Ford, Ernest Horn, Henry Johnson, Jesse H. Newlon, L. C. Marshall, and Charles Merriam. Over the next few years its membership was expanded to include Charles Beard and George S. Counts. A fairly extensive use of subcommittees added others whose names appear in the studies which resulted: Merle Curti, Howard K. Beale, Bessie L. Pierce, and Harold O. Rugg were perhaps the most significant. Merriam's position on the commission as representative of the social scientists was reinforced by the addition of

Isaiah Bowman, a geographer, and Jesse Steiner, a sociologist. The District of Columbia superintendent of schools, Frank Ballou, was appointed to represent the administrative professionals.

Merriam's connections with sources of financing made him an attractive figure on any commission line-up, as did the background of Edmund E. Day, former dean of the School of Business Administration at the University of Michigan whose established academic credentials had made him director of social sciences for the Rockefeller Foundation. Actually several foundations shared in various stages of the study's development. Carnegie gave a grant of $15,000 for initial work, a sum which Krey felt a "comparatively small one."[3] The Commonwealth Fund contributed; but the bulk of funding for the five-year study ultimately came from the Carnegie Foundation.

The sixteen volumes which finally appeared, several of them to become classics in their fields, bore ample testimony to the productivity of the commission, although the bulk, and the rhetoric, conceal effectively the bitter battles generated by personal contention and ideological conflict which split the group into warring factions.

When the final report appeared in 1934, three members of the commission joined Merriam in refusing to sign. A fifth, Isaiah Bowman, signed with reservations. The other three, Frank Ballou, E. E. Day, and Ernest Horn, like all the dissenters, were offered opportunity to present opinions for publication, but only Isaiah Bowman took advantage of the offer. The last meetings of the commission had apparently been too angering. "I had hoped after the prolonged discussion in the last meeting, to say nothing of the emotional outbursts evoked in the course of the proceedings, a different result would have been reached," Merriam wrote, apparently to Day. "I do not intend to sign the Report, and am writing to ask your counsel as to the best course to pursue."[4]

The events leading up to Merriam's decision are interesting to trace because they can be used to reveal some of the profound personal and intellectual differences which split the new social research community.

By 1931 the commission had begun to feel the strong influence of George Counts. Counts's work in American school politics, his interest in educational methods in the Soviet Union, and his very deep respect for John Dewey had led him to conclusions which were to direct his prolific output for the next twenty years, as well as the work of the commission. Specifically, as his writings show, he rejected the child-centered teaching and testing theses of many of his contemporaries in favor of a view of the

189

school as the chief vehicle for socializing the child. Sociology rather than educational science provided him with the methodology of educational reform. Second, he believed that American capitalism was the root cause of American school difficulties and that the schools, by teaching a respect for the necessary mechanisms of social and economic reform to the child at as early an age as possible, could be the major force in the reforming of American capitalism. Finally, he was not a Marxist, though he was often accused of being one. He believed in collectivism; he thought the experiments in the Soviet Union the most exciting of his day, at the same time that he classified Soviet Marxism with totalitarianism. He followed Dewey in looking toward a unique American radicalism which the public schools could help attain.[5]

Beard's backing of Counts indicates the degree to which he, too, had moved toward criticism of capitalism as the source of the difficulties represented by the worsening of the depression. It may also indicate the degree of his hostility to Merriam, the chief among Counts's critics on the commission, excepting possibly the scientific educators who also gave up in disgust. Harold O. Rugg, one of the other central participants in the dispute, described his own experience with the educational battles of the thirties many years later in his affectionate criticism of the man he considered one of his most important mentors, John Dewey.[6] Rugg had been at Chicago, in the aftermath of Dewey's angry departure from the university, working with Charles Judd, who, according to Rugg's recollection, sustained a Chicago tradition of treating Dewey's work as a joke. Rugg then went to Columbia where he was closely associated with Dewey for the next thirty years. Counts also spent several years working in Chicago, where he produced *School and Society in Chicago* (1928), which quickly acquired deserved status as a major work in the study of American urban politics and public education.

The New York community which Rugg and Counts reflected was one ably memorialized by Rugg in the dedication to *Culture and Education in America*, which he published in 1931:

This book is dedicated to a company of creative students of American culture, John Dewey for phrasing clearly the experimental method of knowing, Charles Beard for his documentation of the interrelationships of economic, political, and social life, Louis Sullivan, integrator of American culture, Alfred Stieglitz, the voice of the creative American, exemplified, in "291," "303" and an American Place, Randolph Bourne, Waldo Frank, and Van Wyck Brooks, for launching a creative analysis of American culture, Frederic Howe, for his school of opinion—a pioneer attempt to build a true cultural group.[7]

Some members of the group found William F. Ogburn's concept of "cultural lag" a seminal idea, not simply as a tool for analysis, but for its acknowledgment of a holistic, systematic view of modern culture which recognized technology as a revolution to which social attitudes must adjust. As it did for Ogburn, the concept induced men like Rugg to dream of effectively measuring social change with a precision which would lead not only to scientific understanding but to a scientific management of society far beyond the tentative ambitions of Frederick Winslow Taylor or E. A. Ross. The latter two had both stepped back from the ultimate issues of social control. Both were unwilling to use the state as the coercive agency for bringing about social change.

Rugg and Counts, strongly influenced by the psychological measurement of Edward L. Thorndike ("whatever exists, exists in some amount"), took from Dewey his commitment to the school as the laboratory for the reorganization of all of social behavior but strongly criticized his restriction of himself to the rational, conscious experience of the mind. If one considered unconscious motivation the response to symbols as well as words, and saw in it an opportunity to reorganize unconscious social response as well as conscious social behavior, one could escape Taylor's dilemma and its voluntarism. Most important of all, one could reorganize American society without resort to the coercions of the state—or so it seemed to them. Communities controlled their own schools in America. Teaching teachers to teach the young would eventually produce cultural revolution to match technological change. The schools, not the state, would serve as the machinery to control cultural lag.

As Merriam's dealings with Krey amply testify, it was possible to take his own position in *Civic Education in the United States* as support of many of the points which Counts was seeking to make. While Merriam kept insisting that his own thinking rejected the use of the schools for purposes of propaganda and indoctrination, the fact remained that civic training was a function of the schools from his perspective, and an exceedingly vital one at that. There was a difference, however, and it was a crucial one. What Merriam's schools were to do was to apply modern technical skills to training the young to meet the standards of behavior established by the community of adults—whatever those standards might be. The reform of those standards was a responsibility of politics and leadership, not of the schools. While Merriam's kind of thinking would be criticized as amoral relativism, it was closer in fact to a search for a way to separate responsibilities for reform. The politics of the whole community was the center of democratic reform, not the judgments of experts manipulating the attitudes of future adult generations through an indoctrination of the young. Counts's position, however calmly it might be stated, was, from Merriam's point of view, an effort to generate revolution in the young by separating them from the framework of community values.

In 1931 Counts introduced a translation he had helped make of a textbook for Russian boys and girls, entitled *New Russia's Primer: The Story of the Five-Year Plan*, by M. Ilin. Counts praised Ilin for having "dramatized the Five-Year Plan" and having "sought to evoke those loyalties to the general welfare which have commonly been associated with war in the past." In his opinion, the form of the book was far more important than the content for precisely that point: that it could produce a peacetime fervor for reform through national loyalty and patriotism which Americans, at least, could generate only in the heat of war. "The American teacher will be forced to put to himself the question: Can we not in some way harness the school to the task of building a better, more just, a more beautiful society? Can we not broaden the sentiment of patriotism to embrace the struggles which men must ever wage with ignorance, disease, poverty, ugliness, injustice?"[8]

Merriam, too, believed that social reform methods ideally could be transferred from culture to culture. The civic education series had been designed, in fact, to reveal what these methods might be. Although it had limitations, the basic premise of the series had been the necessity for gathering information which might make such transference possible. Here again, Merriam seemed to sense an inevitable pluralism in historical and cultural background which would limit transfers, while Counts's more enthusiastic internationalism began not from cultural difference but from modified cultural relativism which saw national boundaries as antiquated remnants of barriers to the exchange of humane ideas. His was the internationalism of science, before which the disputes of politics and politicians would have to give way. Merriam's conviction that politics and the state were not the enemies of human progress, or even temporary edifices to be replaced by new scientific systems of controlled behavior, forbade his acceptance of such a utopian position, which he could only have considered dangerous.

Merriam's progressivism had set the balance of government on a relationship between leadership and the aims of the community, with the structures of government a medium through which that relationship could be expressed. It was a delicate balance, to be sure, always in danger of weakening through the temporary absence of leaders or the inability at a given moment to get the best ones through the political thickets; and it was equally endangered by periodic lapses in public concern. The answers, therefore, could not be found in changes in the system to compensate for weaknesses, for that was not where the resources of strength would ultimately be found. To improve the quality of the leaders and the methods available to them and to inform and arouse public awareness were the only ways to rebalance the equations of politics. In a perhaps paradoxical form, Merriam's state did not need to wither away because he had never allowed it the authority which would have made it a threat to the fulfillment of his dream.

The dispute between Counts and the commission broke into the open in December 1931 when Counts presented to the executive committee a plan for a volume on American society in an industrial age. He had been advised by committee members to examine the preliminary reports of the Committee on Social Trends, the educational sections of which were being guided by Charles Judd of Chicago, but Counts was rather blunt in his rejection of them. He did not think they would be of much help, partly because they covered too short a period of time and partly because they were, in his opinion, concentrated statements of factual material rather than ideas. He said further that he was planning collaboration with Charles Beard and that he wished to submit his manuscript to John Dewey for a reading. Some members of the committee suggested that he get another historian for "a less philosophical criticism." Others suggested that he take more account of "the importance of tradition."[9]

Beard was the author of the commission's initial volume, *Charter for the Social Sciences*, a book well received despite Merriam's persistent objections to it. Other members of the commission, too, found Beard's undertone of criticism of approaches to social science which conflicted with his own close to what they chose to consider carping. The seventh volume in the series, also by Beard, *The Nature of the Social Sciences*, confirmed both their point of view and Beard's.[10] In fact Beard was trying to find some area of compromise between two conflicting positions which the commission's work had emphasized: that of the educators whose concern with the potentially "rich and many sided" personality of the child led them to establish education as an architectonic specialization controlling both method and subject matter, and that of the "specialists" in the separate fields of the social sciences who considered their commitment to subject matter the prime factor in any educational argument. Each side presented the other as a caricature, even in the best of circumstances, yet many of their aims were closer than they were willing to admit. Both the educators and the social scientists, for example, emphasized the fundamental role of empirical research and measurement data, yet Counts found the data of *Recent Social Trends in the United States* (the report of President Hoover's Committee on Social Trends) useless because of its purely factual nature—an exaggeration at best—while critics of Counts found his fixed concern with personality and culture too subjective and inaccurate for scientific use.

Beard's support of Counts gave the younger man leverage which crippled Merriam's efforts to modify his effect on the commission's work. The chief objection made by Merriam and others to *The Conclusions and Recommendations* was its seeming radicalism. Although Krey and Beard succeeded in getting numerous modifications in the text to appease critics without offending proponents, the result was still unsatisfactory to many. Indeed, the final document as published is almost a model of complete inconsistency. Scarcely a positive suggestion fails to be met by some later critical denial: every harsh criticism has its apology secreted somewhere in the text.

Merriam was too angry to frame a bill of objections. Another member, commented upon but unnamed in the Preface, submitted objections but withdrew them before publication. Isaiah Bowman signed the report but appended reservations which the commission published in an appendix. He found the "Utopian yearning" particularly objectionable. "I observe that international conflicts and wars take place not alone because of struggles among nations for markets and raw materials," he said, quoting one of the several irrelevant and disconnected economic doctrines which floated through the report. "How can we eliminate such struggles except in Utopia? We can regulate the relations of nations, diminish the intensity of the struggle and come to working agreements with our neighbors. It is not necessary in constructing a framework of good relations that the individualism of nations should be eliminated." Continuing in a line of analysis which, in another context, would have pleased Beard enormously, he argued that "regional diversity is one of the blessings of the world and the boundaries between countries express the idea of neighborhood or region in the large sense."

Noting in some of the reports other internationalist asides, Bowman complained, "Who had the temerity to write that Asia is being brought within a common orbit of civilization? That phrase was written in metropolitan New York and not by one whose shoes still carry the dust of Asia. . . . Its people are not swinging in our orbit in even the modest sense of that phrase."[11] And so it went.

Merriam relied on Bessie L. Pierce for the only clear statement his objections were to receive, and he chose his spokesman well. Professor Pierce wrote to Krey and sent a copy of her letter to Merriam. "On the whole, however, my opinion as to the desirability of publishing a report which apparently has much of a propagandist character in it is much the same as it was here in Chicago," she wrote, referring to the objections she had voiced of earlier drafts at the December meeting. "I think I expressed myself rather freely to you then. I fear very much that should this report with its avowed sponsorship of inculcation of collectivism in the schools be published that it would destroy much of the validity of the other work of the Commission. I am wondering if much more could not be accomplished by omission of the word 'collectivism' which certainly is anathema to many Americans as well as being misunderstood by others."[12]

Given the subject of her volume in the series, her criticisms had a particular relevance which the calm tone of her letter belied. Her *Citizen's Organizations and the Civic Training of Youth* had done a thorough job of laying bare the efforts of citizen, public interest, and private interest groups to influence the quality of public education. The veterans groups, the Daughters of the American Revolution, the Ku Klux Klan, and others stood out on the roster, which also included the National Council for the Prevention of War, the American School Citizenship League, the American Peace Society, and the League of Nations Association. It was a wide range and a balanced one to prove the point that the organized purveying of propaganda in the schools did not ultimately provide any conception of democratic ideals clearer than the one held by the leaders of the Columbia Teachers College, although all, in their Tocquevillian claim to the power of group organization, insisted on the essential democracy of their endeavors. From her point of view, and Merriam's, the writers of the report were as far from the dust of midwestern America as they were from that of Asia.

195

"The efficient functioning of the emerging economy and the full utilization of its potentialities require profound changes in the attitudes
and outlook of the American people," wrote the commission. "Continued emphasis in education on the traditional ideas and values of economic individualism and acquisitiveness will intensify the conflicts,
contradictions, maladjustments, and perils of the transition." And
further, "If the school is to justify its maintenance and assume its
responsibilities, it must recognize the new order and proceed to equip
the rising generation to co-operate effectively in the increasingly inter-
dependent society and to live rationally and well within its limitations
and possibilities."[13]

Krey completely failed to see the basis of Merriam's objections, but
he can scarcely be blamed for the failure. Merriam also talked in terms
of hostility to a commitment to tradition and of the need for a new
approach based on some kind of new order; but he seemed to resent
most efforts to spell it out. As Krey wrote him when the battle was all
but done,

> I cannot help confessing some disappointment at your failure to recognize
> how much your own ideas had gone into the report which we considered
> at Chicago on the 22nd of February. I really thought you would express
> some appreciation of the efforts that I and others had made to incor-
> porate them. Looking back on it now, the only explanation I can offer to
> myself for your failure to do this is that you had not had time to consider
> the revised report before you came to the meeting and that some of the
> remarks which you did make were based upon the original Princeton
> version and not this revision. In view of your many other cares, and
> perhaps illness as well, I can certainly forgive you for failure to express
> this appreciation, but the regret lingers nonetheless.[14]

Merriam was not shamed to mortification, if that was Krey's intent,
but he did express a personal appreciation to Krey. "I have been greatly
outraged, however, first at the failure of the draftsman to interpret the
meaning of the Chicago meeting, and second, the high-handed action
of the AHA as reflected by Con Read. I do not think even the latest
revision represents the solid judgment, perspective and tone of the
Commission, but over emphasizes a special point of view peculiar in
part to Counts and in part to Beard."[15] He went on to accuse Counts
and Beard of having taken over the work of the committee from the
executive group which had been guiding it.

There was sufficient truth to the accusations on both sides to make
the arguments genuinely irresolvable. As executive secretary of the

American Historical Association, Conyers Read did not want to hold up
the final report for further revision—even to try to achieve some kind
of committee unity. Counts knew exactly what he wanted the report to
be and, in a style of academic management which Merriam might have
admired in other contexts because he had perfected much of its operation himself, he made sure he got what he wanted. Counts had wanted
Beard on the executive committee and Merriam could scarcely have
objected. Merriam's ideas were all the way through the report, no
matter how inconsistent some of them might seem to the careful reader
of the argument. Merriam had been badly outmaneuvered.

To have been outmaneuvered by Charles Beard was particularly
painful. Merriam never confronted the problem directly. Neither,
really, did Beard. Yet throughout the period the two men had taken
public positions designed to present to their audiences alternatives they
never allowed to come together as positions to be openly debated. The
Commission on the Social Studies is probably the only instance, even,
of semipublic dispute between the two, and even that seemed puzzling
to most observers, the apparent product of a personal animosity no one
else understood.

Beard's 1926 presidential address to the American Political Science
Association followed Merriam's by a year. Beard entitled it "Time,
Technology, and the Creative Spirit in Political Science" and couched it
as an attack upon the profession, on American universities, and, as
obliquely as he could, on everything Charles Merriam was seeking to
compromise. He opened with an elaborate fable representing a teacher
of moral and natural philosophy in 1783 lecturing to his class on the
revolutionary future yet to come, a sequence of upheavals to culminate
in modern industrial technology. It would all be very threatening for
that old professor, and it would all illustrate the tragic difficulties of
adjusting to change. It would all, too, contrast sharply with the optimistically benign tone of Merriam's vision. Where Merriam saw
compromise and cooperation, Beard saw disagreement and conflict.
Where Merriam sought the construction and expansion of professional
identity, Beard saw the pitfalls of parochialism. Where Merriam praised
the expansion of resources for independent disciplinary work, Beard
pointed out the continuing servility to wealthy donors and politicians.

Most important, perhaps, was Beard's attack upon the narrowness of
scientific research—he used all the adjectives, "myopic," "barren,"
nothing was left out—and the attendant, even consequent, destruction
of imagination. Modern technology required creativity as much as it

required measurement. Nor were historians exempt from attack. They were conservative, like Beard's professorial prophet of 1783 fearing any future which violated their sense of the past.

Beard seemed, in his final sentence, to equate much of the kind of social research Merriam was seeking to support with a stepping away from important inquiry, a fearful withdrawal from the hard realities of political, social, and economic life. He might have been addressing Wesley Mitchell's 1920 doubts about the relation between facts and hunches. "Let us put aside resolutely that great fright, tenderly and without malice," Beard concluded, "daring to be wrong in something important rather than right in some meticulous banality, fearing no evil while the mind is free to search, imagine, and conclude, inviting our countrymen to try other instruments than coercion and suppression in the effort to meet destiny with triumph, genially suspecting that no creed yet calendared in the annals of politics mirrors the doomful possibilities of infinity."[16]

By 1931 both Merriam and Beard were prepared to take stands which nonetheless represented firm continuities with their earlier commitments. Beard was the more radical, Merriam the more conservative, but only in relation to one another, not with regard to the basic framework they shared. Merriam spelled out the elements of that framework with what one must assume was a deliberate intention in the Cutler Foundation lectures which he delivered at the University of Rochester in March 1931. Published under the title *The Written Constitution and the Unwritten Attitude*, the lectures constitute one of the most important and succinct statements of the last major phase of his career.

"The Constitution of the United States was one of the most revolutionary documents of its day—a shock to the sense of propriety in the established political and economic order of the time," he said in his opening statement. Pushing aside Beard's contention about the relation between property ownership and the Constitution, Merriam emphasized the overthrow of the hereditary basis of power. "The wealth of the time was in land; and land and political power went along together in the line of family descent. To break any link in this line was to break the chain that bound government together." And he presented as a major proposition of his argument the belief that "the United States Constitution was revolutionary, experimental and adventurous in nature."

Merriam traced the origins of the conservative view of the Constitution to Woodrow Wilson, quoting Wilson's words in *Division and Reunion:* "The Federal Government was not by intention a democratic government. In plan and structure it had been meant to check the sweep and power of popular majorities." Merriam placed Beard with J. Allen Smith in Smith's contention that "the Constitution was framed in a reactionary spirit by conservatives who deliberately made the document difficult to amend, in order that propertied minorities might be better protected." Merriam was left, then, with his own statements in his *History of American Political Theories* to explain, and he invoked a mild repudiation: "In writing my volume again, I should make the emphasis somewhat different."[17]

Part of the difference lay in seeing the Constitution in a more international light.

> If we look at the field from the world point of view, the Constitution was in reality a revolutionary document of the most disturbing character; and its makers were fully aware of this. They were willing to break with the old Articles of Confederation which provided for an unalterable union except with unanimous consent of all the states; to break with the world's political traditions; and to abandon the narrower precedents of the English establishment. They were ... eager to adjust the forms and procedures of government to the actual forces and facts of their time. They were not unmindful of the business advantage of having a Constitution, but they were willing to work out this new government in terms of experiment and innovation.[18]

With regard to the difficulty of amendment, Merriam points out that the remarkable thing is not the difficulty of amendment, but the fact that the provision for amendment was there at all.

Merriam sought to criticize both the rigid adherence to constitutional structure and the equally rigid belief that changes in constitutional structure would have a useful effect on American political life. As he tried to point out, the Constitution established methods of government, not ideas of government. It would not protect against injustice or illiberalism except insofar as public attitudes pressed it to. Merriam gave his belief in civic culture, not formal organization, as the basis of American political life, its most eloquent statement.

Here, too, one can see the philosophical basis of his objection to the report of the Commission on Social Studies. For an educational system ould preserve a civic culture by seeing that it received its best articulation from one generation to the next, but it could not create such a culture in opposition to or as a revolution against one which already existed without violating the whole concept of civic culture: that it was *civic*, produced by the community itself, not imposed upon that community by an ideological elite.

Merriam's final statement in the lectures appeals to the essential optimism with which he sought to counter a sense of the need for enforced, revolutionary change.

> That the statesmanship, the industrial leadership, the scientific ability which has produced modern civilization will fail to find solutions for these new problems the pessimist may aver and may point out that thus far this has not been done, and that government lags behind modern progress. The optimist will look forward to a fruitful period of readaptation in which intelligence will be able to deal with the problems of ignorance and greed and evolve new and more beautiful forms of democratic cooperation.
>
> It is, of course, easier to organize the hates and prejudices and greeds of mankind, to scatter the flames, to sow tares among the wheat while others sleep, to appeal to passion and prejudice than to organize human friendliness and the spirit of cooperation. But the history of modern civilization is the history of this slow process, and there is no reason to believe that the limit of human intelligence in cooperation has yet been reached, or very nearly approximated.[19]

The democratic revolution in America could be traced, now, to the governmental origins of modern American society and its roots to the culture Americans had built. The answer to cultural lag was written in the Constitution itself. No future revolution was needed; no new ideology could justify such a revolution.

Beard was not calling for revolution either; but he was hinting at the need for changes in the social and economic order more radical than anything Merriam was willing to accept. Was he using Counts as a stalking horse for his radicalism? Was Counts, by any standard common among American intellectuals in the 1930s, a proper radical? The fight between Merriam and Beard, the shadows of figures behind a screen, did not answer such questions, and it was not at an end. When *Recent Social Trends in the United States* appeared in January 1933 with Merriam as one of its authors, Beard was ready again for the polite attack.

11

The Social Sciences and Mr. Hoover: Recent Social Trends

By the close of the twenties Merriam held extraordinary power in the management of the nation's complex of communities engaged in social research. The SSRC, the Spelman Fund, plus the interlocking relationships with such groups as the Brookings Institution, the National Bureau of Economic Research, and the Institute for Public Administration all assured him a prominence on the national scene which promised influence and authority on a scale few others could match. Locally, the Department of Political Science at the University of Chicago, which he continued to head, as well as other social science departments which he could influence through the Local Community Research Committee, combined with an authority within the university in general and its supporting community of influential local citizens to expand the base of power in the city. Merriam the Progressive politician acquired the status of a legend and his deeds were recounted to each entering class of students. His past continued to be useful to him.

The utility of active politics for the expansion of social research, however, had to be revised. Progressive politics had heralded the utility of scientific research for social reform; but Progressive politics had failed. The Harding and Coolidge presidencies had paid a certain amount of lip service to the utility of scientific research, with Secretary of Commerce Herbert Hoover bearing most of the practical burden of sustaining the concern; but this kind of support raised as many questions as it answered for the social scientists of Merriam's generation. The latter continued to consider the ultimate aim of social research to be social change; and many of them continued to see partisan politics as the major enemy. The drawing of analogies to biological and physical science, medicine and engineering, only served to emphasize the disputed role of politics in achieving the utopian aims of social research.

Merriam's politics in the 1920s did not offer him much support for a clear-cut decision of his own. Mayor Thompson's control of the city and of the local Republican regulars had forced Chicago Progressives to align themselves with the Democrats. When George Brennan, one of Chicago's leading Democratic politicians, asked Merriam to prepare a plank attacking Republican corruption for the Democratic platform of 1928, Merriam complied.[1]

Intellectually speaking, Merriam's interest in the city was in the process of transformation from the more local view of his earlier years to a wider concern with the nature of urbanization. His writings throughout the period reflect an increasing awareness of the role played by urbanization in the national political system. One can begin to see the transition from the "home rule" arguments based on the protection of the city from the politicians of the state, to predictions of a "city state" entity, a metropolitan regionalism which would create urban areas as effective political units on their own. Merriam's persistent and continuing effort to turn research findings into practical politics led him into a familiar set of difficulties.

Throughout the 1920s Merriam carved for himself a role in Chicago politics which compromised his ambitions and raised some questions about the scientific objectivity of his intellectual interests. Alderman Dever's success in the mayoralty race of 1923 had led to the temporary eclipse of Big Bill Thompson and enabled Merriam to establish a working political relationship with the growing Democratic machine. The Chicago studies of the Local Community Research Committee had served purposes which extended beyond the development of the new research methodology for which they were known throughout the profession. Methodology and its application were obviously of prime importance to writers like Harold Gosnell and Carroll Wooddy; but they were applied to themes of the corruption in America's most internationally known city of corruption, thus giving them a drama and a color which lightly veiled the reform motives without concealing them entirely. Readers calmly threading their ways through the cool statistical tables and analytical commentaries were also reading about the St. Valentine's Day Massacre in their daily tabloids and preparing whether they knew it or not, to transfer the images of gangsterism and lawlessness to the international scene when it became appropriate to do so.[2]

In his Preface to *The Case of Frank L. Smith*, after likening dictatorship in Europe and disrepute of urban government in the United States, Wooddy thanked Julius Rosenwald for his "generosity and civic interest," Charles Merriam for his guidance, Harold F. Gosnell and S. McKee Rosen for their reading of the manuscript, Luella Gettys for her aid in assembling the material, Samuel A. Stouffer for his collaboration in the preparation of the statistical materials, and Harold L. Ickes and Donald R. Richberg for their criticism. As a list of the Chicago school of reform, old and new, it documents a group which had created for their leader, Charles Merriam, a role his previous approaches to politics had failed to achieve.[3]

Students swarmed over city hall, examining the workings of Chicago government, commenting, advising where it seemed appropriate, publishing the results of their research in forms and in language which made no pretense of avoiding judgment. Theirs was no morphological analysis. They were more like doctors identifying the causes of an illness whose seriousness they judged from the behavior they observed. The term "corruption" was used freely to indicate any and all violations of "public trust"; and the manipulators of machines were simply "bosses." What one can detect as a new line of argument, however, is the general avoidance of an automatic identification of "bosses" and "corruption." It was this change that marked Merriam's new role in politics; and while it is not altogether clear yet in his writing, it is amply demonstrated by his behavior. Nor is it inconsistent with his own political past. "Power" could not always be circumscribed by traditional ethical boundaries; and politics, as he had long been arguing, was a world with many sides to it and an indefinite future.[4]

Anton J. Cermak, as president of the Cook County Board from 1922 to 1931, had built a Democratic machine as carefully organized and as precisely calculating of the relation between patronage and compromise as the traditional Republican organization had been. He saw in Merriam's approach a degree of sympathy with and a realistic appreciation of the harder and irreducible core of politics which was Cermak's profession. Merriam toyed briefly with the idea of running for the office of mayor himself and then came out for Cermak in the election of 1931. In a bitterly fought campaign in which Thompson played heavily on ethnic hostilities, Merriam again returned to the hustings, speaking a language he had not used so volubly since his campaign of 1919. Cermak won; but Merriam and Chicago were never to know just how effectively the new-style boss would be able to maintain control over the old-style machine. A bullet meant for President-elect Roosevelt killed Cermak in early 1933. Cermak was succeeded by Edward J. Kelly, whose alliance with county chairman Pat Nash created the famed Kelly-Nash machine, the organization of which rebuilt Chicago politics a step away from Thompson, to be sure, but in an all too familiar direction. Merriam had had no illusions about Cermak's essential commitment to the traditions of Chicago politics; but he thought he could, through his influence, modify the shape, if not the direction, of that control. Cermak, on the other hand, had served together with Merriam on the Chicago City Council at intervals from 1912 to 1918. He had no fears about the political sensitivities of the professor, as reformer or as politician.

Although Merriam's own political ambitions had reached their nadir in the defeat of 1919, the turning away from that career to the management of the emerging profession of social research had been accompanied, over the decade, by an increasing concern for the ultimate political effect of social research. Unlike Wesley Mitchell and others among his contemporaries, he had never really withdrawn from his sense not only of the appropriateness of politics as the end of political research but of the inevitability of politics as the vehicle of all reform. Nor was this a grudging acceptance of some harsh reality. As he would continue to say in his writings over the next decade, political power was no dark, malignant force except insofar as men determined to use it that way. His utopia, as one can define it from his writing, was a utopia of rational, scientific political dispute.

The application of such intellectual positions to local community reform was a tradition in American politics significant only, perhaps, for its lack of continuing effect as reform ferment declined and new systems aged. The search for a national system of social reform, or at least the effort to transform dispersed local concerns into national programs, had never been as easy as some of the more enthusiastic descriptions of local-national reform movements had made it sound. The dispersion of progressivism in the 1920s was an example and the national political mood of the period underscored the difficulty. Under the Harding and Coolidge administrations the national Republicans seemed to be doing little to maintain the support of the local Progressives, particularly the younger group who held a reverential respect for Woodrow Wilson from their service in World War I and who, like Merriam, were inclined to see the domestic reforms of the first Wilson administration as the real triumphs of progressivism. Again like Merriam, they seemed disinclined to look to the federal government for further reform but were interested in local reorganizations; whether that position stemmed from a preference for local reform or from lack of faith in national leadership is open to question. Certainly Merriam and his contemporaries in their laments about the state of national leadership expressed the latter feeling, at the same time that they continued to debate the virtues of the local leaders they saw around them as potential national figures.

Merriam and Harold Ickes had been watching the careers of a number of Democrats, among them Al Smith of New York and World War I administrators William G. McAdoo, Newton Baker, and Franklin Roosevelt. Splits in both parties combined with more realistic appraisals of the Progressive debacle to support a disenchantment with party reorganization as the route to reform. At the same time, a national leader who could embody a publicly acceptable version of the intellectual's concern with scientific reform seemed hard to define.

The career of Herbert Hoover throughout the 1920s was virtually a model of the skills requisite to assuming the leadership of the progressives of both parties. The extent of his skill can be seen not only in the kinds of people who committed themselves to his carefully structured campaign but in those who did not, for the debate between his adherents and his enemies touched the heart of postwar progressivism. It has always been tempting to suggest that had Hoover chosen to ally himself with the Democratic party—waiting perhaps until the campaign of 1932 to make his bid—he could hardly have failed to achieve the goals of significant leadership he set for himself; but such speculation may conceal the very question one needs most to examine: Hoover's relation to the politics of the 1920s.

Those who worked with Hoover during the period of 1914 to 1920 came out of the experience with a definite opinion of him, though they were by no means agreed. An interest in scientific management, industrial technology, or related subjects tended to unify attitudes among the engineers, who had professional reasons to respect Hoover,

205

and progressive publicists and journalists whose fascination with the possible social extensions of Frederick Winslow Taylor's Scientific Management filtered through the articles they wrote for magazines such as *The Survey, World's Work,* or *The Metropolitan Magazine.* Franklin Roosevelt, one of Hoover's wartime friends, wrote to Hugh Gibson, a mutual friend, "I had some nice talks with Herbert Hoover before he went west for Christmas. He is certainly a wonder, and I wish we could make him President of the United States. There could not be a better one."[5]

He had also the appearance, at least, of a committed nonpartisanship which led interested managers in both parties to seek out his political aims. Colonel House questioned him on his attitude toward the presidency as early as December 1918 and received a thoroughly noncommittal reply—he would acknowledge only a firm belief in progressivism—a statement Hoover then circulated in press releases.[6]

Merriam was not sure. He'd seen enough of Hoover during the war to know that he did not find him attractive; but he was not sure just why, and his own correspondence ran counter to his personal impression. Morris Llewellyn Cooke, an engineer and one of the urban progressives with whom Merriam maintained correspondence, wrote that, though he was not altogether sure he would vote for Hoover, "there is a possibility if he is elected, as he probably will be, that Herbert Hoover may show us how to shed politics in some large way in the demonstration of a democratic form of government."[7] He did not like him either, apparently. "If he only had Al Smith's personality and his own training," he lamented, "I believe you might look forward to having a government-Pasteura." That was it. Aseptic politics could be the answer—but not for anyone who knew American politics as Merriam did.

"I agree with you that if Hoover had Smith's personality he would make a remarkable demonstration of democracy," Merriam replied; but then he drew back. "He is more inclined toward a dictatorial type, however, and I do not know what the result will be if he takes over the enormous power of the presidency. He does not take opposition kindly and there will be some heavy clashes."[8]

While Merriam did not challenge Cooke's view of scientific politics, he did not subscribe to such a view. Writing of his four leaders in 1926—and he had designated them as "party leaders"—he had acknowledged the necessity of intelligence of "a high order, in most cases of an unusual kind." But he went on to specify that intelligence in ways which would not have appealed to a number of his social science contemporaries. "This intelligence was not critically scientific as much as it was parliamentary, poetical, prophetic in nature."[9] Few of those who supported Hoover's candidacy would have called him either parliamentarian or poet; but that he possessed, at least, a critically scientific cast of mind was the attribute most commonly ascribed to him.[5]

John Merriam thought his brother a bit hard on Hoover. John had watched his own respect for the secretary of commerce develop well beyond anything he might have anticipated, even during the hurried days of the war when Hoover seemed the brighter among the younger administrative stars which the emergency had revealed.

John's move to Washington in 1920 to head the Carnegie Institution had given him much more direct contact with government there than Charles had, and considerably more funds at his disposal, at least initially. His continued involvement with the National Research Council had put him closer to scholars not only in the natural sciences but the social sciences as well, as the NRC broadened its interest in research in state and local government. As a group pressing for the expansion of research, the NRC quite logically watched its interests drift perceptibly and familiarly into politics. Natural resources reform, particularly for one as experienced in California politics as John Merriam had become during his years on the Berkeley campus, had always been inextricably bound to politics; and John Merriam's interest in various aspects of environmental preservation—the concept of "conservation" broadened rapidly after the war—made the shift to the national scene easy enough. In addition, as the NRC responded to advice from proponents like Secretary of Commerce Hoover and sought funds from private industry to further research, it found itself touching the complex boundaries of the economic politics involved in trade associations and tax-exempt foundation research. Industrial "philanthropists" could scarcely miss the point that a tax-free gift to a university for research purposes might produce profitable even if taxable results.

It is significant, perhaps, that John was first to press for bringing the SSRC to work for President Hoover. Charles was reluctant, initially. Recognizing that the state of research in the social sciences was primitive, however much he may have underestimated the time it would take to improve it, he wanted the time. Hoover as president, too, saw the spotty condition of anything that could be called "research," but, like John Merriam, he saw no reason to wait if the personnel could be assembled and the appropriate time allotted to improving the condition.

As secretary of commerce, Hoover had promised a continuation and expansion of the cooperation between industry and science that the war had indicated might be possible; and his exhortations to his colleagues in the engineering field, his work with the NRC, and, most important of all, his obvious desire to use the Department of Commerce as the chief clearinghouse for industrial-scientific development pointed to the possibility of a new and exciting future for American research. Actually, what Hoover had done was to recognize the potentialities of the War Industries Board and to shift functions and personnel as quietly as possible into the small department he had taken over.[10]

Hoover's faith in the nonpartisan professional was taken directly from the Progressive tradition which had produced the city-manager movement and the myriad reforms which now went under the name of public administration. The marshaling of the new professionals for government service—and he saw enlightened business leadership as the center of the same new professionalism—became one of the central aims of his Department of Commerce years. He maintained, too, the same Progressive view of public service financing that had dominated Merriam's earlier Chicago years: organized philanthropy rather than government should back the research studies on which reform would be built. Eager to draw on the new university talent, he began almost immediately to press those academics he had been in touch with during the war years to move into government. The economist Wesley Mitchell was one of his first targets, but Mitchell refused.[11] Indeed, the war years had taught Mitchell and Merriam quite a different lesson from the one learned by Hoover. The academics left Washington with suspicions about the capacity of government to accumulate and use scientific ideas as well as with a view of wartime "voluntarism" somewhat different from that of Hoover and others even more inclined to romanticize the war experience.

In 1923 Secretary Hoover accepted the chairmanship of the President's Conference on Unemployment. Edward Eyre Hunt, one of his chief assistants in the department, asked John Merriam whether or not the new social research group, the SSRC, which his brother headed might be interested in serving as consultant, in some form, to the conference.[12] John was enthusiastic about it, but Charles was not

Charles conceded the argument advanced by both Hunt and John: such a study would carry much more weight and prestige if it were "scientifically conducted," but he saw the distinction between the actual state of his social sciences and their rapidly expanding popular image. He discussed the proposal with his colleagues on the council and came to the conclusion that "the Council might be of considerable help in planning the investigation and finding the best personnel to carry it on. But I do not think that the Council is in a position to assume the responsibility for the actual carrying on of elaborate researches."[13]

Hoover's apparent sense of urgency was not an unrealistic response to conditions which he probably saw more clearly than many other Americans, given the position he had held for the past eight years. His planning for his presidency was extensive for its day, certainly, and interesting. Although he was in no position to elaborate a revolutionary thesis—as a Republican succeeding a Republican he could scarcely have risked a "progressive" campaign—he nonetheless moved quickly and quietly to establish a progressive program which, if implemented, would, by the election of 1932, be able to serve both as the subject of a campaign document exploiting his presumably successful first administration without the threat of intraparty dispute and the basis for a very real and practical program for the future.

But Charles Merriam's reluctance to encourage SSRC participation indicates an awareness of the nature of national reform politics Hoover would have done well to understand. No one who had experienced so closely the fights of social researchers with urban politicians could have any illusions about the relation between practical politics and scientific research. The war experience had suggested at least one possible conclusion: hasty or badly conducted research could be damaging to both the public good and the public image of research. Hoover's background in American politics was virtually nonexistent; and if his war experience had aroused any suspicions about the utility of scientific research for solving social problems, his general successes in the Washington bureaucracy of the 1920s had wiped them away. Hoover knew—or thought he knew—what scientific research could do for industrial efficiency. The transference of the industrial model to social organization seemed as obvious to him as it was urgent. But whether social research and industrial research were of the same order, and whether either of them was properly "scientific" were questions clearer, in part at least, to Merriam than to Hoover.

Merriam knew, too, that the temptation would be strong among his social scientists to become advisers to the President of the United States, thereby certifying themselves as the experts they believed themselves to be, even at the risk of failing to produce the science their researches were intended to generate. The dependence of scientific research on empirical investigation was certainly part of Merriam's whole approach to both social science and social reform, but given the necessary base in local research which had not yet been built, the leap to federal and national research was premature. At the same time, as his experiences also demonstrated, the public and private backing of social reform rested on the publicity given the researchers and their programs by those who held the most prominent public pulpits. And what better pulpit was there than the presidency? His agreement, finally, to help provide social science research for the Hoover administration was the beginning of a new attempt to confront the issues.

Hoover's plan for his "Great Society" was to be built out of the studies prepared by the President's Research Committee on Social Trends, which he appointed in December of 1929. Financed by the Rockefeller Foundation and utilizing the academic resources of the SSRC, its purpose was to survey the whole of American society, to break apart the piecemeal tradition of social research and reform so that the issues of environment and natural resources, unemployment and industrialization, education, old age, medical care, crime, the full panoply of both the new and the traditional reform concerns could be viewed from a rational, scientifically organized vantage point for the first time. Hoover's ambitions ran high, but his confidence in the sources of his program ran higher. It was in the Hoover administration that the era of scientific progressive reform seemed destined to come of age.[14]

Although Mitchell and Merriam were to serve as chairman and vice-chairman of the committee, the chief academic movers of the project from the beginning were William F. Ogburn and Howard W. Odum, director and assistant director of research, respectively. Ogburn and Odum had been the initial contacts made by the White House through presidential assistant French Strother, and it was they who urged Merriam and Mitchell to accept the president's invitation. Hoover was well acquainted with Mitchell from his Commerce Department days, when Mitchell had headed the Bureau of Economic Research. Merriam was head of the SSRC, and so both men were more in command of both the president's attention and the necessary resources than either Ogburn or Odum. Odum had his own research institute at Chapel Hill and was the editor of *Social Forces*. The skepticism of Mitchell and Merriam, however, is important for the differences it reflects. Mitchell felt that so crucial a study could not be done in such a short time in any case. Merriam was less concerned about that factor and more concerned about the assumption of so directly political a role by the young SSRC. Knowing of the Rockefeller family's increasing reluctance to involve itself in anything which would draw attention to it as seeking political influence, he had been a persuasive force in preventing a total withdrawal of the various Rockefeller philanthropies into purely scientific and medical research. Interestingly enough, he did not believe that the new generation of Rockefeller sons was going to get involved in politics, and so he feared for the future of Rockefeller engagement in social reform. Most important, perhaps, Merriam respected Hoover's managerial capacities enormously. Future groups of students thought his defenses of Hoover feeble and joking rather than serious statements of his own point of view. They were right about the weaknesses, but not about the seriousness.

Ogburn and Odum were far more deeply committed to the absolute objectivity of social research than was Merriam, yet far more willing to move directly to the service of the president as, somehow, the nonpartisan representative of the nation as a whole. Mitchell and Merriam, although in different degrees, respected political involvement as a part of social research, yet shied away from making the social science community an instrument of presidential policy making. All four had come out of the generation that had fed liberally on James Bryce's injunction that the only source of real political knowledge was politics itself and action in politics the only true method of attaining such knowledge. Yet how to promote the utility of social research without tainting the purity of the research with partisanship would play an increasingly divisive role among the four.

Conceived in the full bloom of the boom optimism of the twenties—the introductory dinner with the president took place on 26 September 1929—the committee carried on its researches and formulated its analyses on the full downward slide of the depression years. Its report was published in January 1933 as the country sat out the puzzling interregnum apparently trapped between a president who would not act and a president-elect who could not, or maybe it was the president who could not and the president-elect who would not—the historiographical clamor which emerged from the New Deal effectively obscured the issue by making the question irrelevant. For a brief period the reviews heralded the monumental achievement of more than three years of work by the largest community of social scientists ever assembled to assess the social condition of a nation; but, again, the coming of the New Deal and the insistent demolition of the crumpled remains of the Hoover reputation covered it over, not in the critical derision which marked the many other commentaries on the Hoover administration, but with a silence which was, in its way, far more effective.

The program which the committee presented to the president on 21 October 1929 set out the initial premises. "After some three weeks of investigation [it] has found that there exist data in sufficient quantity and accuracy to give assurance that a survey of recent social changes in a number of important fields is possible." They listed some twenty-four separate fields, from "population, food, and natural resources" to "public administration," all encompassing what was intended as a thorough analysis of the "kind of people" who inhabited the United States, and the nature and the quality of their lives.[15]

It is hard to see how Merriam could have agreed to such an assertion except to convince Hoover and his assistants of the desirability of the program. Certainly such men as E. E. Day of the Rockefeller Foundation, one of the likeliest targets in a search for financial support, were more sophisticated. But Ogburn had said, after his initial meeting with presidential assistant French Strother, "Hoover wants us to tell him what he wants," and that was what they were doing.[16] The degree of faithfulness to the state of knowledge among the social scientists involved had to be stretched for such purposes.

Whether such data actually existed nonetheless reflects a dilemma which social research groups continually faced in their efforts to cope with the tension between the reform tradition of collecting information to support a position already obvious to the reformers and the new aim of dispassionate objectivity. Part of that dilemma had been the need to convince patrons in advance that a research project was feasible—feasible not necessarily in the research terms of the experts but in the reform terms of the patron. Herbert Hoover had been president of the United States for only eight months; but he had been a kind of patron of scientific research for almost two decades. In a foreword to each of their supplemental monographs the committee informed readers how they had tried to safeguard their conclusions against bias.

The researches were restricted to the analysis of objective data. Since the available data do not cover all phases of the many subjects studied, it was often impossible to answer questions of deep interest.... Discussions which are not limited by the severe requirements of scientific method have their uses, which the committee rates highly. Yet an investigation initiated by the President, in the hope that the findings may be of service in dealing with the national problems of today and tomorrow, should be kept as free as possible from emotional coloring and unverifiable conjectures. Accuracy and reliability are more important in such an undertaking than liveliness or zeal to do good. If men and women of all shades of opinion from extreme conservatism to extreme radicalism can find a common basis of secure knowledge to build upon, the social changes of the future may be brought in larger measure under the control of social intelligence.[17]

The effort to analyze one's own society required, by the committee's standards, some kind of objective separation of a responsible sense of citizenship from the demands of "pure" social research, not to mention the holding of a firm conviction that such a separation was possible. Keeping the collecting and interpreting of data apart from the issues of reform did not preclude their use in reform measures, but it did complicate the committee's sense of its own purpose.

To refrain from expressions of approval and disapproval, not to make propaganda for any cause, is difficult for the student of social changes, for as private citizens, the Committee's collaborators have their individual scales of value, and some are eager advocates of certain reforms. But, as sharers in this enterprise, one and all have striven faithfully to discover what is, and to report their findings uncolored by their personal likes and dislikes, or by their hopes and fears of what may be.[18]

These statements were being written while Merriam and Beard were engaged in their struggles over propaganda and the objectivity of the educators. Merriam should have been achieving in the scientific atmosphere of the social trends group the very objectivity he was arguing for in the social studies group, but he was not. As the debates show, he was finding himself faced with what appeared to be the opposite extreme.

In the case of the study of social trends, the reform pressures came from outside the group of social researchers rather than from inside it, but the source was a significant one, incapable of being ignored: the president of the United States. Although previous presidents had used research committees for similar purposes, Hoover was breaking new ground in his insistence that this committee be his, that he be deeply involved in its deliberations from its initial financing to its final conclusions. Presidential assistant Strother had written George E. Vincent, president of the Rockefeller Foundation, on the day the committee's prospectus was received. He assured Vincent that President Hoover "long had in mind, as one of his chief opportunities for service to the country ... the conscious organization of all possible practicable means by which the Government might inspire, promote, or guide both public and private thought and action of benefit in the field of social problems." In his search for method, Strother explained, Hoover had requested the advice of a "small group of eminent sociologists and social workers.... They were to provide a plan which, if carried through, would produce a rounded and explicit picture of the whole American social scene, with such a wealth of facts and statistics and conclusions as to form a new and unique basis of thought and action for social scientists, social workers, and those officers of government who, like himself, have a special responsibility in relation to such problems." Strother attached the committee's report, and, in his effort to make Hoover's desire for specific responsibility in the matter clear, continued: "The President would wish to assume responsibility for the prosecution of the researches, and to sponsor the reports and experiments supplementary to them. He regards them of as fundamental importance, and certain to be of the highest public as well as scientific value."[19]

In some respects, what Hoover was doing in sponsoring the committee himself and requesting the funds for it in his own name was no different from what he had done in the Commerce Department, where he had employed the same techniques, nor was it different from the sort of thing Wilson had done during the war. But to translate those methods to the presidency in peacetime might not be regarded as a reasonable carryover. Once again, President Hoover and Secretary Hoover were to come in conflict. Everything in the Progressive tradition supported Hoover's belief in the presidency as an administrative office. Whether the political traditions of that office would provide similar support was another matter.

Interestingly enough, Merriam and Ogburn came to disagree because of a curious estrangement in their respective attitudes toward the relation between the presidency and a report such as that of the social trends committee. Merriam, by far the more political of the two, had begun to object in August 1931 to the turning over of preliminary materials to President Hoover. Ogburn saw nothing wrong with such a procedure and indeed seemed to revel in the close relation to the White House which his correspondence with Edward Eyre Hunt, the committee's official liaison figure with the president, gave him. Hunt delayed circulating the minutes of the August meeting until December, and when he did, he omitted Merriam's objections. Merriam wrote him to clarify his point and to insist on its incorporation.

> My position was that if the President asked to see the work in progress, he was entitled to. But that it would be better not to submit piecemeal or unfinished reports to the President for the following reasons: that the President would get a better impression of the comprehensive work of the Committee if he first saw the Report and the conclusions as a whole. That the President would be in the most favorable situation, if he could say that he had seen none of the Reports until they came to him as the finished product of the technicians selected for the task. That the Committee would be saved the embarrassment arising from any suggestions for change, to which it could not agree, or from being charged with having made such changes, even if in fact not true.[20]

Merriam's view of the relation between the committee and the president did not at all conform to the understanding that Hunt had from the president or from Ogburn; and Merriam's apparent distinction between "work in progress," which could be turned over to the president, and "piecemeal or unfinished reports" did not help to clarify the matter. Indeed everything in the preliminary planning of the committee's work indicates that Hoover could well have thought exactly the opposite: that he commanded a research staff which would provide him with materials to help him exercise his national leadership.

It is equally clear that Hunt did not agree with Merriam. Objectivity and scientific purity to the contrary notwithstanding, Ogburn also saw no threat in the president's involvement in the formulation of the report. Ogburn was willing to give Hoover a leeway which Merriam would later be willing enough to give to Franklin Roosevelt; for the moment Ogburn was enjoying a personal relationship with the White House similar to that which Merriam would have with FDR. Equally important, Merriam was growing increasingly restive with the "coolness," so to speak, of the language of the report. Even there, however, their differences of opinion could not be organized along clear lines.

Hunt wanted the style to be somewhat more popular in its appeal, as did the president; and he suggested a publicity campaign to hint, at the very least, at some kind of forthcoming report. Howard Odum objected. For one thing, Hunt had sought in his statement to underplay the concept of "social welfare" by arguing that the term as used by the committee had meanings quite different from those that critics of the president might attach to it. "We are certainly dealing with dynamite," Odum remarked irritably, "when we ourselves send out a statement negating the whole claim of social science for accurate terminology and interpretation. . . . At the present writing all evidence, as I see it, is against this preliminary publicity."[21] Merriam, on the other hand, would not have objected to the publicity if its purpose were to prepare the public for the report by providing useful background. He had done such things all through his career and saw no danger in it.

A meeting of the committee was called for mid-March 1932 to clarify the issue—or at least to determine the relationship between the committee's report to the president and the one problem which, oddly enough, had not been anticipated at the beginning but was gradually engrossing the committee's attention: the November election and the anticipated bitter campaign. The White House had apparently continued to entertain the possibility of using the committee's materials in the campaign; but that would have necessitated beginning early in the spring at the very latest. Committee manuscripts would not be available for publication until October, which further emphasized the need for a long preliminary buildup—if there was to be a buildup at all. Both Strother and Hunt had been using their magazine and newspaper contacts to drop hints about a forthcoming great announcement, but the committee's refusal to allow publicity that far in advance—or finally any publicity at all prior to publication of the summary report—stopped all such hinting or any other plans for an announcement. Both sides could agree that a sudden bombshell in October or even September would do no one any good. From the president's view, it would look like a last-minute gambit and only confirm the criticisms of those who saw similar motives in his various commissions and conferences. From the point of view of the social scientists, they would all be called politicians, which, regardless of the fact that some of them were still ardent supporters of Hoover, would have violated totally the very scientific objectivity they were struggling to achieve. Yet, as many of them would have agreed, the presidential campaign was becoming ever more important in the judgments they themselves were beginning to make about the nature and the quality of their work.

As the committee's work reached its final stages, the disagreements grew more critical. As chairman, Mitchell was responsible for writing the final report and Merriam, as vice-chairman, the concluding essay on government. In those positions Mitchell and Merriam seemed to squeeze Ogburn in an increasingly uncomfortable vise. But they were not the only critics of Ogburn's position. Mitchell spent the spring of 1932 in England reading mimeographed drafts of the reports and trying to support Ogburn against Hunt's critical remarks. "It will take a serious minded reader to go far with it," he wrote Ogburn. "My guess is that you will go down in history as the editor of a good national inventory of value to future historians, and not as the chief author of a best seller. . . . My introduction might perhaps point out in advance as tactfully as possible the superior merits of such a job, and make a possible reader ashamed to acknowledge that he cannot get excited about sober statements of facts."[22] It was a good try, but August in New York did not help. Merriam was there, but in a hospital with an attack of quinsy. Robert S. Lynd, who was increasingly becoming known for a view of the social sciences far more functional, not to say reformist, than Ogburn's or Odum's, annoyed Odum with a criticism of the committee's work. Said Ogburn soothingly, "You must not take any of Lynd's remarks personally. He is a very zealous young man and sometimes forgets the personal equities."[23]

Confidence ebbed and criticism mounted. Ogburn's attempts to maintain an Olympian editoral pose above the battle, shaping and guiding, only sharpened issues, and the correspondence is filled with asides covering such details as "nervous" excuses, illness, secretarial inefficiency, and the like. But Ogburn knew what he wanted: evidence, not impressions, and in the final analysis, not even their positions as chairmen of the committee could keep Mitchell and Merriam from the criticism of their director of research. Merriam had finished his chapter on government in May. Ogburn's criticisms of the draft pointed to differences between them reflecting a deep intellectual opposition between Ogburn's positivism and Merriam's politics. After praising the general tone and scope, Ogburn opened his attack. "It seems to me, however, that you have paid a price for these high achievements and this

217

price, I think, would be the outstanding criticism which I would make. It is a lack of equivalent richness and evidence and data to support your observations and statements."[24] Hunt joined him, accusing Merriam of writing a "political essay" in which "the statement of problems seems to rest on your authority, rather than on the data."[25]

Although Merriam ignored most of Ogburn's criticism, he grew restive as the committee debates dragged on and complained about the report's suspension above history and events. "No one would ever suspect there was such a man as Dewey from reading this. You would never know there was any such person as Giddings or Small. You would never know except for a few pages ... that there were men like Roosevelt and Wilson or any of the other thinkers who instituted these educational or other changes." The lack of reference to international relationships also struck him. "We take a rather provincial attitude as if there were no other country in the world except the United States."[26] He was still trying to be optimistic, but it wasn't easy. "I am more than ever encouraged to believe that the outcome of our long effort is likely to be made something socially significant and vital," he was willing to say in March. "Perhaps Mr. Strother is right in saying that we ought to have more faith in the outcome than some of us seem to have."[27] But by August it was getting harder. He thought it might be a good idea to survey the reviews of Mitchell's *Recent Economic Changes* to see if they pointed to any pitfalls which might now be avoided. "I have heard several times that Recent Economic Changes ... was too optimistic in view of what had happened since, and that there was not enough warning of what was to come. No doubt the business depression was pretty hard to foresee," he wrote in the letter accompanying the clippings Ogburn sent. "They are certainly very interesting," he replied after he read them, "but also tend to make the Depression more depressing."[28]

Optimism and depression—terms relatively new to interpretations of aggregate social behavior—had bothered the members of the committee since January, at least. "A substantial proportion of the chapters that have been turned in," Ogburn wrote in a staff memorandum, "have been criticized by a fairly large number of the staff and others as having *too optimistic a tone*," and he underlined the phrase to make sure that it impressed everyone as much as it had impressed him. Optimism, he conceded, could not be measured scientifically; and there was also the fact that it might suggest "an interpretation in the mind of the reader rather than an exact determination in an objective manner." He was still willing to struggle with the problem. "Again, optimism and pessimism vary according to different persons." Fundamentally, however, he felt that "in so far ... as the author sticks to the measurement of the trends without evaluation the optimism would seem to be read into it by the reader, except, of course, as to the selection of the data."[29]

In the final drafting, Mitchell and Ogburn remained in utter disagreement. Ogburn substantially rewrote Mitchell's first draft of the basic "Introduction and Findings," and Mitchell bridled. He disliked Ogburn's language and pressed him to return to the original draft, suggesting that he get good editors if he wanted to. But language alone was not the issue, although Ogburn first tried to state it that way, and the debate continued. Ogburn found others who would agree with him that Mitchell's statement was too long, not sufficiently interesting, diffuse, discursive—he sprayed adjectives about with abandon; and he charged finally that there were not enough facts.[30] Even that blow glanced off the by then adamant Mitchell and the report went through as he wrote it, replete with the elegance and grace which were the mark of Mitchell's mind, facts or no facts.

The real issues were more below the surface than anyone cared to reveal, but there was a clear enough indication of conflict. For ten years Merriam had been solidly and effectively arguing the fundamental compatibility of the basic positions in American social science, and others seemed to agree. But in the final analysis, the disagreements were sufficient to provoke an intensity of heat attributable more easily to personalities than to an incompatibility of the issues themselves.

Ogburn, for example, saw no contradiction in his willingness to soft-pedal matters which were politically sensitive—race, birth control, the relation of immigration to crime—and his worship of scientific objectivity and facts. He wanted the report to be as useful as possible to the president; so he saw nothing untoward in letting Hoover be involved in every stage of the investigation if that was what he wanted. On the other side, the degree to which an increasingly partisan disenchantment with the Hoover presidency influenced such disagreement as that voiced by Merriam cannot be measured, but it was there.

More important, perhaps, are the inferences one can draw of more fundamental conceptions of the relation between leadership and social science which mark a distinction between Merriam and Ogburn in their

219

views of Hoover and the presidency. "I have an idea," Odum wrote Ogburn a week before the election, "that President Hoover is going to value these volumes about as much as anything he has done. Barring a miracle, it does seem now that the volumes will be the first of a series of factors which will start the historical estimates of his work as ex-president. It is certainly a great thing that studies can now be looked at as studies and not as something to be shot at by politicians."[31] Ogburn's hearty agreement with Odum's point of view can be seen in the letter he wrote Strother the day after the election. "This is the dark hour for 'the Chief,'" he moaned, using the affectionate title which only the inner staff applied to Hoover, "and I am truly sorry. I doubt if we've ever had a man in the White House who ever labored more courageously or more intelligently, or who fought better than did Mr. Hoover. . . . I should say roughly that Mr. Hoover did 100 times as much against a depression as any other President has done before. The people were not voting against Mr. Hoover, they were voting against the business cycle. . . . [T]he only type of man who could have saved himself . . . would have been a man of spectacular histrionic ability— an actor, a 'gesticulator.' . . ."[32]

Hoover, too, was worried about his rapidly disintegrating reputation. He had written his preface to the report in October 1932; but when the public issuance came in January 1933, the full impact of the campaign led him to supplement his comments.

> I wish to add to the foregoing the observation that the significance of this report lies primarily first, in the fact that it is a cooperative effort on a very broad scale to project into the field of social thought the scientific mood and the scientific method as correctives to undiscriminating emotional approach and to insecure factual basis in seeking for constructive remedies of great social problems. The second significance of the undertaking is that, so far as I can learn, it is the first attempt ever made to study simultaneously all of the fundamental social facts which underlie all our social problems. Much ineffective thinking and many impracticable proposals of remedy have in the past been due to unfamiliarity with facts in the fields related to that in which a given problem lies. The effort here has been to relate all the facts and present them under a common standard of measurement.[33]

Wesley Mitchell opposed the man of hunches, William Ogburn resisted the man of spectacular histrionic ability, and Hoover feared the undiscriminating emotional approach. But by whose orders and with what system of laws could scientific moods and methods become correctives? John Dewey enthusiastically suggested the report was more than the mere fact-finding critics were wont to see. Here, he said, "the facts are presented—sometimes implicitly, sometimes explicitly—so as to make *problems* stand out, and that, in my judgment, is the proper function of statements of facts. Hence the volumes are an arsenal. And I would rather have an arsenal of authoritative knowledge than such a premature firing-off of guns as would make a lot of noise and emit great amounts of smoke."[34] To hunches, histrionics, and emotions, Dewey added noise and smoke.

Although Dewey's distinction between facts and problems plays through the committee discussions, it was joined, ultimately, by a third term which neither Dewey nor his intellectual sympathizers on the board would have been willing to include at the beginning: programs. The committee had explicitly refused to accept the responsibility of recommending programs of action, acknowledging this as the province solely of the president. Yet through the depression years, only gradually being defined as the crisis they had so clearly become by 1933, the awareness of the need for programs, for crisis leadership rather than social management, had lent a certain heat to the discussions of the committee and a particular tone to a text initially conceived as dispassionate, objective, and, as some of its critics were inclined to argue, essentially colorless.

From within the new administration, A. A. Berle pointed out the problem in terms which would become a continuing criticism of the branch of social science which Merriam tried to lead into the New Deal. Berle thought the evidence irrevocably tied to 1929 and therefore to a now rejected past. This was not the case, as the committee's persistent search for the most recent available data might have testified; but Berle's misunderstanding is a result of a deliberate stance chosen by the committee in its presentation of its materials. The committee had decided to play down the sense of crisis, to avoid undue optimism, to be sure, but at the same time to project a calm and hopeful America against the background of revolutionary world politics.

Berle thought the report opened up endless tempting vistas. "[H]ere is a compilation of source material of the first importance. It has the authenticity of well conserved and well directed scholarship. It has the barrenness of quantitative theory and statistical measurement. It indicates what happened; makes a fair attempt to explain why it happened; and through sheer force of limitation stops short of the question of whether it must continue to happen." And in a crucial critique, Berle attacked the self-imposed limitation "under which academic students today place themselves—their endeavor to be objective, non-controversial; to state facts, rather than to interpret them or plead a cause. One may regret that the academic community has fallen out of the habit of interpreting its data; feel (as perhaps many academicians do feel) that the desire for objectivity has been carried entirely too far." He went on to acknowledge the possibility, indeed the hope, that "a master who is not one of the authors, or who might perhaps be one of the authors acting in a different capacity, may perhaps reduce much of the work to a serviceable tool."[35]

Berle touched the central issue: that the value of the work would depend on a "master" acting in a capacity different from that of the authors, or an author acting in a different manner—but who, and above all, how? The committee had assumed from the beginning that it need not determine that point. It was the president's committee, although the image of the "master" had begun to fade early in the project. Dewey was right in pointing to the essentially conservative base of the report, its dependence upon the logic of planning; but in an era of revolution, an "arsenal of authoritative knowledge" which did not make a certain amount of noise and emit a reasonable quantity of visible smoke might end up being as effective as a toy gun.

Charles Beard's criticisms of the committee's report reveal once again some of the very crucial differences of opinion which separated him from his generation of social scientists but which, interestingly enough, can be used to show some of the problems in point of view which divided members of the Committee on Recent Social Trends. It is quite likely that some of Beard's concerns were strikingly similar to some of the questions which were troubling Merriam; but in this case Merriam's apparent commitment to the committee hampered his voicing of them publicly.

In a review of the report which he published in the *Yale Review* Beard began to spell out his objections. Praising the effort which went into the work—like many others he made the error of assuming at the outset that "undoubtedly the work will serve as a mine of materials for statesmen, editors, students, and everyone else who has occasion to seek orientation in the fields surveyed"—he continued: "It seems safe to assume that this monumental treatise will mark an epoch in the history of social thought in the United States—perhaps the end of an epoch.

And for two reasons. First, no such vast undertaking is likely to be authorized or financed again along the lines here laid down. In the second place, the results, highly valuable as they are in detail, reflect the coming crisis in the empirical method to which American social science has long been in bondage." That crisis, he felt, was built on what he considered the basic error Americans were making: their belief, as he put it, "that when once the 'data' have been assembled important conclusions will flow from observing them—conclusions akin in inevitability to those of physics or mathematics."[36]

Beard concluded a second critical review of the report with relatively oblique criticism of Merriam.

> ...the relation of trends in government to "broader social and economic tendencies" is an admirable enterprise and it would be difficult to discover anyone in the United States who could do a better job than Mr. Merriam, but that undertaking cannot be handled in terms of causation; on the contrary it is an intellectual operation in historical and social philosophy which transcends the listing of changes and the plotting of gradients.... The scientific method is only a method. Dreams, plans, purposes, and collective will must come from the human mind and heart. Where they exist, science can discover the facts that condition realization and furnish instrumentalities for carrying plan and purpose into effect.... A revolution in thought is at hand, a revolution as significant as the Renaissance: the subjection of science to ethical and esthetic purpose. Hence the next great survey undertaken in the name of the social sciences may begin boldly with a statement of values agreed upon, and then utilize science to discover the conditions, limitations, inventions, and methods involved in realization.[37]

In many ways, this was precisely the point, and few men in the United States had the basic experience to be as sensitive to the issue, or as central to the basic conflict generated by it, as Merriam and Beard. Both had sought, in different ways, a leadership in an academic community which each acknowledged was facing a crisis in the definition of common values. In some senses, Beard was far more zealous in his demand for—if not his search for—precise definition of those values and clarification of statement; but he seemed virtually suicidal in his separation of himself from the sources of power and authority which might have provided him with what he sought. He would have to establish his ideas without outside funding, without an institutional base, and above all, without a continuing flow of students to give a firmer foundation to his best intuitions.

Merriam had all those things, but at what Beard often rightly saw as a very high price. To an important extent, however, Beard's price, from Merriam's point of view, was equally dear. To separate oneself from the sources of real power was an impossible price to pay for the articulation of the aims of power. Merriam's continued wielding of his authority depended upon his recognition of the point which Beard refused, apparently, to acknowledge: that there was no central statement of values powerful enough to organize a comprehensive program of social reform which would conform to the traditional values of the many regional and ethnic groupings comprising American society. If Beard wanted to recapture the systems of values explicit in theology, he would have to find a unity implicit in an American tradition which could provide it. He thought he could, as his beautifully prophetic imagery so often testifies, but to the degree that his prophecies attacked segments of the community of American reformers—and the social scientists were certainly among them—his eventual isolation from the community he sought to unify was determined by his commitment to the formulation of a unifying American ideology.

Merriam, in contrast, built his political power in that community on his ability to describe a sense of unity which could organize for some kind of purposive action, however temporary that organization might prove to be. Yet Merriam's descriptions of the content of that sense of unity remained obscure, pointing at best to examples of the effects of temporary unity in his frequent rhapsodic descriptions of the success of projects being undertaken by his researchers. Disputes like that within the Social Studies Commission and the differences which riddled the last compromise of the Social Trends group were, from Merriam's point of view, anomalies rather than the signs of basic conflict, yet, as Beard might have demanded, What was the norm and where the foundation of unity?

When all was said and done, however, there was far more to unite Merriam and Beard with each other than there was to unite either of them with many of the positions in the community for whose leadership they competed. Their opposition to determinism, their support of what each persisted in calling "pluralism," their spiritual nationalism and traditional Americanism, their driving small-town Protestantism, and their basic sense of the useful innovation inherent in science and technology gave them a far broader base on which to unite than either of them ever was willing to admit. Merriam was no social control behaviorist, fascist or otherwise, and Beard knew it. Beard was no economic determinist, communist, socialist, or what have you, and Merriam knew it. Yet each saw in the other the threat of the extreme which each conceived of the other as representing.

Merriam's own view of the Committee on Recent Social Trends was not that far from Beard's. Although he continued to point to its work throughout the remainder of his career as the beginning of a new relation between the social sciences and the presidency, he himself stepped away from most of its essential principles as reflected in the work of Ogburn, Odum, and even Wesley Mitchell. Merriam's acceptance of the problems of politics, programs of action, and direct participation of social scientists in policy making was resolved in the New Deal only in the sense of a tacit agreement to stop debating the issue as though scientific objectivity were the only god to be appeased. In that sense, the atmosphere of crisis which circumstances and the Roosevelt leadership created around the New Deal served a purpose for Merriam too. Emergencies could lay debates on principle aside, leaving them for later, though no less painful, reckoning.

12

Planning and the New Deal

Merriam's role in the New Deal touches issues as complex for the analysis of his career as for the study of the intellectual history of the period itself. Roosevelt's persistent if unsystematic search for advice from the new social scientists could scarcely have avoided turning up Merriam, given his prominence in the profession; but there is more to it than that. In addition to Merriam's work with organizations for social science, he had been engaged throughout the twenties in the building of a system of associations of local government officials. The purpose of such an organization was to be the same as that for social science: exchanges of information, the creation of machinery for research, interchange and identification of personnel. To the extent that the New Deal involved a new bureaucratization of the federal government in its relation to state and local government, Merriam's efforts to structure the governmental professions and to center their professional associations on the campus of the University of Chicago gave him an important position in the training and staffing of the new bureaucracy.

The state governors of the twenties who had interested themselves in administrative reform were all familiar with Merriam's efforts. The governors included Frank Lowden of Illinois, Harry Byrd of Virginia, and, of course, Franklin Roosevelt of New York. As leaders in the Conference of State Governors, they provided an important cross section of influential state and local America. Any of them, as president, would have found Merriam's influence in that community and its preoccupation with new ideas extraordinarily useful.

In addition, Merriam had retained his place among the old Progressives through his friendship with Harold Ickes. There were others, too, with whom Merriam exchanged lists of prospective leaders throughout the twenties, lists accompanied by pungent commentaries ticking off virtues and defects important to their efforts at prophecy. Among the Democrats still available in 1932 they liked Newton Baker most of all, although Roosevelt's gubernatorial victory in 1928 and his magic name moved him higher on the list than an estimate of his intellect would have placed him. True to their heritage of Victorian hypochondriacal health worship, they admired his victory over polio, not only for the feat itself and its seemingly obvious indication of superior character, but also for the mystical evidence it provided that something new had happened to him as a result of the disease. Suffering had developed his insight, had transformed the handsome young aristocrat whom Merriam and others remembered from World War I into a wiser and more sensitive democrat. From the vantage point of their progressivism with its dependence upon the philanthropist-politician for leadership, the combination was almost too true to be good. Like great charismatic figures in any day, Roosevelt drew together two generations: the men of his own past who saw in him the promise of rebirth, and a younger group just coming to politics to seek new answers to current dilemmas. With respect to the academic and governmental communities which he influenced, Merriam helped in the bridging of the generations, using Harold Ickes and their joint glorification of a progressive Roosevelt to bring a younger, modern generation to power.

The chief vehicle for Merriam's approach to the New Deal through the Chicago center for state and local government was his friendship with Louis Brownlow and the organization of the Public Administration Clearing House (PACH) at 1313 East Sixtieth Street. Merriam's association with Harold Ickes led to the second entree to the New Deal through the planning group which came to be known as the National Resources Planning Board. The two of them, PACH and the NRPB, represent the transformation in the New Deal of the two major groups from Merriam's Progressive past: the public service professionals who had managed the research bureaus and the reform agencies of the older era, and those academics whose interest in conservation and environment, economics, and social control had led them to construct a reforming and reformed social science.

Merriam's friendship with Louis Brownlow was perhaps the closest of his career. Brownlow represented the practitioners of the new public administration, the non-academics who viewed the universities with a certain suspicion; but Brownlow, an unschooled, self-taught ex-journalist from a country town in Missouri, admired academia and saw in Merriam something he might have been himself. Brownlow had served as commissioner of the District of Columbia during World War I and had joined the new city manager movement. He had turned a recent battle as Knoxville's first manager—he suffered a nervous collapse under the political pressures of the job—into a parable of an administrative Samson outmaneuvered by political Philistines. Like many of the enthusiasts for the new reform method, he developed the biblical method of glorifying defeat as a lesson necessary for the ultimate victory.

The two men worked together without the competition which could have cooled an academic or administrative friendship for either man, given their personalities. Merriam enjoyed the myth that he had given up politics and governmental administration for the life of the scholar. Brownlow relished the title of "Doctor" which an honorary degree conferred upon him, but often remarked that the only "exam" he had ever taken was for a driver's license. This was part of his ritual of self-mythology, He knew his public administrators, and he knew the bases of their suspicions of academics. Above all, he knew that scientific knowledge, no matter how "true" it could be proved to be, had to be integrated with the administrator's experience before it could be made functional. Brownlow's representation of this fact to the academics was the basis of one part of his success. The other part rested on his capacity to keep his constituency among the professional public servants convinced of the necessity of continued association with the academic community as one of mutual benefit. The conflict in point of view could be made productive if the threat of each to the other were moderated by a sense of community which did not violate the independence of each member of the association. Brownlow, through PACH, managed the building, its resources and facilities, its joint reference library, its publicity and public relations. Merriam, through the Spelman Fund, managed Brownlow, in effect, by providing him with funds to facilitate the forming of new associations and the backing of research programs and publications. Idea man Beardsley Ruml played his role in philanthropy, the business community, and, for a period of time, as dean of the Social Sciences Division at the University of Chicago. The power generated by the three men was based on discovering what needed to be known, encouraging research, and controlling the financial resources. In the preceding generation such entrepreneurial roles had been played by a much smaller elite: the presidents and trustees of the universities. Merriam, Brownlow, and Ruml took over the management and aided in the transfer of control to the practicing professions themselves.

The problem of how to use such a system was far more serious than the structure of the system itself made it appear. PACH had to become a financially self-sustaining operation, over and above any seed money it received from its donor. Its chief sources of income were to be the fees paid by the organizations it served: state and local government, the federal government, and the associations of public officials for whom it solicited projects for study and funds for research or to whom it provided office and administrative services. It was a more complex example of a method used by other governmental research agencies which were privately endowed and operated. While it was thus, technically speaking, a corporation organized not for profit, it was an institution purveying services for which it expected to be paid. Unlike a philanthropic foundation supporting its own costs of the distribution of money, the Public Administration Clearing House was to sustain itself by the sale of its services.

Ultimately, not only the utility but the continuity of the system Merriam and Brownlow were controlling depended upon the willingness of governmental officials, political and administrative alike, to use the advisory services provided. Foundations, following traditions established by their philanthropist creators, judged the efficacy of the research institutions they supported by their actual rather than simply their hypothetical utility. If they were intended to give government useful advice, then government had better be willing to find that advice useful. Thus, it was absolutely necessary for Brownlow and Merriam as entrepreneurs to get government to listen to the advice, indeed, to request the advice, even though the cost of the service was privately subscribed by a foundation. While the relative independence of the Spelman Fund from the Rockefeller Foundation gave Merriam and Brownlow a remarkably free hand in their use of its funds, the board of PACH, interlocked with the Spelman Fund and the Foundation and including Frank Lowden and Harry Byrd among them, required Brownlow to make systematic reports, which he did in the form of a daily diary recording his activities from November 1933 until the eve of World War II. It is a record of what, in another context, might be called influence peddling. Brownlow, in effect, ran a "brains lobby" whose function it was to convince departments of government that they needed the advice of the groups he represented.[1]

For example, when the War Department needed a study of the managerial problems of the Panama Railroad Company and its relation to other government agencies, Brownlow suggested that the University of Chicago and PACH were in a position to finance such a study, provided it be along lines acceptable to the managers of research. An internal administrative study of such a company would not do. Professor Marshall Dimock of the University of Chicago happened to be working in the direction suggested. Of course, that was what Secretary of War George H. Dern and Governor Julian L. Schley of the Canal Zone claimed they had wanted all along, and once Brownlow was able to convince Governor Schley that Dimock had no railroad investments, it could be managed.[2]

The method—and it was to be the central one for the advisory program Merriam would plan for the later New Deal—was built on a scheme which deliberately and systematically sought advisers who were outside government and could be counted upon to remain so. As one diary entry reads in November 1933, Harry Hopkins wanted Paul Betters, secretary of the American Municipal Association, to become his principal assistant in the operation of the Civil Works Administration in Washington. Betters was running the American Municipal Association in Chicago at that point, but much of his time was going into the problem of Civil Works. Hopkins's suggestion was logical enough, but Brownlow spent an evening talking Betters out of it. Instead, Brownlow suggested that Betters set up a Washington office for the American Municipal Association to concentrate on Civil Works, establish himself there as consultant to Hopkins rather than assistant, hire someone else to run the main AMA office in Chicago, and apply to the Spelman Fund for $10,000 with which to pay for the new man in Chicago. Brownlow had that sum in unexpended funds which would be lapsing on 31 December, and he knew the transfer could be made. The principle was clear enough: the independence of the consultant guaranteed government and consultant alike freedom from the bureaucratic entanglements which could so easily and so subtly shift emphasis away from Betters's specialization—Civil Works—to the problems of being a government administrator. The separation of the source of advice from the administrative structure in which the advice would be used was to be assurance of a needed measure of professional objectivity. "Nonpartisan" and "objectivity," as well as "professional" and "social science," were terms on which Merriam and Brownlow easily agreed, they suggested professional and financial independence from the entangled careers of politician and administrator. Their younger associates, already beginning to enjoy their new political power, were more inclined to be skeptical.[3]

By preventing the absorption of advisers into the administration of government Brownlow also achieved the continuing independence of his and Merriam's advisory system. If the system itself was to be constantly losing personnel to government, operating as a selection and training service for government, its own continuity would be in jeopardy. Advisers who entered government service would become identified not simply with the specialization which qualified them as advisers in the first place but with the partisan politics of the administration. While Merriam and Brownlow did not seem to see any way in which this would necessarily threaten the positions of specialists in the organizations to which they would need to return, they did see the danger to the continuity of social research which partisan identification could make. By the end of the New Deal–Fair Deal years when the almost total alliance of the Democratic party and American academics would blot out the pre–New Deal years, insistence on nonpartisan independence seemed a little quaint to younger critics. But they did not realize how effectively the twenty-year dominance of the system Merriam and Brownlow established had obscured the older generation's experiences with partisanship and its problems.

Roosevelt's appointment of Harold Ickes as secretary of the interior provided Merriam his most direct route into the New Deal. Ickes's inclination to isolate himself from influences he suspected—and to view an attempt to influence as itself suspicious—gave Merriam's long-standing association with him an authority it might not otherwise have had. Ickes knew that Chicago was the base of his political power as well as the background of his political experience and that an important part of both were represented in the career of Charles Merriam. Roosevelt's appointment of Ickes as secretary of the interior was also the most effective means of bringing the still viable fragments of the old progressivism into the New Deal. The Department of the Interior had been Hoover's choice as the base of his never-to-be-launched program of social reform. It had been the focus of the

231

conservation movement and some of the earlier American environmentalists' bloodiest controversies.

That presidents with surprising regularity saw the Department of the Interior as a center for a new redistribution of wealth or new energy for reform is attested to in part by the men who preceded Harold Ickes. Columbus Delano and Albert Fall were two of a kind, to be sure, but then so were Carl Schurz and Ray Lyman Wilbur. All past, present, and future planning for the uses of the country's treasure of natural economic resources, other than those which could be clearly designated as private industry and agriculture, were controlled by the Department of the Interior. And the complex interlocking with industry and agriculture complicated the department's position, as did the rapidly developing controversies over hydroelectric power.

Franklin Roosevelt's decision in July following the passage of the National Industrial Recovery Act to separate the NRA provisions of the act from the public works provisions and his appointment of the secretary of the interior as administrator of public works thus represented a fundamentally traditionalist view of the administration of American government. The public aspect of the Public Works Administration was to be sharply distinguished from private industrial recovery. The Department of the Interior provided a public counterbalance to the government's continued support of a national "private" industry. The division also assured Congress control of its version of public interest through the very involved committee structure produced by the years of overseeing the activities of the Department of the Interior. Supporters of the Army Corps of Engineers, for example, like the rivers and harbors bloc, would continue to influence the affairs of the department, as would defenders of the policies of the National Park Service.

By placing public works in the hands of a secretary of the interior whose entire career had been involved in the progressive opposition to the domination of the public interest by private industry, Roosevelt certified a traditional, progressive management of public works. By placing the administration of public works in the hands of a secretary of the interior committed to the progressive view of political reform with its condemnation of the life blood of classical politics—patronage—Roosevelt also perpetuated the conflicts with Congress which that department could generate. The route of public works programming from Washington to the vast jumble of state, county, and city boards, commissioners, and offices would have to follow the well-worn paths of congressional and political prerogative, past the public troughs and pork barrels.

Roosevelt hedged his concession to old-line progressivism by giving Harry Hopkins a collection of mandates which could override Ickes's brand of reform with the less systematic, more compassionate mechanisms of politics, but this was a matter filled with conflicts and confusions. Party organization in the urban areas where public works and unemployment had the most meaning and the most potential depended upon patronage and its distribution. To threaten that would have been destructive of the very nature of modern urban politics and, at the same time, of the most immediately available conduit for the distribution of public employment. On the other hand, the possibility of turning public works into a scandal surpassing those of the Grant and Harding administrations combined was a danger not worth risking. In some respects Harold Ickes was ideally suited to his position between the two dangers. He would struggle to prevent victories by either side, and he would accept his inevitable defeats with loyal, if disgruntled, resignation.

The relationship between Merriam and Ickes beautifully, at times even brilliantly, epitomized the contradictions. For Merriam, Ickes was a friendly and direct route to power. For Ickes, Merriam was a trusted and respected source of access to a knowledgeable academic and professional community. The key was in their friendship and trust, sufficient to render disagreement harmless, even when both men felt strongly on a subject. When Merriam pleaded with Ickes that he negotiate with the Chicago Sanitary District trustees for the building of new sewers, for example, Ickes refused. He blasted that "rotten bunch" (the trustees) who wanted to get its "dirty fingers" on $120,000,000 of federal money without supervision. Merriam had no illusions about Chicago Sanitary District politics which needed dispelling by Ickes, but he thought the jobs more important,[4] and the Sanitary District was not going to employ work crews as the fall of 1933 approached. Ickes obviously didn't agree, but he was quick to soothe whatever hurt feelings his friend might have suffered by the heat of his reply and assured him that they really could have their disagreements.

Between March and July, Merriam gave Ickes reports of Chicago politics which Ickes could pass on to the president. This was a practice which became increasingly important in the months following Anton

Cermak's assassination as the temporarily disorganized Democrats continued to tilt with the recently unseated Republicans for control of the state. On Merriam's advice, Ickes informed Roosevelt as early as June that the Democratic situation in the state was bad and that the appointment of the right Democrats to fill the right patronage openings in the state would be crucial. He threatened a backward swing of the political pendulum, as he put it, if he were not allowed to exert influence over any appointments.[5]

Through 1933 FDR sought ways of using Merriam in the administration, communicating them through Ickes. Ickes thought Merriam ought to have been tempted by the offer of the commissionership of Hawaii, where he could do more good "in formulating a colonial policy for the U.S. than by attending all the dry-as-dust committee meetings that you seem to thrive on." And in December 1933 when Roosevelt asked, again through Ickes, whether Merriam might be willing to accept an appointment to the Civil Service Commission "with a view to drafting a new Civil Service law along broader lines," Merriam used the occasion instead for his first face-to-face meeting with the new president and to press the appointment of Leonard D. White in his stead. The meeting with FDR impressed Merriam deeply. The president's informed and extensive knowledge of civil service was, from Merriam's point of view, remarkable, for it extended backward into the Progressive tradition from which the reform movement had sprung and forward into the kind of systematic managerial analysis which Merriam knew the future required. It was the president's awareness of technical needs beyond his own immediate competence that might most have impressed a man like Merriam, not simply in itself, but in its combination with a fearless sense of his own political responsibility to manage and control, regardless of what his experts might consider his degree of comprehension.[6]

For a brief moment in the aftermath of the Cermak assassination, Merriam entertained the possibility of another mayoralty campaign. Key Chicago newspaper figures, Colonel Knox and Victor Watson, were eager to move Merriam into position as the consolidator of the victory over the Thompson forces which the Cermak election had been presumed to have been. They approached Ickes, who, in turn, discussed the matter with Merriam. "This may offer a real chance," Ickes wrote his erstwhile candidate, "which I trust you will not hesitate to take advantage of." Merriam was willing enough; but the consequences of his party affiliations were still to stand in the way. Governor Henry Horner, a Democrat and many thought the creation of Cermak, wanted none of this Republican turned Progressive turned—reformer was about the jist of Horner's opinion. He told Watson that Merriam was too conservative, that he would seek to abolish gambling in Chicago and that Chicago wouldn't be able to take that. The idea was absurd; but its practical effects were clear enough. As Ickes reported to Merriam, FDR would have been willing to refrain from backing Boss Kelly—particularly in view of the possibility that Big Bill Thompson would be one of the opponents—but he would not be able to come out openly for Merriam.[7]

Merriam's work for the New Deal began on 20 July 1933, with the appointment of the National Planning Board. Speed in the planning and distribution of public works once the National Industrial Recovery Act went into effect was the problem. The difficulty in arriving at priorities and criteria of judgment pressed on Ickes as administrator of public works the necessity of making decisions in the face not only of the demands of local communities seeking federal funds but also of the urgency for employment of work forces throughout the country. For an old-line progressive it was an utterly satanic temptation, as Ickes found himself surrounded by all the evils he had ever known.

His first solution was an advisory board which he could chair. He chose two men with Chicago backgrounds, his friend Charles Merriam and, to serve with him as vice-chairman, the president's uncle, Frederic A. Delano. Wesley C. Mitchell was appointed to the committee on the advice of Louis Brownlow. Mitchell was less well known to Ickes, and if his connection with *Recent Social Trends*, the report of the Hoover administration's committee, was known to Ickes, it seems not to have troubled him. To appoint such a board had been one of the ideas in the concluding deliberations of that committee with which Merriam can be directly associated. It is certainly the case that for Merriam, Delano, Mitchell, and Brownlow the concepts of planning as envisaged by the committee's report were what they had in mind from the beginning as they arranged for the formation of the board.

Ickes's sense of emergency had produced the entering wedge for the development of a planning agency at the very top echelons of government, within the president's cabinet, where politics and administration met. The placing of the board in that sensitive a position, together with the problems of Ickes's personality, set the issues with which the board would have to contend: the politics of planning by experts in areas

235

crucial to the pork-barrel problems of government spending, and the influence of academic policy advisers on high-level policy makers whose responsibilities derived from presidential appointment.

What seems clear enough is that Ickes saw the board as *his* board, made up of his advisers, and that the board saw itself according to the mandate of *Recent Social Trends*, embryonic, to be sure, and limited in its initial conception, but on its way toward becoming the nation's first presidential agency for social planning. The potential for conflict between the traditional presidential advisory system which the cabinet had become and the new advisory system generated by the development of the social sciences was clear at the outset.

From the early stages of the board's operation, Merriam's handling of Ickes used the old friendship to new advantage. In a letter from Chicago early in August Merriam began issuing his warnings. He thought TVA needed stronger executive direction. As "the most difficult of all the 'plans' " it could easily become "a grand flop of prize dimensions. Watch your step." He suggested that Ickes use his work on the "advisory planning board," as he called it, as the model for the cabinet advisory board, where he thought there would be a danger of interference with the necessary immediate actions. "There is danger that they also may get in the way and gum up the situation with too much discussion, and too long and perhaps fatal delay." He then went on to suggest the crux of the matter: that Ickes give Colonel Henry M. Waite, whom on Brownlow's advice he had placed in charge of public works, fuller responsibility; "lean on Colonel Waite and hold him responsible, subject to your general direction."[8]

Merriam's peroration is interesting because it illustrates the method of praise and threat which he alone could use in addressing Ickes.

Hon. Harold L. Ickes is taking over powers and responsibilities *such as no Cabinet officer has ever held* in time of peace, and if we are to preserve your health and usefulness, you must be relieved of too much detail and placed in a position where only the most important decisions must be made by you. . . . As I said when you took me for a ride, it seems imperative to *reconsider your whole position* in the light of the new and amazing developments which make you a super Cabinet officer. You will have to protest against too much detail being thrust on you, and get in a position to deal swiftly and effectively with the incredible problems which are rising up thicker and thicker every day and *will continue to come*, owing to your talents.[9]

The underlinings (here printed as italics), the fawning sycophancy, are all calculated to deal with problems being described to Merriam by

Brownlow, who was in Washington watching the potential for debacle of Ickes's refusal to delegate. Brownlow gave Merriam his interpretation of the effect of the letter on Ickes—which was not encouraging. In an effort to help matters, Brownlow tried to prevent Waite from giving up hope and started a chain of messages from Rexford Tugwell to Louis Howe and thence to the president, who was to try to get Ickes to slow down and to delegate authority. Brownlow's final refuge, like Merriam's, was in the threat of breakdown. "I am very much afraid that if he does not change his system there is a danger of physical breakdown within a very short time. I hope that if you have an opportunity to see him again that you will do what you can."[10]

By October Merriam was frantic. In another confidential letter to Ickes he warned of a serious congressional threat to the whole public works program. Blaming the slowness of the program, he recommended the appointment of an accelerator to speed things up, acceptance of decisions of state boards as final where the amounts involved were under $100,000, and, as he had in his previous letters, a variety of technical mechanisms he thought might help. But slowness was not the main issue, and he knew it; he boldly attacked the real problem in his middle paragraph, following the form now taken by most of the Merriam-Ickes letters: open with concern, suggest details, wallop Ickes's refusal to delegate, end with soothing praise.

> The details of these projects, such as most personnel, small expenditures and sundry, like matters should not be loaded on you or come over your desk, but be left to your subordinates.... I am afraid you are dealing with altogether too many minor questions, which must be trusted to someone, especially in an overwhelming emergency such as this. If you cannot let go of some of these details, it seems to me that you are likely to collapse and the plan with you. I am saying this in all seriousness, taking the liberty of an old friend and companion, deeply solicitous for your welfare and success, as well as that of the common cause.[11]

Ickes's reply opens with "My dear Charlie" and proceeds to a far more reasoned defense than Merriam's letter might have received had it been written by anyone else. He liked the idea of an "accelerator," but argued that the delay was not in the stage of approving projects but in getting them started after the allocations were made. The chief difficulty was in the recruitment of lawyers. He defended himself against the charge that he was supervising every detail, insisting that, "believe it or not," he was actually signing important contracts involving millions of dollars without even pausing to read them cursorily. He concluded once again by voicing his appreciation of Merriam's friendly concern and helpful suggestions and asking him to feel free to write at any time.[12]

As Merriam was to learn, that aspect of the problem was insoluble, though familiarity with it made it somewhat more surmountable than it had seemed at first. By 1935 dealing with Ickes had become a kind of obbligato which Merriam and his colleagues played while their main attention centered on the ultimate solution of the problem. In his diary Ickes comments on a visit from Frederic Delano in which Delano purports to detail a recent argument among members of the board to decide which of them would tell Ickes that he was working too hard.[13] They still used affectionate terms designed to appeal: the poor overworked man, the threat of breakdown, the old ethic hammered out. Delano even claimed to have taken the secretary's side against his colleagues on the issue of whether the board would become an independent agency, or at least so Ickes remembered it when he confided to his diary. The reply from his colleagues which Delano relayed to the secretary was neatly devised to conceal the truth. "His colleagues agreed with him so far as I was concerned but remarked that they didn't know who the next Secretary of the Interior might be." Ickes's ego swallowed whole the morsel well prepared to be the opposite, almost exactly, of the truth. If one were to stay with the cabinet setup as the primary planning organization, a secondary planning agency in the Department of the Interior was not a wholly impossible idea, at least in 1935; but with Ickes as secretary, it was probably hopeless.

In the late battles of the New Deal as Roosevelt struggled against Congress and the Court, Ickes observed the defections of the progressives with an emotion as close to nostalgia as his manner ever allowed him to come. "It is funny how men move in and out of politics," he wrote in his diary in mid-February 1937. "Hiram Johnson stayed in until a week ago Monday when he moved out on the Court issue, and unfortunately other Progressives moved out with him. One thing about my old friend Charles E. Merriam is that he has been the most consistent liberal of them all. I have always known where to find him. There have been times when he and I seemed to be all that was left of the old Progressive movement."[14]

While Ickes was not Merriam's only access to influence in the New Deal, the relationship was significant in its reflection of the transition the New Deal brought about in the role of the social sciences in government: from advice to management, from influence to control, from the progressive hostility to politics and its separation from administration to a newer concept of that relationship. Merriam was bringing to power a new generation whose drive for independence from the limitations Ickes represented would produce serious conflict in the social sciences and in government. Again, Merriam's sense of the utility of compromise won out. The groups were the same though the context was different. The SSRC academics, the Brownlow group of practitioners, the new planning professionals, and Harold Ickes as the last of the old progressives could all be brought to some measure of agreement in some limited set of areas. Merriam was still convinced that it could be done, that it had to be done, and that Franklin Roosevelt agreed. The planning group which Ickes formed in the Public Works Administration served Merriam's purpose, but not without some serious strains.

"If we cannot think of any better lines of social control," Merriam had written his brother in September 1933, "it is not unlikely that violence will settle the lines of social organization for a generation or so, and without being an alarmist there is a chance that the whole of western civilization will be pulled down."[15] Both Merriams respected experimentation, both had praised pragmatism, and both were willing to give the new administration every chance and every hope; but the new Roosevelt magic had seemed a flimsy protection for a democratic society which was going to have to trudge through yet another depression winter. Were the new programs helping? It was impossible to get more than a babble of responses. Germany had fallen once again, and the oceans of 1933 were scant protection to the generation which had crossed them in 1918. It was a threatening backdrop against which to view the beginnings of the disorganized struggle for recovery which the New Deal was rapidly becoming.

The National Planning Board met in Washington in October 1933 to try to give more shape to the program it had begun the previous summer. Its chief focus at the beginning was on the establishment of contacts with the state and local planning groups organized in various parts of the country over the previous fifteen or twenty years. If the requests for public works projects could be channeled through recognized groups whose interests were in rational planning, the understandably anguished cries for federal funds could be translated into some kind of order less subject to a sense of emergency.

Both Merriam and Mitchell reminded the assembled group of their relationship to the Committee on Recent Social Trends but pointed to

239

differences between the mandate from Hoover and that which they already considered themselves to have from FDR. According to Mitchell, Hoover's emphasis had been upon the finding of facts out of which he would build programs, while Roosevelt wanted plans of action. Equally important, Mitchell considered one of the most relevant consequences of *Recent Social Trends* to be its emphasis upon coordination of plans and the interrelation of effects, the consciousness that changes in one area produce changes in others. At the same time, the board's emphasis was and would continue to be on a distinction between coordination and control. Following much the same kind of decentralization and regionalization that Merriam and his colleagues used in the organization of the SSRC, the board concentrated on building up and investing power in state and local planning groups whose work would then be coordinated nationally.[16] This kind of regionalization and decentralization had two important virtues. Writers such as Howard W. Odum and the authors of *I'll Take My Stand* had emphasized the cultural and historical nature of America's regions, not as the basis of fixed political differences, but as the basis of social and geographical differences bound to the history of cultural settlement and the organization and development of natural resources. The nonpartisan—or, it could be argued, antipolitical—base of *Recent Social Trends* had implied at least some kind of escape from politics to scientific rationality. The planning board of the New Deal was to be built on an effort to push that idea further.[17]

The second virtue of decentralization rested on a practical ground which in some important respects was not altogether consistent with the first. State and local governments were to provide the legislative and administrative bases for the local planning agencies of the National Planning Board. The creation of these agencies assured the national board of continuing attention to local needs and conditions and, thereby, continued local support for planning. Local governments could also be assured of their continued tap on available federal funds—once they submitted to being coordinated. This was the same kind of carrot-and-stick approach which Merriam and Brownlow used in their relationships with philanthropists and local government professionals. It was also an important ingredient in the American practice of federalism. The seeming inconsistency, however, stems from the persistent conflict with the fact that the process of regionalization had to take place through the traditional political agencies—state and local governments—which were often most likely to be threatened by such rationalization. Merriam's answer here was the traditional two-pronged Progressive method: persuasion and education. For Merriam, local politics and political structure were the continuing reality of American federalism. They were not, in the foreseeable future at least, to be got rid of by reform; and this was no grudging concession. Local politics was the ultimate protection of democracy and the most effective vehicle for its continuity. A scientific democracy which foresaw the end of politics, even in the interest of social efficiency, was a dangerous delusion.

Opponents of Merriam's position were not hard to find, although they constituted a group as fraught with internal dissent as they were sustained by their common opposition to what the planning board came to represent. Agencies of the federal government already established to oversee natural resources in the states could ally themselves with scientific management adherents who saw the federal government as the only effective controller of national resource policy. At the same time, cabinet officers overseeing administrative needs of agencies under their control were bound to be torn between the professional advice of their subordinates and the political needs of constituent pressure groups threatened with "coordination" by a planning board.

One opinion which Merriam and Mitchell shared from the outset was that the board's effectiveness depended upon its proximity to the president. Yet it can be suggested that the closer the board got to the president as the nation's chief politician, the better target it made for its political and administrative opposition. From 1933 until 1939 the planning board existed under the uncomfortable protection of a cabinet group which mediated its access to the president. Freed by the reorganizations of 1939 and 1940 and established in the newly created Executive Office of the president, the board aroused congressional opposition sufficient to end it in 1943.

The War Department's fight with the planning board assumed several shapes from the beginning. In September 1933, Assistant Secretary of War Harry Woodring denounced Ickes's nonpolitical appointments to oil boards and other advisory boards. The next year, the very meaning of coordination and cooperation was called into serious question by Secretary of War Dern and Secretary Ickes, with the planning board the center of the dispute. In April 1934 Dern tried to argue the superiority of the Army Corps of Engineers for water resource planning on grounds which opponents of that group's planning had always found indefensible, but to which Dern held deep commitment. A single plan was not a good idea, he kept insisting.

> For example, putting an end to stream pollution seems to have little or no connection with improving the streams for navigation, flood control, power or irrigation, because it is chiefly a matter of the construction of sewage disposal plants, which so far has been a municipal question.... Reforestation plays an important part in flood control and soil erosion but it may be carried on quite independently of river improvement works.... Each of these activities is a special problem, to be handled by a special group of experts if satisfactory results are to be obtained. Here is a place where too much coordination, or the coordination of unrelated activities, might prove harmful instead of beneficial.[18]

Given the philosophies of integrated planning espoused by the planning group, it is hard to see where compromises with Dern could have been made. As his letter makes clear, the War Department and the Army Corps of Engineers were committed to accepting as given the administrative and political conditions of the local environments in which they worked. This fact was the better part of political wisdom and it was ultimately to help defeat the board. But it reduced the concept of coordination to a piecemeal provision of mechanistic solutions to one problem at a time, and it virtually denied the possibility that problems might arise unexpectedly out of the relation of solutions to one another. What Mitchell believed to be the fundamental contribution of the approach to planning set forth by *Recent Social Trends* was thereby denied. Dern argued, quite rightly, that the army engineers had far vaster resources of data and technical skills for making the studies the president wanted made; but the point of view would always produce the same results—more politically appealing results, as Dern pointed out.

In 1934 the board published the document which bore the title *Final Report*, summarizing its first year on the eve of its transformation from the National Planning Board into the National Resources Committee. The depth of Merriam's concern shows clearly through the pages of what was, in significant part, his own prose. The dilemma is clear enough even over the familiar tone of Merriam's prophetic certitude. Planning was to be seen as a familiar ingredient in American history: Hamilton's *Report on Manufactures*, Albert Gallatin on internal improvements, Clay and and the American System, and on through a litany of names which included Theodore Roosevelt and Woodrow Wilson, as well as, of course, Herbert Hoover. But history was only half the story. Planning existed elsewhere in the world of 1933 and not in forms American would find acceptable. The report lists "the systematic efforts of Japan, Russia, Italy, and more recently, of Germany." England and France are mentioned briefly, but the thrust of Merriam's argument is that American planning rests on democratic decentralization, on local and national freedom, on the absence of regimentation. "It is clear that an undertaking such as that now in process among the Soviets, the Nazis, or the Fascists is not adapted either to the governmental organization of this country or to economic and technological conditions widely different from those found there." And he goes on to characterize American planning as "experimental, evolutionary, and at times undoubtedly somewhat illogical.... To those who think only in terms of one or another set of 'isms', the American system appears socialistic or individualistic or confused and illogical, as the observer looks at one or another phase of our national life."[19]

The effort to give the term "national planning" an acceptable public meaning was to be Merriam's task over the next few years, and indeed, for much of the decade. That his efforts appear to have been something of a failure—by the end of World War II the term would be carefully excised from popular governmental vocabulary and in use only with respect to military or foreign policy programs where the concepts it seemed to embody were more acceptable—is easily misunderstood out of context. In repeated tributes to scientific management and to the efforts of Hoover, the *Final Report* points to the urgency for coordinated planning apparent since World War I, treating the depression as the ultimate event in the catalog of premonitory experiences going back to the 1880s and prefigured by the emerging progressive consciousness of the greater need for organization, direction, and control. At the same time events of the thirties had already begun to demonstrate a willingness on the part of the American public to accept irrational planning concepts—Huey Long, Francis Townsend, and Father Coughlin appear to have been the most dangerous leaders—which threatened everything that social science progressivism had sought to represent.

In addition, Merriam knew early in the game what position former President Hoover was going to take, and while he did not overestimate Hoover's public appeal by then, he knew what following he would continue to represent. The last dinner of the Recent Social Trends group with Hoover took place in late September 1933, and Merriam relayed Hoover's views to Ickes in some detail shortly thereafter. Indeed, for Mitchell more than Merriam but for Merriam more than

243

most, Hoover's opposition to the New Deal would present the dilemma in its most acute form: that scientific planning was America's first order of governmental business but that the New Deal was a harsh regimentation of American life which was leading to a European form of tyranny. Both Merriam and Mitchell reviewed Hoover's *The Challenge to Liberty* when it appeared in 1934, Mitchell with far greater sensitivity to the problem than Merriam. Mitchell sent an advance copy of his review to Hoover and corresponded with him about it, raising the issue which troubled committed nonpartisans like Mitchell. "I suggest that though you frequently couple national planning with regimentation in your book, you are really an exponent of deliberate and thorough national planning." The letter and the review led Hoover to a whole sequence of replies, angry, disordered, unclear. In one burst of his characteristic form of argument he wrote,

> A National planning board of your concept would need be either governmental or non-governmental. If governmental it would need be either appointed or elected. If appointed today its purpose would be to create a Socialist State—or at least a Regimented one. The Germans tried to elect such an organism. Nearly every government in Europe has tried to create some sort of such organism, and they have atrophied or died. As a matter of fact, the whole scheme of democratic government is an attempt by Parliaments, Congresses, Executives, and Courts to include "National Planning." Your trouble, as I see it, is a lack of faith in these organisms. I will not dispute your justification.[20]

In his reply Mitchell acknowledged the "emergency" nature of the programs of 1933 but expressed a strong feeling that the board which the committee was about to recommend to the president would avoid that, would return to the spirit of *Recent Social Trends*. It was clear that Hoover did not understand, and it would apparently become clear to Mitchell that Roosevelt did not understand, either. Mitchell conceived of federal planning as a full-time professional responsibility. Despite struggles in that direction—and the direction was by no means as clear to others as it was to Mitchell—the planning board never achieved that form.

The planning board spent its first year traveling about the country to stimulate interest in planning in local communities and among groups of state and local government officials. Merriam's rhetoric shaped the tone of the debates with its frank confrontation of the issue of ideology.

This sound and reasonable planning is the very safeguard [against] what many people fear, planning accompanied by violence, tyranny, by harsh repression, the working out of a blue-print in a frame, and planting it down on the soft flesh of a people. Sound planning is a way to prevent that.... I have never been convinced that wisdom died with John Stuart Mill and Karl Marx.... There is a middle ground in America.[21]

A meeting of the National Planning Board in Knoxville in May 1934 was addressed by TVA directors Arthur Morgan, H. A. Morgan, and David Lilienthal. The lengthy transcripts of those meetings illustrate far better that anything else the depth of difference being compromised in the intense, if brief, mood of cooperation which, in its initial stages, the planning group was able to achieve. Arthur Morgan's commitment to a Bellamy-like concept of industrial modernization confronts H. A. Morgan's Turner-like belief in the rejuvenation of a geographical-agricultural tradition, while Lilienthal presents the power reformer's sense of a public interest in the modernization of natural resources for democratic purposes, the balancing of output against need. Meetings could sound in their way like the camp meetings of old, with model conversions to planning cited as examples to potential converts and threats to potential backsliders. Vincent Miles, district chairman for District Six, told his story. "I sent circular #5 to the five Governors and received no reply except from the Governor of Missouri. He replied that he had turned the whole matter over to Mr. Harry Truman of Kansas City. Immediately the Missouri Planning Board was established....I have used Missouri as an example throughout the other states."[22]

Within a year there were many successes to be pointed to in the effects of the planning board as a stimulator of local planning. Not only the board's own statements, but the presidential files indicate the extent. A letter in early 1935 from Governor Landon of Kansas asks for an added grant from the board for the encouragement of state planning and to make it easier to obtain adequate appropriation. Governor Talmadge of Georgia appointed a planning board for the state, and Ickes was beginning to ask Roosevelt for more money.[23]

Roosevelt had already indicated his own interest in the continuity of the board and, initially, his willingness to see it removed from the Department of the Interior and placed more directly under his control, a step recommended by the *Final Report*. Roosevelt wanted the term "planning" removed from the title, and the board members began to

make suggestions. Charles Eliot suggested "natural resources" bu
Mitchell thought that tended to exclude "human resources," which
were, from his point of view, perhaps America's largest resource. This
distinction also illustrates the beginnings both of the need to express
openly the sense of restriction felt by some board advocates because of
the emphasis upon water and land resources and of the pressures to
enlarge the board's planning mandate to include economic and social
issues. When Merriam suggested "national resources," the president
agreed at once.[24]

At the meeting of 26 July 1934 the president outlined his own view of the
board's mandate: that it formulate a long-range program, with a plan
strong enough to withstand congressional pressures. A water and land
report by the first of December would leave time for public discussions
of it before Congress returned. Implied in the president's view of the
board was its potential use as a bulwark against pork-barrel demands, a
hedge against the irrationalities of local political pressure. He objected,
however, to the report's discussion of "informational and educational"
programs, which he felt would be "too much like propaganda,"
although he wanted the Executive Order setting up the board to "specify
everything including the kitchen stove and such other matters as may be
directed by the President." For the moment at least, the president had
completely agreed with the planning board's concept of planning: but it
was a brief moment, as board members were to discover.[25]

Competition between the planning board and the cabinet had been
going on almost from the beginning. Since the initial board was entirely
under Ickes's control as administrator of public works, he had run
interference for it when necessary. In February 1934 Delano, as
chairman of the board, asked Ickes to explain what relation the board
would have to the president's recent announcement of a cabinet
committee to produce a water use national plan. Ickes's explanation was
clear enough, but it could scarcely answer the question of why such a
project should be set up without preliminary consultation with the
secretary's own planning group.[26]

Like many of the programs Roosevelt was pressed to create in ad hoc
form, the Committee to Develop a Water Use National Plan was the
direct product of pressures from congressmen threatening to fill
legislative hoppers with demands for flood control projects. The
president's rough calculation already indicated a possible total of $3
billion for the project, which, given the complex nature of American

water resources and their frequent crossing of state boundaries, could become one of the biggest unintended boondoggles of the century. Roosevelt called for a twenty-five-year plan, and Senator Norris introduced a resolution to create the cabinet committee to produce it. The secretaries of interior, agriculture, war, and labor were to establish six subcommittees of technicians for the six major water regions to study the problem. The board's relation to the committee and sub-committees, as Ickes described it, would be through its executive officer's work with the committees.

"The Planning Board should be cock of the walk and take over this proposition and run it in cooperation with the Cabinet Committee," Ickes explained in terms which must have filled his planning board with considerably less enthusiasm than he might have wished. Whatever plans they had begun to formulate for removing themselves from Ickes's control were about to be effectively thwarted; but they still wanted to fight. Even so, their June meeting with the president had given them every reason to believe they had won. They had sent the following telegram to the president the day before the meeting:

Judging from the information coming to us we believe the ideas of a joint committee of nine Cabinet and independent members would prove cumbersome and ineffective. Under the original theory of our Government the Cabinet was to be the National Planning Board. That proved disappointing despite the high general character of the men and also because the Cabinet men were naturally interested in their own departments. Our draft report handed to the President recommended a Board of not more than five disinterested individuals reporting directly to the President. We are personally interested in the cause, not at all in the appointment.[27]

Had Ickes been the sole opponent to independence for the board, the board might still have prevailed, but there were others. A letter quickly circulated by Frances Perkins and signed by her with the names of Henry Wallace, Harold Ickes, and Harry Hopkins, all of whose authorizations she had hastily obtained, voiced very strong objections to the appointment of such a planning board and asked for an immediate conference with the president. "Politically such a board would be open to very heavy fire; executively it would find itself in a very difficult situation. It would be in the position of making plans of the most far reaching importance without the responsibility for carrying out these plans."[28] The letter emphasized the cabinet members' high regard for the members of the planning board but objected to the form of the appointment. Although even in the original plan cabinet members were to be given consultative status in relation to the board, that was clearly insufficient.

The final order creating the National Resources Board was a compromise which in some respects combined both plans, the cabinet committee and the board, but under the control of the cabinet and with Secretary Ickes as chairman. Delano, Merriam, and Mitchell were made members of the cabinet committee but were also appointed to an advisory committee which Delano chaired. They had lost, to be sure, but had they looked back from the vantage point of 1943 to the cabinet complaint which won the day in 1934, they might have felt some sense of prophetic warning in the prediction of heavy political fire. If the first year of the board's existence seemed to demonstrate an American willingness to accept overall national planning as an American concept, it was an attitude which was not to be sustained. Planning was a necessity; the concept of planning was a threat. Where could you go from there?

Over the decade of its operation, the board was to conform to none of the generally accepted historical analyses of the New Deal. Its seventy or more major documents and studies effectively complete the aims of *Recent Social Trends* although they go far beyond that seminal study in comprehensiveness and sophistication of method. Yet if the New Deal was benevolent pragmatism operating without system or ideology, the planning board was system and order committed to an articulate and articulated doctrine of welfare capitalism. If the New Deal sought to center in Washington the responsibility for maintaining a social and economic order, the planning board sought a rational regionalization of the United States which would keep the wellsprings of planning in local communities responding to local needs. If the New Deal was a freewheeling political circus ringmastered by the shrewdest political manipulator of them all, the planning board was the center of a scientific antipolitics devoted to the outlining of true realities—social and scientific ideals, if you will—and dependent not upon what was politically possible from state to state and Congress to Congress but upon economic, geographical, and social conditions as they could be shown to exist. Finally, if the New Deal was the foundation of modern professionalization and bureaucratization of the federal government, the planning board was the vehicle for sustaining the influence of nongovernmental professionals on local and national policy making.

Planning and the New Deal

While the ultimate programs of the New Deal in all the areas where the planning board was active bore the inevitable shape of Roosevelt's politics, the reports of the planning board often served to inform supporters, inflame opposition, and establish the parameters of problems, if only by coordinating the channels of dispute. For those who wanted to see a planning board at the center of the wheel of government, guiding policy and serving as the focus around which all action revolved, the board was a failure from beginning to end; but this was not its function or its effect. The board was intended from the beginning to operate more as a source of highly organized systematic energy whose function it was to counterbalance with available knowledge and direction the pressures and demands of political urgency and need. As such, its failures were always partial successes to the extent that it could be shown to have influenced political programming in more rational directions, while its successes were always partial failures to those whose commitment to systematic analysis led them to see a system battered and brutalized by political maneuvering as an instance of intellectual tragedy. The reports of the board were an effort to bring the best contemporary method to bear on the outlining of what the New Deal programs ought to have been, while the position of the board insured that the programs which were politically possible at any given moment would not be hampered by their critical deviations from the ideal. In that sense, the board can be seen as the measure of the New Deal, in effect, a counter-New Deal. One can consider the board a model of the progressive, nonpolitical side of Roosevelt's mind.

Some aspects of Merriam's view of the board are central both to the exposition of his own beliefs and to the historical significance of his generation of "planners." Chief among them is his insistence that board members be appointed from outside the government and that they serve part time for limited compensation. While the offices of the board were to be in continuous operation under the direction of the executive officer, Charles W. Eliot 2nd, actual meetings of the board were to take place at intervals of four to six weeks, its non-Washington members assembling in Washington from other parts of the country to make policy. Wesley Mitchell's resignation from the board in 1935 was based on his belief that the work of such a board required the full-time attention of its members and he wanted to address himself more fully to his own research. But it is difficult to accept such a reason. That the board was not giving full-time attention to its functions was by

249

Merriam's firm intention, not by any accident of overcommitment on anyone's part. Mitchell's resignation could be interpreted as a criticism of Merriam's concept of a planning board, though Mitchell chose not to state it that way. In addition, for the full decade of the board's existence, Merriam and Charles Eliot maintained a relationship which was considerably less than cordial and on several occasions openly hostile. Personalities aside, there were reasons for difference which stemmed from the conflicting loyalties of a man whose full-time occupation was the overseeing of the board's activities and the development of its programs and of a man who had deliberately designed his role as that of overseer from an extragovernmental, nonpolitical vantage point. Could one maintain a permanent governmental institution which did not focus and professionalize the intellectual loyalties of those whose sole occupation it was to manage it?[29]

Put in another form, the question was this: could the system of local participation in community management which Merriam and Brownlow knew from their childhoods, which they had fostered in their professional careers as community advisers, and which they believed the wartime government of Woodrow Wilson had raised to a high industrial order be transferred to a peacetime federal government? They thought it could, but not simply because of their faith in their own past experience. They also felt deeply that the transfer was not only a useful possibility but an unavoidable necessity. The future of American democratic government rested on it. If planning were to become a federally controlled program which utilized and created federal planners, the democratic experiment would be at an end. As Merriam knew, scientific analysis which conflicted with regional-historical tradition was doomed.

Merriam's chief writing during this period provides us with considerable insight about his reasoning, although the point he was trying to make was not one of the ones his students seemed inclined to pick up. *Political Power* appeared in 1934. The trilogy of which it is a part included *World Politics and Personal Insecurity* by Harold D. Lasswell and *Beyond Conscience* by T. V. Smith. Although the three volumes were initially published separately, they constitute together a summation of the philosophic motivations which underlay Merriam's view of his Chicago School.

The experience of those pre–New Deal years had led to the development of Merriam's own concept of a civic culture for Americans, a culture which would serve as the necessary foundation for a continuing, self-reforming modern industrial community. His interest in civic education and the recurring concern with national loyalty had led him to seek some attempt to reconcile the revolutionary demands of the new social science and its virtual rejection of history with his own increasing awareness of the psychological base of political commitment. That base had to include the individual's awareness of and desire for power, as well as the community's sense of the meaning and purpose of power. The latter sense was built on history, not necessarily the historian's history, but, more importantly, the community's sense of its history. Ceremony, ritual, and myth made far greater contributions to the history of culture than the data collections or scientific analyses of historians, although, in an ideal sense of course, accurate history could aid the process if it chose to.

Merriam's political science began in a self-expulsion from history. John Dewey, as the prophet of the social science movement which turned pragmatism into an affirmation of present experience, became the useful figure—not necessarily by his own choice—in a view of the past as the threat to reform. Yet Merriam, leading political science and espousing much of what Dewey represented, kept recognizing the dangers of an antihistorical view of science.

Political Power seeks to restate the view of sovereignty with which Merriam's own writing had begun and to find bases for power which would depend upon persuasion and participation rather than force and obedience. In a much quoted chapter entitled "The Poverty of Power" Merriam argued that the use of violence is a sign of the weakness of power, not its strength, for violence will produce violent reactions which will keep authority under continuous threat. "Law Among the Outlaws" and "The Credenda and Miranda of Power" contain his discussions of the community nature of power, its dependence upon common customs, ideals, and aspirations. Merriam deals with "culture" as a combination of analytically rational order, disordered fragments of tradition, and emotional attachment to individuals, rituals, and myths. As Merriam recognizes, what makes modern man willing to give his life for the good of the community may transcend scientific reason and violate tradition without being the result of mad emotional fervor. What could make the modern American willing to do so might involve factors even more difficult to describe. The pragmatic foundations of self-sacrifice could well be the ultimate American dilemma.

Chapter Twelve

The reconciliation of an individualistic ethic with an acceptance of the necessary authority of the state required, then, a third factor, which begins to emerge in *Political Power*. This is "civic education," the use of the schools to train the young, propaganda to educate the public, and the maintenance of a public morale different from the more formal mechanisms of education and propaganda in that it provides a sense of assurance, well-being, and competence of leadership and direction summed up by the term "confidence." Confidence in leadership is the only assurance that the rational and irrational components of civic culture could be kept in balance. The dependence of "confidence" on the process of democratic selection is the sole assurance of the continuity of democracy.

Making the whole process rest on the selection of leaders rather than the education of the young, or the mechanisms for managing public opinion, provided the argument with its essentially populist core, although the term was not one which Merriam would have used to describe it. The term "leadership" did not designate presidents alone but the whole range of political officialdom which managed local, state, and national politics. Emphasis upon popular political leadership effectively short-circuited the power of educators and expert technicians, limiting their control to what political leadership would ordain. Political leadership could also remain free of the restrictions of certification and professional authorization which the technical professions needed to use as the definition of competence.

The proper power of a planning board, then, from Merriam's point of view was not political power. The cabinet letter objecting to the original plan for an independent board stated the confusion as clearly as it could be stated. "It would be in the position of making plans of the most far reaching importance without the responsibility for carrying out these plans."[30] That presumed defect was precisely the point. No planning board in Merriam's view should have the responsibility for carrying out its plans. Yet that the board did not have such responsibility would continue to be the problem. As the board's ideas developed larger intellectual constituencies and began to influence legislative programs, the line between a commitment to scientific ideas and the need to influence political programming became more difficult to draw. It was long-standing tradition among government agencies to develop lines of communication and influence legislative programs— "to inform" they would have said—but could a planning board find a place in this tradition? Merriam thought not, and though he was far from unwilling to use personal influence where he thought it would work, he did not want the board's staff to undertake lobbying. Particularly where Congress was concerned, Merriam insisted on absolute avoidance of any contact. Eliot, whose presence in Washington kept him much more involved with the normal flow of gossip about attitudes on the Hill, felt that the use of more carefully directed information and influence would have helped programs the board was backing, but Merriam was adamant. When Eliot finally did get approval for meetings with a senator willing to consider the board's point of view, the board members sat stiffly and silently, speaking when spoken to, answering questions only when asked.

In addition to the fact that being in Washington had its inevitable effect on Eliot's view of his role—a predictable response which had led other associations of public officials to seek different national locations—Eliot's background as a planner, like that of Delano, had given him a view of the relation between planners and politicians that made the sharpness of the lines separating them less intelligible. Whatever deference Delano felt toward Merriam's point of view—apparently a good deal—Eliot did not. Although Merriam had the distinct impression that Roosevelt did not want the board to engage in politicking on the Hill, the president was not of one mind on that subject at all times and could easily have given different impressions to others. Certainly Merriam himself felt strongly about the matter, and Roosevelt did not tend to contradict anyone's strong commitments.[31]

In short, Roosevelt's attitude toward the board was probably like his attitude toward many of the other groups with which he dealt. He liked the board's personnel and found it an enormously useful entrée to a significant group of Americans whose advice he might use—the American academic community. Unlike the ad hoc arrangements made by later presidents or the piecemeal advisory agencies authorized by later Congresses, the planning board of the New Deal was an overall planning agency which sought to collect relevant social science and natural science experts to make studies directly for and give advice on programs directly to the president. Still, Roosevelt wanted to make his own plans, and, like Merriam, he trusted his own democratic populism, no matter how mystical that may have seemed to others. Also like Merriam, his trust of intellectuals was limited by a kind of public faith which was personal and real. Very late in the career of the New

Deal—it was 1943 and the war was in progress—Delano sent his nephew a copy of a report on the "Perfect Union" which Louis Brownlow had written. "I have read it at the rate of one page per minute," FDR told his old uncle. "He has not got the answer yet. I don't think anyone has." And then he concluded affectionately, half-jokingly, half-perceptively, "I am a bumblebee. I am going to keep on bumbling!"[32]

Similarly, Merriam, throughout his decade of service on the planning board, retained one curiously persistent pose: that he was not a planner. It became a stock joke for him, an amusing self-parody which had a purpose. As he told a meeting of the University of Chicago Planning Club in 1950, he failed to qualify for the American Institute of Planning because he was neither an engineer nor a landscape architect, and he had fulfilled none of the training prerequisites to full membership in any of the related planning professions. It was the kind of drawling denial with which he and his friend Brownlow fended off the potential charge of meddling which their involvement in the rapidly proliferating service professions could entail.[33]

In their later years both men became household gods to the groups they had helped create, and they would be brought forth on holidays to tell stories about the past and to be wined and dined and generally celebrated. Such honored positions were established, however, during the New Deal years when they wielded the power of selection and the funds for support which created the groups and defined their functions. The key characteristic of their roles was that neither of them ever qualified for membership in most of the professions they were seeking to create and that, at the same time, they tried to represent qualities necessary to the continuing utility of the profession. Brownlow called himself a "generalist," and Merriam called himself a "political scientist." Both men served as exemplars, not of the professional forms they were trying to bring into existence, but of the system of values which those professions would have to sustain.

Brownlow acted out his role as "Brownie," the boy from the Ozarks whose supposed lack of education made him the eternal democrat. But Merriam worried about the problem in a last set of efforts to construct an American political theory. "The value systems of the world have a deep political meaning which cannot be ignored in any examination of the realm of the political," he wrote in 1939. "These values are the fiery core of patterns of cohesion, of loyalty, of allegiance; and they form a massive resistance to the wayward trends toward the satisfaction of the individual at the expense of the functioning of the group of which he is a part." Yet he saw very real dangers to the continuity of values under change. "The content of these values at a given moment may seem imperishable, but their special magnetic centers change with time and with new tensions. . . . It is in this 'fading' of the old picture into the new that some of the most serious problems of political adaptation arise. Here are problems of the adaptation of new techniques to the older value systems—or, putting it another way, the creation of new value systems to replace the old as they fade away. It is when value systems fade and fail and no others come in rapidly enough that the equilibrium of the society is shaken most." And on the eve of the emergence within his profession of viewpoints which in their various ways would laud the inherent democracy of American government—its implied "consensus"—Merriam worried: "The most tragic moments in human life are those in which the value systems are unreconciled—when one cries out against another; the family against the state, the state against the church, the neighborhood against the distant capital, life in the broader sense against nonlife or narrow life—against the end of life."[34]

Merriam's generation, which had sensed its first burst of maturity in the Progressive period, came to an end in the New Deal. Whether what that generation was passing on to the generation edging in for its turn at the controls was what the older generation thought it had been carrying was another matter. In that sense, Merriam in the New Deal shares at least one significant characteristic of the entire period. His work on the National Resources Planning Board, his late writings, even his management of his beloved Department of Political Science, were all eventually to bear the marks of the end of something—an era, perhaps. He could sense it in his own physical decline and the attendant anxieties.

All of Merriam's career had been built on the belief that the American voting public could be persuaded to want what it needed, that a reconciliation between self-interest and the public interest was possible under a system of public virtue which made that reconciliation an act of national commitment. But the relation between the thrust of his progressivism and the reform capacities of American government was, for the second time in the twentieth century, left unresolved by the interposition of a devastating international crusade. For the second time in the century, too, the Progressives' route to the White House was the Democratic party, the party with the strongest commitment to regional autonomy, legislative hegemony, and suspicion of eastern industrialism. Yet, progressivism's banners were nationalism, rational executive authority, and industrial modernization. Progressive ideals and the political reality through which they would be achieved were set in an opposition which seemed tied irrevocably to the structures of American politics: federalism, the two parties, the separation of powers. Yet the New Deal, in spite of its conflicts with those structures, served to affirm them to the generation Merriam was leading far more effectively than for the progressive generation which he represented. The younger generation would be left with the fixed belief that what was needed was a return to the New Deal in order to insure continuity. Merriam's generation was less sure, but they were not going to live forever and they were tired.

For Merriam and Brownlow the New Deal had proved only one thing for sure: that in American government great leadership could move mountains. What they continued to worry about was whether the moving of mountains was the most efficient way to govern a technological society. Questions of that kind had led many of their contemporaries to abandon politics as the method of approach. Their own continued affirmation of politics is what gives their joint and individual function in the New Deal as defenders of planning and social research the particular significance it has.

Throughout virtually its entire ten years, the planning board was forced to occupy itself with two major sets of problems; the complex relation between them illustrates succinctly the planning dilemma in American government. The first was, on the surface, the most obvious. The board had been formed to gather data relevant to the planning of public works, to analyze that data in accordance with the best current methods, and to coordinate and propose programs. The nature of public works—from roads and hydroelectric dams to schoolhouses and hospitals—indicates the potential breadth of the concept of public works and the mixture of natural and social planning which could be touched upon. The multitude of reports turned out by the board is ample testimony to the thoroughness with which it did its job and to the success of the board in drawing on the best available data collections and methodology.

The second set of problems involved the necessity of the board's establishing its own continuing relationship with the government, defining as it went along the role which planning would play in

American government and perhaps more important, attempting to construct the administrative mechanisms for establishing that role as one of the federal government's essential functions. It is in this second set of problems that Merriam's role is central, not because he was not involved in the specialized studies—the selection and oversight of the various technical committees whose function it was to conduct the research and produce the reports—but because the establishment of a role for planning was central in his own view of his contribution to his times.

The relation between the two sets of problems is important. The reports themselves are the planning board's lasting memorial, in a way, for purposes of historiographical inquiry. Like *Recent Social Trends,* they are a remarkable social documentation of their times. But the board was ultimately abolished, a historical fact too obvious to be ignored. As Hoover shrewdly predicted in his critique of New Deal planning, the reports themselves would become clumsily antique in their time, the "facts" made irrelevant by unpredicted innovations, the predictions made absurd by the emergence of new facts.[35]

But he touched the problem which Merriam's view of planning and his sense of the future of the board were trying to resolve. The necessity of separating planning as a process from a judgment of the effectiveness of each plan was essential to the attitude Merriam was trying to create. While technicians committed to the plans they had worked out and governmental administrators committed to studies of efficiency and effectiveness were understandably seeking their own standards for measuring the practicality of planning, Merriam kept searching for a more general concept which would be consistent with his own experience in politics and government. Such a concept would place much greater emphasis upon the process of planning—the fact that it was going on at all and the coordination of the methods by which it was carried on—than on fixed judgments about the efficacy of planning. Rejecting the idea that planning governed the future in any totally predetermined form, Merriam searched for a view of planning which would also protect society from the technologists' tendency to deny any limitations on prediction. At the same time, the real necessity for the continuous outlining and testing of technical programs and their relation to one another had to be recognized. The problem was particularly acute for American society where natural, social, and regional heterogeneity preserved potential conflicts which might be

257

revealed only by the imposition of national programs. The whole tendency of national government in the twentieth century had been toward increasing involvement in area after area of local reform. Some of the conflicts could be predicted—the southern attitude toward race was the most obvious one—but the vast majority of political disputes showed themselves only in the process of hammering out programs with politicians who were to legislate them into existence and administrators who were to carry them out.

Not only were the problems difficult to predict, but their partisans were equally hard to envisage in advance. At one of the planning board's earlier meetings Administrator Ickes found himself suddenly and unexpectedly in a showdown with Secretary Perkins over the mountain people in the Shenandoah National Park. Ickes wanted to move them out of the park, using the Subsistence Homestead Act as his lever, but the law forbade him from doing it unless he could prove that he was relieving industrial unemployment—which was scarcely applicable. Madam Perkins balked. "Why do you want to move them?" she asked testily. "Because they don't fit into the picture and are more or less dangerous," Ickes replied; and then summoning up his urban reform prejudices, he fumed, "they are inbred, and should be moved out of the hollows where they have been living ever since the Revolutionary War." That did it. "I have always felt the way they do," she retorted. "You could not move me out." And she suggested that Ickes find them something to do in the park.[36]

The tradition of American reform had been skillful in concealing the rhetoric of moral improvement which the new scientists were rapidly adopting, transforming it into a language of general welfare. But the reformers had rarely been in agreement. Administrative and political constituencies had been able to join suddenly and unexpectedly with proponents on new technical ideas to support or oppose moves perfectly consistent with the logic of some plan but totally out of keeping with a group's perceptions of its needs. The process of planning forced such discrepancies to surface and Merriam's view of the process of planning assumed an inherent flexibility, coordination, and openness to revision which could resolve them. The question was whether this model was as logical in the American system of politics as Merriam wanted it to be. In some crucial respects, the New Deal was ultimately to prove him wrong.

Merriam's joking insistence that he was not a planner, therefore, has some significant truths which are worth examining. To paraphrase his own title to the first committee's *Final Report*, "A Plan for Planning," he was a planner of planning. More than any other member of the board, he was seeking to find a role for planning in the federal government which would entail not only finding a place for planning but also reorganizing the government to give that place genuine effect. The fact that his initial mandate from Ickes was not that at all was a constant drag on his efforts, but it did not stop him. For twenty years he had been one of the central figures in the construction of a scientific system of social reform whose direction had always been toward national implementation and toward the presidency as the vehicle. Though Merriam was far less intolerant of the legislative process than most of his contemporary Progressives, there is no doubt that Congress was, from his point of view, the expression of local interest and the staging area for conflicting political aims. Few in his generation were inclined to pick up the advice that even Woodrow Wilson had been forced to drop after 1890: that the efficient reorganization of Congress was the only viable route to reform. For Merriam, however, the legislative branch was an essential ingredient in the political process, and he was committed to the sustaining of politics as the essential means of order and improvement in the human community.

John Dewey saw the problem in his 1939 review of American social planning; but he did not see the New Deal's efforts as an occasion for celebration, let alone optimism. He articulated Merriam's basic insights much better than Merriam had when he said that "an immense difference divides the *planned* society from a *continuously planning* society. The former requires fixed blueprints imposed from above and therefore involving reliance upon physical and psychological force to secure conformity to them. The latter means the release of intelligence through the widest form of cooperative give-and-take. The attempt to *plan* social organization without the freest possible play of intelligence contradicts the very idea in *social planning*. For the latter is an operative method of activity, not a predetermined set of final 'truths'"[37] Merriam could not have agreed more; but Dewey had praised *Recent Social Trends* and had become one of the New Deal's most profound intellectual critics. Merriam by 1939 had established another set of principles with which to relate himself to the concepts of social science which had moved him through the era of the twenties, or he had transformed the debate over principles somewhere along the way. His students discussed the problem as they watched him in these later years, his faith in science and democracy seeming ever more mystical against the dark background of the world.

13

The Purposes of Planning

The students who worked with Merriam in the late thirties reaped the benefits of a system of social research some twenty-five years old, and centered in a personality that charmed and entertained—and puzzled. Merriam persisted in radiating an optimism which no longer seemed to light the way toward a unified concept of social science as sharply for them as it continued to for him. The base of the Chicago School was beginning to crumble, in some respects under the weight of its success. Specialized research led to particularized interests which left little time or enthusiasm for the level of Merriam-like generalization which had been the initiating force. Robert Maynard Hutchins cast a shadow over the celebration of the tenth anniversary of the Social Science Research Building when he suggested a test of the social research ideal of ten years earlier by the experience of the world around them.[1] Hutchins had shared the reformist enthusiasm of Merriam's generation, having been raised in it himself; and quite conceivably he recognized the contradiction lurking underneath Merriam's concern for progressive social change and his promotion of the objective social sciences.

Beyond the local scene, too, one could see in the New Deal of those years an increasing suspicion of the distance between promise and achievement. The overwhelming victory of Roosevelt in the election of 1936 had been followed by a succession of defeats in Congress. They were defeats which seriously threatened any view of comprehensive change in the management of social reform. The planning board concerned itself with the production of rational frameworks whose need had been revealed in the first New Deal administration. These ranged from general issues of American government—regionalization of the federal system and reorganization of the executive branch—to more

260

particular issues of water resources and land use, urbanization and population distribution. By the end of the period the NRPB, under the umbrella of postwar planning, projected programs for a complete restructuring of the American concept of welfare, work, relief, and social security. Again Congress would reject whatever utopian dreams the president shared with his planners. As the weight of the public opinion studies undertaken by the planning board revealed, the public was more inclined to see the congressional view as the best support of its interests.

Merriam continued to fight for his utopianism. In late afternoon cocktail sessions in the bar of the Shoreland Hotel near the university— the first air-conditioned bar opened after the repeal of Prohibition returned Chicagoans to the legal enjoyment of their habits—Merriam held court with students and colleagues celebrating the signs of success and explaining the evidences of failure. He was suffering a fair amount of disgruntlement in those years which had little to do with his professional interests, although he was not always inclined to see it that way. His never very sturdy marriage was again in a temporary state of disarray, taking its toll on a man much in need of affection. He complained, joked wryly about the gossip he seemed inadvertently to invite upon himself, and advised others on the details of their lives and the complexities of their careers. Like his friend Brownlow, he was far more dependent upon his family as the center of attachment to the life from which he had come than any of the younger generation observing him in post-Prohibition Chicago or New Deal Washington were likely to understand, though they understood his dissatisfactions clearly enough.

From the point of view of the intellectual activity he generated and the institutional support for that activity he was able to sustain, Merriam came closer to the fulfillment of his ideals during those years than he had come during the previous decades. The work of the planning board, its tightly interlocked relation to the SSRC and PACH, and its increasing proximity to the president were all part of an expansion of influence and control which made Merriam one of the most influential social scientists in the country. One cannot trace that influence like an economic theory affecting specific decisions. Merriam was the leading architect of a system of academic influence in policy formation. The most influential idea as such was his view of planning. It was also the idea most subject to rejection by the conservative reaction which spread through Congress and the public in the "recovery" period after World War II.

From the beginning Merriam's approach to the decentralization of planning was intended as a middle ground between federal control and localized chaos. The method was one which academics of his stature had been working with, in effect, for most of their professional lives. The creation of a national academic system without a national university system—indeed, in seeming abhorrence of a national university system—had been based on distinguishing between the scholar as a national professional and the scholar as a faculty member in a particular institution. While the resulting schizophrenia was to produce periodic identity crises for academics and their universities as each strove for competitive recognition, the system had produced an important compromise which spread able people around a large and diverse country to provide astonishingly uniform levels of quality education at key private and public educational institutions throughout the nation. Within states and within regions the quality of education would show a widely varying range, but the nation as a whole could point to reasonably well distributed and generally well recognized peaks, region by region if not always state by state. Merriam had no intention of promoting a single hierarchy in education, although he would support the competition of his Chicago School for national prominence over the traditional eastern establishment and seek influence for his colleagues in a national reform administration.

The SSRC had been formed as a super-academic association. The developing model for the NRPB was, in its turn, a super-government research association. Like the associations in the hierarchy of which it was a part, its function was not to dictate standards or to execute the policies it formulated, but to coordinate, to communicate, and to plan. While a central part of its funding would come from the federal government, its ultimate dependence would be upon the work of the groups whose efforts it coordinated. From Merriam's point of view, the successful performance of PACH in its role of coordinator and manipulator of the administrative associations gathered in the building called "1313" in Chicago proved the workability of the method. But so, then, had the experiences of his entire career. The planning board brought the method to an important peak; but it also raised all the basic questions in their most complex—even insoluble—forms.

His work on the board can be defined in three stages which reflect his overriding interest in establishing the place of overall planning in the American political process. The first stage was his "plan for planning" marshaling the natural and social sciences communities into a national advisory system. Merriam assumed that such a cooperative relationship would be possible and the position of his brother John among the natural scientists seemed to assure it. The basic plan of the *Final Report* had provided for a report from the National Academy of Sciences; and John Merriam had chaired the committee which produced it. The academy's report tried to face the basic questions of utility—the relation between pure and applied research—and in a sense it succeeded in finding the rhetorical dimensions, at least, of the problem. But the cooperation began and ended there. The social scientists' demand for utility, buttressed by their correct assessment of the president's attitude and the political demands of Congress, drove the natural scientists even further into protecting the purity of their research. Delano conferred with Karl Compton of MIT in 1934, at the president's request and with John Merriam present; and Delano came out of the meeting confirmed in his belief that the natural sciences had had more than their share of government backing (the Geological Surveys appear to have been his model) and would have to wait until the social sciences caught up. A dinner meeting between representatives of the various natural and social science organizations was held at the Cosmos Club, but the evening seemed only to exacerbate the mutual suspicions aroused by the recurrent questions of utility and application.[2]

The social scientists' sense of prediction offended the natural scientists in the academy. "There is, of course, great danger in making predictions concerning discovery," academy president Frank R. Lillie wrote William F. Ogburn in March 1936, "and I do not think any committee of the Academy would run the risk of appearing ridiculous in this matter."[3] Out of the uneasy cooperation between the social and the natural scientists were to come such important board reports as *The Problems of a Changing Population* and *Research—a National Resource*; but the problem of definition and agreement on ends remained unresolved. The dropping of the atomic bomb brought physics back into the group of "useful" sciences in an almost grotesque parody of the debates of the mid-thirties.

The second stage of Merriam's effort to establish planning in American politics can be found embedded in the 1935 report of the National Resources Committee, *Regional Factors in National Planning*. The report recommended a division of the United States into twelve administrative districts with movable boundaries, depending on the function being divided. The federal functions then distributed among many centers were to be consolidated into the administrative centers of these districts. All districts would report to a national coordinating agency responsible directly to the president. Emphasis upon the centers would lessen the problems which could arise from the flexibility of the borders.

The report pointed to the evil of 192,000 units of government spread out among the forty-eight states. It recommended rational restructuring but insisted that this entailed nothing revolutionary beyond the efficient ordering of chaos. Yet what would happen to the states? The states, their boundaries and their governments left untouched, were to be encouraged to utilize more fully their own resources for local planning and their power for initiating compacts with other states—even given the general agreement that the compact was a complex and cumbersome device. At the same time, the idea of centralizing administrative responsibility in the president and decentralizing it in regional centers might well have given pause, and there were those who did wonder just how Congress, with its traditional dependence upon the states as the basic source of the power distributed by it, was going to respond to a redivision of the nation's resources along executive and administrative rather than congressional and political lines.

The report's compromise on the issue of the states is in striking contrast to the general dilemma of local government in the thirties. The enthusiasm for reform in the predepression years had not been sustained in the economic and political realities of local governments stretched well beyond capacity by the persistence of the depression. Whether or not this condition was permanent—could the states and cities ever undertake the control of agricultural and industrial relief and reconstruction—was only half the question. The other half was equally difficult. Would the federal government's assumption of general responsibilities constitute a dangerous or inefficient or un-American adventure in coercive centralization? Hoover's reluctance to take powers from the states can scarcely be said to have been matched by Roosevelt's willingness to see such powers permanently centralized in Washington. Roosevelt covered the indecision by an emergency attitude which ultimately wore thin. The report's concept of region was an effort to compromise the two halves of the question by providing a unit of government which would have practical and flexible utility with respect to the problems it had to solve but no political identity which would throw it into competition with either local or federal traditions. And meanwhile, what were the states to do? "Wither away," a cynical American Marx might have muttered.

The third stage, the reorganizing of the presidency, took place outside the immediate direction of the board. Its chief purpose was the reshaping of the presidency to include planning as an executive function and to draw the system with which Merriam was working into the White House itself. Increasingly through Roosevelt's first term the necessity of promoting the direct presidential role of planning dominated Merriam's point of view. By 1936 he had the means. While the President's Committee on Administrative Management, the Brownlow Committee, was not a subcommittee of the National Resources Committee and was, in fact, independent of the NRC, it was a direct consequence of the experience of the NRC. Roosevelt had decided that to turn the project over to the NRC would complicate matters by involving the cabinet members of the NRC in reconstructing their own functions, and would have included other members of the NRC as well. Although Brownlow had frequently met with the NRC and was a continuous influence on its discussions, his nongovernmental position as director of PACH gave him a particularly useful role to play on such a governmentally sensitive committee as the Committee on Administrative Management. Merriam served on the committee; Brownlow was head of it. It proved to be the culmination of the careers of both men, and it marked the outer limits of what their generation was to accomplish.

In some crucial respects the line one can draw from the Committee on Recent Social Trends to the National Resources Committee reached its culmination in the President's Committee on Administrative Management. The differences are the consequences not only of four years of the New Deal but of the personality of FDR, and these differences are by no means to be gainsaid. The continuity, however, has to be noted and accounted for. Although as the later Hoover Commission studies tend to indicate, Hoover's point of view would have strengthened the executive branch rather than seek, as the Brownlow Committee did, to strengthen the president himself; but even that crucial difference should not obscure the essential similarity: that it was the reorganization of the administration of the federal government which was at stake. The emphasis upon executive government which had been essential to the development of industrial progressivism had taken as its traditional enemy the various American forms of legislative control. Legislatures were blamed for the evils of corruption and patronage, local myopia and self-interest, political parties and partisanship, inefficiency and mis-management.

By giving Merriam and Brownlow central roles to play in the reorganization of the presidency, Roosevelt assured at least one line of continuity with the past. Both men had spent their lives trying to reconcile the views of politics with which they had been raised with the realities of modern urban and national life. Unlike their urban counter-parts in many cases, they loved the past as they remembered it, and their reforms were reconciliations, not rejections. Luther Gulick, the third member of the President's Committee on Administrative Management, was far closer to the industrial progressivism of Hoover and the scientific social science of William F. Ogburn than he was to either Merriam or Brownlow. The organization of the committee therefore insured the closest possible relationship with the broadest reaches of the social science communities and the public service communities which the three men represented.[4]

For the moment at least, free of the cabinet politics which the assigning of the task to the NRC would have entailed, the President's Committee on Administrative Management represented a rebirth of the concept of extragovernmental advisory systems for the president, plus one step beyond. The Committee on Recent Social Trends, although appointed by and directly responsible to the president, was financed entirely by private funds. And although government aid in the form of significant amounts of research assistance and supplementary staff was a significant factor in the production of its report, *Recent Social Trends*, this was, in a sense, support outside the control of Congress. The President's Committee on Administrative Management, although first intended as an adjunct of the National Emergency Council, was refused authorization by the comptroller general. In a series of negotiations with committees of the Senate and the House, Roosevelt got appropria-tions for the committee's work. To be sure, much of that work was already prepared and continued to be managed by money provided by the SSRC and PACH, the latter for foreign studies which it was simply assumed Congress would refuse to fund; but the procedure had finally been reversed. A peacetime Congress had been pressed into the financing of social research for a presidential report, and the private sources of funds—very largely the Rockefeller Foundation—would be behind the scenes. Hoover had been proud to announce that private industrial funds were financing governmental research. Roosevelt felt embarrassed by it. So might Hoover have felt in 1936.[5]

While Merriam's influence touched all aspects of the report of the committee, his chief importance was in establishing a base, practical as well as philosophical, for continuing relationships between the presidency and the academic research community. Merriam's structuring of a National Resources Planning Board for the Executive Office of the president was intended to give the president direct access to the academic community with funds of his own to pay for the advice, but two points of view, to which both Merriam and Brownlow were deeply committed, protected this proposal. First, the members of the NRPB were not to be professional planners but outsiders chosen by the president from private occupations relevant to planning. Second, the members of the board were to be nonsalaried, to serve at the pleasure of the president. The president's research money was to be for research, not for a permanent staff of researchers. While the executive officer was to be a government service officer, the rest of the board was not. These two themes—the persistence of independent groups of private citizens representing private institutions to the government and the awareness of the need for a counter-bureaucratic influence on the presidency—form an important core of dissent which Merriam and Brownlow both represented in the communities which they led. This dissent reflects, in a crucial sense, their basic populism in its modernized form—not a fundamentalist anti-intellectualism, but a necessary protection against the failures of science to know what it claimed to know and against professional elites to lead where the public was not prepared to go.[6]

Appearing before the Joint Committee on Government Organization, the three members of the President's Committee on Administrative Management took characteristic positions. Brownlow provided history and general rationale, Luther Gulick provided technical explanations, Merriam provided what he was increasingly calling "philosophy."[7] In Roosevelt's jovial approach to his relationship with the committee, Merriam was indeed coming to represent the philosopher. The president would ask Merriam to remain after meetings so that he could "talk philosophy." Merriam was "Chawles" in those conversations, not "Doctor Merriam," as the president referred to him in public meetings, or "Uncle Charlie," as the students called him behind his back. Roosevelt would talk about political power in a manner which sometimes startled the political scientist. There was a sense of distance in his approach which Merriam found unusual in his experience with professional politicians, an objectivity—"as though he were not involved in it," Merriam told his students.[8] The planning board was therefore providing

Roosevelt something he appreciated, a set of programmatic ideals, practical enough in their technically established relationship with American government and society not to be utopian but utopian nonetheless in their projection into the future of possibilities inherent in the present.

Merriam's work on the board and his writing during this period served as culminations of a philosophical position which he had taken throughout his career: that the projection into the future of present tendencies in American national life could reveal continuing ideals realizable without revolution and built on the base of what American government was rather than on what it would need to become. Yet, as congressional response to the report of the Committee on Administrative Management and to subsequent NRPB reports would amply demonstrate, such projections filtered through congressional apprehension would always seem to threaten revolution. Even supportive congressmen could easily twist an evolutionary concept into a revolutionary shape. Had not a report of the board recommended the regionalization of Washington, setting up new federal capitals around the country? one man asked. No, Merriam tried to explain, regionalization did not mean that, and he offered to send the regionalism report to members of the committee. Senator Joseph O'Mahoney of Wyoming had read William Bennett Munro's suggestion that the states be abolished, and Merriam tried simply to ignore the point. The Brownlow Committee's use of the word "abolish" reverberated around the hearing room with an unexpectedly threatening sound; and the technicians had to stop and explain what they meant by their curiously nonmoral use of the word "responsible."[9]

The committee based its entire rhetorical position on the necessity of preserving democracy in a world in which democracy was under serious threat. Merriam recounted the experience which he and Brownlow had had the previous summer in Poland where fascist country representatives to a conference on government tried to put the group on record as opposed to legislative control of executive government; but the comparison itself raised the inevitable threat. The American awareness of the need for executive reorganization and, indeed, the responsible recognition of it, had long preceded the European dilemmas of the postwar era. Merriam even called attention to that in a shrewd exchange with Senator Byrd, one of the report's most committed opponents. As governor of Virginia Byrd had been one of the leaders in executive reorganization and had used the advice of many of the same technical experts—Gulick among them—in achieving it. "Senator Byrd recoiled somewhat from the paternity of this plan, apparently," Merriam chided, letting his humor drift toward the spittoon tradition of American political debate, "but we have the goods on you, Senator, we have your fingerprints, or your blood test, or whatever it is. This child looks to you as its father." The senator was not beyond going along with so obviously flattering a joke. "You cannot disinherit your own child," he agreed. The last laugh was going to be his in any case.[10]

The fundamental issue was never one of ideology, despite the fact that ideology would serve as the only fear capable of producing unity. The reorganization of the presidency was not going to make Roosevelt a dictator, and the continuation of a national planning board was not going to turn the country into a communist state. What they were going to do was what Roosevelt had wanted them to do in the first place, from the beginning of his appointment of a planning board in the Department of the Interior. They were going to limit the access of Congress to influence on decisions made by administrative agencies of the government. The demand for access had derived a great deal of its impetus from the pork barrel; but to see it in that form alone can misstate the case. Congressional leaders, particularly given the effects of the seniority system, were men who could spend entire careers watching presidents and cabinet officers come and go while they, the legislative branch, conducted the business of government. Every attempt by a president to limit the power of Congress was thus, from the president's point of view, a desperate need for an increase in his administrative efficiency, from the Congress's point of view, another sally from yet another fresh set of troops, which had to be taken seriously, but which could nonetheless be expected to go away. Progressives old and new could continue to place their faith in executive leadership; but it was Congress who controlled the works.

However aware Merriam was of the subtleties of congressional politics, he was significant in his generation for his awareness of the increasing role which leadership actually did play in democratic government and for his efforts to formulate some definition of that role. He and Brownlow kept trying to define public administration as something besides charts of organization and refinements of budgeting techniques. With all their powers, legislative bodies could not generate a public sense of leadership, or civic culture. As Roosevelt was amply to prove, a president who could generate confidence could succeed in sustaining his leadership of the nation whether or not he could lead Congress to act. He could even, in the final analysis, give justification and purpose to congressional programs which mutilated the logic and justice of his own plans. Indeed, his leadership of Congress could consist not simply in his willingness to take his lickings, but in his ability to project to the public the impression that he was enjoying them. Congress could never be a symbol of national purposes; the president had to be, and their dependence upon each other hung on his capacity to symbolize something which only they in their chaotic compromises of local interests and national needs could define.

In those respects, and very importantly, Merriam and the National Resources Planning Board were as close to a philosophy as such a system could get. They could present to the president the logical rationalities which were scientifically and technologically possible and he could present to the Congress whatever of them he thought politically possible. Congress in turn could present him with what it considered consistent with its own collective conception of the national interest and he would have to decide whether he would reject it, allow it to become law quietly and without fanfare, or celebrate it as what he had wanted all along.

The creation by the Reorganization Act of 1939 of the National Resources Planning Board in the Executive Office of the president brought Merriam and the board the independence they had wanted. Although it formalized within a structure of governmental operations a staff which had been working together for six years, it also continued the more widespread set of academic contacts which the organization of the Social Sciences Research Council had set up for Merriam many years earlier. One need only thumb through the agenda for the meeting of the directors of the SSRC in September 1938 to see what was involved. Sixteen committees of scholars reported on the studies being undertaken, approaching publication, and published over the previous year. Other committees appraised the results of research and projected future proposals. John Commons discussed Berle and Means's *Modern Corporations.* The Committee on Freedom of Inquiry, including C. H. Judd as chairman, E. S. Furniss, James B. Conant, Lynn Thorndike, and Merriam, was set up "to prepare a book which shall give in fully documented form an account of contemporary cases in which freedom of inquiry and teaching has been attacked." Through its Committee on Industry and Trade, the council financed the National Bureau of Economic Research in studies resulting in such books as Simon

Kuznets's *Commodity Flow and Capital Formation*, the first volume of which appeared in June 1938. The Committee on Personality and Culture was responsible for research and publication of works by Melville J. Herskowitz, Louis Wirth, Ralph Linton, and Leonard Doob during the course of the year. Louis Brownlow's chairmanship of the Public Administration Committee had led to a variety of significant studies: John Gaus on the administrative problems of the Department of Agriculture, Arthur Macmahon and Gladys Ogden on the administration of the relief program of 1935, Herman Finer and Herman Pritchett on TVA, Don K. Price and Harold A. and Kathryn H. Stone on city manager government, V. O. and Luella Gettys Key on American, Canadian, and British programs of grants-in-aid, Gordon Clapp on training for public service, and a variety of other works eventually to appear as significant contributions in their various fields. Of the total funds available for 1937–38, some $950,000, the council had spent approximately half by July 1938, with all but $50,000 of the remaining half committed to continuing work.[11]

By 1939 the NRC had a total of a little over a million dollars to spend for planning and research, a sum which does not include the talent made available to it by the SSRC, PACH, and the network of universities willing to grant time off to faculty for research on projects. The peak of the board's organizational activities was reached probably in 1941 when a full planning staff included the board members, Delano, Merriam, and George F. Yantis, advisers Henry Dennison and Beardsley Ruml, Director Charles W. Eliot, Assistant Directors Thomas C. Blaisdell, Frank W. Herring, and Ralph J. Watkins, and an executive officer, Harold Merrill.

From the beginning of the board's elevation to independent status in the executive office of the president—indeed, as a part of the fight to achieve that status—the board's continued existence had never been more than precarious, although Merriam's intense ambition for it seems to deny that. Congressional hostility, particularly in the House of Representatives, could easily be mobilized to trim appropriations, if not to threaten their cutoff entirely. Roosevelt liked Merriam; he trusted Uncle Fred Delano; and he enjoyed reading the board's reports. He had told Merriam on several occasions that he wanted the reports put in more digested, popular form, because such a form would make them useful for circulation among congressmen as well as to the interested public; and, beginning in 1939, this was done.[12]

Even where direct recommendations of the board were not followed,

ideas generated by the board had a triggering effect on the president'
plans. In November 1938 Delano forwarded to the president a lette
from Ogburn, written after four months in Germany. Ogburn recom
mended a study of war industry which would be concerned with socia
and civil problems rather than military alone, something to serve a
protection against the increasingly warlike developments on the Conti
nent. "This is an interesting letter from Dr. Ogburn," Roosevel
replied. "I think some study along this line should be made, but befor
anything is decided on, will you talk with Assistant Secretary of Wa
Johnson, and Harry Hopkins, and Henry Morgenthau, Jr.?"[13] While i
took some time, a Committee on National Defense Power under Loui
H. Johnson did come into being the following fall.

Nonetheless, the reorganization fight over the creation of the NRPI
had begun to make it clear to FDR that the cost of his advisory boar
was going to be high. The dispute was not initially over the ideologica
issue of a planning board, but over the board's interference with th
aims and intentions of the "powerful Rivers and Harbors bloc," a
Representative John J. Cochran put it in reply to pressure from FDR o
the inclusion of the board in the reorganization bill. Quoting Represen
tative Lindsay Warren, another of the board's opponents, he suggeste
that "Certain interests have had a great deal to say in references t
Rivers and Harbors authorization and appropriations. Organization
retain men in Washington during the entire period of Congress lookin
after their interests."[14]

Roosevelt still continued to press to protect his board, although onc
the successful Reorganization Plan of 1939 brought it out from unde
the relative protection of the cabinet, protection became more difficul
Writing to a group of the board's opponents in the House, he argue
that the NRPB did not conflict with the work of the Army Corps o
Engineers, and that its water resource planning did not duplicate th
work of any other agency. But the engineers were lobbying against th
board, and their protectors in the House were easy to convince. Afte
all, a planning board responsible only to the president was not a
subject to influence as was an administrative department. In th
original plan for the board Congress had tried to exert its control b
insisting on the retaining of cabinet members on the board and o
subjecting board appointments to the advice and consent of the Senate
Roosevelt opposed both provisions, but succeeded in blocking only th
first. "Will you tell Fred Delano and Merriam to get after the Hous

conferees and tell them to reject the conferees provision?'' he wrote to presidential assistant Pa Watson in a rare effort to involve the board members in politicking for their interests.[15]

Part of the running opposition between Charles Eliot and Merriam rested on the apparent necessity of a continuous battle with House opposition and the role to be played by the board members in that battle. The aging of Delano put increasing responsibility on Eliot to manage the daily affairs of the board, both in the board's offices and in its relationships in the White House and on the Hill. Merriam opposed not only political activity on the part of the board but Eliot's efforts at what he considered lifesaving. In March 1940 as the board's appropriation went through its yearly test of fire in the House, Roosevelt continued his efforts on the board's behalf, succeeding finally in getting $170,000 of the $1,060,000 originally requested through the Independent Offices Act of 1940; but the House attached the provision that the board could perform only functions authorized by the Federal Employment Stabilization Board under the Employment Stabilization Act of 1931. Although the board's original creation in 1934, after its initial selection by Ickes, had been based on the provisions of that act, it had certainly expanded its activities well beyond the 1931 view of planning. The discrepancy was ultimately used in attacks on the board's work.

Roosevelt's use of the board was in many respects like his use of the earlier Brains Trust. He relied more on the individual advice of men he trusted, and he used it in his own political way. The board, through Merriam, examined the Selective Training and Reserve Act of 1940 to analyze its relationship to WPA and Social Security and to begin some preparation for a veterans' program, if there was to be one. The president allocated funds from the emergency provisions of the Army and Navy Appropriations Acts for a compilation of a Register of Scientific and Specialized Personnel in cooperation with the Civil Service Commission. The board's contacts with agencies engaged in concerns with housing and urban development also made it useful and a center of suggestions for coordinating work, arousing awareness of conflicts, and the like.[16]

The board's role as a presidential "think tank" rather than as a direct planning agency had evolved out of a combination of the Rooseveltian manner of using ideas and the congressional opposition to the board. Roosevelt could have used a more systematic planning agency from his own point of view, and his efforts to retain the board in that form make it clear that he knew it. The board also had such an image of its own role. As early as January 1937 Gardiner Means had spelled out the ambition in a memorandum to Merriam. "In its earlier activity, the NRC took a position on thin ice jutting out from the solid background of city planning and resource conservation. Now that the ice is solid under the Committee and a more advanced position is tenable, the question arises whether the next steps should only move the Committee further toward the center of the pond or should move it out to cover the center." His estimate of the firmness of the ice suited the conditions of 1937 far better than those of the reorganization settlement two years later when the committee had indeed moved itself closer to the center of the pond, where the ice was much thinner. The closer they got to where they wanted to be, within earshot of the president, the more they subjected themselves to the protection of his politics. It was the least safe position they could have held, but it was the one they chose, and it was the one Roosevelt wanted for them.[17]

Roosevelt made his intention to use the board and his method of using it clear in his conference with the board on 17 October 1939. He asked them not to participate as members of interdepartmental committees since he planned to submit to them the reports of such committees and felt it better that they not be involved in the production of reports which they would then be asked to judge. The memorandum of that meeting prepared by board member George F. Yantis gives a picture of Roosevelt the administrator which differs considerably from the general views of his administrative practices. His concern with coordination, with not "stepping on toes," with proper clearance with other groups working on similar or related projects, and with not running "crosswise with others," does not sustain the image of an administrator who liked to assign the same projects to different people without telling one of the other's involvement. Whatever unconscious inclinations he might have had in such directions, it is clear in his instructions to the new board that efficient coordination was to be their mandate.[18]

What is also impressive in the report of the meeting is Roosevelt's concern as early as 1939 with postwar planning. He specifically enjoined the board from becoming tangled in wartime activities or programs. He wanted them to concentrate on normal, peacetime conditions. With regard to the problem of transportation, for example,

The Purposes of Planning

he told them that he would like a study indicating what transportation ought to be in 1949. He was interested in a superhighway program which would combine public and private investment through the use of tolls. On the question of the board's studies of taxation and national income, Roosevelt had told Merriam that he wanted them to lay off so politically sensitive an issue, but Merriam had explained that the board's intention was to produce not a detailed study with attendant publicity and a legislative program but rather an effort "at keeping au courant with all Federal tax proposals affecting national planning programs." Roosevelt approved the project but once again enjoined them to "have due regard to studies by the Ways and Means Committee of the Congress, and studies by the Treasury Department, avoiding conflicts with both." Again and again, the attention to clearance with others, coordination, and communication is emphasized.

Delano sent a memorandum to the president on 1 July 1942, calling his attention to discussions which the board had organized with members from various relevant agencies which could be expected to have interests in the process of demobilization of the armed forces. He wanted Roosevelt to issue a memorandum asking for the opening of further discussion of the subject. Roosevelt was reluctant to do so. "This is a little like the problem put up to me by the State Department," he replied. "They want a full-fledged, publicized survey on postwar international, economic and other problems, and said that they had many people in and out of the Government who are 'rarin' to go." His chief concern was that "there will not be any post-war problems if we lose this war. This includes the danger of diverting people's attention from the winning of the war." He did, however, recognize the need for preparatory discussions and saw no harm in an unpublicized, off-the-record examination of the subject "but without any form of an official set-up." He did not want a committee as such, he said, "but you might ask four or five people, in whom you have confidence, to work on this in their spare time." The informal Conference on Post-War Adjustment of Personnel which Floyd Reeves chaired was the result of the board's work, and the GI Bill its ultimate product.[19]

The board's appointment of the Committee on Long-Range Work and Relief Policies in 1939 marked the beginning of postwar planning, although the term "post-defense" was obviously a preferable designation at that stage. As his support of the planning board indicates, Roosevelt's concerns through 1940 and 1941 were divided between

275

planning for the war production and personnel and planning for postwar continuity. The latter assumed the continuation in the postwar period of the prewar conditions of economic and industrial stagnation and therefore acknowledged the need for postwar public works programs. Economist Alvin H. Hansen's memorandum of January 1941, "Financing Post-Defense Public Improvements," is characteristic of attitudes of many of the social science advisers. Among the problems of prediction which grew out of the influence of the depression was the conviction among population experts influential in the planning board that "the nations with the highest level of living and the greatest scientific resources stand at the threshold of population decrease.... [T]he United States is definitely tending toward the cessation of population growth and a subsequent period of population decrease."[20] The consequences, the author felt, were cause for alarm and a further indication of the need for careful planning.

Cautiously, given the amount of work actually underway, the president introduced the "Four Freedoms" in his State of the Union message in January 1941: freedom to speak and to worship, freedom from want and from fear. A new public conservatism reflected in congressional elections and the artificial full employment and production prosperity produced by the war itself did not encourage liberal optimism. Merriam's generation knew the New Deal to be a dramatically unfinished operation which had never had the chance to succeed, but they were not giving up. A memorandum to the president signed by Delano and Merriam on 17 March 1941 indicates just how far they were pushing their limited mandate. It lists what it calls "10 promises of American life." They are: adequate food, healthful shelter, decent clothing, medical care, education, especially for youth, work through the productive years, regular rest from work and a chance for recreation, release from full employment of the aged, the youth, the sick, and mothers with children, opportunity to advance on the basis of merit and effort, and the four freedoms. The final report of the board, issued in January 1943 and transmitted to Congress by the president in March, carried a similar list, designated "A New Bill of Rights."[21]

The list and part 1 of the full report for 1943 begin with what undoubtedly is the fullest statement of Merriam's American plan. Part 2 and particularly part 3, which is the report of the Committee on Long-Range Work and Relief Policies, spell out in detail the ways in which those aims can be achieved. Nothing which social and political reformers over the next thirty years would struggle with, in large part unsuccessfully, is omitted—from the suggestion of the need to move to an incomes policy for welfare benefits to the realization of the need to compensate for tax base inequities state by state, in the financing of public education; from the idea of reorganizing transportation to that of controlling environmental pollution. Read in the 1970s, the documents stand as a kind of indictment of current American relations between social ideas and public policy, not only in the public and governmental failure to realize what was obvious thirty years ago, but in the fact that the community which produced such reports and which has sought responsibility to provide continued thoughtful efforts in facing those problems forgot completely that such a program was ever researched and presented.

The basic principle of the report which can be most associated with Merriam's lifetime aims are stated in the board's introductory material and emphasize one point: that the American form of government can, without denying its past or revolutionizing its future, provide as a right the mass benefits of progress to all Americans. In a comprehensive analysis of the sources of inequality in American society, their rooting in regional differences and natural circumstances for which no individual can be held responsible, the board and its committee faced realistically the subtle problems of adjusting the necessity for change to the true puzzle of a heterogeneous collection of communities committed to acting as a nation. The issues established by geography, by the random location of fundamental resources, and by the cultural traditions which had grown out of historical expansion on the vast and varied continent were explored as the basis for reform. The new social science reformers, both buoyed and blinded by the internationalism which America's involvement in World War II had produced, assumed a cultural nationalism which had, by some mystical process they would soon be calling "consensus," been achieved all along. It wasn't so, and the neoprogressives of the New Deal knew it. What they had seen was a nation choking on natural resources which it could not organize or control, refusing to use a perfectly adequate political system, seemingly bent upon sacrificing historic ideals in defense of outmoded habits. Americans feared the destruction of their way of life by internal subversion and international design. What they faced was the threat of its destruction by accident.

The public response to the "cradle to the grave" program was ambivalent, as far as any of the board's efforts to test that response were able to reveal. Newspaper editorials opposed it two to one. Popular journals such as *Time* and *Newsweek* labeled it a campaign program for 1944 and the much predicted fourth term. Delays in publication made the report appear to be an American imitation of Great Britain's Beveridge Plan, although the work had preceded the British program by some time. The committee's energetic director of research, Eveline M. Burns, had worked at the London School of Economics, was familiar with the work of Sir William Beveridge, and had come to the United States in 1926 to join the faculty of Columbia University. Unfortunately for the report's public relations, she had also studied German relief policies in her successful effort to establish herself as one of the world's experts on international relief problems. A hostile headline in the Knoxville *Journal* put it, "Dr. Burns, Student of Nazis, Works on NRPB Post-War Dictatorship."[22]

Merriam and Brownlow had both worked through the war to take advantage of the potentialities in Anglo-American cooperation in future research programs of government administration, their chief contact being Sir Henry Bunbury. It may be one of the ironies of the period that American social and governmental planning was taken far more seriously in Great Britain, where a century of communication and exchange had created habits of mutual professional respect, than it was possible for it to be taken in the United States.[23]

After an initial flurry of debate, the idea died as far as most Americans were concerned. The immediate emphasis upon the planning of demobilization—and specifically the GI Bill—emphasized simpler aims, a return to "normalcy-plus," however one wanted to define it. In many respects, the congressional reaction was typical in its brusque misunderstanding of the issues, and in its crude reflection of public attitudes. Congress abolished the National Resources Planning Board by refusing to approve its appropriation. In one sense the whole concept of planning, which Hoover and his followers had identified with regimentation, had survived the fears of totalitarianism but not the experience of the war. The war was a national regimentation, however clumsy, and that was enough. The war was also a kind of prosperity, and fully employed American workers were not inclined to view the future with apprehensions carried over from the depression.

Although commentators tended to blame the demise of the board on a variety of causes—the rivers and harbors bloc, the Army Corps of

Engineers, the welfare and security program, congressional desire to get at the president through slapping his Uncle Fred—none of those causes was really very new. They were all true enough, but they had all been there from the earliest days among some groups hostile to all or part of the New Deal. Judging by the succession of votes which ultimately killed the board, a search for the cause can begin simply in the increasingly conservative complexion of Congress after the elections of 1942. The rhetoric from congressional opponents Rankin of Mississippi and Smith of Ohio is obvious enough in its railing against the threat of communism, feudalism, totalitarianism, and the like; but this was nothing new, though it would take on new forms in the years to come. What seems more striking in the debates is the general level of ignorance of the meaning of planning, the functions of the board, and, most important of all, the threat which a planning executive seemed to pose to a Congress seeking to reassert authority seemingly lost in the war. Even over and above the hostilities to Roosevelt and the New Deal, the fear of an all-powerful executive usurping the authority of the legislative branch looms larger. What killed the NRPB was the same opposition that had hampered its activities all along. What that opposition had in 1943 was the margin for victory it had lacked in previous battles.

Contrary, also, to a good bit of commentary then and since, Roosevelt recognized the value of the board and fought to keep it. It seemed to no one that he was doing enough, and in the press of affairs at that late stage in his career, that is probably true. His letter of 16 February 1943 to Clarence Cannon, chairman of the House Appropriations Committee, is worth quoting for its summary of the issues.

> Since my return from Africa, I read in the papers that the Appropriations Committee has, in effect, abolished the National Resources Planning Board by recommending no appropriations for it after June 30th of this year.
>
> I do not want to raise any public discussion in regard to this . . . but I have no objection if you wish to read this letter to other members of the Committee.
>
> I hear a lot of people talking about the necessity of doing things after the war is over, in order to prevent a sudden crash when the munitions factories close and when the troops and sailors are mustered out. They want some kind of cushion during the transition period and, as you all know, I have been building up what I call "a shelf of projects"—most of which are deferred projects—which the Congress could consider appropriating money for when the time comes. . . . The National Resources Planning Board, in connection

with other agencies, such as the Army Engineers, has done, and is doing, a wonderful job not only in the actual details of planning but also in the consideration of other problems created by the war. . . . The amounts of money involved are very large—billions of dollars—and I, having been a Legislator, know that after the war mere appropriations will not save emergencies quickly unless the planning has been done beforehand.

The amount involved in keeping the National Resources Planning Board at work while the war lasts is not great.

If the Congress wants to abolish this Board and set up another Board with different personnel, they have a right to do so. In other words, if the Congress does not like the individuals who have been doing this work for many years, all they have to do is say so quite frankly.

The point is that in keeping the Board going I think the nation will save money—lots of it—billions of it in the years after the war. In this matter at least I hope your Committee will recognize that I am trying to be economical.

And in a postscript, Roosevelt added, "By the way, I hope the Committee realizes that the National Resources Planning Board is very largely instrumental in keeping state, county and city planning at work. Lots of counties and cities have their own planning commissions and we are getting a very well integrated system for almost every part of the United States."[24] "I am much upset over the Congressional attitude toward the National Resources Planning Board," he wrote Delano. "The need for such studying and planning as your Board is doing is so obvious that I am very hopeful that the Senate will restore the appropriation." He urged them to present a strong argument to the Senate Appropriations Committee for the full $1,400,000 which had been requested.[25]

Cannon sent Roosevelt copies of the *Congressional Record* for 25 February giving his remarks in support of the board, but one did not have to read far to come across the statements of familiar enemies like Representative Taber of New York. "The National Resources Planning Board throughout its entire life has been made up of people without a practical viewpoint of life," Taber complained. "It has been made up of those whose theory of life is that it is absolutely impossible for the economic system of America to take care of our people after this war is over, and that we must have some kind of fake employment or employment on public works that we cannot afford in order to provide the daily bread of our people." And in a statement which may reflect the deepest opposition of all to the board's insistent recollections of the painful thirties, he continued, "The implication of the continuance of the National Resources Planning Board is that America is dead. It represents an attitude of defeatism. It represents an attitude that there is no future for America."[26] If the frontier was closed, Mr. Taber didn't want to hear of it, and neither did anyone else.

On the fifteenth of March, Roosevelt wrote again to Carter Glass, chairman of the Senate Appropriations Committee, arguing against the supposed "duplication" which the work of the board was claimed by its opponents to reflect. And on the twenty-fourth, in a joint letter to Cannon and Glass he argued the money-saving utility of the board.

> In view of the fact that many Federal agencies in planning their work from month to month are increasingly asking the advice of the National Resources Planning Board toward the elimination of duplication, they will have, after July first, no place to go in the Government to get expert advice either for the present or for the post-war period.... I have spoken many times of the simple fact that in existing planning, and especially in post-war planning, the Federal Government can save millions and millions of dollars to the Federal Government, to state governments, to business, to industry and to labor—an amount far in excess of the relatively small cost of maintaining the National Resources Planning Board.... I am very definitely opposed to the principle of "Penny wise, dollars foolish."[27]

On 2 May, the president met with members of the board to plan their strategy. Among other things, he asked Charles Eliot to send him a rundown on attitudes of the various congressional committee members toward the board, and specifically that of Senator Glass. Glass's opposition to Roosevelt was certainly familiar by that point, but the quotation Eliot chose to send as evidence may have sharpened the point a bit. Glass fumed about Delano's blocking the authorization by a priorities unit of a $7 million apartment hotel in Arlington, Virginia. As chairman of the Park and Planning Commission, Delano had the influence with the priorities board to do just that. "I will tell you one thing they are engaged in," Glass blustered as Eliot tried to answer a question concerning the activities of his staff, "which is to carry out the whims of Mr. Delano.... Mr. Delano thought that [the apartment hotel] interfered with his esthetic ideas." "To conform to his esthetic taste? " Senator Bankhead asked. "Yes Sir," the chairman confirmed. Merriam tried to explain that Delano's activities on the Park and Planning Commission had nothing to do with the work of the National Resources Planning Board, but to little avail.[28]

And so the battle ended. Angrily, Congress specified that the board's functions not be transferred to any other agency. Some members of

Congress even tried to pursue the staff members as they were quietly shifted to other agencies of the government. The hostility was deep, the anti-intellectualism profound, the reaction far broader in scale than the relatively small budget of the little group merited. Roosevelt gave up trying to defend it.

The president did not see the board members again. On 24 August 1943, the NRPB went out of existence. The three members of the board tried to pay a call on the president to deliver their final report; but he was not available. "Mr. Delano wants to be sure that the President's attention is called to the fact that they personally brought this report to the White House," the secretary's memo reads, and it was.

"The National Resources Planning Board wishes to extend to you, Mr. President, its heartiest appreciation for your continuing support of national planning as a means of attaining democratic goals, and of the National Resources Planning Board personnel during its ten rough years of existence," the covering letter read. "We can at least say that we went down with all available guns firing and the Captain at his proper station."[29]

Charles Eliot drafted the president's final letters to the members of the board. Merriam's began "Dear Charles," and Merriam cherished it. To Eliot's concluding "sincerely yours," Roosevelt added "very." Eliot opened the letter to Delano, "Dear Uncle Fred," and Roosevelt changed it to "Mr. Delano," and then back again to "Uncle Fred." Eliot concluded the letter "Affectionately," and Roosevelt changed that to "very sincerely yours." There was nothing left to manipulate but the words.[30]

The manipulation of words— There had to be more to it than that, although later analysts of the careers of both Roosevelt and Merriam could scarcely avoid puzzling at the relation between rhetoric and action. The rationalist conception of progressive democracy on which the two men built their respect for each other had at its core a belief in popular education and political process. The term "behavior" linked popular politics with scientific politics. "Behaviorism" made it possible to see in the American voter both the sensate being satisfying his needs and the responsible citizen serving the interests of the community. The conflicts which Merriam's students were finding in that linkage were conflicts which neither Roosevelt nor Merriam could see as central to the social and political structure of American life. Harold Lasswell's political psychology and V. O. Key's voting studies threw the alternatives into sharper relief than Merriam found comfortable. Lasswell and

Key both retained Merriam's optimism, but in vestigial form which made it all the more difficult to understand. As in the case of Merriam's earliest efforts in political theory, one could dispute the priority of Locke and Rousseau in the formulation of American political ideas. One could find no American Hobbes.

Merriam's progressivism, like Roosevelt's, had its origins in a simpler state of American nature, and Merriam's academic career had been devoted to transcending those origins. The transcendence involved no repudiation of progressivism and no apology for it. It demanded no recognition of error and no espousal of new truth. As a method of social reform, science was infinitely superior to many of the canons the Progressives had relied upon; but it had been one of their methods, and its move to first place had never been, for Merriam, a revolution against the progressive past. That it would become so for his students was a consequence he began to see only in his late years. That he himself had helped cause that change was a charge he would most vigorously have denied. Progressivism died with him—not in him but with him. The Chicago School rested on his faith in an American system of values, but it was his faith, not his science; and that made all the difference.

14

Planning the End

Merriam was not scheduled to retire from his professorship at the University of Chicago until 1940, but he began the planning of his retirement years well ahead of time. Two projects vied for his attention. One was the return to his earliest major interest; the writing of a systematic politics, the title he had chosen many years before. The other was an autobiography. That the two were closely related in his thinking was a point he did not always explain. He persisted in leaving the impression that *Systematic Politics* (1945) was based on a manuscript he had had in hand since 1907. There was no such manuscript, though the fable contains other, subtler truths. The two themes, political theory and the self-conscious living of a political life, were perhaps the irreconcilable counter-themes of his career. The ultimate success of one, whichever it had been, would have canceled out the other. The autobiography was never destined to be, though not for want of his trying.

As early as February 1936 he wrote to John Gaus that, "encouraged by H. G. Wells, *Experiment in Autobiography*, I have been setting down notes from time to time on a similar experiment of my own." He was going to title it: "A Professor's Tael: Or Silver and Gold Have I None, But Such as I Have Give I Unto Thee."[1] Had he checked Acts III:6 he would have found that the phrase was "Give I Thee," but he didn't. The memory on which he relied had been formed long before his academic years, and he would not have felt the need to check it. Gaus, too, would have caught the reference. It is an interesting one, given Merriam's career, and one which reveals perhaps a bit more than he intended. Peter said it to the lame beggar pleading for alms, and what the beggar received was the miraculous return of strength in his legs. Merriam had spent his lifetime working with America's alms-givers, and what he wanted to give to the lame was not money but government and the power to use it for themselves. The professor's coinage was obvious to him, but in 1936 he was even beginning to feel the concern which would create in the declining decade of his life still another Merriam out of the materials of the previous ones. The autobiography was to be a final, useful experiment in making his life functional in some symbolic, emblematic sense.

He divided it for Gaus into books: "Book I, The Book of Youth; Book II, The Book of Politics and War, Book III, The Book of Building (futile and other organizations), Book IV, The Book of Books (intellectual life and contacts), Book V, The Book of Carlo (being the book of my sub-conscious)." His use of the phrase "futile and other organizations" is an example of the recurring depression he was to feel in those last years as he watched many of the organizations he had built slip from his grasp. In a later letter to Gaus he elaborated on the "Carlo" theme. "The Book of Carlo is to be disguised as reveries or dreams, so that you will never know whether you are reading what your old friend did or what he thought about."[2] Carlo, as he was to explain to audiences on numerous later occasions, was a childhood pet. Merriam's sometimes public preoccupation with his canine subconscious has a deceptive quality, more fox than dog, the tracks laid on to facilitate the chase but to frustrate the capture.

In a restatement of his myth published as part of the autobiographical introduction to the collection of essays in his honor which his students published, he describes Carlo as his mischievous friend, undisciplined and playful, less interested in theory than in people. "And will this Carlo ever learn to leave me? Who knows? In our Fourth Reader there was a story of a faithful dog who lay upon his dead master's grave, refused to move, and perished there. But what complications ensue nowadays. My body goes to the Medical School . . . and who knows, indeed, with all the numerous institutions of the higher healing, the entrances and exits to and from, he might mistake the proper place to lie in his masterpiece of dogged devotion."[3] He does not tell them about the California trip and the grieving dog who had to be destroyed, or about his feelings about California. His last years were to have as a persistent obbligato running throughout the projects he continued to fight, an at times almost urgent desire to reveal himself to others in a carefully managed narrative of his life. As he said to Gaus, "you will never know whether you are reading what your old friend did or what he thought about," and that comes close to being the way it was.

The Future of Government in the United States: Essays in Honor of Charles E. Merriam appeared in June 1942. In his Preface, Leonard White, the closest of all of the Chicago School to sharing a contemporary friendship with Merriam, tried to describe for the "students" represented in the volume the attitude toward Merriam which all of them felt.

> To all these students he gave faith in the capacity of man for a better life through tolerance and reason coupled with a willingness to fight for progressive ideals. This faith he gave because of what he was and is. The central quality of his contribution to this generation is confidence in the future and certainty of the values of democracy. . . . In these essays Merriam's students testify to their debt to him. For them he has been an extraordinary—sometimes a baffling—combination of the scholar, the practical politician, and the statesman. . . . His activities and achievements created educational values of a high order. They set an impossible standard to attain, but it was possible for his students to try with what powers they possessed. Along their various roads they are making their way, with a warm recollection of years spent in touch with a kindly, if at times an exacting, personality.[4]

In addition to the autobiographical essay by Merriam and an essay by White, the volume included papers by Harold D. Lasswell, Albert Lepawsky, John A. Vieg, Leo C. Rosten, Harold F. Gosnell, Louise Overacker, V. O. Key, Jr., Joseph P. Harris, Hymen E. Cohen, and Frederick L. Schuman.

Although the influence of the Chicago School on American political science had at least another thirty years to run—if one judges by the succession of officers in the American Political Science Association—Merriam's control over its course at the university was beginning to wane. A philosophical antipathy to Merriam's functional views of political research was summed up in Chancellor Hutchins's opinion of Merriam as looking like a faddist. Hutchins had told him his department was full of "monuments to his passing whims,"[5] a judgment patently unfair both to Lasswell and to Gosnell, against whom it had apparently been directed. Political science at Chicago, even at its peak, had always depended more on the quality of the other social sciences at the university than the rhetorical stance of the department tended to concede. The presence of "1313" and Merriam's involvement in Washington affairs called attention to a frankly political point of view which could not always be justified as scientific simply by insisting that it was nonpartisan. In the years before the term "policy science" would enter the vocabulary as still another attempt to give academic status to political participation, public administration bore the burdens of intellectual justification, but in ways which kept political science relatively free of the open accusation that it was no science at all but rather a thinly disguised training ground for political reformers. Merriam could be highly respected and admired for his accomplishments in the field of policy formation and advice without being respected as a social scientist by sociologists, economists, and anthropologists who used the opportunities he provided for them but elaborated programs and methodological techniques more refined than anything directly associated with Merriam's own research. Hutchins could thus find Merriam a man to respect and admire without finding his political science acceptable.

Merriam's political science also stood closest to the critical line dividing public from private in efforts to define the proper public role of the university. Hutchins was far more sympathetic to Merriam's defenses of the faculty's freedom to engage in social research, however reformist the aims of that research might be. Both Hutchins and Merriam had been called upon throughout the 1930s to defend university faculty from attacks by the state legislature, the *Chicago Tribune*, and various aroused vigilante groups of local citizens.

In 1935 drugstore millionaire Charles R. Walgreen accused the university of teaching communism to his niece, opening a critical phase in what Merriam saw as a much larger effort to ally anti–New Deal sentiments with a crusade against the major universities whose faculties were supplying the New Deal with policy advisers. Never before in American history had the universities been so directly engaged in the support of a presidential administration; and the consequences of a successful campaign against that involvement threatened the basic concepts of planning Merriam had spent his career building. "It occurs to me that the President himself might be interested in this organized movement to attack all of our colleges and universities on the ground that some of their members are friendly to and have been active in the present Administration," he wrote Ickes in April of 1935. The political science department and Frederick Schuman in particular were under attack; but Merriam saw even more dangerous possibilities. The conservatism of most university presidents around the country—Ickes asked Merriam to check on this for him following the election of 1936—and the dependence of universities on trustees and donors whose attitudes toward the New Deal were becoming increasingly clear, raised basic issues where the future of any kind of private advisory system was concerned.

When Merriam and Hutchins persuaded Walgreen to endow a lecture series in defense of American institutions they achieved something in the nature of a major victory; for the series and the books published in it over the next twenty-five years constituted a far better testimonial to the patriotic responsibilities of the academic community than any of them might have anticipated.

"What we tend to subvert," Merriam argues in his defense of the university, "is not American institutions but misunderstanding, injustice, corruption, graft, waste, special privilege in American public life."[6] The periodic rhetorical victories did not always conceal the nagging fear that there was more to come, that it might even get worse. Merriam had even discussed with Ickes and other friends the possibility of his own resignation as a public gesture of concern. The war years masked the intensity for a time, but only barely. As in the case of the reaction against the NRPB, the protection was thin and disturbingly temporary.

The reaction against the reforms of the 1930s was considerably more profound than the kind of ignorant congressional rhetoric with which the NRPB was attacked or the fumings of the *Tribune* and downstate Illinois legislators. "Liberal" was coming to be a term much more subject to anti-intellectual opposition than "Progressive" had ever been and even more easily linked to the American fear of radicalism. By the end of World War II the emergence of an intellectually acceptable conservatism within the academic community began to pose issues new and threatening to Merriam's generation, a conservatism solidly based on European social thought at least partially outside the training of the older generation.

Within the University of Chicago itself a group led by John U. Nef and his wife, Elinor Castle Nef, had formed the Committee on Social Thought in 1941. From Hutchins's point of view, the committee offered an opportunity to counterbalance the supposed Germanic orientation of the professionally conscious faculty by cutting across departmental lines; and its sympathies with the postwar revival of British conservatism in the United States were strong. One of its functions during these years was to serve as a center for European émigrés like Friedrich von Hayek, the economist, and expatriate T. S. Eliot, both of whose positions were, by standards being redefined, conservative. Held together by a common concern for a moral order capable of transcending the horrors gradually being revealed in Hitler's Germany and their relation to the origins of the war, the committee and its guests in varying ways sought the application of a new international sophistication to American intellectual life and tended to see New Dealers like Merriam as misguided provincials, caught in a naive interpretation of the nature of man.

In part, the migrations of the war period hastened a process which had in fact been underway since World War I, at least; and Merriam had been part of it throughout his career, encouraging the visits of European scholars and the sending of Americans abroad. World War II, however, introduced an element of permanence which had been only peripheral to the earlier experience. The shocks reverberated throughout the American academic community as Europeans examined the conditions to which circumstances beyond their control had committed them and as Americans discovered the consequent problems of the new collegiality. There was a fair amount of provincialism on both sides as teaching and research in every field adjusted to the biggest transformation since the introduction of graduate education. The so-called Atlantic migrations produced upheavals in the social sciences and the humanities as revolutionary—and often explosive—as those which rocked atomic physics and as full of the same responses: the first a gratified embracing of new riches from old Europe, the second a horrified reaction to the consequences of ideas foreign to the context of American academic life and threatening to the system which two generations had produced. The new migrants accepted the cultural superiority of their own positions, measuring the sometimes strange American environment against their idealizations of prewar English and European culture. In fields like music and art history—a prewar tradition of "appreciation" in the arts was given an intense infusion of European historicism by the migrations—the disputes between the new immigrants and the American schools were to be as intense as they were in every other area of intellectual activity. The new internationalism was producing changes too rapid even to be charted, let alone directed.[7]

Merriam's most disturbing experience with the problem came with the publication of Friedrich Hayek's *The Road to Serfdom* in 1944. Unlike the work of many of the other émigrés, Hayek's book achieved spectacular success. Digested for general consumption by the *Reader's Digest*, it fed a public hostile to the New Deal and the growing postwar reaction to reform. The book made the best-seller list of the *New York Times*, while its publisher, the University of Chicago Press, struggled under the weight of unaccustomed success. Although advertised as an academic monograph, the emergence of a new kind of "professor" on the academic landscape, the book's popular triumph was no accident. Chapter titles like "Why the Worst Get on Top" opened serious attacks on administrative bureaucracy which could be read as frankly anti-intellectual. References to "regions of lower moral and intellectual standards where the more primitive and 'common' instincts prevail" spoke to an audience concerned with problems of social control but also concerned with the intellectual elitism Hayek, then on the faculty of the London School of Economics, espoused. The success of the book and its appearance on his home territory gave Merriam cause for concern. He had had few other occasions in his career to feel so threatened from within his own world. Not even Beard's popularity posed serious conflict in principles of reform. Hayek's did.

Merriam confined his first explosion to a review in the *American Journal of Sociology*. "On what meat does this our Caesar feed in his 'political book,' ... derived from certain ultimate values?" Merriam sneers. "The only home of freedom in the Hayek philosophy is the open market place. Unmindful for the moment of monopolies, cartels, depressions, economic concentrations, and exploitations, he finds the market the source from which all blessings flow."[8] Merriam's attack on the book continued to be intense and well outside any attempt at systematic analysis of what Hayek and others in his school of thought were beginning to say. He focused his greatest energy on Hayek's use of the term "planning," for it was in his attack on this concept that Hayek most threatened Merriam's position.

The use of the term became the central focus of a remarkably angry confrontation between Merriam and Hayek on the staid Sunday morning broadcasts of the University of Chicago Roundtable in April 1945. Maynard C. Krueger, then assistant professor of economics at the University of Chicago, was serving as national chairman of the Socialist party and had been vice-presidential candidate on the Socialist ticket in 1940; he took the role of moderator, though the term scarcely fits. Listeners must have been puzzled at the speed with which hostilities began, without prior introduction of the dispute and virtually without explanation throughout. What they did not know is that the six-hour warm-up session the evening before had been considerably more heated than was normally the case and that Merriam and Hayek were scarcely on speaking terms as the program opened.[9]

Krueger began by calling the book "a general attack on socialists of all varieties" and asked the author to restate the main thesis of the book. Hayek said that it was not "really" an attack on socialists but was rather an attempt to persuade them that they were mistaken in the methods they were using for achieving their aims. "I am opposed to government direction, but I want to make competition work." He could have quoted Merriam in agreement with the second part of his statement and a good bit of the first. Merriam's opening statement was equally curt, concluding, "I find that this book is not particularly significant in our field except that it tends to confuse men in regard to the meaning of planning in this country."

The meaning of planning was indeed the issue, but it was unresolvable. Hayek accused Merriam of reducing the term to meaninglessness by identifying it with government activity of any kind. Hayek disliked being pressed into a position of opposing all government activity. Merriam's use of the term seemed to Hayek too personal to be of general use and he said so. He tried to get some agreement on a technical use of the term which would satisfy both of them; but that was not the purpose of Merriam's objection. Whatever Hayek thought he meant by the term, Merriam knew that the book was being used by others as an attack on Merriam's interpretation of the term. "I read a comment only today of your book which said that 'this will be an antidote to well-meaning and sentimental planners and socialists' without any discrimination whatsoever—anymore than you make any discrimination in your book." That was, of course, the point. The use of the book by American readers had already been established by its sales. "It must be a disappointment . . . to have a man, an American planner, tell you that we do not use your word in that sense and that we do not like the way you push it on us," Merriam argued, allowing a touch of xenophobia to enter the dispute, while Hayek continued to insist on the "meaninglessness" of Merriam's use of the term.[10]

Merriam accused Hayek of doubting the efficacy of democracy, and Hayek's efforts at gentlemanly response cracked. "I am saying that people like you, Merriam, are inclined to burden democracy with tasks which it cannot achieve, and therefore are likely to destroy democracy." There had been few occasions in Merriam's career for confrontation which hit so close to the center of his beliefs. For Merriam the overburdening of democracy was an impossibility as long as the machinery ran efficiently and the leadership worked intelligently and the public had faith. The New Deal had proved this, if not entirely in itself, then certainly by contrast with Hayek's Europe. He could not see it otherwise, although the intensity of his response to the success of Hayek's book reveals in its own way the degree of uncertainty surrounding his conviction. Merriam's acute sensitivity to his times indicated to him that Hayek represented something more serious than a temporary excitement. The New Deal was over. The problem was, where to go from there.

Truman's accession to the presidency in April 1945 was a significant stage in the bringing of the last representatives of small-town midwestern America into positions of power. With all the wartime rhetoric of internationalism and the certainty—again the certainty—that America's international role was determined once and for all, it was still hard to say how much things had really changed. A look at the Senate and the House showed some familiar faces, even if the names were changing gradually. Everett Dirksen was representing Illinois and Kenneth S. Wherry, the "merry mortician," had replaced George W. Norris of Nebraska. It was easy for a man of Merriam's age to realize that a scant twenty years separated two similar periods. Truman, as a successful member of the Senate establishment and a party regular of significant skills, brought a shirt-sleeves informality to the presidency as well as a manner and an accent which should have been far more satisfying to Merriam and Brownlow than Roosevelt's patrician joviality, but it wasn't, not at least at first when all of his contemporaries, eager to give him the help they thought he so desperately needed, still thought of him as "Harry." "Our worthy President is slipping fast and is at dead center now," Merriam wrote his son Robert in October 1945. But unlike his friend Ickes he did not give up.[11]

Merriam spent the later years of his friendship with Ickes trying to keep him from carrying his anger so far that it damaged a record which he knew, as few others really did, was much worthier of praise than most of the lauded ones. Ickes sent the manuscript of his autobiography to Merriam in 1942 and Merriam tried to dissuade him from publishing it. "It seems to me beneath the dignity of the Secretary of the Interior and Administrator of many things; and further to give an entirely wrong impression of your own character and activities," he wrote. "You have fought a long series of battles for definite principles. ... All this stands out the more clearly in contrast with previous administrations of the Interior. If you set out to build yourself up as a curmudgeon just for literary purposes, that is one thing, but a very unwise thing in my judgment." Merriam suggested that he eliminate the personal attacks and develop his own constructive record. That, he told him, would not "sell as many copies perhaps, but it would constitute an honorable and accurate record of your career." The book appeared the following year, its tone intact as Ickes wrote it, solidifying his image.[12]

Ickes sought Merriam's aid in an attempt at a "dump Truman" move, or at least an effort to revive progressivism, as he saw it, in some form; but Merriam was not sympathetic. In many ways, perhaps, the basic characteristic of Ickes's political experience was that, fundamentally speaking, it taught him so little. He learned no more from his failures than he did from his successes and could therefore be counted upon to move in his initial direction for as long as his energy lasted. Roosevelt could use people like that; others could not.[13]

Merriam was determined to retain his optimism. In the privacy of his poetry he lamented the loss of power entailed by aging. Like most Americans he had to struggle to find satisfaction in retirement and faced the signs of approaching senescence with none of the relief that characterizes the classic literature of old age. True, his speaking schedule through the last years of his life remained gratifyingly heavy, but there were moments when it was clear to him that many of his most cherished ideals were coming under attack. The chief among these was the relation between social science and progress, for it was that relationship that served as the base for his optimism.[14]

In 1946 Luther Gulick sent Merriam the manuscript of an article he was publishing in the *Municipal Review.*[15] Gulick had set himself the task of reexamining some of the cities described by Lincoln Steffens in his *Shame of the Cities,* and the results of his examination were not, to say the least, encouraging. It was even harder to see the accomplishments of reform by 1946 than it had been for Steffens over a decade earlier when he had reviewed the era himself in his autobiography; and Steffens had the Soviet Union to look to as his hope. Gulick didn't.

Merriam was disturbed and told Gulick so. "I thought your general tone was very pessimistic—unduly so it seemed to me," and, as he went on to say, Gulick was not alone in arousing this response in him. He had criticized a paper by Philip Hauser, of the University of Chicago's Department of Sociology, in a similar fashion, he said, and he characterized Hans Morgenthau's recent writing as making "the human 'blues' very evident." "Your indictment seems to be directed not only against cities but American politics and political standards," he complained. And in an avuncular tone he wrote, "I cannot avoid the conclusion, Luther, either that you had a bad day when you wrote that or that in your journeys around the world you have caught some virulent germ of Pessimism. Cheer up!"[16]

William A. Dunning had writted such a letter to Merriam several years before his death, but in his obituary of Dunning, Merriam had thought him pessimistic about the future. In some ways, perhaps, pessimism about the future was one of the luxuries of old age, but it was extremely unattractive in those still engaged in active life.[17]

Gulick had explained to Merriam in his covering letter that

> I am inclined to believe that we have no reason for thinking that human beings have changed in the past forty years, or for that matter over the centuries, as to their inherent intellectual capacity or as to their disposition to behave socially as distinguished from selfishly, that is as to morality. If this is true do we have any right to be disappointed that governmental corruption shows over and over again the same patterns of individual dishonesty, appetite for power and neglect of individual sacrifice for the public welfare? If man is pretty much a constant, then we would seek improvements in government not by making men "smarter" or "better," but by (a) releasing the social and intellectual drives, while holding the anti-social impulses and ignorance in check, and by (b) elaborating the tools of social and intelligent action.[18]

Along with Hayek's "new conservatism," a "new realism" was emerging in a younger generation reading Joseph Schumpeter's economics and Reinhold Niebuhr's social philosophy and combining the two to produce a sense of social responsibility which would see as its opposition the optimism and idealism that Merriam's generation—and Merriam in particular—had fought to sustain. The small-town Americanism of the Progressive period would have to be stripped of its Protestant fundamentalisms and its individualist frontier mythology. American internationalism would have to be purged of its Wilsonian naiveté and its restrictive commitment to legalism.

The threat posed by Hayek was far clearer, from Merriam's point of view, than the problems of the emerging realism. In the 1950s writers such as Richard Hofstadter, Daniel Boorstin, and Louis Hartz were crudely classified as "new conservatives" by some of their critics. The positions they represented in their search for a "real" American intellectual doctrine in the postwar world of ideological hostilities constituted a far more important effort than the use of the term "conservative" indicates to understand shifts in direction which were making the progressive Americanism of Merriam's generation unsuitable for the international role postwar America was being called upon to play. But the fact that Merriam's progressive Americanism reflected something which could be called a majority position in American society necessitated that the "new" Americanism would have to be just as "American" as the old. Thus, even for the critic Niebuhr, "our democratic civilization has been built, not by children of darkness but by foolish children of light."[19] It was not an altogether unfamiliar lament.

Merriam's relation to the Progressive tradition, however, had never rested on that tradition's preoccupation with process. A pragmatist in the classic American definition of the term, and committed to exploring the practices of government, Merriam nonetheless sought the establishment of relationships not only with what he kept calling "theory" but with the clearest possible definition of ends. The publication of both Niebuhr's book and, possibly more importantly, Harold J. Laski's *Faith, Reason, and Civilization,* which appeared the same year, 1944 (also the year of the publication of Hayek's book), signaled disturbing alternatives to Merriam's optimism. For a refusal to accept the responsibility for defining ends was, from Merriam's point of view, a cynicism that invited the pessimism against which he felt himself necessarily arrayed. "It is important to paint a picture of the attainable future in verifiable terms, showing what the gains of civilization are likely to be and holding out definite hope to man," he wrote in *Systematic Politics.* "This is the opposite of pessimism, defeatism, drift."[20]

The essential revolution in Merriam's concept of science rested, in effect, on making sure that science transformed the utopian tradition from its mystical reliance upon fantasy and imagination into a force for the practical realization of the future. Realism consisted not in a rejection of utopia but in a recognition of the existence of the practical tools for its attainment. The key lay in the continuous construction and reconstruction of that utopian image in accordance with the development of those tools. "The advance of the human spirit since the dawning recognition of the dignity of man, his possibilities, and high destiny may be set forth against prophets of pessimism and disaster, and the future of human ideals and idealisms portrayed in colors as vivid as they are true. For the first time in history utopias need not be woven from fancy and hope but may be constructed from a wealth of science and reason to show indisputable opportunities lying before mankind at this very hour."[21] For Merriam there was no longer a need to choose between the miracle of Christ and the pragmatic realism of the Grand Inquisitor. One could describe a future and plan for its realization in a world in which bread and miracles came from the same source, the talents and skills of men. And in a world just beginning to reel under the impact of the atomic bomb, Merriam would remind his audiences that the wonder of atomic power was not that it existed in nature, but that the mind of man had discovered it. In the catalog of the miracles of nature, man's intelligence still stood first.

The necessity of portraying the future "in colors as vivid as they are true" is thus the essence of planning as it moves from the mechanisms of scientific technique to the reaches of prophecy. A future which could not be described could not be planned for. A public which could not be told where it was headed could not be led there. A leader who could not see the future and describe it had nothing with which to lead and nowhere to lead. No matter how hard men tried, they could not make a utopia out of materials and methods alone; they would still have to dream.

The postwar realism against which Merriam directed his aging concerns was in many ways like the frustrating period of the twenties. The emerging materialism was not simply the product of a consumer energy suppressed by the depression and wartime controls but a more profound denial of ideas and ideals alike, a glorification of pragmatism in the reification of a Roosevelt unlike any he had known, and a growing public dread of ideology, a dread fed by intellectual justification of an American history happily bereft of conscious self-controls. It was in some respects a baffling replay of the twenties with the intellectual's commitment to reason and justice in strong opposition to the public's search for scapegoats, but the two extremes existing, somehow, on a continuum as irrevocable as it was inexplicable. His own views of communism had not changed. He saw no possibility, let alone utility, in any withering away of the state. He viewed economic interpretations of history as a once useful corrective to the lack of awareness among preindustrial social theorists of the effects of economics on history but old-fashioned in a post-industrial age. And he saw the postwar conflict with the Soviet Union as the product of competing nationalisms.[22]

Nonetheless, the utopianism of the twenties, like that of the progressive period, had a more open appreciation of social idealism and had, in that respect as much as in any other, given the New Deal its moral energy. Could one condemn all ideology without threatening something profoundly central to the moral base of a culture? In the fragmented writings of his last years Merriam kept trying to return to his concept of civic education and the need for shaping cultural development not only for the young but for all the citizenry. Moral responsibility and cultural self-control were inherent in man, he kept arguing, but they were not automatic responses. No matter how much he and his contemporaries had glorified the small town, even trying to reproduce it in city neighborhoods, he knew there was nothing automatic about the things he had learned there. His education had been designed, guided, and controlled by people who were convinced that they knew what they were doing and why. He could not reproduce that, but he respected it for what it was: civic education.

The postwar period was not destined to produce a point of view compatible with Merriam's last insights. Hayek's right-wing liberalism threatened, but then so did an emerging liberalism of the left, dedicated to an anti-ideological social reform. Ironically, Merriam himself would be credited with originating an American version of a value-free behaviorism, but that had never been what he meant. His emphasis upon the necessity of an empirical approach to theory was not intended to destroy theory any more than it was intended to deny the function of values; it was intended rather to determine that theory be verified by continual empirical testing. He believed, undoubtedly, that such verification would demonstrate the truth of the values he and his generation held. The problem was the protection of those values and their transmission to succeeding generations.[23]

He had once argued with Theodore Roosevelt, he told his students, over the question of the relation between justice and order. Roosevelt had said that, if forced to choose between the two, he would come down on the side of order. Merriam disagreed. Justice so fragile as to be permanently damaged by the periods of disorder to which mankind had been traditionally subjected, could scarcely be called true justice. Order which required injustice as its support, he had contended in every definition of the power of the state he constructed, was too fragile to be worth supporting. Indeed, the persistent testing of the relationship between justice and order was probably what his empiricism was all about.[24]

In the last years of his life Merriam was once again given an opportunity to serve the federal government, this time in defense of justice, he thought, though his closest friends tried to persuade him to let this opportunity go by. Asked to serve on President Truman's Loyalty Review Board as one of a group of some twenty-three "distinguished" citizens, he accepted, along with his friend Arthur Macmahon of Columbia's political science department. The Loyalty Review Board was originally intended to serve as a court of appeals to the regional and local loyalty boards which the Truman security program had set up in response to pressures to protect government from what were presumed to be subversive influences. At his first and only meeting with the initially appointed group, Truman assured them that their purpose was to protect justice in an atmosphere of intemperance and insecurity. That the legal system of the boards and their review board did not assure that purpose was clear from the beginning in the absence of procedures which would have protected due process, the chief weakness being the utter secrecy in which reports accusing defendants of subversive activities and associations were kept; Merriam's initial judgment, however, was that the review board was Truman's inner circle of executive protection for a system whose outer circle it was assumed would raise serious questions of justice. Indeed, it might have been that way had the president in fact extended his protection over a system which was, again in fact, under his direct jurisdiction; but he didn't. The board's chairman, Seth Richardson, quite probably without initially intending to do so, allowed the review board simply to become the senior witch-hunter supervising the lesser witch-hunters. Instead of acting as a counterforce balancing the already known tendencies of its subsidiaries, it reinforced the system, giving it, in effect, the backing of the White House itself, however reluctant that backing might have been.

Brownlow was then closer to Washington politics and knew that this would be the case. He pleaded with Merriam to turn down the appointment. Unlike later critics of the period who would see the post-World War II red scare as the opening campaign in the cold war, Merriam and Brownlow both knew that the New Deal had not been a period in which radicalism had been given its head, and both men knew that no president—even FDR at his peak—could have withstood pressures generated by a fear of radicalism. Brownlow's sense of the advantages possible in a political environment led him to predict clearly enough that nothing could be done about it, that it would have to be endured.[25]

Undoubtedly, the possibility that he was needed again, that he could be drawn from retirement like some lesser Cincinnatus to defend the republic, appealed to Merriam. Certainly the issue of loyalty and its meaning held an interest for him which was already less clear to younger men in his profession than it seemed to him. Like many of his generation, he considered loyalty the product of a community endeavor to generate a sense of common purpose, and he wondered how the new attitudes, encouraged by the propulsion of the nation into international responsibility, would work to sustain the older, dying system. Discouraged by the the way things were going, he resigned from the board after a period of less than a year, without fanfare or public statement—he was old enough to get away with that and committed enough to Truman not to want to make an issue out of something which seemed so far beyond control. He worried about the problem, however; he wanted the problem studied, and he referred to it frequently in his own public statements.

Speaking at a luncheon of the annual meeting of the American Society for Public Administration in March 1948, he returned to basic themes.

> Loyalty does not flourish on neglect, injustice, inequality.... [W]e cannot build true allegiance by means which destroy the very basis of these lofty aims.... It is vitally important to recall again and again the indispensable importance of loyalty to loyalty, of loyalty to the principles and purposes of loyalty. The *means* of producing loyalty must not be such as to destroy the very *ends* for which loyalty exists. Otherwise what looks like the granite of irresistible authority may turn out to be putty and crumble in the hour of crisis.[26]

As he had said so many times, authority which rested on artificial or coerced patriotism was not true authority, could not be sustained, and would lead ultimately to the destruction of confidence which was the beginning of revolution.

Merriam accepted his retirement years with a reasonable amount of grace and a skill which few who watched it realized was as conscious and controlled as it was. Both he and Brownlow shared with the leaders they admired, Roosevelt and Hoover among them, an awareness of the necessity of the continuous training of the generations which were to carry on. A clear enough process where the youngest generations were concerned, despite the conflicts over educational theory, it was a subtler process when applied to those taking over the instruments of one's own mature and hard-earned powers. Machinery which both men had built from raw material available to them in their time was often accepted as antiquated and consigned politely to oblivion without regard for the functions it had served or how the world might get on without it. Lest they be accused of preserving the past and be forced into a world of lonely aging, they adjusted themselves to transitions which would leave their spirits intact in the continuing affections they could generate among the young lords, with moments of very gratifying opportunity to remind them that they had been warned—but not too often, not too harshly, and never too bitterly. One needed the young in those years, not just the grandchildren one dandled on one's knee, but all the young who had taken over one's world and were running it. Entertaining them was a different matter and in many ways much more important to aging men. Unmoved and unmovable by the ticking of a pocket watch held up to the ear, they could still be touched to response by stories of the past and by reminders—more essential than anyone seemed able to admit— of the values on which the crusading search for facts had rested. In that sense, the real prophecies came at the end, though they had been implicit from the beginning.

At the end, too, came what was perhaps the most gratifying—if Merriam thought about it this way, perhaps one of the most profoundly gratifying—experiences of his old age. In 1947 his youngest son, Robert, published a book, *Dark December*, a combat history of the Battle of the Bulge in World War II, and won his first aldermanic campaign in Chicago. The old men gathered to watch and, where they could, to advise, but mostly to comment to one another. "Dear Merriam," Carl Sandburg wrote from his North Carolina farm on the eve of another Independence Day, "I've been reading your boy's book. *Dark December*. This is a rare achievement.... It is brilliant yet also solid. It must be something rich in your life that in the same year he has this worthy book published and goes to town in his first aldermanic campaign." And like the others, Sandburg began to remember. "It has thrown me back to those old days when I saw you often and you risked

your life and forsook the abstractions of scholarly living to work out a
report on crime in Chicago, a report which is alive today. I heard you on
the Round Table when you drove Hayek from corner to corner ... I
hope the coming year we can get together for an hour or two about our
yesterdays and tomorrows. Just now I am sentimental about this son who
has something of your face and your drive and integrity. The likes of him
give me a surer feeling about the tumultuous world future."[27]

Merriam and Brownlow struggled to keep their hands off "young
Bob's" career, but like aging Trojan generals sitting on the battlements,
they discussed it endlessly, a pair of Machiavellis trying to educate a
Prince. Through the war years Merriam had kept up a correspondence
with his son. "The problem of a political or governmental career always
starts an argument which in the end is settled by the taste of the
individual," he wrote in an effort to analyze a question as puzzling to him
at the end of his career as it had been at the beginning. "An
administrative career is more secure but not so exciting in some ways.
Elective office has many advantages but also many hazards when things
go the other way." Times had changed since his father's Iowa days, but
what were the alternatives? "It used to be a short step from the law to
political office, but law is more and more specialized and the clients
don't care so much for 'politicians.' A high ranking administrator of the
type of Emmerich or Brownlow or MacLeish, or an advisor like Harry
Hopkins has a very broad influence although not so spectacular.
University work is midway between them." It was almost a summary of
his career as he outlined it in quick, dry, unemotional terms. "Leadership based on elections is possible, as has been seen, but has many
hazards, and if you are in the wrong district at the wrong time, it may
be just too bad; or on the outs with dominant factions in the party.
However we are in great need of men who are willing to take such
chances, and have the necessary qualities to make it go."[28]

The question was money, and Merriam knew it. A major career in
politics rested on an ability to finance not only the mechanisms of
campaigns—sizable sums in any day he had known, and even more in
the new days of mass media—but the financing of one's own life in the
days between victories and after successes. Merriam saw no reason to believe that his early judgments of business leadership and its political acu-
men had changed much. "It is a great argument for democracy and the
soundness of the judgment of the mass of the people," he wrote his son
during the war, "that the so called 'better sort'—the wealthy and well

born who, as John Adams said, are the 'natural rulers of mankind' are so often wrong, as in the case of FDR, TR, Wilson, Lincoln, Jackson, Jefferson, Washington—defending the stamp tax, against the income tax, defending slavery, opposing regulation of monopoly, against social security, against all forms of planning, willing to trade the League of Nations for Harding's election."[29] The list extended interminably, but not without its protections. The masses did tend to be right and they did win.

If hopes for his son's political career rested on money, Merriam was going to try to provide at least some of that himself, and so he set out on a joint project with Bob to produce a textbook which would use the Merriam name, perhaps to capitalize on the one possibility of an academic career he had up to that time avoided, the writing of a money-making textbook. None of his books had produced significant royalties, except perhaps the histories of political theory, and Merriam and Merriam was destined to be no exception. It was too late.

Merriam spent his last years enjoying his family more perhaps than he had earlier. The years of hypochondria in an odd way paid off. Prepared for suffering by fantasies richer than any reality could have been, he faced aging as the only really justifiable disease he had ever suffered. He sought predictions from his doctors on the useful years available to him, recording their measurements as he had his adolescent muscles, and issuing progress reports on the planning of his last future. He survived a first stroke in 1950, but a second one a year later left him paralyzed for eleven months of what was to be a final frustration. Unable to speak and angered by the gadgets given him to communicate his wants—there were none worth communicating in that state—he fought as long as he could the last efforts to keep him alive.

Merriam spent his last months in Washington, D.C., in a nursing home. When he died, on 8 January 1953, the city was preparing for the inauguration of Dwight Eisenhower. Merriam had selected Arlington National Cemetery as his place of burial. He may have thought as he told his students and colleagues of his intention to commit his body to medical experiment that he actually intended to do that—or at least he ought to have—but it was the last of the useful myths. He had spent his life among his scientists. He wanted his eternity to be with his heroes. It was the last of the symbols with which and through which he had lived his life.

In those late concerns with loyalty—worse were yet to come, but he wouldn't know that—he would still retain, not simply the optimism, the awareness of the necessity of building a genuinely humane loyalty, but the hostility to pessimism, all of which were in some ways the things he most wanted to force beyond the limits of his own existence. "There are those who in their confusion or from the faintness of their hearts conclude that the age of loyalty is dead," he wrote. "They find that the competing forces of modern life are too powerful and eccentric to bring together. Even Rebecca West loses the way at the end of her splendid volume on The Meaning of Treason.... Others are driven by gloomy forms of pessimism inherited from Schopenhauer, Nietzsche, and Spengler to the most dismal forms of despair. Pessimism and violence are often happy companions.

"We reach higher forms of human loyalty as we come more nearly to the realization of our ideals of liberty, justice, welfare, and the banishment of fear and want." And he concluded, "When justice and authority are united in government, then the ways and means of loyalty may find expression in that full measure of liberty which is the end for which loyalty exists."[30]

Notes

Preface

1. For a complete bibliography of the writings of Charles E. Merriam through 1942, see Leonard D. White, ed., *The Future of Government in the United States: Essays in Honor of Charles E. Merriam* (Chicago, 1942). Although Merriam published several later essays and *Systematic Politics* (Chicago, 1945), referred to in my text, it seemed needless to duplicate the bibliography in this volume simply in order to bring the previous one up to date.
2. Bernard Crick, *The American Science of Politics, Its Origins and Conditions* (London, 1959). But see also V. O. Key's criticism, "Issues and Problems of Political Science Research," in *The Status and Prospects of Political Science as a Discipline: Papers Presented at the Fiftieth Anniversary Celebration of the Department of Political Science at the University of Michigan. April 8-9, 1960* (Ann Arbor, 1960).
3. Tang Tsou, "A Study of the Development of the Scientific Approach in Political Studies in the United States—with Particular Emphasis on the Methodological Aspects of the Works of Charles E. Merriam and Harold D. Lasswell," Ph.D. dissertation, University of Chicago, 1951. A published article, "Fact and Value in Charles E. Merriam," *Southwestern Social Science Quarterly* 36 (1955-56): 9-26, summarizes the basic position with regard to Merriam, and presses the systematization of his thought about as far as it can be pressed.

Chapter One

1. Family background comes from the following sources and will not be documented throughout. In addition to much family correspondence, the Merriam papers contain a large collection of autobiographical fragments prepared initially for the collection of essays in Merriam's honor edited by Leonard D. White, *The Future of Government in the United States* (Chicago, 1942) and expanded over the years by Merriam himself until his last

305

illness. The papers of John C. Merriam at the University of California Berkeley, and the Manuscripts Division, Library of Congress, Washington contain extensive family correspondence. A family genealogy was prepared in 1892 by W. S. Appleton, *The Family of Merriam of Massachusetts*. It traces all American Merriams, with both one *r* and two, to three brothers who arrived in Massachusetts in 1638, settling eventually in Princeton, Massachusetts. That "Meriam's Corners" is the true location of the "shot heard round the world" is a matter of family pride much recounted in Charles Merriam's day.

2. See William R. Ferguson, "Life of Lenox College," *Palimpsest* 28 (September 1947): 257–88.

3. As A. Hunter Dupree was kind enough to point out to me, the California state survey was probably the significant beginning of this interest. Gerald T. White's *Scientists in Conflict: The Beginnings of the Oil Industry in California* (San Marino, 1968) leaves no doubts about the complex and sometimes bitter relation between the development of the science of geology and the industrial exploitation of natural resources. See also William H. Goetzmann, *Exploration and Empire: The Explorer and the Scientist in the Winning of the American West* (New York, 1966).

4. William Emerson Ritter, *Charles Darwin and the Golden Rule* (Washington, D.C., 1954) contains some interesting autobiographical fragments. See also Ritter, *The Probable Infinity of Nature and Life* (Boston, 1918); Joseph Leconte, *Autobiography of Joseph Le Conte* (New York, 1903), and *A Journal of Rambling through the High Sierras of California by the "University Excursion Party"* (San Francisco, 1875).

5. "I am a Californian, and day after day, by the order of the World Spirit . . . I am accustomed to be found at my tasks in a certain place that looks down upon the Bay of San Francisco and over the same out into the waters of the Western Ocean. . . . With these problems [of metaphysics] I shall seek to busy myself earnestly, because that is each one's duty; independently, because I am a Californian, as little bound to follow mere tradition as I am liable to find an audience by preaching in this wilderness." Josiah Royce, "Meditation before the Gate," unpublished MS quoted in Dr. J. Loewenberg's Introduction to *Fugitive Essays by Josiah Royce* (Cambridge, Mass., 1925), pp. 6–7. For an important general account of the California experience in this era, see Kevin Starr, *Americans and the California Dream, 1850–1915* (New York, 1973).

6. See Henry Adams, *The Education of Henry Adams* (Boston, 1918), pp. 309–13; Clarence King, *Mountaineering in the Sierra Nevada* (Boston, 1872); A. Hunter Dupree, *Asa Gray, 1810–88* (Cambridge, Mass., 1959), pp. 406–9. Wallace Stegner, *Angle of Repose* (New York, 1971) offers in fictional form a fascinating account of western engineering exploration and the development of a western intellectual life.

7. See John C. Merriam, *Science and Human Values* (New York, 1936), and *The Garment of God* (New York, 1943).

8. The University High School in Berkeley was something of an innovation for its time. It was essentially a college preparatory school, the first such

school to be accredited in the state (1884), and was dominated by the university until the term of President Wheeler (1899). See S. D. Waterman, *History of the Berkeley Schools of the Town of Berkeley* (Berkeley, 1918), *Annual Report of the Public Schools of the Town of Berkeley* (Berkeley, 1892); William Warren Ferrier, *Berkeley, California: The Story of the Evolution of a Hamlet into a City of Culture and Commerce* (Berkeley, 1933); Writers Program of the WPA, *Berkeley, The First Seventy-five Years* (1941).

9. See Louis Brownlow's *The Anatomy of the Anecdote* (Chicago, 1960) for examples of one of the most prominent practitioners of the form. Brownlow and Merriam were close friends and would, in private company, compete with each other in such storytelling, correcting details, adding color, though Brownlow made a considerably more public display of his skills.

Chapter Two

1. See William R. Ferguson, "Life of Lenox College," *Palimpsest* 28 (September 1947): 271.

2. Wilson was much concerned with the problem of the relation between the legal profession and the rest of society, and he continued to write and speak on the subject after he had abandoned the profession himself. See "The Legal Education of Undergraduates," address to the American Bar Association, 23 August 1894; "The Lawyer and the Community," address to the American Bar Association, 31 August 1910; "The Lawyer in Politics," address to the Kentucky Bar Association, 12 July 1911, all in *College and State: Public Papers of Woodrow Wilson*, ed. Ray Stannard Baker (New York, 1925), 1:232–45, 2:245–68.

3. Cornelius Bontekoe, "Development of the Social Studies in the State University of Iowa, 1856–1906." M.A. thesis (1936) in the library of the State University of Iowa, Iowa City; Karl D. Loos and Helen Loos Whitney, "Isaac Loos" *Centennial Memoirs, University of Iowa* (1947); the catalogs of the State University of Iowa and the announcements for the years 1893 to 1899 give an interesting account of the course changes that accompanied Loos's transformation of the program. See also Nellie Slayton Aurner's "Benjamin F. Shambaugh" in the *Centennial Memoirs* of 1947.

4. Merriam details many of the elements of this decision in the chapter of his memoirs devoted to his Columbia years. MS Merriam papers. At the time he was writing it, of course, the interest in the German origins of American academic development was still under the influence of the anti-German sentiments of World War II, though a great deal still comes through Merriam's analysis.

5. A useful and insightful general study of the German aspects of the issue can be found in Jurgen Herbst, *The German Historical School in American Scholarship* (Ithaca, N.Y., 1965). For the Wisconsin background see Merle E. Curti and Vernon Carstensen, *The University of Wisconsin, A History, 1848–1925* (Madison, 1949), especially vol. 1, chap. 22. As in the

case of Columbia and Johns Hopkins, the various publications series during the period give the best description of faculty and research work, but see also *Herbert B. Adams, Tributes of Friends, with a Bibliography of the Departments of History, Politics, and Economics of the Johns Hopkins University, 1876–1901* (Baltimore, 1902). The memorial to Adams, who had just died, by Richard Ely epitomizes a point of view. Adams is quite rightly given more credit for involvement in the less "historical" social sciences than Merriam seemed to credit him with. The intense institutional nationalism of Columbia University produced a longer and wider-ranging list of historical accounts. The ones used here and in succeeding sections of this chapter are, in chronological order, Brander Matthews, John B. Pine, Harry Thurston Peck, Munroe Smith, and Frederick P. Keppel: *A History of Columbia University* (New York, 1904), particularly Book II, chap. 2, p. 267. Nicholas Murray Butler, *The Rise of a University*, vol. 2, *The University in Action*, ed. Edward C. Elliott (New York, 1937). R. Gordon Hoxie et al., *A History of the Faculty of Political Science* (New York, 1955), particularly the chapter on the Department of History, by Richard Hofstadter.

6. Background on Low is taken from Benjamin R. C. Low, *Seth Low* (New York, 1925). Low's Columbia presidency is covered in some detail in Matthews et al., cited above.
7. "An American View of Municipal Government in the United States," chapter 52 of James Bryce, *American Commonwealth* (New York, 1888).
8. Matthews et al., p. 277.
9. Adna Ferrin Weber, *The Growth of Cities in the 19th Century* (New York, 1899).
10. Class notes of Charles E. Merriam, 1897–98, Merriam papers. See also Burgess's posthumously published memoir, *Reminiscences of an American Scholar* (New York, 1934), as well as the essay on Burgess by William R. Shepherd in Howard W. Odum, ed., *American Masters of Social Science* (New York, 1927).
11. James W. Garner et al., *Studies in Southern History and Politics* (New York, 1914); C. E. Merriam and Harry Elmer Barnes, ed., *A History of Political Theories, Recent Times* (New York, 1924). See Odum, *American Masters of Social Science* for Merriam's essay on Dunning.
12. William A. Dunning, *Truth in History and Other Essays*, Introduction by J. G. de Roulhac Hamilton (New York, 1937), p. xxviii.
13. Burgess's clearest analysis of the relationship between Germany and the United States, as he saw it, can be found in *Germany and the United States*, an address delivered before the Germanistic Society of America, 24 January 1908, and published by the society (New York, 1908). See also in the *Reminiscences* his inaugural address as the first Theodore Roosevelt Professor of American History and Institutions at the University of Berlin (27 Oct. 1906). Woodrow Wilson's dislike of Burgess might also be noted. It provides some further views on the distinction between English and German influences. The editor of the *Atlantic* offered Wilson the opportunity

to do an anonymous review of Burgess's *Political Science and Comparative Constitutional Law* when it appeared in 1891. The Wilson review was a polite but strong condemnation. "He has strong powers of reasoning, but he has no gift of insight. That is why he is so good at logical analysis, and so poor at the interpretation of history." The review and his notes in the margins of his copy of the book are reprinted in *The Papers of Woodrow Wilson*, ed. by Arthur S. Link (Princeton, 1969), 7:169–77, the letter to Horace E. Scudder, 7 February 1891, p. 165, and the text of the review, pp. 195–203. The quotation is on pp. 201–2. Once the war started, Burgess was active in producing book and pamphlet literature: *Causes of the European Conflict* (Chicago, 1914); *The European War of 1914, Its Causes, Purposes, and Probable Results* (Chicago, 1915) (also published in Germany the same year); *America's Relation to the Great War* (Chicago, 1916). Dunning, too, was active: William A. Dunning, *The British Empire and the United States*, with introductions by James Bryce and Nicholas Murray Butler (New York, 1914). The influence of Friedrich A. J. von Bernhardi's *Germany and the Next War* (New York, 1914) had been one of the factors prompting Dunning's analysis. Bernhardi had written that England had made the unpardonable blunder from her point of view in not supporting the southern states in the Civil War. "What the Prussian general calls an 'unpardonable blunder,'" Dunning retorted, "was the scornful refusal of The British nation— a practically unanimous refusal— to take advantage of the division in a kindred people and set back the cause of human freedom" (p. xxxiii). Once the battle of the historians was joined, the norms of historical analysis suffered.

14. *American Political Science Review* 16 (1922): 692; *Journal of the American Bar Association* 7 (1922): 87–89.
15. As vol. 12, no. 4 (New York, 1900).
16. For an important analysis of Burgess's position from a different perspective, see Bernard E. Brown, *American Conservatives: The Political Thought of Francis Lieber and John W. Burgess* (New York, 1951). The current interest in biographies of American social scientists has produced, in addition to Ray Allen Billington's magisterial *Frederick Jackson Turner* (New York, 1973), such useful examples as Daniel M. Fox, *The Discovery of Abundance: Simon Patten and the Transformation of Social Theory* (Ithaca, N.Y., 1967); Benjamin G. Rader, *The Academic Mind and Reform: The Influence of Richard T. Ely in American Life* (Lexington, Ky., 1966); Dorothy G. Ross, *G. Stanley Hall: The Psychologist as Prophet* (Chicago, 1972); and Julius Weinberg, *Edward Alsworth Ross and the Sociology of Progressivism* (Madison, Wis., 1972). Albert Somit and Joseph Tanenhaus, *American Political Science: A Profile of a Discipline* (New York, 1964) places both Burgess and Merriam in the historical context of the development of the discipline itself.
17. The best and most extensive analysis of the development of higher education in America during this period is Laurence R. Veysey, *The Emergence of the American University* (Chicago, 1965).

Chapter Three

1. Richard J. Storr, *Harper's University: The Beginnings* (Chicago, 1966) covers the period described here; but readers should also consult Thomas W. Goodspeed, *A History of the University of Chicago* (Chicago, 1916). A recent account of a fuller range of the university's history is the brief but well-illustrated catalog of an exhibit of materials from the university archives, *One in Spirit* (Chicago, 1973). The Harper mythology ranges from Milton Mayer, *Young Man in a Hurry* (Chicago, 1957), which is less concerned with an accurate accounting of Harper's career than with narrating what Chicagoans tend to believe happened, to the more veiled fictional account of Robert Herrick's novel *Chimes* (New York, 1926) and the attack contained in Thorstein Veblen's *The Higher Learning in America: A Memorandum on the Conduct of Universities by Businessmen* (New York, 1918). Herrick conceals Harper's Chicago under the name "Eureka" and John D. Rockefeller as a millionaire lumberman, called reverently, and frequently, "The Founder."
2. W. A. Dunning to Merriam, 27 May 1902, Merriam papers. (Unless otherwise indicated, all letters to or from Merriam cited in this book are in the Charles E. Merriam papers, University of Chicago Library.)
3. W. A. Dunning to Merriam, 13 May 1903. The McLaughlin review appeared in the *Political Science Quarterly* 18 (1903): 327-28.
4. *American Historical Review* 8 (1902-3): 727-69. James W. Garner reviewed it favorably in the *Annals of the American Academy of Social and Political Science* 21 (1903): 469-70.
5. W. A. Dunning to Merriam, 6 March 1903.
6. Merriam's dissertation had been criticized as a Dunning product, in effect, by Benjamin Shambaugh in the *Annals of the American Academy of Social and Political Science* 17 (1901): 123-24. "In view of the fact that he had to pursue his study without a satisfactory system of political philosophy, afforded by recent writers or constructed by himself, Dr. Merriam's monograph is certainly a meritorious production." Although Merriam had specifically disclaimed any attempt to do more than describe the history, that was still insufficient justification for Shambaugh, who suggests in his review that Merriam ignores Woodrow Wilson's injunction to make judgments about the meaning of sovereignty.
7. Charles E. Merriam, *A History of American Political Theories* (New York, 1903), p. 334.
8. Ibid., p. 349.
9. W. A. Dunning to Merriam, 6 March [1903].
10. *American Political Theories*, p. 302.
11. "State Government," *New York State Library Bulletin, Review of Legislation*, 1902, pp. 711-16.
12. W. A. Dunning to Merriam, 8 June 1904.
13. "Helen Culver," *The National Cyclopedia of American Biography* 17:178 (not in the 1920 edition).
14. Charles E. Merriam, *Municipal Revenues of Chicago* (Chicago, 1906).

15. Merriam to Dean Butler of the University of Chicago School of Education, 1 March 1909.
16. "Home Rule Features of the New City Charter," Merriam in debate with the Hon. Edward T. Noonan, *City Club Bulletin* 1, no. 13 (19 June 1907): 152-56. See also Charles E. Merriam, "The Chicago Charter Convention," *American Political Science Review* 2 (1907-8): 1-14.
17. Merriam to W. A. Dunning, 10 June 1907.
18. *Report to the Mayor and Aldermen of the City of Chicago by the Chicago Harbor Commission* (Chicago, 1909), John M. Ewen, Chairman.
19. *New International Encyclopedia* (1904), 14:16-17; "State Central Committees," *Political Science Quarterly* 19 (1904): 224-35; M. Ostrowgorski to Merriam, 27 October 1908; Merriam to Ostrowgorski, 14 November 1908.
20. Henry Jones Ford to Merriam, undated note enclosed with questionnaire.
21. Charles E. Merriam to John C. Merriam, 10 January 1907; John C. Merriam to David Starr Jordan, 18 October 1905; John C. Merriam to Dr. W. J. Sinclair, 19 February 1907, all in John C. Merriam papers, University of California Library, Berkeley. See also John C. Merriam to Bernard Bienenfeld, 20 December 1916: "The significance of research may be measured in some cases in the economic sense; in other cases the value may be aesthetic, intellectual, or of some phase not easily measurable although of the highest importance. The Committee desires to lay before the Commonwealth Club the best illustrations bringing out the significance of scientific investigation, and to show the relation of such work to the vital and fundamental needs of the community." John C. Merriam papers.
22. Merriam to Judson, 2 February 1909.
23. Allen Burns to Merriam, 4 October 1907.

Chapter Four

1. Unpublished autobiographical fragment, Merriam papers.
2. Deneen to Merriam, 24 February 1909.
3. See Clarence A. Wood to Merriam, 27 February 1909.
4. Dunning to Merriam, 26 February 1909.
5. Discussions of the structure of Chicago government and politics over the period covered here can be found in the *Annual Preliminary Reports* of the Municipal Voters' League, Chicago, as well as in the *City Club Bulletin*, published weekly by the City Club of Chicago. See also Steven J. Diner, "A City and Its University: Chicago Professors and Elite Reform, 1892-1919," Ph.D. dissertation, University of Chicago, 1972.
6. Forrest MacDonald's *Insull* (Chicago, 1962) presents a picture of Insull quite different from that held by men of Merriam's generation, to whom Insull was to the scandals concerning public utilities what Charles Tyson Yerkes had been to the traction scandals. At no point in his writings does Merriam ever credit Insull with any of the useful technical and legal innovations of American public utilities development.
7. The Merriam papers contain folder after folder of correspondence giving

the range of an alderman's involvement in the city. In addition to the obvious questions of permits for lighting and surfacing of streets, licenses and jobs, school transfers and tax rebates, there are also the beginnings of discussion about movie censorship (its desirability, not its infringement of rights) and much correspondence with officials of other cities, as well as questions from research bureaus or agencies in various universities and cities around the country.

8. Joel Arthur Tarr's *A Study in Boss Politics: William Lorimer of Chicago* (Urbana, Ill., 1971) is an admirably thorough analysis of the career of William Lorimer and its impact on party politics in the period.

9. The account of the campaign comes from several sources: unpublished autobiographical fragments in the Merriam papers; Charles Edward Merriam, *Chicago: A More Intimate View of Urban Politics* (New York, 1929); Harold L. Ickes, *The Autobiography of a Curmudgeon* (New York, 1943). Ickes sent the manuscript to Merriam for correction and censorship; Merriam did both. Carter Henry Harrison, Jr., told his side of the story twice, first in *Stormy Years* (Indianapolis, 1935) and then, in somewhat different form, in *Growing Up in Chicago* (Chicago, 1944). The latter account had apparently been sparked by publication of Ickes's version. Harrison refers to Ickes as "Ishy" throughout.

10. Richberg to Merriam, 5 April 1911. In a letter to Raymond Robins, Chicago social reformer, Deneen denied complicity in Merriam's defeat. "I had also volunteered my services in the campaign for Mr. Merriam and had been refused," he argued, and he accused Robins and the Merriam staff of financial irregularities. Deneen to Raymond Robins, 11 May 1912, Robins papers, Wisconsin State Historical Society, Madison. I am grateful to Joel A. Tarr for sending me a copy of the letter and sharing with me several other documents and materials from his research on Lorimer.

11. Harrison, *Stormy Years*, p. 294.

12. Cleveland to Merriam, 5 April 1911.

13. W. Clyde Jones to Merriam, 10 June 1911.

14. Robert M. La Follette, *Autobiography* (Madison, Wis., 1913), pp. 516–20.

15. E. B. Fletcher (a downstate Progressive Republican organizer) to Merriam, 1 July and 6 July 1911.

16. Walter S. Rogers to Walter L. Houser, telegram, 23 February 1912, copy in Merriam papers.

17. "Address of Charles E. Merriam, Temporary Chairman, State Convention, Progressive Party, August 3, 1912," Ms in Merriam papers.

18. Merriam to Theodore Roosevelt, 19 November 1912.

19. Roosevelt to Merriam, 23 November 1912. As late as 1941 Harold Ickes still worried about the problem of Perkins: "Who Killed the Progressive Party?" *American Historical Review* 46 (January 1941): 306–37.

20. Roosevelt to Merriam, 11 April 1913, Roosevelt Memorial Association Collection, Harvard College Library.

21. Roosevelt to Merriam, 18 April 1913, Roosevelt Memorial Association Collection, Harvard College Library.

22. Hiram Johnson to John Callan O'Laughlin, 13 July and 16 July, 28

November 1916, O'Laughlin papers, Roosevelt Memorial Association Collection, Harvard College Library. O'Laughlin was in charge of the *Chicago Tribune* Washington office. He had been assistant secretary of state in 1909. His letters to his wife give a useful account of the effects of the report of the Chicago Vice Commission.
23. Roosevelt to Lowden, quoted in William T. Hutchinson, *Lowden of Illinois*, 2 vols. (Chicago, 1957), 1:282.

Chapter Five

1. Family materials in the Merriam papers provide a large part of the background for this chapter. I am particularly grateful to Harold Lasswell for his recollection of visits in the Merriam home. Through most of his life Merriam wrote poetry in which he expressed his feelings about himself and life around him. A number of them are in manuscript form in the Merriam papers and I have drawn on them for some of the description here.
2. An account of the incident can be found in the introduction by Morris Janowitz to *W. I. Thomas on Social Organization and Social Personality: Selected Papers*, ed. Janowitz (Chicago, 1966). For the story of Merriam's involvement, I am grateful to Edward Shils.
3. See Brownlow's account of his experiences with the Haskin service and quotations from his writings during the period in Louis Brownlow, *A Passion for Politics* (Chicago, 1953).
4. The still standard account of the work of the Creel Committee is J. R. Mock and Cedric Larsen, *Words That Won the War* (Princeton, 1939).
5. Charles E. Merriam, "American Publicity in Italy," *American Political Science Review* 13 (1919): 541–55.
6. For a description of the American embassy in Rome during the war years see Norval Richardson, *My Diplomatic Education* (New York, 1923). Richardson was an embassy attaché.
7. Two telegrams relating to American propaganda in Italy are in the Department of State central files in the National Archives: Will Irwin to Gabriele D'Annunzio, 6 June 1918 (file 103.93/370f); Merriam to Irwin, 19 June 1918 (file 103.93/406). The remaining materials are in the Committee on Public Information files in the National Archives (CPI 20-A5, CPI 20-A3, CPI 20-A2).
8. I am indebted to Walter F. Wanger for sharing with me his recollections of the period. Memorandum to author, 28 August 1963.
9. George Creel to Colonel House, 25 September 1918, Edward M. House papers, Yale University Library.
10. 6, 12 November, 10 December 1918, House diary; R. S. Baker to House, 1 November 1918, House papers. Baker's long report is dated 22 November 1918.
11. Baker to House, 1 November 1918, House papers, Wanger memo.
12. Ibid.
13. 16 December 1918, House diary.
14. Mock and Larsen, p. 288.

15. Naval Attaché, Rome, to Representative of Public Information in Italy, 2 October 1918; John Hearley to Commissioner Charles E. Merriam, Rome, "A Report on Lieut. Tedeschi, Liaison Officer of Col. Buckey, American Military Attaché at Rome," 21 September 1918; Nitti to Gaetano Pietro, October 1918, Merriam papers.
16. Mock and Larsen, pp. 289–90.
17. House diary, 1 January 1919; Page to Creel, 16 September, 30 December 1918, Box 2 A2, Papers of the Committee on Public Information, National Archives.
18. For discussions of the career of William Hale Thompson, see John Bright, *Hizzoner Big Bill Thompson: An Idyll of Chicago* (New York, 1930). The book carries an introduction by Harry Elmer Barnes and is dedicated to Walter Lippmann. More recently, and popularly, Lloyd Wendt and Herman Kogan, *Big Bill of Chicago* (Indianapolis, 1953).
19. Speech to the Men's Club of St. Peter's Parish, Chicago, 13 January 1919, Merriam papers.
20. Merriam tried to interest publishers in his work on the Committee on Public Information, and the lack of reponse puzzled and disturbed him. He corresponded with Bruce Bliven about studies of new media and continued to defend the work of the committee. See letter of Gordon Laing to Merriam, 4 April 1920, rejecting a study of Italy in wartime, and Merriam's letter of 18 June 1919 to John Spargo, in which he comments on the failure to use the data compiled by Spargo and others. See also correspondence with Edward Pierce, Secretary to E. A. Filene, with reference to the 1924 Washington Conference on International News and Communication, Merriam papers.
21. Charles E. Merriam, *The American Party System* (New York, 1922).

Chapter Six

1. New York *Evening Post*, 8 April 1920; quoted in Lucy Sprague Mitchell, *Two Lives* (New York, 1953), p. 337.
2. *American Political Ideas* (New York, 1920), p. 453.
3. Herbert Croly to Merriam, 19 October 1921.
4. W. A. White to Merriam, 16 November 1923; Merriam to White, 18 April 1926; White to Merriam, 21 April 1926.
5. *American Political Science Review* (hereafter cited as *APSR*), 15 (1921): 173–85.
6. Ibid., pp. 173–74.
7. *APSR* 15 (1921): 487.
8. *APSR* 15:176.
9. Ibid., p. 184.
10. Ibid., p. 185.
11. Ibid.
12. See Lucy Sprague Mitchell's *Two Lives*, a biography of her husband and herself and one of the classic works of the period.
13. Herbert Heaton, *A Scholar in Action: Edwin F. Gay* (Cambridge, Mass., 1952). Gay was Mitchell's immediate superior in the War Industries

Board. Heaton's description of the war years is very useful.

14. Wesley C. Mitchell to John Maurice Clark, 9 August 1928, quoted in Lucy S. Mitchell, "Personal Sketch," in *Wesley Clair Mitchell, the Economic Scientist*, ed. Arthur F. Burnes (New York, 1952), p. 95.
15. Mitchell, "Quantitative Analysis in Economic Theory," in *The Backward Art of Spending Money and Other Essays* (New York, 1937).
16. Mitchell, "Economics, 1904-1929," ibid., p. 392. The political scientists' debate on the purpose of undergraduate training in their field is beautifully summarized by Frank G. Bates in "Instruction in Political Science on Functional Rather Than Descriptive Lines," *APSR* 21 (1927): 402-5.
17. The collections of essays in his honor include statements from as diverse a group of economists as Arthur F. Burns, Paul Douglas, Alvin Hansen, and Milton Friedman. See *Economic Essays in Honor of Wesley Clair Mitchell* (New York, 1935) and *Wesley Clair Mitchell, the Economic Scientist*, cited above.
18. *APSR* 20 (1926): 199.
19. *APSR* 19 (1925): 179.
20. Mark DeWolfe Howe, ed., *Holmes-Laski Letters* (Cambridge, Mass., 1953), pp. 4-15, 573, 710, 795. The review in the *New Republic* appeared on 1 April 1925.

Chapter Seven

1. *APSR* 16 (1922): 315.
2. *APSR* 18 (1924): 574-600. Merriam's section of the report appears in this issue as "The Significance of Psychology for the Study of Politics."
3. Ibid., p. 309.
4. Merriam to John Merriam, 10 July 1925.
5. *New Aspects of Politics*, 3d ed. (Chicago, 1970), p. 245.
6. Seager to Merriam, 6 June 1922.
7. Mitchell to Merriam, 19 March 1923.
8. Haskins to Merriam, 5 December 1922.
9. Cheyney to Merriam, 20 March 1923; Merriam to Cheyney, 22 March 1923.
10. Haskins to Merriam, 10 May 1923.
11. Jameson to Merriam, 11 May 1923; Merriam to Jameson, 14 May 1923.
12. Allen to Merriam, 29 June 1923; Allen to Crane, 2 August 1923, copy in Merriam papers.
13. Crane to Allen, 19 July 1923, copy in Merriam papers.
14. Mary Van Kleeck to Merriam, 7 February 1923; Merriam to Van Kleeck, 9 March 1923, drawing Professors Robert Park and Ellsworth Faris into the project; Merriam to Van Kleeck, 20 March 1923, reporting SSRC response, and continuing involvement through 1924. See also the memorandum of 5 October 1925 and Edith Abbott to Merriam, 22 September 1925, for a more detailed analysis of the scope and nature of the Human Migration Study.
15. Correspondence between Merriam and Bruce Bliven, 1924-25.

16. James Angell to Ruml, 24 December 1921, Ruml papers, University of Chicago. The Ruml papers contain materials for an autobiography.
17. "Mr. Russell told Mr. Hurley that the University was planning a campaign and that he might wisely consider how much he could give because we were a worthy institution that needed funds badly; that we no longer had Mr. Rockefeller's personal support, etc. etc. Mr. Hurley replied that he would give something but that he would give more if we taught more practical politics." Harold H. Swift to President Burton, 16 October 1924, copy in Merriam papers.
18. Merriam to Raymond Fosdick, 17 April 1922.
19. Transcripts of this and subsequent meetings are in the Merriam papers. They are verbatim, and constitute an extraordinary account of the intellectual transition taking place. It should be pointed out that the 1920s was a period when numerous such gatherings took place. The "News and Notes" sections of the *American Political Science Review* give a sampling. In 1924, for example, the New York Academy of Political Science held a conference on wealth, debt, and taxation, with E. R. A. Seligman, Dwight Morrow, Albert Shaw, T. I. Parkinson, and a special assistant to the secretary of the treasury in attendance. The Williams College summer Institute of Politics had, as a visitor, Sir Paul Vinogradoff. The Graduate School of Economics and Government at Washington University in St. Louis planned to secure correlation with research work in Washington, D.C., through the Institute of Economics and the Institute for Government Research, transformed that same year into the Brookings Institution and separated from Washington University.
20. See annual reports of the SSRC.
21. *APSR* 20 (1926): 1–13; reprinted in Charles E. Merriam, *New Aspects of Politics*, 3d ed., pp. 331–52, quotations on p. 338.
22. Ibid., pp. 336–37.
23. Ibid., p. 341.
24. Ibid., p. 350.
25. Ibid., p. 352.

Chapter Eight

1. Merriam to John C. Merriam, 16 April 1921.
2. Nicholas Murray Butler to Merriam, 13 December 1922; Merriam to Butler, 16 December 1922; Merriam to John C. Merriam, 17 December 1922.
3. Telegrams: Burton to Merriam, 26 January 1923: "President [Judson] assures me practically certain invitation to other man will be declined. Conditions proposed by you this morning satisfactory and will put them into effect. Earnestly request you not to commit your self to New York but await my arrival five twenty five Monday afternoon." And, 9 February 1923: "Would you be willing to indicate terms on which you would remain if California situation clean [sic] up satisfactory?" And, 12 February 1923: "Statutes limit professor salary to eight thousand. At first trustee meeting after February twenty will recommend you receive this amount beginning July this year.... Hope you appreciate my position as not yet in office.

Honestly hope you will consent to remain on these terms and faith in the future of university. In any case, do not accept New York till you have answered this and heard from me again. Very important for reasons you will understand to avoid campus discussion far as possible till after twentieth." Also, Nicholas Murray Butler to Merriam, 2 February 1923.

4. Merriam to Butler, 15 February 1923; Merriam to Howard Lee McBain, 15 February 1923; McBain to Merriam, 21 February 1923. Correspondence between Dever and Merriam during the same period supports, certainly, Merriam's view of their relationship. Harry Elmer Barnes wrote Merriam on 12 June 1923, "It would be extremely irritating and humiliating for you to have to work under [Howard Lee] McBain as Chairman of the Department. I have also heard indirectly that the situation at Chicago will be much more pleasant for you in the future." Lindsay Rogers's account of the incident and its consequences can be found in an article entitled "Notes on 'Political Science'" in the *Political Science Quarterly* 79 (1964): 227–29.

5. Harold Lasswell describes this eloquently in his Preface to the 1964 edition of Merriam's *Political Power*.

6. See, for example, Lasswell to Merriam, 4 August 1923.

7. *The American Party System* (New York, 1922), p. 433 n.

8. The "News and Notes" sections of the *American Political Science Review* through this period are ample testimony to the method. The tone throughout is one of an almost frenetic cooperation.

9. As I have tried to indicate in the Preface, some of those Merriam students I interviewed found it difficult to justify intellectual distinction in Merriam. The problem was undoubtedly complicated by the number of years since his death and the closeness of many of them to the end of their own active careers. Whether Merriam created them or they he is a much more interesting problem, perhaps, than I could indicate without going into critical evaluations and lapses of confidence which seem to me unwarranted.

10. Merriam to Frederick Jackson Turner, 18 October 1922. Turner's article appeared in *Yale Review* 12 (1922): 1–21.

11. See Charles E. Merriam, Spencer Parratt, and Albert Lepawsky, *The Government of the Metropolitan Region of Chicago* (Chicago, 1933); Howard W. Odum and Harry Estill Moore, *American Regionalism: A Cultural-Historical Approach to National Integration* (New York, 1938); *I'll Take My Stand,* by Twelve Southern Authors (New York, 1930).

12. Local Community Research Committee, Financial Statement, 1926, Merriam papers.

13. Claudius O. Johnson, *Carter Henry Harrison I, Political Leader* (Chicago, 1928); Leonard D. White, *The City Manager* (Chicago, 1927); Harold F. Gosnell, *Boss Platt and His New York* (Chicago, 1924); Marietta Stevenson, "William Jennings Bryan," Ph.D. dissertation, University of Chicago, 1926.

14. Confidential memorandum from Leonard D. White to Merriam, 1 March 1929.

15. Reprinted in *New Aspects of Politics*, 3d ed., p. 352.
16. *Political Science Quarterly* 41 (1926): 604.
17. The Ogburn papers at the University of Chicago contain extensive materials, designs, and results of letter questionnaires sent by Ogburn to academics around the country.
18. Edward Sapir to Ogburn, 25 October 1928, Ogburn papers.
19. Various versions of this quotation in various edited forms can be found in the Ogburn papers. No one, to my knowledge, has actually traced it to Kelvin. It appears in the Ogburn papers first in a handwriting other than Ogburn's, without textual reference, accompanied by an equally unsculptural quotation from Laplace.
20. See "Program of the Dedicatory Exercises on the Occasion of the Formal Opening of the Social Science Research Building, 1126 East Fifty-Ninth Street, December Sixteenth and Seventeenth, Nineteen Hundred Twenty-Nine," Ogburn papers.
21. This account is dependent in large part on the extensive diaries kept by William E. Dodd throughout the period, letters exchanged between Dodd and his wife and children, and correspondence between Merriam and Dodd, all in William E. Dodd papers, Manuscripts Division, Library of Congress. I am grateful to Paul Glad for pointing out to me the existence of these materials.
22. Dodd diaries, 5 May 1928.
23. Dodd diaries, 10 May 1928; Dodd to Merriam, 1 September 1928, Dodd papers.
24. Dodd diaries, 21 and 25 May 1928.
25. Dodd diaries, July 1928; Merriam to Dodd, July 1928, Dodd papers.
26. Dodd to Merriam, 27 July 1928, Dodd papers.
27. Merriam to Dodd, July 1928, Dodd papers.
28. Dodd to Mrs. Dodd, November 1928, Dodd papers.
29. Embree to Swift, 19 March 1929, copy in Dodd papers, with covering letter, Embree to Dodd of same date, Dodd papers.
30. Dodd to Mrs. Dodd, December 1928. Mrs. Dodd was in Europe, and Dodd's correspondence with her provides an additional running commentary.
31. Dodd diaries, 1 January, 13 February, 7 March, 9 March 1931.
32. *New Aspects of Politics*, 3d ed., pp. 33-48.
33. Speech #328, 12 January 1944, Speech file, Hutchins papers.
34. Rockefeller to Hutchins, 16 December 1929; 23 January 1939; Hutchins to Rockefeller, 29 January 1930, Hutchins papers, University of Chicago.

Chapter Nine

1. Carl Brinkmann, *Recent Theories of Citizenship and Its Relation to Government* (New Haven, 1927).
2. Merriam to Brinkmann, 10 February 1928, 1 November 1929, 5 June 1931; Brinkmann to Merriam, 21 June 1931.
3. Merriam to Michels, 24 May, 2 November 1926; Michels to Merriam, cable, 19 November 1926.
4. Merriam to John Gaus, 26 May 1926.

5. Merriam to Michels, 17 July 1927; Michels to Merriam, 19 October 1927.
6. Michels to Merriam, 1 July 1927.
7. Kosak to Merriam, 7 July 1927.
8. Merriam to Kosak, 5 April 1927.
9. Merriam to Brooks, 14 November 1927; Michels to Merriam, 26 October 1927.
10. Merriam to Michels, 28 February 1929.
11. Michels to Merriam, 18 March 1929; Merriam to Michels, 2 April 1929; Michels to Merriam, 18 April 1929; Merriam to Michels, 26 July 1929; Michels to Merriam, 2 July 1931.
12. Brooks to Merriam, 20 March 1928; Merriam to Clough, 9 April 1928.
13. "Mussolini, Prophet of Pragmatism," *Political Science Quarterly* 41:161, 184.
14. *Four American Party Leaders* (New York, 1926), pp. 100–101.
15. Harold F. Gosnell, *Boss Platt and His New York Machine* (Chicago, 1924); Claudius O. Johnson, *Carter Henry Harrison I, a Political Leader* (Chicago, 1928); Marietta Stevenson, "William Jennings Bryan," Ph.D. dissertation, University of Chicago, 1926.
16. Graham Wallas to John Gaus, 28 March 1927, copy in Merriam papers.
17. See Roberto Michels, "Some Reflections on the Sociological Character of Political Parties," *APSR* 21 (1927): 753–72; William Kilborne Stewart, "The Mentors of Mussolini," *APSR* 22 (1928): 843–69; Luigi Sturzo, *Italy and Fascismo* (London, 1926); Guiseppe Prezzolini, *Fascism* (New York, 1927); Luigi Villari, "Fascism," in *Bolshevism, Fascism, Capitalism* by George S. Counts, Luigi Villari, Malcolm C. Rorty, Newton D. Baker (New Haven, 1932: published for the Institute of Politics, Williams College, Williamstown, Mass.). The most interesting general study of the American response to Mussolini is John P. Diggins, *Mussolini and Fascism: The View from America* (Princeton, 1972).
18. Lasswell's review appeared in *Journal of Sociology* 34 (1929–30): 134.
19. Mussolini reviewed Roosevelt's *Looking Forward* when it appeared in 1933. The American embassy sent Roosevelt a translation of the review, which was generally favorable, even though it asked if Roosevelt believed the crisis to be *of* the system or *in* the system. "Roosevelt and the System," PPF 434, Franklin D. Roosevelt Library, Hyde Park, N. Y. (hereafter cited as FDRL).
20. Arthur Woods to Merriam, 13 October 1926; Ruml to Merriam, 23 December 1926, enclosing memorandum of the Executive Committee meeting of 21 December.
21. Merriam to Ruml, 15 November 1927.
22. In all fairness to Merriam, it should be noted that he also purchased the Brinkmann manuscript but did not publish it.

Chapter Ten

1. Quoted in Edgar Dawson, Secretary of the National Council for Social Studies, "The History Curricula Inquiry," *Historical Outlook* 15 (June 1924): 6. The American Historical Association had also appointed a Committee of Fifteen in 1894, a Committee of Seven in 1899, and a

Committee of Five in 1910. The report of the last of these committees had led to a dispute with the American Political Science Association over its substance.

2. See Charles A. Beard, Review of *The New Democracy and the New Despotism, APSR* 33 (1939): 884-86.

3. Krey to Merriam, 9 February 1927. The initial request to Merriam to join the committee is dated 18 January 1926. The group was formed at the Christmas meetings of 1925.

4. Merriam to "Dear Dean," 9 December 1933.

5. See George S. Counts, *The American Road to Culture: A Social Interpretation of Education in the United States* (New York, 1930); *Dare the School Build a New Social Order* (New York, 1932); Gerald L. Gutek, *The Educational Theory of George S. Counts* (Columbus, Ohio, 1970).

6. Harold O. Rugg, "Dewey and His Contemporaries," in *John Dewey in Perspective*, ed. A. S. Clayton (Bloomington, Ind., 1960).

7. Harold O. Rugg, ed., *Culture and Education in America* (New York, 1931), p. iii.

8. M. Ilin, *New Russia's Primer: The Story of the Five-Year Plan*, translated from the Russian by George S. Counts and Nucia P. Lodge (Boston, 1931), p. ix. The book had been sent to Counts by a "Russian friend," and he found it "a document of rare quality.... Practically every page carries the marks of genius." P. v.

9. Minutes of the Executive Committee, 6 December 1931, Merriam papers.

10. Charles A. Beard, *A Charter for the Social Sciences in the Schools* (New York, 1932); *The Nature of the Social Sciences in Relation to Objectives of Instruction* (New York, 1934).

11. Report of the Committee on the Social Studies, *Conclusions and Recommendations* (New York, 1933). Bowman's critique appears as an appendix.

12. Bessie L. Pierce to A. C. Krey, 18 December 1933, copy in Merriam papers.

13. Ibid., pp. 34-36.

14. Krey to Merriam, 6 March 1934.

15. Merriam to Krey, 9 March 1934.

16. *APSR* 21 (1927): 1-11.

17. Merriam, *The Written Constitution and the Unwritten Attitude* (New York, 1931), p. 4.

18. Ibid.

19. Ibid., pp. 87-89.

Chapter Eleven

1. Merriam read the plank to Dodd. See Dodd diaries, 23 June 1928.

2. See Carroll Hill Wooddy, *The Chicago Primary of 1926: A Study in Election Methods* (Chicago, 1926).

3. Carroll Hill Wooddy, *The Case of Frank L. Smith: A Study in Representative Government* (Chicago, 1931).

4. See Merriam, *Chicago: A More Intimate View of Urban Politics* (New York, 1929).

5. FDR to Gibson, 2 January 1920, Hoover papers, Herbert Hoover Presidential Library, West Branch, Iowa. Gibson forwarded the original to Hoover, who kept it, no doubt, as a rather ironic momento of their friendship.
6. House diaries, 19 December 1918, Yale University Library. Richard Hofstadter refers to the press release in his Hoover essay in *The American Political Tradition and the Men Who Made It* (New York, 1948), p. 286. The so-called Bible in the Hoover Library at West Branch, Iowa, is a dramatic source of reference to all of the articles on Hoover during the period.
7. Cooke to Merriam, 30 July 1928.
8. Merriam to Cooke, 14 August 1928.
9. Merriam, *Four American Party Leaders* (New York, 1926), p. 98.
10. See in particular Hoover's speech *The Vital Need for Greater Financial Support of Pure Science Research,* National Research Council, Reprint and Circular Series, no. 65 (1925).
11. Hoover to Mitchell, 29 July 1921; Mitchell to Hoover, 3 August 1921, both quoted in Lucy Sprague Mitchell, *Two Lives* (New York, 1953). "If this Department is to become the economic interpreter to the American people (and they badly need one)," Hoover wrote, "it has simply got to be stiffened up with stronger economic operators. We have a myriad of problems on which I do not feel myself capable of passing, we have no one in the organization who can competently handle them and we need you to come to Washington to give us a hand." Pp. 364-65.
12. Hunt to John Merriam, 15 December 1932, John Merriam papers, Library of Congress.
13. Charles Merriam to Hunt, 9 January 1924.
14. Hoover planned to center research in natural and social resources in the Department of Interior under the rubrics "Division of Public Works" and "Division of Education, Health and Recreation." Ray Lyman Wilbur, medical educator and college president, was appointed secretary of the interior. He soon noticed the resemblance between being a university president and academic entrepreneur and being a cabinet member, both in the gentle "art of extracting funds" and in seeing familiar names on the list of private sources upon whom he could depend—such as Rockefeller, Rosenwald, Carnegie, Brookings. Hoover's plans are outlined in *The Memoirs of Ray Lyman Wilbur,* edited by Edgar Eugene Robinson and Paul Carroll Edwards (Palo Alto, Calif., 1960). Also see undated correspondence between French Strother and Edward Lowry, container 1-G/961 600, Hoover Library, West Branch. A fuller discussion of the committee from a somewhat different point of view is "Presidential Planning and Social Research: Mr. Hoover's Experts," by Barry D. Karl in *Perspectives in American History* 3 (1969): 347-409. The following also add some useful insights and information on Hoover's methods: Craig Lloyd, *Aggressive Introvert: A Study of Herbert Hoover and Public Relations Management, 1919-1932* (Columbus, Ohio, 1973); and Carolyn Grin, "The Unemployment Conference of 1921: An Experiment in National Cooperative Planning," *Mid-America* 55 (1973): 83-107. An interesting study of the whole issue of

social science and American industry can be found in Loren Baritz, *Servants of Power: A History of the Use of Social Science in American Industry* (Middletown, Conn., 1960).

15. [Preliminary] Report of the President's Committee on Social Research, with letter of transmittal, Wesley C. Mitchell to French Strother, 21 October 1929, container 1-G/967, Hoover Library, West Branch.

16. Ogburn to Mitchell, 6 September 1929, Ogburn papers, University of Chicago.

17. Quoted in Leonard D. White, *Trends in Public Administration* (New York, 1933), p. vi.

18. President's Research Committee on Social Trends, *Recent Social Trends in the United States* (New York, 1933), p. xciv.

19. Strother to Vincent, 22 October 1929, container 1-G/967, Hoover Library.

20. Merriam to Hunt, 10 December 1931, Hunt papers, Hoover Institute for War and Peace, Palo Alto, California.

21. Odum to Ogburn, 5 March 1932, Ogburn papers; Odum to Hunt, 21 November 1932, Hunt papers.

22. Mitchell to Ogburn, 8 May 1932, Ogburn papers.

23. Ogburn to Odum, 26 February 1930, Ogburn papers.

24. Ogburn to Merriam, 11 May 1932, Merriam papers.

25. Hunt to Merriam, 4 May 1932, Hunt papers.

26. Committee minutes, 4, 20 June 1932, Ogburn papers.

27. Merriam to Hunt, 17 March 1932, Hunt papers.

28. Merriam to Mitchell, 12, 19 August 1932, Merriam papers.

29. Committee memorandum, 25 January 1932, mimeographed, Merriam papers.

30. See Mitchell to Ogburn, 10 August 1932; Ogburn to Mitchell, 6, 9 September 1932, Ogburn papers.

31. Odum to Ogburn, 28 October 1932, Ogburn papers.

32. Ogburn to Strother, 10 November 1932, Ogburn papers.

33. News release, 2 January 1932, container 1-G/967, Hoover Library, West Branch.

34. Review in *International Journal of Ethics* 43 (1933): 344.

35. *Saturday Review of Literature* 9 (1933): 533–35.

36. *Yale Review* 22 (March 1933): 596.

37. *Social Forces* 11 (May 1933): 510.

Chapter Twelve

1. Complete sets of this diary, which runs to some seven volumes, are in the Brownlow papers in Harvard Library and in the Merriam papers. It is a remarkable document of this aspect of the workaday New Deal. Published sources for the development of PACH are, chiefly, Louis Brownlow, *A Passion for Anonymity* (Chicago, 1958), and Barry D. Karl, *Executive Reorganization and Reform in the New Deal* (Cambridge, Mass., 1963). There are, however, several unpublished manuscipts which provide crucial details. One, by Herman Pritchett, was commissioned by Brownlow and is in Brownlow's papers. The late Herbert Emmerich wrote another account

with Don K. Price, a copy of which is in the Merriam papers. Finally, Emmerich commissioned a study by Ruth Grodzins, which he lent to me and which is now presumably in his family's possession.

2. Brownlow diaries, vol. I, p. 7, 13 November 1933.
3. Ibid., p. 1, 12 November 1933. The diaries of Herbert Emmerich, Brownlow's successor at PACH, overlap this period enough to provide an interesting view of a younger man watching the old lions at work. He often disapproved of the lavish entertainment they provided themselves.
4. Merriam to Ickes, 28 October 1933, Ickes papers, Library of Congress.
5. Merriam to Ickes, 17 March 1933, Ickes papers; Ickes to FDR, 16 June 1933, PSF Box 21 FDRL.
6. Ickes to Merriam, 20 November 1933; Roosevelt to Ickes, 28 December 1933; the meeting between Merriam and the president took place on 6 January 1934, Ickes papers.
7. Ickes, *The Secret Diary* (New York, 1953–54), 1:245–46; Ickes to Merriam, 10 March 1933, 15 March 1933, Ickes papers.
8. Merriam to Ickes, 2 August 1933, Ickes papers.
9. Ibid.
10. Brownlow to Merriam, 4 August 1933, Merriam papers.
11. Merriam to Ickes, 2 October 1933, Ickes papers.
12. Ickes to Merriam, 4 October 1933, Ickes papers.
13. *The Secret Diary*, 1:281.
14. Ibid., 2:77.
15. Merriam to John Merriam, 7 September 1933, John Merriam papers.
16. Merriam to the Board and Mitchell to the Board, Minutes of meeting of 22 October 1933, NPB Box 193, National Archives.
17. Twelve Southern Authors, *I'll Take My Stand* (New York, 1930); Howard W. Odum, *The Regional Approach to National Social Planning* (New York, 1935).
18. Minutes of meeting of 30 July 1933; Dern to Roosevelt, 20 April 1934, OF 1092, FDRL.
19. National Planning Board, *Final Report* (Washington, D.C., 1934), pp. 27–29.
20. Lucy Sprague Mitchell, *Two Lives*, pp. 370 ff.
21. St. Louis, Mo., 23 October 1934, NPB Box 201, National Archives.
22. Meetings of 4–6 May 1934, Knoxville, Ténn., NPB Box 194, National Archives.
23. Landon to Roosevelt, 19 February 1935; Talmadge to Roosevelt, 18 April 1935; Ickes to Roosevelt, 4 May 1935; Roosevelt to Ickes, 17 May 1935, OF 834, FDRL.
24. Notes of the meeting of 26 June 1934 with the president were taken by Merriam and Charles W. Eliot. Both sets of notes are in the NPB papers, National Archives.
25. Ibid., Merriam's notes.
26. 18–19 February 1934, NPB minutes, National Archives.
27. Delano, Mitchell, and Merriam to Roosevelt, 25 June 1934, OF 1092-A, FDRL.

28. Wallace, Ickes, Perkins, and Hopkins to Roosevelt, 26 June 1934, OF 1092, FDRL.
29. Mitchell's letter of resignation was dated 23 September 1935, but the president asked him to stay until 1 December. Mitchell believed that "proper performance of the exceedingly responsible duties assumed by a national planning organization requires the full time and strength of the ablest men available." Henry Morgenthau commented at a meeting that Mitchell had been disturbed by the board's emphasis upon natural resource planning rather than economic and social planning, and that, too, may have influenced his decision. Mitchell to Roosevelt, 23 September 1935; Roosevelt to Mitchell, 1 November 1935, OF 1092, FDRL. Meeting of 29 November 1937, Morgenthau Diaries, vol. 99, p. 211, FDRL. I am grateful to Dean L. May for calling my attention to this last reference.
30. See note 29 above.
31. Interview with Charles W. Eliot 2nd, February 1966. The meeting was with Senator Wagner of New York, as Eliot remembers it. There is certainly plenty of evidence that the president wanted it both ways. His experts could make good witnesses before congressional committees, if they were as skilled as Merriam; but that was not always the case. See, for example, Roosevelt to Watson, 30 June 1939: "Will you tell Fred Delano and Merriam to get after the House conferees and tell them to reject the conferees provision?" OF 1092, FDRL.
32. Roosevelt to Delano, 22 February 1943, Delano papers, Box 3, FDRL.
33. Comments to the University of Chicago Planning Club, 17 April 1950. Manuscript in the Merriam papers. Brownlow's autobiography, *A Passion for Anonymity* (Chicago, 1958), provides an excellent description of their method and the style.
34. *Prologue to Politics* (Chicago, 1939), pp. 81–82.
35. Lucy S. Mitchell, *Two Lives*, p. 372.
36. Minutes of the meeting of 28 November 1934, NRB papers, Box 198, National Archives.
37. "The Economic Basis of the New Society," in *Intelligence in the Modern World*, ed. Joseph Ratner (New York, 1939), pp. 431–32.

Chapter Thirteen

1. Address by Robert Maynard Hutchins in Louis Wirth, ed., *Eleven Twenty-six: A Decade of Social Science Research* (Chicago, 1939), pp. 1–4.
2. John C. Merriam to Frederic A. Delano, 2 May 1934; Delano to J. C. Merriam, 18 July 1934; Delano to Col. Marvin McIntyre, 26 December 1934, copy to J. C. Merriam, John C. Merriam papers, Library of Congress. See also the excellent account of these problems in Gene M. Lyons, *The Uneasy Partnership: Social Science and the Federal Government in the Twentieth Century* (New York, 1969).
3. Lillie to Ogburn, 31 March 1936, Ogburn papers.
4. For extended discussion of the work and effect of the President's Committee on Administrative Management, see Barry D. Karl, *Executive Reorganization and Reform in the New Deal* (Cambridge, Mass., 1963),

and Richard Polenberg, *Reorganizing Roosevelt's Government* (Cambridge, Mass., 1966).
5. See Louis Brownlow, *A Passion for Anonymity* (Chicago, 1958), chap. 28.
6. Philip W. Warken, *A History of the National Resources Planning Board, 1933–43*, Ph.D. dissertation, Ohio State University, 1969 (University Microfilms, 1970), gives a useful account of the background, organization, and work of the board. A forthcoming study by Albert Lepawsky should provide a comprehensive account of the board in the context of the American view of planning. Merriam's own discussion of the experience can be found in "The National Resources Planning Board: A Chapter in American Planning Experience," *APSR* 38 (December 1944): 1075–88.
7. U.S. Congress, Hearings before the Joint Committee on Government Organization, 75th Congress, 1st session, 16, 18, 24 February; 8, 9, 11, 29, 31 March; and 1, 27, 29 April 1937.
8. Remarks by Charles Merriam to the University of Chicago chapter of the American Society of Public Administration, 9 May 1950: "I've never seen anyone who could discuss power as objectively as he would—as if he had nothing much to do with it; as if he were looking into a picture, seeing what was happening, but himself out of it." Merriam papers.
9. Hearings before the Joint Committee on Government Organization, p. 132.
10. Ibid.
11. SSRC Agenda, September 1938, Merriam papers, quotation from p. 3.
12. Ickes to Roosevelt, 1 November 1938 on the subject of abbreviated reports. At its peak the board began to undertake radio broadcasting. OF 1092, FDRL.
13. Roosevelt to Delano, 1 December 1938; Delano to Marvin H. McIntyre, 14 December 1938.
14. Cochran to Roosevelt, 8 February 1939, OF 1092, FDRL. By 1939 Senator Clark was accusing the board of being the means whereby J. P. Morgan, Wall Street, and the munitions makers would control the money.
15. Roosevelt to William M. Whittington, Joseph J. Mansfield, Clifton A. Woodrun, 14 February 1940; Memo to Watson, 12 February 1940; Delano to Roosevelt, 20 March 1940; Roosevelt to Watson, 30 June 1939, OF 1092, FDRL.
16. Merriam to FDR, 13 August 1940, Merriam papers.
17. Means to Merriam, 23 January 1937.
18. Report of Conference of National Resources Planning Board with the President at the White House, 11:40 A.M., 17 October 1939, OF 1092, FDRL.
19. Delano to Roosevelt, 1 July 1942; Roosevelt to Delano, 6 July 1942, OF 1092-D, FDRL. For a full account of these discussions and their outcome, see David R. B. Ross, *Preparing for Ulysses, Politics and Veterans during World War II* (New York, 1969).
20. Frank Lorimer, "Population Policy and Social Planning in a Democracy," in George B. Galloway and Associates, *Planning for America* (New York, 1941), pp. 348-49.

21. Merriam and Delano to Roosevelt, 17 March 1941, OF 1092, FDRL.
22. Quoted in Warken, *A History of the National Resources Planning Board.*
23. See Memorandum on Chateau D'Ardenne Conference, 20–25 September 1937, prepared by Charles E. Merriam, transmitted by Roosevelt to James F. Byrnes and returned.
24. Roosevelt to Cannon, 16 February 1943, marked "personal," OF 1092, FDRL.
25. Roosevelt to Delano, 22 February 1943, OF 1092, FDRL.
26. *Congressional Record, House*, 1943, p. 373.
27. Roosevelt to Glass and Cannon, 24 March 1943, OF 1092, FDRL.
28. Charles W. Eliot to Roosevelt, 4 May 1942, OF 1092, FDRL.
29. Delano, Merriam, and Yantis to Roosevelt, 24 August 1943, OF 1092, FDRL.
30. Interview with Eliot, cited above, chap. 12, n. 32; Roosevelt to Merriam, 21 August 1943; Merriam papers; drafts of letters in OF 1092, FDRL.

Chapter Fourteen

1. Merriam to Gaus, 28 February 1936, Gaus papers, Harvard University Library.
2. Merriam to Gaus, 9 March 1936, Gaus papers.
3. "The Education of Charles E. Merriam," in *The Future of Government in the United States: Essays in Honor of Charles E. Merriam*, ed. Leonard White (Chicago, 1942). The quotation is from p. 2.
4. Ibid., pp. v–vii.
5. Hutchins to the author, 13 November 1970.
6. Merriam's testimony was reprinted in the *University of Chicago Alumni Bulletin*, May 1935.
7. Donald Fleming and Bernard Bailyn, in *The Intellectual Migration, Europe and America, 1930–60* (Cambridge, Mass., 1969), have assembled a remarkable display of the problem and its complexities. See in particular the autobiographical essay by Paul F. Lazarsfeld, "An Episode in the History of Social Research," which could serve as model for dozens of other experiences in as many fields, some of them remembered with less reflective humor and touching sensitivity.
8. *American Journal of Sociology* 50 (1944–45): 233–35.
9. "The Road to Serfdom," A Radio Discussion by Friedrich Hayek, Maynard Krueger, and Charles E. Merriam, 581st Broadcast in Cooperation with the National Broadcasting Company, No. 370, 22 April 1945. Merriam wrote Ruml a description of the "6 hours" with Hayek the night before the broadcast, and included a line count of the discussion: Hayek 210, Krueger 135, Merriam 108. Merriam to Ruml, 5 April 1945, Ruml papers.
10. Ibid.
11. Merriam to Robert E. Merriam, 21 October 1945.
12. Merriam to Ickes, 19 October 1942. See also Ickes to Merriam, 7 November 1942.
13. Ickes to Merriam, 4 March 1948.

14.   "The Flame of Life is burning low
And ever lower
Nor will it ever rise again
With upward reaching grasp
Embers may burn in ashen eyes, but not for long
Their day is done
Their night is near
Perchance these fires have scattered sparks
And set new blaze aflame—somewhere
Perchance the torch is now a forest fire
That roars its way of devastation
Perchance enshrined as an eternal fire
Fed by the undying devotion of enkindled souls
But now the flaming eye that fiercely
     glared at the world
Has lost its challenge
Now it can only defy its own weakness
That mightily envelops ebbing strength
As the wolf pack closes in upon the fallen.

"The old time baleful glance fades to a watery stare
Deceiving no one
The faded eye no longer summons awe or fear or quickly
     springing response
Nor love nor hate
But only the sputtering flashes of dying powers
Parlono gli occhi
But the eyes are dumb
In vain the towering will despatches its messenger
Ashes to ashes Dust to Dust
These are the epitaph of the eyes burned out
In three score years and ten—or less or more."

"When the Flame in the Eyes Dies Down: On Seeing an Angry Old Man Trying to Scowl," unpublished Ms, Merriam papers. Among the lectures during those years are two sets of Walgreen lectures, excerpts of which appeared in journal articles, but the bulk of which remain unpublished, and a set of lectures delivered at the Maxwell School of Syracuse University in 1947. Mss, Merriam papers.
15. Gulick to Merriam 27 November 1946, Merriam papers.
16. Merriam to Gulick, 29 November 1946.
17. Dunning's statement is worth quoting. "I am sorry that at your early age you have fallen into pessimism. Pull out quick! No one has a right to admit that he is there before he is 60. It is very doubtful if there is wisdom in admitting it even then!" Dunning to Merriam, 8 February 1922. Merriam, "William A. Dunning," *APSR* 16 (1922): 692–94.
18. Gulick to Merriam, 27 November 1946.

19. Reinhold Niebuhr, *The Children of Light and the Children of Darkness* (New York, 1944), p. 10.
20. *Systematic Politics* (Chicago 1945), p. 338.
21. Ibid., p. 339.
22. Merriam was at work on a manuscript entitled "Government and the Economic Order" at the time of his death. Aged and repetitious, it seemed too incomplete even to sympathetic family advisers to be published after his death. Nonetheless, read in the context suggested here, it is a rich and often brilliant source of a very late philosophy.
23. See Tang Tsou, "Fact and Value in Charles E. Merriam," *Southwestern Social Science Quarterly*, June 1955, for a position which differs somewhat from that presented here. Tsou argues that Merriam returned in his later years to a position from which he had shifted in mid-career. Tsou's dissertation, "A Study of the Development of the Scientific Approach in Political Studies in the United States—with Particular Emphasis on the Methodological Aspects of the Works of Charles E. Merriam and Harold D. Lasswell," University of Chicago, December 1951, is a most useful approach to the study of the period.
24. Unpublished autobiographical fragment, Merriam papers.
25. My own conversations with Brownlow over the period of his writing the autobiography provided a number of the points made here. The published literature on the Loyalty Review Board emphasizes, quite properly, the way the board actually did work, rather than the way in which Merriam and Macmahon hoped it would work. In order of publication these works are Walter Gellhorn, *Security, Loyalty, and Science* (Ithaca, N.Y., 1950); Eleanor Bontecou, *The Federal Loyalty-Security Program* (Ithaca, N.Y., 1953); Alan D. Harper, *The Politics of Loyalty: The White House and the Communist Issue, 1946–1952* (Westport, Conn., 1969). A general study of the issue which is particularly important as both a product of the period and a product as well perhaps of Merriam's influence, is Morton Grodzins, *The Loyal and the Disloyal* (Chicago, 1956).
26. "Some Aspects of Loyalty," *Public Administration Review* 8 (1948): 81–84.
27. Sandburg to Merriam, 3 July 1947.
28. Merriam to Robert E. Merriam, 2 September 1944.
29. Merriam to Robert E. Merriam, 5 December 1944.
30. "Some Aspects of Loyalty," p. 84.

Index

329

Index

Culver, Helen, 51, 68
Curti, Merle, 188
Cutting, R. F., 26

Dartmouth College, 38, 134, 144, 161
Darwinism, 10
Daughters of the American Revolution, 170, 195
Day, Edmund E., 161, 189, 212
Delano, Columbus, 232
Delano, Frederic A., 55, 235, 238, 246, 248, 253-54, 263, 271-72, 275-76, 280-82
Democratic party, 5, 8, 28-29, 55, 66-68, 70-71, 76, 79, 89, 97, 202-3, 231, 234-35, 255
Democracy, x, 7, 21, 41, 48, 57, 82, 104, 121, 171, 178, 192, 200, 206-7, 241, 243, 250, 254, 255, 291, 295, 301
Deneen, Charles S., 61, 67, 70, 71, 73-74, 78-79, 97
Dennison, Henry, 271
Dern, George H., 230, 241-42
Dever, William E., 142, 202
Dewey, John, 44-45, 96, 106, 109, 180-81, 189-90, 193, 218, 221-22, 251, 259
Dimock, Marshall, 230
Dirksen, Everett M., 292
Dodd, William E., 157-60, 162, 165, 167
Doob, Leonard, 271
Douglas, Paul, 34
Dunne, Finley Peter, 137
Dunning, William A., 25, 31-32, 34-36, 38-41, 46-50, 53, 55, 58, 61, 109, 118, 140, 294
Durkheim, Emile, 146

East Side House, 31
Economics, 21-22, 37, 111, 113, 124-25
Eisenhower, Dwight, 302
Eliot, Charles W., 2nd, xiv, 246, 249-50, 253, 271, 273, 281-82
Eliot, T. S., 289
Elliott, William Yandell, 115, 178, 180-81
Ely, Richard T., 23, 26
Embree, Edwin R., 161
Emmerich, Herbert, 301

Fairlie, John A., 52, 119-20
Fall, Albert, 232
Faris, Ellsworth, 152
Fascism, 131, 174-78, 181, 225, 243, 268

Federal Employment Stabilization Board, Employment Stabilization Act of 1931, 273
Filene, E. A., 130, 182
Finer, Herman, 271
Fisher, Walter L., 73
Fleming, Walter L., 34
Flexner, Abraham, 132
Ford, Guy Stanton, 134, 188
Ford, Henry Jones, 57-58
Fosdick, Raymond, 132-33
Frank, Waldo, 190
Frankfurter, Felix, 135
Freud, Sigmund, 146
Freund, Ernst, 44, 144
Furniss, E. S., 270

Gale, Henry G., 157-58
Gallatin, Albert, 242
Garfield, H. A., 181
Garner, James W., 34
Gaus, John M., 172, 174, 180, 271, 284-85
Geological Surveys, 263
George, Henry, 15, 28-29
Gettys, Luella, 57, 203, 271
Giddings, Frederick, 26, 34, 218
Gierke, Otto, 37-38, 46
Glass, Carter, 281
Godkin, E. L., 48
Gompers, Samuel, 93
Gomplowicz, Ludwig, 146
Goode, J. Paul, 56
Goodnow, Frank, 34-35, 39
Gosnell, Harold F., ix, 144-45, 147, 152-53, 179, 202-3, 286
Grant, Ulysses S. 2, 65, 233
Gulick, Luther, 266-67, 269, 293-94

Hall, A. B., 112, 114, 121
Hamilton, Alexander, 242
Hansen, Alvin H., 276
Harding, Warren G., 65, 95, 98, 100, 201, 205, 233
Harper, Samuel N., 172, 175
Harper, William Rainey, 27, 38, 42-44, 46, 54, 59, 87, 160, 167
Harriman family, 26
Harris, Joseph P., 286
Harrison, Carter, Jr., 66-69, 71-72, 79, 81
Hartz, Louis, 295
Harvard University, 162-63, 166
Haskin, Frederick J., 88

331

Index

Haskins, Charles Homer, 126-27
Hauser, Philip, 294
Hayek, Friedrich von, 289-91, 295, 297, 301
Hayes, Carleton J. H., 172
Hearley, John, 92, 94, 95
Herrick, Robert, 44
Herring, Frank W., 271
Herskowitz, Melville, 271
History, 21, 25, 33-34, 105, 125, 152
Hitler, Adolf, 178-79
Hobbes, Thomas, 283
Hofstadter, Richard, 295
Holmes, Oliver Wendell, 116
Holst, Herman von, 173
Hoover, Herbert, 69, 100, 104, 120, 122, 182, 201, 205-6, 208-12, 214-15, 220, 231, 240, 242-44, 257, 264, 266, 278
Hoover Commission, 265
Hopkins, Ernest Martin, 161
Hopkins, Harry, 230, 233, 247, 272
Hopkinton, Iowa, 1, 2, 5, 6, 9, 13, 14, 16, 18, 30
Horn, Ernest, 188-89
Horner, Henry, 235
House, Edward M. 90, 92-95, 206
Houser, Walter L., 74-75
Howe, Frederic C., 190
Howe, Louis M., 237
Howitt, John, 93
Hughes, Charles Evans, 61, 81, 122
Hull, Charles, 51
Hunt, Edward Eyre, 208-9, 215-18
Hutchins, Robert M., 142, 160-67, 260, 286-88

Ickes, Harold L., 53, 66-67, 69-72, 78-80, 97, 203, 205, 226-27, 231-39, 241, 243, 245-48, 258-59, 273, 287-88, 292-93
Ilin, M., 192
Independent Offices Act of 1940, 273
Institute for Public Service, 128
Institute of Public Administration, 133-34, 150, 201
Insull, Samuel, 63
Interior Department, 56
International City Managers Association, 145, 183
Irwin, Will, 91

Jackson, Andrew, 40, 302
James, Edmund J., 44-45
James, William, 181
Jameson, J. Franklin, 44, 127-28

Jaszi, Oscar, 172
Jefferson, Thomas, 302
Jernegan, M. W., 152
Johns Hopkins University, 25, 158, 160
Johnson, Claudius O., 152, 179
Johnson, Henry, 188
Johnson, Hiram, 81, 102, 238
Johnson, Louis H., 272
Jones, W. Clyde, 72-75
Jordan, David Starr, 58
Judd, Charles H., 190-91, 193, 270
Judson, Harry Pratt, 38, 44-46, 50, 58, 59, 140-41, 144, 166

Kelly, Edward J., 204
Kelvin, W. T., Lord, 155
Kenna, Michael, 72
Kerwin, Jerome G., 144
Key, V. O., Jr., ix, 271, 282-83, 286
King, Clyde L., 119
Knox, Colonel Frank, 234
Kosak, Paul, 172, 175-76
Krey, A. C., 186, 188, 191, 195-96
Krueger, Maynard C., 290-91
Ku Klux Klan, 195
Kuznets, Simon, 271

La Follette, Robert, 65, 73-75
La Guardia, Fiorello, 91
Laing, Gordon, 157, 159
Landon, Alfred, 245
Lansing, Robert, 93
Laski, Harold J., 116, 295
Lasswell, Harold D. ix, 145-46, 153, 175-76, 181, 250, 282, 286
Laughlin, J. Lawrence, 44
Law, 21-22
Leadership, 30, 101-2, 179, 191-93, 206-7, 221, 227, 252, 269-70, 301
League of Nations, 123, 182; League of Nations Association, 195
Le Conte, Joseph, 8, 11, 12
Lenox College, 6, 8, 18-19
Lepawsky, Albert, 286
Lieber, Francis, chair, 33, 140-42
Lilienthal, David, 245
Lillie, Frank R., 263
Lincoln, Abraham, 2, 94, 179, 302
Lingelbach, William E., 188
Linton, Ralph, 271
Lippmann, Walter, 48, 96, 98, 103, 114, 119
Local Community Research Committee, 150-52, 165, 201-2

Index

Index

336